Spy Television

Spy Television

WESLEY BRITTON

The Praeger Television Collection
David Bianculli, Series Editor

PRAEGER

Westport, Connecticut
London

Library of Congress Cataloging-in-Publication Data

Britton, Wesley A. (Wesley Alan)
  Spy television / Wesley Britton.
    p. cm.—(The Praeger Television Collection)
  ISBN 0–275–98163–0 (alk. paper)
    1. Spy television programs—United States.   2. Spy television programs—Great Britain.
  I. Title. II. Series.
  PN1992.8.S67B75   2004
  791.45′658—dc21   2003053634

British Library Cataloguing in Publication Data is available.

Library of Congress Catalog Card Number: 2003053634
ISBN: 0–275–98163–0

First published in 2004

Praeger Publishers, 88 Post Road West, Westport, CT 06881
An imprint of Greenwood Publishing Group, Inc.
www.praeger.com

Printed in the United States of America

The paper used in this book complies with the
Permanent Paper Standard issued by the National
Information Standards Organization (Z39.48–1984).

10 9 8 7 6 5 4 3 2 1

Contents

Photo essay follows page 123

Acknowledgments

What could have been the tedious and meticulous side of this intelligence-gathering process became one of my greatest pleasures as I sought out the help of what turned out to be an international support group of knowledgeable people who both checked, double-checked, and sometimes triple-checked various chapters for this book. In some instances, information was hard to come by. In others, the dilemma was sorting through mountains of material to verify facts and dates. The blame for errors rests with this agent, but to give gratitude where it is due, my deepest thanks go to many fans, writers, and researchers.

In particular, Mark Dawidziak, author of books on *Columbo* and *The Night Stalker*, guided me to resources and suggested directions on how to put together a TV book. He also sent along some press kits of more recent series and made contacts for me with a string of potential publishers. Without him, this book wouldn't have made it outside of my office. Through my actor friend, Bill Irwin, who shares father-in-law duties with Robert Conrad, I was able to interview the star of *The Wild Wild West* and gain helpful notes on that series and other Conrad spy projects. I must thank Robert Vaughn, who graciously gave me interview time at an antiques show in Gaithersburg, Maryland.

Ian Dickerson, honorary secretary of *The Saint* Club, vetted two drafts of my chapter on *The Saint* and corrected some errors I'd picked up from less reliable sources. Jon Heitland, author of *The Man from U.N.C.L.E.: Behind the Scenes of a Television Classic*, gave me many suggestions on my chapter about that show. Scriptwriter Danny Biederman graciously answered questions regarding projects to which he'd contributed and provided information regarding his "Spy-Fi" collection display at CIA headquarters in 2000. British mastermind Alan Hayes, who has worked on the impressive *The Avengers*

Forever website, went over Chapter 4 and provided me a lengthy critique, including needed corrections. Alan also gave me details about shows seen only in England and asked the creator of the *Avengers Forever* website, David K. Smith, to give Chapter 4 yet one more review. Jim Benson, owner of Jim's TV Collectibles in San Diego and coauthor of one book on *The Night Gallery*, sent me helpful information on one of his favorite shows, *The Equalizer*. *It Takes a Thief* fan Ed Johlman provided many details that beefed up my file on that series.

I Spy fans were especially helpful, many feeling their show had been slighted in previous studies. Much useful information came from Chantal Ni Laoghaire, S. J. Dibai, Mike Rupert, and Debbie Lazer. Other indispensable fans and editors included Ellen Druda, Caroline Williams, Catherine Ferreday, Jennye Jackman, Mary Couldron, Marcia Colpan, Amanda Haverstick, and Amanda Lewis. I cannot credit all the fans who provided me details, sources, and insights on various LISTSERV® host sites, but I must compliment the Yahoo groups Channel_D and "The Wild Wild West@Yahoo" for being both lively and intelligent.

Diane Wiedemann, the master of interlibrary loans at McCormick Library at Harrisburg Area Community College in Pennsylvania, was immeasurably helpful. Pat Somers, volunteer coordinator at Tri-County Association for the Blind in Harrisburg, helped me out by having two of her volunteers, Dottie Kirkpatrick and Karen Corrigan, record two books on *The Saint* for me. I must thank my Dad, Royce Britton, who had more fun than he expected checking out many useful online databases.

Most of all, I must thank my wife, Betty, who shared many selfless hours on this project, despite her total disinterest in the world of fictional espionage. Because of my visual impairment, she read many photocopied and text pages to me when she'd rather have been doing almost anything else. Without the support of this non-fan, this book wouldn't exist.

Introduction

In the 1960s, American popular culture depended more on "begats" than any book in the Old Testament. On the television screen, one success inevitably begat another. If a fair-haired young Dr. Kildare captured viewers, so would a dark-haired Ben Casey. If a beautiful blonde housewife turned the world on with her twitch in *Bewitched*, so too could a blonde girlfriend in *I Dream of Jeannie*. We were asked to *Make Room for Daddy* because *Father Knows Best*. The ghoulish humor of *The Addams Family* begat *The Munsters*. The cornpone jokes of *The Beverly Hillbillies* begat *Green Acres* and *Petticoat Junction*. The World War II action of *Combat* begat *The Rat Patrol*, *Hogan's Heroes*, and *McHale's Navy*. Private eyes operated on the coast (*77 Sunset Strip*), on tropical islands (*Hawaiian Eye*), and underwater (*Sea Hunt*). The science fiction of *The Twilight Zone* begat *The Outer Limits* begat *The Invaders* begat *Star Trek*. The most pervasive genre of the era was the Western, *Gunsmoke* begetting *Wagon Train*, *Wyatt Earp*, *Maverick*, *Bonanza*, and a host of others. And all of these programs aired on only three networks.

Into this American mix came a double-edged British sword. After the Beatles landed at New York's LaGuardia Airport in February 1964, they begat the Rolling Stones, the Dave Clark Five, Petula Clark, and seemingly any British Islander who could play an instrument or carry a tune. Suddenly, even the Americans wanted to speak with British accents. Neither could Broadway escape the British Invasion when Julie Andrews, Richard Burton, and Rex Harrison graced the stages of *Camelot* and *My Fair Lady*.

The other side of the British sword came in 1962 with the release of *Dr. No*, the first of the most successful film series in motion picture history. Although James Bond was a product of the 1950s, his first appearance in print being *Casino Royale* in 1953, the Bond of Ian Fleming's books and Sean

Connery's films came to prominence in 1960 when *Playboy* magazine published a Fleming story and when U.S. president John F. Kennedy listed *From Russia with Love* as one of his favorite novels in a 1961 *LIFE* magazine article. In 1964, *Goldfinger* became the first international megahit in film history. Not only did New York theaters run back-to-back screenings of *Goldfinger* twenty-four hours a day to meet the demand, a cornucopia of imitators filled both large and small screens in cinemas and televisions around the globe.

For example, Fleming's own *Casino Royale*, not available to the official Bond movie production team, became a Bond spoof allowing actors from David Niven to Woody Allen to portray six different comic 007s in one film. Saltzman supplemented his Bond success by producing three films based on spy novelist Len Deighton's character, Harry Palmer, in *The Ipcress File*, *Funeral in Berlin*, and *Billion Dollar Brain*. Another successful writer of spy stories, John le Carré, created a gritty world with ambivalent Cold War morals in *The Spy Who Came in from the Cold*, which was also made into a 1965 film starring Richard Burton. Even Sean Connery's brother Neal took his turn in the Italian-produced *Operation: Kid Brother* (1967), playing 007's younger sibling.

The Americans struck back, attempting to out-Bond Agent 007 in the *Our Man Flint* and *In Like Flint* series starring James Coburn. Taking the genre to silly heights, comic Dean Martin portrayed a singing secret agent in the Matt Helm series. Fellow Las Vegas Rat Packers Sammy Davis Jr. and Peter Lawford also took up the mantle, playing the wisecracking team of Salt and Pepper in 1968. Another singer, Robert Goulet, played David March in the television series *Blue Light*. In 1968, the former Ben Casey, actor Vince Edwards, became a swinging spy in *Hammerhead*. Even the musical beach bum charmer Frankie Avalon took his turn defeating the nefarious Dr. Goldfoot in *Dr. Goldfoot and the Bikini Machine* (1965).

Nowhere was the success of the Bond bonanza more evident than on network television. Espionage capers exploded as *The Man from U.N.C.L.E.*, *The Avengers*, *Secret Agent*, *The Champions*, *I Spy*, *The Wild Wild West*, *The Prisoner*, *Mission: Impossible*, *The Saint*, *The Man Who Never Was*, *Jericho*, and the inevitable parody, *Get Smart*, took over American living rooms. Popular anthology series of the era showcased espionage adventure, such as "Memorandum for a Spy," broadcast on *Bob Hope Presents the Chrysler Theatre* in 1965. The first made-for-TV movies included spy dramas, notably *The Scorpio Letter* (1967) starring Alex Cord. Saturday morning children's shows became spy happy as well, as Secret Squirrel worked with Morocco Mole, Winnie the Witch, and Squiggly Wiggly to battle Yellow Pinkie. *Lancelot Link, Secret Chimp*, featured live chimpanzees playing all the characters. Other shows without espionage elements rethought their approaches. From September 1965 to April 1971, *Hogan's Heroes*, although not a direct link to the spy boom, was espionage oriented with the World War II Stalig 13 underground cell blowing up bridges, kidnapping German generals, and smuggling secret agents in—and secret plans out—of Germany. The popular 1963 ABC program *Burke's Law*, in which Gene Barry portrayed a Los Angeles chief of detectives, was restructured as *Amos Burke, Secret Agent* in 1965. The same network offered Anne Francis as Honey West, a feline private investigator using Bondian gadgets. Spies visited on *The Beverly Hillbillies* and *My Favorite Martian*. Barbara Eden in *I Dream of Jeannie* frustrated enemy agents attempting to steal NASA's space secrets. In 1968, the otherwise innocent dolphin Flipper helped prevent a spy from delivering an aborted rocket's instrument panel to a hostile power. Nothing on television seemed able to avoid one connection or another to the 007 avalanche.

This spy boom was a gold mine for tie-in merchandising. Toys, colognes, games, and trading cards would become a collector's dream in subsequent decades. To move off drugstore shelves in the 1960s, toys didn't need to be associated with any particular spy, merely secret agents in general. Secret Sam was a multipurpose attaché case equipped with a gun that could become a long-barreled rifle, a periscope, and a hidden camera. 0-M Sonic Blaster was a plastic air gun designed for playground counterespionage. Secret agent motifs sold products unrelated to the genre as in TV spots using sexy trench-coated women driving Aston Martins to promote Max Factor's Sheer Genius with 005-5 Secret Moisturizing Agents. Theme songs from films and television became chart hits, including the themes to *Secret Agent* and *Mission: Impossible*. For those hungry for literary adventures, paperback racks were filled with the good, the bad, and the ugly imitators of Fleming, Deighton, and le Carré alongside novelizations based on the hit television series. In addition, Gold Key comics issued illustrated stories of TV's favorite agents. Gold Key, Marvel, and DC Comics created superagents of their own from Nick Fury of S.H.I.E.L.D. and T.H.U.N.D.E.R. Agents to Sarge Steel, the secret agent with a literal iron fist. Characters from the Golden Age of radio were reactivated as in a Shadow comic book where Lamont Cranston became a superhero working with C.H.I.E.F. Even the Three Stooges got into the act. In one Gold Key comic, Larry, Curly, and Moe were recruited as spies by N.E.P.H.E.W.

As the 1960s wound down, the heyday of the spy was also on the wane. But the heroes of old continued to have long lives in popular culture and continue to influence television to the present day. In the 1970s, spies became gimmicky comic book characters in *A Man Called Sloane* and *The Six Million Dollar Man* or became demoralized figures on PBS's *Tinker, Tailor, Soldier, Spy*. In the 1980s and 1990s, most of the earlier television series had reunions in one form or another. Many, such as *The Wild Wild West*, *The Avengers*, and *Mission: Impossible*, came to the large screen in new incarnations as a new century dawned. By the first years of the new millennium, new spies appeared again in every guise imaginable, notably in sci-fi series like *The Invisible Man*, *VR.5*, and The *Secret Adventures of Jules Verne*. Even before the September 11, 2001, attacks on the United States, a new interest in the actual world of espionage developed as three new TV series, *The Agency, Alias,* and *24,* were already set for their fall debuts. Even with the end of the Cold War, espionage thrillers, both realistic and campy, still have a place in our culture. One question seems obvious: Why?

It would be too easy to dismiss the affection for old heroes and the interest in new versions of them as mere baby boom nostalgia. The many faces of James Bond demonstrate that each new generation discovers a love for old spies. Characters such as the Saint, who first appeared in print in the 1920s and reappeared on the screen in 1997, must have something that gives them longevity beyond Hollywood's long-noted laziness in looking for new ideas. Just what made the spy genre what it was, what it is, and what it may become is worthy of some exploration.

The following chapters will primarily focus on both the forgotten as well as the immortal characters from television's past and present, as the world of James Bond himself is already well chronicled in an increasingly expanding collection of analytical books and articles. Nevertheless, 007 casts a wide shadow over TV spies, and few chapters here will fail to mention Bond in one form or another. I will take it for granted anyone who has taken up this book has some interest and knowledge of Ian Fleming's characters, but I will also assume most readers are far less knowledgeable about the worlds of U.N.C.L.E., John Steed and his partners, or the other fictional spies discussed here.

Not surprisingly, I've dealt with each series and era quite differently from chapter to chapter. For example, because shows like *I Spy* and *Mission: Impossible* broke new ground in television history—notably with the inclusion of minority lead characters—their impact on entertainment culture will be an important aspect of those discussions. In the chapters discussing shows from the 1970s to the present, I've devoted considerable space to programs like *The Six Million Dollar Man, La Femme Nikita,* and *The X-Files,* which were all successful in their own right and influential on the television milieu of their decades. Series that lasted a season or less, of course, warrant much shorter overviews. The more-than one hundred TV spy series discussed in this book make for a wide palate of colors and approaches, so I cannot help but follow where they lead.

To adequately discuss TV spies in the wider context of popular culture, I've been unable to avoid making literary connections between novels that influenced the genre and storytellers who were, in turn, influenced by broadcast spies. TV does not work in a vacuum, so characters like Harry Palmer, George Smiley, and Jack Ryan deserve at least passing mentions here. In all instances, I've attempted to trace the cumulative and individual influences each show had on subsequent generations, demonstrating that fifty years of espionage adventures are a family history that is engaging, interesting, and important beyond the behind-the-scenes production notes that reveal much about the creative process of television as a whole.

One important concern to me while compiling the information for this book was accuracy, reliability, and credibility in what follows. While considerable—and enjoyable—research went into this project, this book was written for as wide an audience as possible. I know some readers will have special interest in particular shows, but I hope they will enjoy the other chapters, as many themes relevant to the spy genre are traced here from old radio to TV movies and miniseries made in the new millennium. I've endeavored to make each chapter self-contained, but naturally overlapping is inevitable. If you have a shelf of videos and DVDs of these shows, I suspect you'll come away with a new appreciation for the adventures you've enjoyed. If some of these names and faces are new to you, as many were to me, I sincerely hope you'll begin a search of your own to delve into a realm that has entertained so many for so long. Even experts will meet new friends here, and there will be ample surprises for living-room detectives to begin fresh hunts for adventures they never knew were filmed or written. Enjoy!

CHAPTER 1

Defining a Genre

LONE WOLVES, PROFESSIONAL INVESTIGATORS, AND SECRET STRIKE FORCES

We operatives have different styles of course: some work in patent leather and some prefer hobnails. But we are as one in fighting the fight for high ratings.

—David McCallum (quoted in Wolfe 1965)

Within the bounds of a convention, there is still room for novelty and surprise. And that is what we should be striving for, all the time.

—Leslie Charteris's advice to TV scriptwriters
(quoted in Barer 1993, p. 136)

In 1966, author Leslie Charteris claimed he worried about issuing new editions of his Saint books capitalizing on the growing fame of Roger Moore, whose picture would adorn the new paperbacks. In his foreword to the new publication of his 1931 *Alias The Saint*, Charteris wondered if he should update the old tales. He admitted the archaic telecommunications and transportation technologies in the Saint's early adventures had changed significantly. In a similar foreword to his 1965 edition of *The Saint Overboard* (1935), Charteris said his Jules Verne–like machines used by mad scientists were outdated as quickly as the books went to print, making his futuristic aqualungs and bathyspheres commonplace and uninteresting thirty years later. So Charteris said he was reluctant to bring out new editions thinking readers would be better served by new books with new settings and new topical references.

After his editors assured him new readers would want to backtrack through the years and see how the Saint had evolved, Charteris changed his mind. In the various apologies opening his mid-1960s editions, Charteris said many readers should simply see his novels as historical fiction. After all, how could he alter the adventures of yesteryear satisfactorily, he wondered, and how often would the updates need to be updated themselves? Would the Sherlock Holmes stories be as durable if they had been translated from the idiom of hansom cabs to helicopters or a jet-powered antigravity belt? Perhaps our tastes have grown more subtle, he speculated, our monsters darker, and our panoramas larger. Such questions were not Charteris's alone; however, many would wonder how to preserve, continue, update, and create anew the very sorts of adventures Leslie Charteris had done so much to popularize.

Such questions have much to do with the chapters that follow, but before exploring the history, production, and contexts of TV spies, we must come to some understanding of what defines a secret agent in the broadcast media. For example, many might wonder how Simon Templar, Leslie Charteris's Saint, can be considered a secret agent when he is largely remembered as the "Robin Hood of modern crime." As explored in Chapter 7, we shall see that the Saint was indeed as much a secret agent as any other crime fighter in the genre. In fact, Simon Templar was an agent of the British Secret Service in the 1930s long before Ian Fleming began his first James Bond novel in 1952. Certainly, many fictional spies throughout the decades were professional agents working for real or imagined law enforcement agencies from MI5, the CIA, the National Security Agency (NSA), U.N.C.L.E., or unnamed, mysterious organizations. In other cases, as in *Mission: Impossible*, secret agents were semiofficial investigators and saboteurs who were apparently only part-time spies.

In many cases, such agents worked outside of legal charters because their goals were to obtain extralegal results when sanctioned law enforcement was powerless due to official constraints. Like the Saint, many secret agents were "gentlemen amateurs" pulled into clandestine service as were the first three partners of John Steed in *The Avengers*. Drawing from the "Clubland" tradition of the novels of Eric Ambler, Graham Greene, and John Buchan, many such spies were morally driven or patriotic adventurers stumbling into espionage and foreign intrigue by chance rather than official design. One notable trend that virtually defines the spies of the 1970s to the present is the tradition of reluctant secret agents coerced into government or quasi-government service by threat or trickery.

Some secret agents are lone wolves. Others work in pairs. Others, in the spirit of *Mission: Impossible*, work in strike forces in which various specializations are brought together in ensemble casts. Some agents primarily deal with East versus West political battles; others work against various Mr. Bigs threatening commercial interests more so than governmental matters. In some cases, secret agents are international globetrotters; in others, as in *Scarecrow and Mrs. King*, professional and amateur sleuths alike work primarily in settings close to their home base. Another important concern when discussing TV spies is the overlapping of creative concepts. Crossovers between genres can make it difficult to label a given television series any more specifically than as "action adventure." For example, in Mark Phillips and Frank Garcia's *Science Fiction Television Series* (1996), the authors profiled a number of programs with both secret agent and science fiction (SF) elements, including *The Bionic Woman*, *The Champions*, *Wonder Woman*, and *World of Giants*. Such connections had long been established, as in Gary Gerani and Paul Schulman's *Fantastic Television* (1977), which discussed *The Prisoner* alongside series like *The Twilight Zone* and *The Invaders*. Later series like *The X-Files*, *VR.5*, and *7 Days* were also both fantasy oriented and secret agent adventure, continuing to blur the lines between genres. Credit should go to Hollywood scriptwriter Danny Biederman for coining the term defining these series—"Spy-Fi."

Another quasi-sci-fi series, *The Wild Wild West*, was also often as much Western as spy drama. Much of the continuing success of *Get Smart* can be attributed to the fact that it was a situation comedy in the mold of *Bewitched* or *The Addams Family*, giving the series a double life in the syndicated re-run market. More straightforward police shows like *Hawaii Five-O* (1968–1980) also employed espionage themes, beginning with its pilot about the death of an intelligence agent murdered by Chinese spies. In this episode, Steve McGarrett (Jack Lord) was stuck in a yellow scuba suit and placed in a sensory deprivation tank to be brainwashed. This circumstance was more typical of secret agents than cops. More complex are the overlapping characteristics between overt espionage shows and the even more popular private investigator (PI) genre. As Symons noted, most espionage literature in the mid-twentieth century resulted from crime writers grafting spy elements onto detective stories to give murders and related crimes a greater scale of consequence (Symons 1972, 241). On one side, secret agents were often more international crime fighters than true undercover operatives. On the other, many private investigators, such as McGill in *Man in a Suitcase* and *The Equalizer* in later decades, were ex-spies looking for work related to their skills and backgrounds. Still another approach was shown in the 2000 Tom Clancy's Op-Center novel, *Divide and Conquer*, by Jeff Roven, in which a CIA operative described himself as a "diplomatic private investigator." Because of such variations on standard models, for some observers, the lines of distinction between independent private eyes and secret agents are virtually nonexistent.

For one thing, the narrative structure of such shows, whether spy or PI, often seem to be roughly the same, inspiring the numerous parodies of the often too-predictable plots. One typical plot, first seen in John Buchan's early novels, was to transport a code, person, or device from point A to point B, getting past any number of obstacles. The spy was often uncertain about his or her mission's goals, so the viewer learned what was going on just as the agent did. According to Robin Winks, usually the agent didn't know friend from foe and was as worried about the local law enforcement as the opposition (Buchan 1988, iv–x). Often, he couldn't seek help as this would compromise his cover, and there was usually a time frame with an ominous deadline. Typically, both then and now, investigators sought out messages or tips from fellow agents or a snitch, only to find the informer was murdered before he could reveal the missing clue.

The more detective-oriented shows emphasized scientific methodology and the follow-up of puzzling clues or leads (Cawilti and Rosenberg 1987, 34). When a team of investigators was involved, one partner usually took the direct approach while the other surreptitiously blended into the background. Typically, the evil "Mr. Big" captured one of the investigators and interrogated and tortured him or her, always to no avail unless an innocent civilian was on hand to be threatened instead. The villain then left the unguarded prey in a diabolical death trap just before the commercial break—a device still employed today.

Escapes and chases followed such encounters, with the hero or heroine rescuing a partner or a kidnapped innocent civilian or a scientist or political leader from being manipulated or coerced into doing the villain's bidding. Inevitably, the conflict ended with shootouts or physical fights and, in the world of secret agents, the utter destruction of the villain's headquarters.

But the enemies of TV spies came in many molds and were not always predictable. Bad guys were not all deluded villains with clearly evil intent. True, spies dealt with defectors, mercenaries, assassins, revolutionaries, hijackers, rebel guerillas, bogus religious leaders, double agents, and the obligatory literal double—exact duplicates of the agent. Still, Patrick McGoohan's John Drake was likely to be found infiltrating the Irish Republican Army (IRA) or Israeli commandos debating terrorist ethics with pleas for legal rather than vigilante justice. In *Danger Man* scripts, opposition agents duped innocent civilians into thinking that they all were working together for England. Other double agents were torn between love and duty to their masters.

Many adversaries didn't see themselves as evil or criminal but rather as exponents of new and improved world orders or defenders of the ideology of their homeland. When John Steed dealt with his Russian counterparts, each side clearly viewed the opposition as paid professionals who happened to work on different sides of the chessboard. During the 1960s, both heroes and villains lost the stereotypical trappings of decades past, with agents on both sides as svelte and seductive as the other (Newcomb 1997). There were friendships and love affairs between agents, with numerous regrets that their governments happened to be at war.

Secret agents often worked hand in hand with criminals whose wrong-doing was illegality rather than villainy, whose goals were unlawful gain, not devastation. For example, James Bond hooked up with criminal bosses in *On Her Majesty's Secret Service* and *For Your Eyes Only* when the greater good demanded such allegiances and when the criminal demonstrated redeeming characteristics, such as avoiding drug trafficking. When *Octopussy* told 007, "We're two of a kind," she was on target, as independent operators were frequently crossing legal lines as often as their prey (Black 2001, 100).

In this climate, especially in the British novels, films, and TV series, a tone of civility was seen in images of gamesmanship such as animal hunts, chess, card games, and jigsaw puzzles (Newcomb 1997). Agents fought deadly obstacle courses in literal mazes. *The Avengers* wasn't the only series in which villains forced their prey to engage in contests to both test their own abilities and give the hero a "sporting chance." Such sportsmanship was merged with elegant style, as in one episode of *The Avengers* when a professor of assassins praised John Steed's grace and flair in the least of all gentlemanly arts, surrendering.

In the mold of Ian Fleming, many secret agents or their counterparts, like the Saint, were either wealthy or comfortable with the trappings of wealth. For other spies, money was rarely an important incentive for their actions, rather they were inspired by personal or political ideals or simple professionalism. Most fictional spies were portrayed as operating from higher motives than materialism, with greed and lust for power necessarily being the domains of their opponents. More often than not, rather than fighting foreign powers, government agents battled private criminals whose goals threatened the health and wealth of a nation.

WORKING CONDITIONS

From the beginnings of the espionage genre, the boundaries between commercial crime and political intrigue overlapped. In addition, having secret agents serve as crime fighters rather than international spies helped keep television networks out of political hot water. According to Eric Barnouw, the secret agents programs of the 1960s inevitably reflected the limitations handed to scriptwriters by the networks, which preferred euphemisms for Communist countries to avoid becoming entangled in international relations. Some countries, like China and East Germany, were fair game. More likely, however, spies would battle THRUSH, KAOS, unspecified "oppositions," or simply "the enemy." Barnouw noted first drafts of some *Mission: Impossible* scripts used specific locations that were modified later to suit the various teams of censors from networks or sponsors (Barnouw 1990, 370).

No matter who the enemy might be, the secret agent often worked for a government or quasigovernmental agency that could give them extensive and expensive support with gadgets and helpful secondary characters. When producer Chris Carter described his *X-Files* agents as those called in to investigate crimes or situations defying established techniques or confounding conventional investigators, he emulated the missions of teams like *The Avengers*, who dealt with "extraordinary crimes against the people and the state." More often than not, the organization behind the scenes was mysterious and apparently part of a shadow government, as in *I Spy* and *Mission: Impossible*, where it remained a mystery for whom the spies worked. In *I Spy*, *Secret Agent*, and especially *The Prisoner*, undercover operatives often questioned the motives and methods of such agencies.

In the realm of Flemingesque espionage, issues were more gray than black and white, a notable shift from the anti-Communist G-men of the 1950s. Such concerns provided a variety of dilemmas for scriptwriters. For example, to justify government agencies' use of dirty tricks, according to Eric Barnouw, the major premise was that Americans lived in a world of unscrupulous conspiracies requiring a response in kind, allowing agents to employ the same means of deceptions and violence used by the enemy (Barnouw 1990, 369). Although some saw spy films as aggrandizing a contemptible business, one May 1952 Sunday *New York Times* reviewer noted such movies were perfect vehicles in which "lone heroes could wander at will in any disguise, through any social milieu, and in which acts of violence and promiscuity were vaguely condoned by the fact that the heroes were always fighting for 'our side,'" without need for elaborate explanation (quoted in Shaw 2001, 57). Later, *Mission: Impossible* enshrined the official lie—the government must be able to disavow its agents' actions. This would prove to be an important issue by the end of the 1960s, when social and political concerns resulted in another important shift in programming as the lies about Vietnam and Watergate made such sanctioned deception more difficult to accept.

SOCIAL SCIENCE FICTION

Another clear distinction between the heroes of the 1950s and the TV series after 1964 was the presence of science fiction motifs. On the surface, viewers were entertained by the new technologies on both sides of the chessboard. Extraordinary adversaries with extracapabilities gave superspies interesting adversaries and obstacles beyond the gray-haired and gray-suited Commies of old. Often, such new wizardry was merely an extension of what Alfred Hitchcock termed "MacGuffins." For the director of numerous films important to the spy genre, a MacGuffin was a plot device unimportant in itself. The missing codebook, secret plan, or new marvel was only the means to start a story. Such MacGuffins didn't need to be explained. What mattered was how the MacGuffin was found, protected, stopped, or destroyed. In "Spy-Fi" terms, such MacGuffins were usually a visually interesting and clever means to dream up new special effects. But in the final moments, these devices were usually utterly destroyed, apparently never to plague scriptwriters or the world again.

On another level, SF and fantasy elements allowed writers to bring in clichés from other genres to spice up story lines. TV scriptwriters reached back as far as Fritz Lang's 1927 *Metropolis*, which featured the first "fembot" (female robot), a sexy device later seen in *The Man from U.N.C.L.E.*, *The Bionic Woman*, and *Austin Powers: International Man of Mystery*. Tapping into the trappings of Gothic horror films, series from *The Avengers* to *The X-Files* had secret agents investigating usually fraudulent supernatural phenomena, from ghosts to golems to voodoo-stricken zombies. Even the rational *Mission: Impossible* conned superstitious adversaries with spirits and ancient curses. Plots and characteristics based on *Frankenstein, Dr. Jekyll and Mr. Hyde*, and H. G. Wells's *Invisible Man* allowed both the SF and spy genre to expand their boundaries. The original nineteenth-century versions of such stories emphasized personal dramas in which the workings of a mad scientist or criminal only affected a small circle of people in one town or locale (Cawilti and Rosenberg 1987, 33). In the hands of adversaries of U.N.C.L.E. or the Avengers, such monsters posed a much greater threat to the world.

To a large extent, the "Spy-Fi" TV series of the 1960s and beyond were also extensions of the monster and space alien films of the 1950s, often cautionary fables about technology in the new atomic age. Likewise, secret agents contended with mind and body switches, artificial intelligence machines gone amok, genetically enhanced plants or animals, miniaturization rays, and deadly laser beams. Before worries about biological warfare became headlines after the September 11, 2001, attack on the United States, TV spies had long fought terrorists of every stripe employing artificially enhanced diseases as weapons. Long before *The X-Files* and the 2001 version of the *Invisible Man* employed new twists in stories about cryogenics, spy shows used the old motif of artificial immortality to resurrect Hitler, transfer scientists' minds into robots or computers, and seek out real and bogus fountains of youth. Ironically, after September 11, much of this imaginative speculation seemed prophetic. For example, when in October and November 2001 powders carrying anthrax germs were found in mailed envelopes, this author immediately recalled that this had been one MacGuffin in a 1969 *Avengers* story, "You'll Catch Your Death."

In "Spy-Fi," Aldous Huxley's *Brave New World* was as influential as Ian Fleming, at least in terms of the goals of modern villains. Supervillains were typically "zealous puritans intent on cleaning up social decadence" and earthly corruption by destroying humanity so that the species could progress (Donovan 1983, 161). Villains in series like *The Wild Wild West* were often social activists to the extreme, with one terrorist wishing to use tidal waves to destroy polluters.

Each week, independent, freewheeling secret agents brought down ego-maniacs who had utopian designs for reshaping and controlling the world. Private investigators solved crimes against particular people; realistic agents solved crimes against society. But secret agents opposing SF masterminds fought crimes against nature. In the 1950s, this notion allowed writers to portray Communism as a force against nature, particularly human nature. The theme reached its height in *The Prisoner,* whose seventeen episodes were designed to be cautionary parables about the rights of free minds in a world seeking conformity and enforced order. Even in the shows created for pure entertainment, themes that warned of the dangers of ill-used technology—chemical and biological tampering with genetics and the environment—took the spy out of the sometimes claustrophobic Cold War atmosphere into wider vistas of adventure. And, as Cawilti and Rosenberg noted, the techno-logical trappings allowed for ambivalent parables about the meaning of new gadgetry. Whatever devices secret agents had were used up before the final confrontations, when one man stood alone against fantastic machines. If technology was the deciding factor, the enemies of law and order would have won (Cawilti and Rosenberg 1987, 138).

EXPANDING VISTAS

In addition, unlike private eyes, the new type of spy worked in a larger palate of exotic, international locations so the viewer could vicariously pick up interesting details about the global village. As in the richly descriptive James Bond novels, the secret agent's preoccupations with expensive clothes, cars, food, and leisure pursuits were a collage of little facts about what to eat, what to wear, and how to behave in a sophisticated world in which few viewers could ever expect to participate. Glimpses into the realms of exclu-sive clubs like London's Blades were accessible to most viewers only in the glamorous films and TV shows starring secret agents. Such agents had to be worldly enough to go anywhere at any time and seem at home no matter the language, customs, or culture. Viewers learned about these agents' tastes and habits, which were often signature trademarks, as in Bond's preference for shaken martinis. In the pop 1960s, the sexy cars of secret agents helped define their characters, from Simon Templar's "ST-1" Volvo to John Steed's Bentleys and Emma Peel's powder-blue Lotus Elan. Such details gave spy stories a degree of realism and credibility (Pearson 1966, 204). To achieve this plausibility, the production teams behind *Danger Man* and *I Spy,* among others, tried to give their adventures a visual travel documentary look by filming on location. In short, the spy genre offered viewers new kinds of heroes, new vistas in which they operated, and an encyclopedia of a world well beyond small-town America. When viewer interest in such trappings diminished in the 1970s and 1980s, the spy genre underwent major changes in character development, an important theme in explored in Chapters 11 and 12.

In a sense, examining all of the espionage-oriented television programs created before, during, and after the1960s spy renaissance is like inspecting wings of a venerable old museum. Each wing has many rooms, and each section represents the times and attitudes of successive generations of spy buffs and the general public alike. In many ways, the Bond bonanza of the 1960s was merely the most visible era in a genre that has been many things in its fifty-year history. Heroes must act out the principles we demand of them, and our desires shape how we perceive the covert world of fact and fancy. But beyond these matters, the political, sociological, cultural, and artistic issues reflected in spy TV series make them more than examples of escapist entertainment. Our attitudes toward McCarthyism, the Cold War, and changing technologies, as well as American values and tastes have all been mirrored in TV spies. Therefore, the fifty years of TV's secret agents must be seen in a wide context, and the following chapters have as much to say about American culture as they do about one television genre.

But I've jumped ahead of the story—to begin where it began, we must return to those thrilling days of yesteryear, to the beginnings of a century when even radio was but an experiment in Mr. Marconi's lab. Before television, literary and broadcast spies had their own fifty-year history, and these radio and book heroes planted the seeds for all entertainment media to follow.

CHAPTER 2

The Roots of a Family Tree:
1900 to 1961

WHEN SPYING WASN'T COOL

> When one country knows something it doesn't want another country to know, a state secret is born. Then the international fight for custody begins, government official versus government official, diplomat versus diplomat, espionage agent versus counter-espionage agent. And the others, the men who never wear striped pants or frock coats and who always carry guns and grudges, those who buy secrets large and small like vegetables on the open market. Men only loyal to the franc, the dollar, the shilling, the mark, the men living among us as one of us but dying among us differently.
>
> —Secret Agent Christopher Storm in *Foreign Intrigue*
> (quoted in MacDonald 1985, 105)

In the opening decades of the twentieth century, few would have imagined that anyone so disreputable as a spy could ever be considered a hero in popular culture. In the literature of the times, spies were largely portrayed as treacherous, duplicitous, and immoral anarchists, revolutionaries, or sexually deviant betrayers like Delilah, Mata Hari, or Benedict Arnold. Most Americans felt spies should be dealt with as suggested in the *Encyclopedia Britannica:* "When a spy is discovered, he is hanged immediately" (quoted in Symons 1972, 230). Judging from dialogue in Alfred Hitchcock's *The 39 Steps* (1935) spies preferred the euphemism "secret agent" to avoid negative connotations.

The U.S. government was equally uneasy about espionage. Diplomats and their aides and attachés were discouraged from intelligence gathering as it was considered unseemly conduct (Richelson 1995, 3). More ominously, in October 1929, Secretary of State Henry Stimson disbanded the most successful covert office in the United States, Herbert Yardley's "Black Chamber" code-breakers, because the new Hoover administration believed "gentlemen don't read each other's mail."

Still, during this era, Hollywood offered its share of spy yarns such as *After Tonight* (1933) and *Espionage* (1937), featuring beautiful Russian spies gifted in the use of invisible inks, secret jewelry compartments, and seductive wiles. But such stories were merely love-conquers-all yarns as the exotic women inevitably fell under the spell of English-speaking men of courage and character (Strada and Troper 1997, 22–25). Simultaneously, action adventures were an entertainment choice in old time radio. Perhaps the first network spy drama was NBC's 1932 to 1933 series *Secret Service Spy Stories*. In 1935, Herbert Yardley's spy work came to NBC in *Stories of the Black Chamber*. Another notable early fifteen-minute serial was San Francisco-based *Dan Dunn: Secret Operative Number 48*. 1938 saw three new radio spy serials, *Spy at Large*, *Spy Secrets*, and Mutual Broadcasting's four-year success, *Ned Jordan Spy Stories*. Although most such shows turned to World War II themes in 1939, surviving copies of that year's *Secret Agent K-7* show there was still listener interest in pre-Nazi bad guys brought down by the G-men of the Treasury Department, Secret Service, and fictional law enforcement agencies. Popular anthology shows also drew from secret agent files. The Lux Radio Theatre adapted *The 39 Steps* in one 1937 broadcast and brought an army intelligence officer onstage to make a pitch for "good spies," that is "patriotic spies versus mercenary spies"—those who ply their wares for mere money.

Meanwhile, long before television shows like *The Wild Wild West* dealt with pressure groups opposed to media violence, prewar radio confronted the same issue on two levels. First, educational, parental, and women's organizations such as the PTA complained about airwave violence. Such groups feared children would emulate Jungle Jim and the Green Hornet. Parents disliked the fisticuffs and gunplay of *Gangbusters*, the eerie stories of *The Witching Hour*, and even *The Lone Ranger* (MacDonald 1979, 45). In response, NBC promised in 1936 to uphold law and order, sobriety, good morals, fair play, democratic principles, and clean living. No James Bond could flourish under these constraints.

Simultaneously, as World War II dawned in Europe, isolationist spokespeople pushed for programming that didn't encourage calls for American intervention. Networks told writers to avoid including sabotage, subversion, or spying inside the United States in their plots. Radio characters couldn't take one side or the other in the war. Such thinking influenced the White House, as President Franklin D. Roosevelt was discouraged from openly working to establish a central intelligence service despite calls from General William "Wild Bill" Donovan and two British envoys worried about

America's lack of awareness regarding European matters. One of these envoys was Lieutenant Commander Ian Fleming of the British Royal Navy.

The indifference ended after December 7, 1941, when every fictional hero was called to war against the Axis powers; now the international gangsters were to be crushed with fists, patriotic zeal, and dime novel wit. Scorn, derision, and overt hatred for Axis agents replaced the earlier squeaky-clean tone of radio dramas. Counterspying on American soil was now both adventure and propaganda. Superman, Tom Mix, and the once disreputable Green Hornet were now expected to deal with Axis spies with maximum prejudice. In movie serials, Batman took on Japanese spies. In England, even Sherlock Holmes worked undercover against Nazi agents on film and radio.

Radio series featuring secret agents now came to the fore, and they came with a vengeance. The *Man Called X* (1944–1952) featured Ken Thurston (Herbert Marshall) as an American intelligence agent sent "wherever intrigue lurked and danger was the by-word." (Dunning 1998, 344). The concept also made for a short-lived syndicated TV series in 1956 starring Barry Sullivan. Known for intrigue rather than romance, one TV episode featured X taking on a gang of female spies. From 1943 to 1944, *Foreign Assignment* established the format of reporters as spies. Other such series included *David Harding, Counterspy* (1942–1957) and *The Man from G-2*, also known as *Major North, Army Intelligence* (1945–1946). Many of these anti-Nazi shows continued after the war, including *Cloak and Dagger* (1950), a series of fictionalized accounts of World War II operatives working for the OSS (Office of Strategic Services), the predecessor to the CIA. Known for avoiding formulas, the tense dramas invariably began with a question by the "Hungarian Giant" (Raymond Edward Johnson): "Are you willing to undertake a dangerous mission for the United States knowing in advance you may never return alive?" Earlier, the juvenile serial *Don Winslow of the Navy* starred Johnson in its 1942 season as a young naval officer assigned to wartime intelligence. One popular anthology series showcasing Hollywood talent, *Intrigue* (1946), cast notable character actors like Vincent Price in a variety of spy outings. In 1948, *I Love Adventure* had Jack Packard (Michael Laseto), formerly of American intelligence, sent to London to work for the top secret "21 Old Men of 10 Gramercy Park." These keepers of international peace met behind a large two-way mirror where Jack could hear but never see them. NBC's *Top Secret* (1950) starred sultry voiced Hungarian actress Alana Massey as a Mata Hari–style operative during World War II. In the same year, radio stalwart Jack Armstrong became *Armstrong of the S.B.I.* for one season working as a counterspy for the Scientific Bureau of Investigation. Most swashbuckling of all was Errol Flynn's 1952 *The Modern Adventures of Casanova*—lover Christopher Casanova that is. Trying to live down the reputation of his famous ancestor, Christopher was a secret agent for "Worldpol." Another Hollywood heartthrob, Douglas Fairbanks Jr., played a variety of federal agents in *The Third Man* from 1951 to 1952.

Other series shifted their targets to Communist infiltrators at home and abroad. Between 1952 and 1954, popular actor Dana Andrews starred as Matt Cvetic in *I Was a Communist for the FBI*, a concept repeated in a number of television series and a 1951 film of the same name. Based on the book by Cvetic, the unabashed plug for the House Un-American Activities Committee featured a heroic Pittsburgh steelworker working undercover to identify blue-collar Communists. One important trend in these formative years was quasi-realism, which helped give films, radio programs, and finally television shows credibility and an excuse to use violence in the name of public information. Many radio series were ostensibly based on true case files with the consultation of police veterans and local law enforcement departments. On both radio and TV, "true life" stories included *Secret Missions* (1948–1949), based on files of the Office of Naval Intelligence and featuring perhaps the first germ warfare scripts on radio. *Spy Catcher*, a 1960-to-1961 BBC radio series was based on the memoirs of Lieutenant Colonel Oreste Pinto of Allied Counterintelligence Services. *Counterspy* and *Gangbusters* producer Philip Lord, who established the recurring tone of praise and tribute for law enforcement agents, created many such shows employing real-life FBI agents who provided introductions and audio wanted posters for the series. Writers for both radio and TV shows with such formats considered themselves lucky. Instead of having to create a new plot every seven days, they merely dramatized already existing files.

These old-time radio series had much to do with the formation of early television and consequently the secret agents in the 1960s and beyond. In television's first decade, writers and actors came from radio, film, and the stage. Private investigator Richard Diamond was originally a 1949-to-1950 radio detective (Dick Powell) before TV featured David Janssen, the legs of Mary Tyler Moore, and Diamond's gal Karen Wells, played by future *Mission: Impossible* temptress, Barbara Bain. *Hallmark Hall of Fame, Suspense*, and *CBS Radio Workshop* music composer Jerry Goldsmith later wrote the theme and background music for *Our Man Flint* and *The Man from U.N.C.L.E.*, influencing all TV spy themes that followed. U.N.C.L.E. cocreator Sam Rolfe had scripted episodes for *Suspense, Hollywood Star Playhouse, Richard Diamond*, and *Sam Spade*. His U.N.C.L.E. production partner, Norman Felton, had been a longtime NBC radio director and producer for such shows as *Author's Playhouse, Grand Hotel*, and *The Guiding Light* (Anderson 1993, 10). Future *Wild Wild West* costar Ross Martin gained early experience in radio's *Cloak and Dagger* and *Lights Out* in 1949. Radio comedy writer Leonard Stern took the tried-and-true technique of radio catch-phrases and kept television audiences laughing with "Sorry about that, Chief" and "Missed it by that much" in his 1965 cocreation *Get Smart*. One script contributor to *Get Smart* was *I Love Lucy* creator Jess Oppenheimer, who'd also written for Jack Benny and George Burns on radio. Television producer Sheldon Leonard had also cut his teeth in radio, as an announcer and voice for various radio characters, notably for the *Jack Benny Show*. When he conceived *I Spy*, he gave his ideas to writers Mort Fine and Dave Friedkin who developed the series and helped shape the characters of Kelly Robinson and Alexander Scott. Fine and Friedkin were chosen for their radio experience in high-adventure shows such as *Suspense*, *Bold Venture*, and *Broadway Is My Beat*, on which Leonard was a stock player.

BROADCAST CENSORSHIP

A number of political and market forces also shaped early television. In 1952, the year Congress established the House Subcommittee of Legislative Oversight to investigate morality on radio and television, networks had little clout. Advertisers dictated programming, and television networks had few affiliates. In 1952, NBC had sixty-four stations, CBS thirty-one, and ABC a mere fifteen. Many markets had but one or two stations on the air, and many only broadcast from dawn until dusk. While networks grew in the 1950s (ABC had sixty stations by 1959), the 1958 and 1959 game show and payola scandals gave the Federal Communications Commission reasons to threaten stations with losing their licenses if they didn't adhere to strict practices of broadcast behavior.

In addition, the Hollywood blacklist, publications such as *Red Channels* and *Counter Attack*, and watchdog groups like Aware had much to do with 1950s TV spies—and all broadcast ventures afterward. TV spies began in fact before fiction. "Real life espionage reached American television screens in the early 1950s when Congressional investigations of Communism went before the cameras . . . The spies were few but viewers did get insights into tradecraft from undercover agents for the FBI." In fact, the McCarthy hearings "drew one of the largest audiences in television's short history" (Polmar and Allen 1997, 547). Bringing both commercial and governmental pressures together, Former Navy intelligence officer Vincent Hartnett became a subversion consultant who compiled lists of suspicious leftist writers and directors. He sold his list to sponsors, who in turn pressured the industry to drop or cancel series with "questionable" ties to Communism. As a result, the spy shows of the era went to great lengths to demonstrate their prodemocracy themes and portray Communism as the dark side of black-and-white programming. McCarthyism created a climate of fear in Hollywood that, according to Eric Barnouw, resulted in an industry shaped by caution and cowardice from which it has never recovered (Barnouw 1990, 217).

As the rise of television began almost precisely with the growth of Cold War thinking, the two new developments in American culture were quickly joined at the hip. America had moved far away from the isolationism of the 1930s and instead was making ever-increasing entries into every corner of the world stage. As a result, one dominant theme of 1950s film, radio, and

TV spies was undisguised propaganda for U.S. interests. One source for this collusion was NBC founder and Brigadier General David Sarnoff, a powerful executive keenly interested in military intelligence and how broadcast technology could assist anti-Communist efforts. As a result, in 1952 NBC trained CIA operatives in overseas propaganda efforts in Europe and the Far East (Barnouw 1990, 190). During this era, more than thirty-five movies dealing with domestic Communism were produced. Production peaked in 1952, when twelve titles were released in a single year (Strada and Troper 1997, 95). In short, to keep the blacklisters at bay and to capitalize on the popularity of "true crime" radio success, television executives quickly aligned themselves with government law enforcement agencies, which resulted in the first major trend in TV spies.

THE FIRST TV SPIES

> These are the stories of America's intelligence agents, our country's first line of defense.
> —Preamble to each episode of *The Man Called X*, 1956

The history of TV spies begins in 1951 with the debut of three series, *Doorway to Danger, Dangerous Assignment,* and *Foreign Intrigue*. First of its kind in many ways, *Doorway to Danger* ran on both NBC and ABC over its three-year run. Narrated by Westbrook Van Voorhis, the show began as a summer replacement series originally titled *Door with No Name* to indicate the secret nature of the agency's work. Mel Ruick, Roland Winters, and finally Raymond Bramley each played the central role of John Randolph who sat in the secret office beyond the entrance of the show's title. In quasi-documentary style, Randolph, an intelligence supervisor, dispatched various agents on international assignments. The program's first and third years featured recurring characters, including Grant Richards and Stacy Harris each playing agent Doug Carter in separate seasons. During the second year, Randolph supervised a new agent each week.

Dangerous Assignment starred Hollywood leading man Brian Donlevy, who played government agent Steve Mitchell, the role he'd created on the 1948-to-1953 radio series of the same name. In each thirty-minute adventure, the "commissioner" of some unnamed government agency dispatched the suave Mitchell to Mexico City, Casablanca, Burma, or behind the Iron Curtain. Mitchell did considerable stunt work, leaping from cars and electrocuting enemies with light sockets (Brooks and Marsh 1999, 233).

A different approach distinguished the syndicated *Foreign Intrigue*. The cast consisted of one hotel operator and four alternating wire correspondents for the fictional Consolidated News Service who each infiltrated European spy rings. Filmed in Europe, the location shooting was the only constant in the series as new characters were based in different cities as they battled unreconstructed Nazis and Communist saboteurs with very clear Cold War overtones. One August 1953 episode had reporter Bruce Cannon pursuing a news story in East Berlin, which led to his helping a rocket scientist defect to the West (MacDonald 1985, 105).

SPYING AS PROPAGANDA

> This is a story, a fantastically true story, from the files of Herbert A. Philbrick, who for nine frightening years did lead three lives—citizen, Communist, counter-spy. And it is now revealed for the first time his secret files concerning not only his own activities but also the current activities of other counter-espionage agents. For obvious reasons, the names, dates, and places have been changed, but the story is based on fact.
>
> —Opening narration to *I Led Three Lives*, 1956

There was nothing subtle about America's use of TV spies in the 1950s for Cold War indoctrination of its viewers. Frederic W. Ziff, a former radio producer for series such as *I Was a Communist for the FBI*, *Bold Venture*, and *Boston Blackie* went to great lengths to associate the 1956 TV version of *A Man Called X* with the CIA. Advertising for the series made overt references to the agency: "The CIA must learn to kill silently when necessary to protect a vital mission . . . secret agents have molded our destiny" (Barnouw 1990, 216). Another example of this collusion was a different Ziff production called *I Led Three Lives*, an infamous "red scare" TV show starring Richard Carlson. It was reportedly a favorite of FBI director J. Edgar Hoover, who saw the series as a public service program encouraging viewers to call in about suspicious neighbors.

Very popular in its day, the one hundred seventeen story lines were drawn from real-life FBI undercover agent Herbert Philbrick, who in fact had infiltrated the American Communist Party for nine years. The series was based on Philbrick's book of the same name, and the first two seasons dramatized events taken from the book. The third season was built on notes and files from Philbrick's office, including the work of other agents. Philbrick wanted the show to appeal to Hoover and told an interviewer in 1974 his job had been mainly to ensure the FBI didn't need to directly exert their own pressures on the series (MacDonald 1985, 102). He reviewed each script for historical accuracy and conformity to FBI practices. Because of the fame generated from the book and series, Philbrick enjoyed a long career as a lecturer on his spy adventures.

I Led Three Lives was far more than escapist fiction, however. In the series, liberals were always suspect. On both the program and in real life, alert mothers called in to report on daughters who resented bombs and wars; pacifism was clearly a Communist infection. In each episode, Agent Philbrick invariably met a contact in a dark alley or abandoned house, whereas the

Communists always met in basement secret cells, plotting sabotage, thefts of trade secrets, and diabolical infiltrations into trade unions, colleges, and churches. Racial unrest and religious discord, often between Jews and Catholics, were either Communist inspired or exploited to further party interests. Double Agent Philbrick often seemed to lead four lives, as the Communists spent as much time spying on each other as on any U.S. interest. For the Communists, the party was the one cause that mattered. Philbrick was most often called at a moment's notice to do some superior's bidding and expected to drop all else to serve the party.

Throughout the series, Carlson narrated each episode to reveal Philbrick's thoughts to the audience as he hid his schemes from his alleged friends and to underline a sense of danger. "You're in a bind now, Philbrick. But you're the only one between the life of that boy and the poison of the party." Philbrick's home life was often in jeopardy because he was forced to deceive coworkers at his advertising agency. At first, his wife, Eva, was in the dark about his double life, but then she too became an FBI agent. In one story, his mother-in-law became certain the Philbricks were Communists, but was assuaged when she saw the children saying their bedtime prayers. As an FBI agent, Philbrick was ostensibly legally bound to operate within U.S. borders, but he occasionally went abroad to Germany and South America. In the latter location, although his FBI contact told him the agency never got involved in other governments' matters, within minutes Philbrick was asked to spy on Communist guerillas and report on their plans, plots, and the location of their jungle headquarters. Patriotism was an overt theme of the show, as at least one plug for democracy occurred in each script, whether it related to the story line or not. Such patriotic sentiments did not play well overseas. The series was barred from distribution in Hong Kong, Australia, Argentina, Venezuela, and Colombia. The Russians were well aware of the effects of such American propaganda against them.

In one Soviet spy's 1950 report, Moscow was advised that the U.S. government was "setting middle-class Americans against the USSR and People's Democracies with the help of anti-Soviet, anti-Communist propaganda through the press, radio, cinema, and the church" (Weinstein and Vassiliev 1999, 120). As a result, when *I Led Three Lives* was aired in Mexico, the Russian embassy filed an official complaint. The British House of Commons debated over the implications of the controversial show. In America, however, the series had considerable influence during its heyday. To boost their patriotic images, oil and brewery companies sponsored reruns of this extremely successful syndicated program into the 1960s. Without question, *I Led Three Lives* influenced all other TV spies of the era.

For example, *Secret File U.S.A.* (1954–1955) was a syndicated series filmed in Europe and featured Robert Alda as American intelligence officer Major Bill Morgan. The settings in this program reflected a view of the globe typical in most such series, that of a disorganized, frightened world in need of

America's guiding hand. In one of the many spoken-word preambles to such shows, the persuasive purpose was made manifestly clear:

> Secret Files U.S.A. is a warning to all enemies of America, at home and abroad planning acts of aggression. This is the story of the gallant men and women who penetrated, and are still penetrating, enemy lines to get secret information necessary for the protection of the United States. This is the story of one of our nation's mightiest weapons past, present, and future, if necessary the American intelligence services.

Similar programs included *Pentagon Confidential*, also know as *Pentagon U.S.A.* Starring Addison Richards, Larry Fletcher, and Edward Binns, this 1953 CBS series was based on army intelligence files. Executive producer William Dozier, later the producer of TV's versions of *Batman* and *The Green Hornet*, created the series. ABC's *OSS* featured the work of *Spiral Staircase* (1945) director Robert Siodmak, who oversaw the filming of location shots in Europe, which were set during World War II. The show, produced by former OSS officer William Bliscu, ran from 1957 to 1958 and starred Canadian Lionel Murton as an OSS chief who sent agent Frank Hawthorne (Australian actor Ron Randell) on dangerous missions behind enemy lines, often in cahoots with the French Resistance (McNeil 1996). *OSS* capitalized on the public unveiling of the actual organizations' files when the OSS was disbanded and its records declassified. The show also served as propaganda for reversing attitudes about maintaining intelligence agencies after the war. For a time, there was little support for organizations like the OSS or CIA, as some feared a new American Gestapo might be the result.

Another program from the same mold was *Crusader*, which featured future *Family Affair* father Brian Keith. He starred as Matt Andrews, an international freelance journalist who fought simultaneously for scoops and against spies. Andrews's mother had been detained in Poland by the Communists, and after her death in a concentration camp, Andrews blamed the Communist regime and dedicated himself to aiding oppressed people who wished to escape to freedom. Like the correspondents in *Foreign Intrigue*, Andrews fell into espionage while doing other things. And again like *Foreign Intrigue*, the show's preamble stated its propaganda purpose:

> *Crusader* records the struggle of democratic people against the enemies of freedom and justice at home and abroad. These are the stories of people who have been helped by the many great organizations that are dedicated to bringing truth to those who are fed lies, aid to those who live in darkness, protection to those who live in fear.

From 1958 to 1959, *Behind Closed Doors* starred Bruce Gordon as Commander Matson, the program's host and occasional participant. The show was based on the files of Rear Admiral Ellis M. Zacharias, a twenty-five-year veteran of naval intelligence. One episode of *Behind Closed Doors* that aired in April 1959, "Assignment: Prague," demonstrated the series' awareness of media usefulness in the Cold War. The setting for this story was a movie studio behind the Iron Curtain churning out anti-American propaganda under the scrutiny of distrustful Communist bureaucrats who admitted their projects were "distorted, perverted, untrue," put together by dedicated and warped producers (MacDonald 1985, 119).

But even during the McCarthy era, moves toward escapist fun were already evident on American television. In 1955, one of the many incarnations of *The Falcon*, an obvious *Saint* rip-off, came to syndicated TV with the gravel-voiced Mike Waring (Charles McGraw). In *The Adventures of the Falcon*, former radio detective Waring became a U.S. intelligence agent. Many reviewers were puzzled by the description of Waring as the "famous undercover agent." How could anyone work undercover and be famous at the same time (McNeil 1996)? One series with elements that would become popular in the 1960s was *Five Fingers* (1959–1960), starring David Hedison, who was soon to appear on ABC's espionage-oriented SF thriller, *Voyage to the Bottom of the Sea*. For fifteen episodes, Hedison played Victor Sebastian, an American counterspy posing as a theatrical booking agent in Europe. Code-named "Five Fingers," Sebastian looked for spies at the same time he was eyeing musical talent in clubs and cabarets (Brooks and Marsh 1999, 349). This precursor to 1960s spy shows combined humor and an ongoing romance between the agent and an aspiring fashion model named Simone Genet (Luciana Paluzzi) who knew nothing of Sebastian's double life. Paul Burke played Robertson, Sebastian's government contact. This series was loosely based on a 1951 film of the same name starring James Mason, and both the movie and TV versions drew from L. C. Moyzisch's book, *Operation: Cicero* (1950).

Similarly, two-fisted Glen Evans, played by Australian actor Rod Taylor, was a government agent pretending to be a correspondent posted in Hong Kong, also the name of a series that ran from 1960 to 1961. Evans fought smugglers, pushers, killers, spies, and slinky women who disappeared behind beaded curtains (McNeil 1996). His contact was Neil Campbell (Lloyd Bochner), and Evans spent considerable time in the Golden Dragon Nightclub owned by Tully (Jack Kruschen). There was the 1960 NBC series *The Man from Interpol*, which was an influence on the later *Man From U.N.C.L.E.* in name only. In the thirty-minute show, Superintendent Mercer (John Longdon) sent out Anthony Smith (Richard Wyler) on assignments requiring border crossings in cases involving smugglers, counterfeiters, and the like. In this series filmed in England, Smith ostensibly worked for the Scotland Yard branch of Interpol, an actual international information gathering and exchange organization that itself rarely was involved in crime fighting or political espionage.

As would be the case in the 1960s, children's programming joined the fray. One 1956 anthology series hosted by Raymond Massey is best remembered for its title, *I Spy*, later used in Sheldon Leonard's much more successful 1960s series. (A fifteen-minute version of *I Spy* was aired on radio, but few details are known. Eight of these shows still exist.) In the TV syndicated stories, Anton, the spymaster (Massey) told tales of history's spies from ancient Rome to World War II. But in all cases the spies tended to be children who accidentally participated in espionage. The first TV *I Spy* lasted less than a year.

Captain Midnight, later syndicated as *Jet Jackson, Flying Commando*, was another program drawn from 1940s radio drama. Jackson (Richard Webb) captained a secret squadron dedicated to establishing justice around the world. Most members of his secret squadron were children in foreign countries. Midnight flew a jet plane and had a hidden mountain laboratory. Over half of the thirty-nine episodes dealt with enemy agents, national defense, military technology, and despots planning to rule the world (Dunning 1998, 136). In one episode, he fought against an island queen who changed her mind about allowing the United States to test atomic bombs on her island. Long before Puerto Rican citizens protested in 2001 against American bombing ranges on their territory, anyone who opposed such privileges was clearly a Communist dupe.

In 1953, *Atom Squad* appeared as a weekday serial in which three government agents thwarted Communist plots. In one adventure, they broke up a scheme by an enemy agent who had created a giant magnet to disrupt American shipping. They foiled an ex-Nazi who planned to destroy the United States with his weather-controlling machine, a MacGuffin later used in any number of TV series and the film version of *The Avengers*. From 1959 to 1964, and in syndicated reruns for decades afterward, Rocky the flying squirrel and his buddy, Bullwinkle T. Moose, fought Boris Badenoff, Natasha Fatale, and Fearless Leader, all agents of an East European country called Pottsylvania. Almost as enduring was the debate over whether or not the cartoon was deliberate anti-Communist propaganda. Chris Hayward, who had worked on the cartoons, later recalled a rumor that the Bullwinkle team had been asked to create Natasha and Boris to make the Russians look bad. According to Hayward, that sort of thinking was exactly the kind of idea that would inspire a *Get Smart* script, a series for which he also wrote (McCrohan 1988, 11). For other observers, it was more than coincidence that 1958—the year before the series premiered—was the year of the Sputnik scare, when the Russians became the first nation to enter the space race. This inspired Congress to pass the National Defense Education Act, resulting in the construction of hundreds of new schools to create a generation capable of out-thinking Soviet science. Intentional or innocent, Rocky, Bullwinkle, Captain Midnight, and the other superspies contributed to youthful attitudes regarding the Eastern bloc in an era when children were being drilled on the importance of air-raid shelters and how to behave in case of enemy attack at school.

INDEPENDENT OPERATORS

In America, most characteristics of 1960s spies were first seen in radio and television series showcasing independent operators, not tough-talking agents in raincoats and back alleys. Shades of spies to come were the gentlemen amateurs who stumbled into foreign intrigues through chance or patriotism. Such characters were typically Americanized versions of British "Clubland" novels by John Buchan, Graham Greene, and Eric Ambler, in which the amateur was a member of upper-crust society with strong moral and social codes. Like the later John Steed in *The Avengers*, a character clearly influenced by the gentlemen amateur, such adventurers solved crimes at night as if playing a game of cricket against former Eton or Cambridge school buddies. "Unfettered by decreed procedures, the amateur, in this tradition, customarily exhibits far more efficiency and creativity than the professional" (Hoffman 2001, 51). Such characters, emulating Sherlock Holmes, had abundant imaginations and eschewed conventional interpretations that, at first blush, pointed to plausible solutions to crimes.

TV outings with these trappings included the first incarnation of many shows called *The Hunter,* which had two brief runs in the 1950s. The first aired on CBS as a summer replacement show from July to September 1952, with Barry Nelson as Bart Adams, a wealthy American businessman and playboy fighting Communist agents. (In a few years, Nelson would become the first actor to star as James Bond in a TV hour anthology series.) *The Hunter* returned on NBC for a six-month run in 1954, starring Keith Larsen as Adams, now a world-traveling master of disguise. Adams was a private patriot who, at a moment's notice, could leave a tennis match at Wimbledon to rush to Romania to assist an anti-Communist informer. Or he would leave a German art display to jet to Prague to help the Czech underground (MacDonald 1985, 108).

From 1952 to 1953, future *Gilligan's Island* skipper Alan Hale Jr. had the title role in the CBS series, *Biff Baker, U.S.A.* Traveling the world with his wife Louise (Randy Stuart) in search of goods for his importing business, Biff was often drawn into international intrigue on both sides of the Iron Curtain. Before Vietnam became known in the average American household, Biff aided a French plantation owner in Saigon fighting off a murderous band.

In this Frederic W. Ziff production, Baker was the perfect mix of American patriotism and commercial interests, but the popularity of the show portraying a businessman as adventurer led to controversy. The sponsor, the American Tobacco Company, received complaints from business groups protesting the implication that American businessmen were spying for the government. These letters were forwarded to the FBI, and the script consultants explained in a trade journal that the FBI, the State Department, and the Commerce Department all approved the scripts. The show's producers stated that the show was intended to be overt propaganda urging the world to move forward in accepting American democracy. Therefore, any attack on the show was an attack on democracy (MacDonald 1985, 105).

Ironically, the casting of a businessman as hero was a reversal of usual fictional trends, in which the wealthy were portrayed as greedy, amoral, and self-seeking gluttons preying on the less fortunate. In the 1950s, however, both films and broadcast media were under the watchful eyes of a Congress that perceived attacks on bankers and businesspeople as sympathetic to Communism. When sponsors received promotional materials for such series as *I Led Three Lives* and *Biff Baker*, they were proclaimed local members of "The Businessman's Crusade Against the Communist Conspiracy." So the moneyed classes, for a time, were only infrequently heavies in fictional dramas.

For some historians, *Passport to Danger* was likely the most obvious precursor to the 1960s breed of spies (Newcomb 1997). Starring Caesar Romero (the future Joker in TV's *Batman*), from 1954 to 1956 Steve McQuinn (Romero) was a diplomatic courier going from embassy to embassy dealing with enemy agents with dash and humor (Brooks and Marsh 1999, 786). Most unusual of all such shows was one precursor to *The Wild Wild West*, 1953's *Cowboy G-men*. Fusing Westerns with secret agents, for thirty-nine episodes Russell Hayden and Jackie Coogan played government agents Pat Gallagher and Stoney Crockett. Another series associated with 1950s spies was the syndicated half-hour drama *Soldiers of Fortune* (1955). It featured Tim Kelly (John Russell) and Teubo Smith (Chic Chandler) as freewheeling troubleshooters, a mix of military intelligence and private eye stories. These two Americans roamed from London to the Far East, solving problems while reaffirming American effectiveness against international mischief. This merging of military talents with detective work would later characterize TV shows from *The A-Team* to *Airwolf* and a host of paramilitary special operations series.

One 1959 private eye series, *21 Beacon Street*, might not seem, at first glance, to be related to the secret agent genre. But in 1968, Filmways Productions sued *Mission: Impossible* producer Bruce Geller claiming plagiarism. On the Boston set of *21 Beacon Street*, brilliant planner Dennis Chase (Dennis Morgan) ran the Chase Detective Agency aided by a specialized cast of assistants. Before Cinnamon Carter, beautiful Phi Beta Kappan Lola (Joanna Barnes) combined sex appeal with a sharp mind. Brian (Brian Kelly) was an ex-Marine law school graduate combining brains and brawn. Jim (James Mahoney) was a clever dialectician and inventor of useful machines and devices—a precursor to *Mission: Impossible*'s Barney Collier. The agency took on cases the law couldn't or wouldn't solve and was noted for out-swindling swindlers. This team intercepted and replaced criminals and used hidden tape recorders, bugs, and radio-transmitting eyeglasses. While the series was short-lived and quickly forgotten, it not only used concepts shared by *Mission: Impossible*, but its innovative mix of styles and characters served as an early example of what the 1960s had in store.

Another such effort was the single-episode adaptation of Ian Fleming's *Casino Royale*, which aired on October 21, 1954, as part of CBS's Climax anthology series. Hoping television would expand the audience for his new Bond novels, Fleming planned to continue these adaptations despite the casting of former *Hunter* lead Barry Nelson as an Americanized "Jimmy Bond." But the network opted not to do any more such live-action Bond stories, and this version of *Casino Royale* disappeared from view until the 1980s, when video versions surfaced on the collector's market. Had not James Bond been involved, the episode would have joined the rest of 1950s television spies lost in entertainment history. In 2003, the televised hour was included as an extra on the DVD release of the 1967 theatrical film version.

However, Fleming didn't give up on television. The novel *Dr. No* and the subsequent film were based on a 1958 Fleming teleplay originally designed for but never aired on NBC starring a U.S. agent, Commander James Gunn (Black 2001, 34). Originally titled "Commander Jamaica," Gunn was to receive his clipped orders from a demanding admiral heard over a hidden speaker in his cabin on his yacht. Pretending to be on a treasure hunt, Gunn was to investigate gangsters trying to deflect American missiles, a direct precursor to *Dr. No* (Pearson 1966, 182).

After CBS indicated new interest in a series starring Bond himself, Fleming began writing fresh scripts in 1958. Three of these unsold scripts became the short stories "Risico," "From a View to a Kill," and "For Your Eyes Only" (Pearson 1966, 310). In one form or another, these plots conceived for TV ultimately were incorporated into Bond films. In 1966, another Fleming TV project was aired as a two-part TV movie, *UN Project*, later known as both *Poppies Are Also Flowers* and *The Poppy Is Also a Flower*. Directed by Terence Young (*Dr. No*), the story involved narcotics agents working for the UN. In October 1962, Fleming met with *Dr. Kildare* producer Norman Felton to discuss a broadcast version of the former's travelogue, *Thrilling Cities*. Their meeting ended these plans, but their talks directly led to the creation of *The Man from U.N.C.L.E.*, as discussed further in Chapter 3.

B MOVIES SPIES

You are about to see one of the most closely guarded secrets and one of the most fantastic series of events ever recorded in the annals of counter-espionage. This is my story. The story of Mel Hunter, who lives in your world, a *world of giants*.

—Title narration for *World of Giants*, 1959

Other harbingers of concepts to come were evident in the syndicated *World of Giants* (1959–1960). In this early fusion of spy genre and science fiction, Mel Hunter (Marshall Thompson) was an intelligence bureau agent who, while spying at a missile site behind the Iron Curtain, fell prey to a strange residue shower after a rocket filled with experimental fuel exploded. His molecular structure changed, and he shrank to six inches in height. He was paired with normal-sized agent Bill Winters (Arthur Franz) and used his unique gift in secret missions, although he was often more plagued by day-to-day circumstances than the plans of America's enemies. Falling pencils were as deadly as the dogs that growled and threatened Hunter as he scurried under doors and up rosebushes and lifted giant phone receivers. He lived in a luxurious dollhouse, exercised on a tiny gymnastics bar, and was carried around in a special briefcase equipped with a trapdoor over which was his built-in seat and seat belt.

The most expensively made series of its day, the thirty-minute black-and-white *World of Giants* was inspired by the success of the 1957 film *The Incredible Shrinking Man*, along with a plethora of other tiny people B movies (Phillips and Garcia 1996, 543). At first, CBS bought the show but then feared the feature-film budgets it required and instead decided to syndicate the thirteen episodes filmed in England through United Artists. Most of the monies had gone into the oversize props before new producer William Alland discovered new uses for trick photography, notably split-screen filming. Marshall Thompson, later Dr. Marshall Tracy of TV's *Daktari*, was perfectly cast, but no one could take his predicament seriously. One producer noted that it's difficult to believe your country could collapse if the hero can't escape a playful kitten. No one could accept the notion of J. Edgar Hoover briefing a micro-agent in his office. (Phillips and Garcia 1996, 543). Both intended and unintended humor appeared in the visuals and dialogue, as in one scene in which a scientist asked Hunter what he most wanted. "A five-inch girl," was the reply. When the series ended, scientists were looking for a cure, but no cure could help a series based simply on a gimmick.

Not surprisingly, across the ocean on 007's home turf, British producers were more on target in terms of what was to come. One 1959 syndicated import on American screens was *The Four Just Men*, which featured a unit of World War II veterans called by their dying commander to come together and fight postwar evil. First as a team, then as alternating leads in individual adventures, the four then-famous stars were cast to reflect international perspectives. The Americans were represented by newspaperman Tim Collier (Dan Dailey), the British by private eye Ben Bradford (Jack Hawkins), the French by lawyer Jeff Ryder (Italian-American actor Richard Conti), and the Italians by hotel owner Rick Opaceri (actor and director Vittorio De Sica). Surprisingly, this major cast didn't take with American audiences, so the show lasted but one season.

For two seasons (1961–1962), British viewers saw London's Associated Rediffusion's early spy series, *Top Secret*. Although filmed in England, *Top Secret* was set in Argentina, starring William Franklyn as Peter Dallas, a British intelligence agent supposedly on sabbatical in South America (Vahimhei 1997). Miguel Garetta (Patrick Cargill), a local businessman with Secret Service links, gave Dallas his mission orders. Garetta's son, Mike (Alan Rothwell), accompanied Dallas on his adventures. Although no copies of this series are known to exist, its theme, "Sucu Sucu," became far more famous than the series itself. It still appears on compilations of music by its composer, Laurie Johnson, who in 1966 wrote the famous *Avengers* title music.

Four years before Sean Connery's debut in *Dr. No*, producer Ralph Smart fused H. G. Wells and Ian Fleming in *The Invisible Man*, England's first fanciful Secret Agent series, running from 1958 to 1961 in both Britain and the United States. Before this casting of a transparent agent as a force for good, a plethora of invisible mad scientists were unseen seeking revenge and world domination in films throughout the 1930s and 1940s. One exception, *The Invisible Agent* (1942), had an invisible spy (Jon Hall) battling Nazis. In the TV incarnation, using a premise later revised in several invisible spy series, Dr. Peter Brady was a British scientist who accidentally made himself invisible experimenting with light refraction. At first, the government feared him and pursued Brady until he proved his loyalty. He became an agent for British intelligence to fight evil spies or organizations throughout the world. Plots were never the point but rather the novelty of viewers seeing car doors opening and steering wheels turned by unseen hands, not to mention bad guys duking it out with invisible fists. In one episode, viewers saw an invisible Brady enjoy a kiss with a Russian agent. Special effects master Jack Whitehead created most of the scenes with wires allowing glasses to rise, chairs to be jerked downward simulating a man sitting, and hats lifting from an invisible head. During one filming of a car driving through London, a stuntman was hidden under a false seat. Passersby thought a runaway car was loose and chased down the vehicle (Fulton 1997).

During the series run, the identity of the actor playing Brady was kept a closely guarded secret as a ploy to hold viewer interest. Ultimately, long after the show's demise, it was revealed that a little-known actor named Johnny Scripps was the on-screen body, a short man who looked through buttonholes on Brady's shirts. Tim Turner provided the voice (Vahimhei 1997). Supporting characters included Brady's widowed sister (Lisa Daniely) and his young niece played by Deborah Watling. Other talents included writers Brian Clemens and Philip Levene, later the major producers for *The Avengers*. Actors Honor Blackman and Desmond Llewellyn, soon to become Q in the Bond series, made early appearances in *The Invisible Man*.

Whereas the fictional spies of the 1950s established the foundations for their broadcast descendants, a variety of social changes accounts for why most disappeared in the mists of history. For one thing, after the McCarthy hearings, a series of espionage trials, and the U-2 Gary Powers incident, Americans had a sense of exhaustion regarding stark Cold War dichotomies seen in such 1950s TV series as *I Led Three Lives*. When the 1960s opened with the inauguration of President John F. Kennedy, American culture was beginning a new era. Shifting perspectives included new views on the clandestine world in the Cold War along with fictional representations of espionage in the entertainment media.

Most important, television in the 1950s had played on America's fears of pervasive Communism and had encouraged faith in government that would steadily erode in subsequent decades. The influence of British films like *No Love for Johnny* (1960) and *Ring of Spies* (1963) began to emphasize themes of cynicism about what was becoming viewed as a claustrophobic secret war far removed from normal experience. The fallout resulting from the 1961 Bay of Pigs CIA cover-up showed television networks that they had been lied to and in turn had misled American viewers themselves on the evening news. Between 1964 and 1966, reports appeared about CIA involvement in coups and international upheavals connected to Cuba, Guatemala, Laos, Malaysia, and Indonesia. In 1963, retired CIA director Allen Dulles published *The Craft of Intelligence*, which was part memoir and part justification for CIA machinations. But other books were revelations of covert actions dispelling the clean, upright image of years past (Barnouw 1990, 369). New attitudes about the Cold War were reflected in films such as *The Ipcress File* and *Dr. Strangelove*, in which terms like trust and certainty had lost meaning (Shaw 2001, 194). While the spies of World War II knew when their work was done, new Cold Warriors were now in a game without end and without clear victories or boundaries (Hoffman 2001, 48). One odd new twist was the fact government agents investigated the creative staffs of *The Man from U.N.C.L.E.*, *Mission: Impossible*, and *Get Smart*, fearing writers and prop men were coming too close to home in their scripts and gadgets. The former attraction between broadcasters and U.S. intelligence had lost much of its glitter. Not until 2001, when the CIA permitted *The Agency* series to film on its Langley premises, could any spy show be considered anything like propaganda for the real-world intelligence community.

Ironically, Ian Fleming's 1961 novel, *Thunderball*, saw Cold Warrior James Bond moving away from his 1950s battles with the KGB and SMERSH and instead beginning his ongoing war with independent operator Ernst Stavro Blofeld and his creation SPECTRE. This move substantially changed the milieu of all TV spies to come. *Dr. No* fortuitously debuted in the States four months after the October 1962 Cuban missile crisis, turning threat into drive-in movie excitement and a new vogue in popular culture. Two years later, the drive for fresh approaches resulted in the first of the American entries into the Bondian world of espionage. *The Man from U.N.C.L.E.* would be the watershed dividing the generations, and TV spies would never be the same.

CHAPTER 3

Bond, Beatles, and Camp: The Men from U.N.C.L.E.

JAMES BOND IN THE LIVING ROOM

If this is an example of the new, modern U.N.C.L.E. agents, I must confess to a moment of disappointment. I find your abrasive interrogations lacking in both subtlety and finesse. Napoleon Solo would ask the same questions but he would do it with style. Illya Kuryakin would chill your blood without revealing a single emotion. They were before your time, of course. I suppose it's a reflection of what's happening around us. It's difficult for a man of flair, urbanity, and style to flourish in this treadmill society.

—Anthony Zerbe as Justin Sefron
in *The Return of the Man from U.N.C.L.E.*, 1983

In October 1962, television producer Norman Felton met with representatives of Ian Fleming to discuss the idea of making a television series based on Fleming's book of travels, *Thrilling Cities*, one of the author's non-Bond publications. Several weeks later, Felton flew to New York to meet with Fleming himself, but he was no longer pursuing the *Thrilling Cities* project. Instead, he approached the author with the idea of creating a new character, a new James Bond for television. Fleming looked over Felton's notes, liked the idea, and suggested a name for the new secret agent—Napoleon Solo. Fleming gave Felton his own notes, which he'd written on Western Union Telegraph blanks, including the name for a female character, April Dancer. After these discussions, Fleming slipped out of his hotel and purchased Felton a gift set of cuff links shaped like a pair of Colt .45 handguns, one of the pistols used by James Bond and planned to be on the display wall in Napoleon Solo's apartment. After completing their talks, the two men shook hands at midnight on a Manhattan street. Felton flew back to California to do further work on this new concept.[1] Felton had closely watched the films of Alfred Hitchcock, especially *North by Northwest* (1959), which featured ingredients he wanted to use in his project. He liked the notion of an innocent being dragged into the world of espionage and the Cary Grant character who was suave, witty, intelligent, and cool. He saw Leo G. Carroll as the Professor, the shadowy head of a secret organization. Felton gave his ideas to writer Sam Rolfe, saying he wanted to move away from the doctors, lawyers, and sheriffs on television and create something fresh. Rolfe liked Felton's notes, especially the idea of using innocent people in a spy drama as a means to separate any new series from the 007 books. In his opinion, imitation showed a lack of imagination and a likelihood for lawsuits, so he worked to avoid overt connections to James Bond (Magee 1986a, 12) Rolfe began creating a prospectus for a pilot for which he had various names, ultimately deciding to simply use Fleming's character name, "Solo."

As word of the Felton-Rolfe project spread, 007 producers Albert R. Broccoli and Harry Saltzman objected to what they heard. They asked Fleming to stop working on "Solo" to avoid any possible legal entanglements. As he was suffering ill health in his final years, Fleming agreed. The legal department at NBC was asked to review each script of the new series to ensure it didn't stray too close to the world of James Bond. The Bond people didn't like the use of the name "Solo," as this was the name of a villain in *Goldfinger,* a film then in production. Thus, NBC stepped in and gave the new show its title, *The Man from U.N.C.L.E.,* a title the producers accepted grudgingly; it sounded too similar to the earlier NBC series, *The Man from Interpol* (1960).

As Felton and Rolfe developed their new drama, it strayed further and further from Fleming's ideas. In the beginning, this was all to the advantage of the new series. Rolfe went beyond the usual practice of creating a "bible" of back stories about the characters to help writers and actors. He drafted an eighty-page prospectus outlining the makeup of U.N.C.L.E., which at first stood for nothing "because the producers originally thought the combination of initials 'provocative' and 'funny,' with familial overtones suited to family entertainment" (Wolfe 1965). After the United Nations insisted some distinction be drawn between it and the fictional organization, Rolfe quickly dubbed his sophisticated creation the United Network Command for Law and Enforcement. According to Jon Heitland's *The Man from U.N.C.L.E.: Behind the Scenes of a Television Classic* (1988), not all of Rolfe's ideas were incorporated into scripts. But Rolfe's elaborate descriptions of headquarters, U.N.C.L.E.'s organizational structure, and character sketches did appear in the twenty-three Ace Books spin-off novels, which gave fans a wide world of knowledge about who these characters were and the milieu they inhabited. This elaborate creation went well beyond the realm of one television hit; Felton and Rolfe had developed the blueprint for many television series to follow.

In Rolfe's prospectus, U.N.C.L.E. was a complex organization. As explained in the opening narration for the first thirteen episodes of the first season, the secret headquarters of U.N.C.L.E. was disguised on a street in New York's East Forties behind innocent-looking brownstone buildings. Viewers saw the secret entrance for enforcement agents as they walked through a special stall in the back of Del Floria's Tailor Shop. A secretary in the hidden building, watching the goings-on in Del Floria's on a closed-circuit TV, presented each agent with a triangular security badge activated by a chemical on her fingers. The voice-over narration told the viewer the United Network Command for Law and Enforcement consisted of agents from all nations, working to maintain political and legal order anywhere in the world. The audience was then introduced to the three main characters, Solo himself (Robert Vaughn), Illya Nickovitch Kuryakin (David McCallum), and Alexander Waverly (Leo G. Carroll).

Napoleon Solo was a character carefully thought out by Felton and Rolfe, although many predevelopment ideas were never reflected in the scripts. In some notes he'd been a Rhodes scholar, was a veteran of the Korean War, had a nautical background, and had a wife killed in a car accident. One grandfather had been an admiral, the other an ambassador. Without question, he was clearly inspired by the Cary Grant character in *North by Northwest*. According to Robert Vaughn, Solo was detached, cool, meticulous, urbane, witty, and structured.[2]

Vaughn wasn't the producer's first choice for the role. He was selected after a list of fifty-three names, including those of former TV spy Barry Nelson and future *I Spy* lead Robert Culp, was whittled down (Anderson 1993, 40). But Vaughn had all the personality Felton was looking for, and he was well regarded in the industry and best known for his role in *The Young Philadelphians* (1959) for which he earned an Oscar nomination. Four years later, he starred in Gene Roddenberry's *The Lieutenant* television series, which fortunately was canceled before the role of Solo became available. Interested in politics, Vaughn earned his Ph.D. in political science while working on *U.N.C.L.E.* His dissertation on the blacklisting era was later published as *Only Victims*. As Vaughn recalled, he was given wide latitude in portraying his character and brought to the part what he considered his own best features, including his "bachelor" approach to women.

David McCallum, born in 1937 in Glasgow, Scotland, had starred in *The Great Escape* and then in *The Greatest Story Ever Told* as Judas Iscariot, the role that brought him from England to Hollywood. Lunching with friend Charles Bronson one afternoon at MGM, Bronson introduced his friend to the pilot director for *U.N.C.L.E.*, who signed McCallum. At one point, future *Mission: Impossible* star Martin Landau was on the shortlist for the role, but he turned it down.

With only two lines in the pilot, Kuryakin was initially conceived as a minor player, essentially a stereotypical Russian agent used to demonstrate how global U.N.C.L.E. was—a nonpolitical entity rather than a force in the Cold War. In the beginning, Kuryakin was a Communist representing his government, and he could be recalled if his country so desired. We saw Illya in Russian military uniform in the first season episode, "The Neptune Affair." From that point on, however, all agents were treated as full-time U.N.C.L.E. employees, not representatives of their native countries. All McCallum was told was that Illya had a suitcase full of jazz records under his bed.

Slowly, the role progressed. Because his character had no background, McCallum turned this into his advantage, portraying Kuryakin as an enigmatic loner, aloof, intellectual, above it all. According to McCallum, Kuryakin emerged very much the enigmatic man because he was scrupulously undefined (Wolfe 1965). Unlike Solo, Kuryakin wasn't a womanizer and showed disgust for Solo's pursuits. In turn, women pursued Kuryakin, but they were not allowed to touch. To the surprise of all, Illya Kuryakin became one of the hottest international teen idols of the 1960s, and his cool aloofness was part of his charm. Vicariously, female viewers saw Kuryakin's unavailability as something they desired and sent letters of protest whenever he got a screen kiss. As McCallum rose to costardom, plans to give him an ongoing romance were dropped to keep his sex symbol status going. At first, he was to be a master of disguise, but when his looks gained the show its young audience, disguises were abandoned in favor of the black turtlenecks McCallum made a national fad. Without Illya Kuryakin, *The Man from U.N.C.L.E.* would never have been elevated to the phenomenon it became.

Finally, there was Alexander Waverly, played by the one actor from *North by Northwest* to join the *U.N.C.L.E.* cast. Leo G. Carroll had the distinction of starring in five Hitchcock films, more than any other actor. Carroll's Waverly was chief of Section I of the New York headquarters, one of five regional U.N.C.L.E. main offices. He was the right age to be the authority figure over his young agents, a proud grandfather with an apparently large family. In early outings, he was both aided by a brother-in-law and frustrated by an identical cousin (also played by Carroll) who reminded Waverly of long-past indiscretions with young women.

Waverly was somewhat seedy and traditional—an old-fashioned British gentleman in contrast to the surroundings reflecting the contemporary fascination with high-tech wizardry. The emphasis of brains over brawn in the characters was seen in the almost sci-fi decor of U.N.C.L.E. headquarters, with the halls and offices lined with the then-new setting of oversize computers. In a sense, the three principal characters represented humankind in a technological world that brought with it both hope and danger.

The danger came from U.N.C.L.E.'s most frequent adversary, THRUSH, a takeoff of Bond's nemesis SPECTRE, a merging of the Gestapo, Mafia, and Russia's SMERSH. But THRUSH was much larger in scale, had a much stronger SF slant, and was the blueprint for all fictional power-hungry organizations to follow on the small screen. After *U.N.C.L.E.*, television's secret agents have rarely battled on real-world chessboards but instead typically fight mirror opposites of themselves in the mold of THRUSH. Rolfe's THRUSH gave U.N.C.L.E. an elegant and sophisticated organization, an equally organized opponent with equal power. THRUSH provided the show with an ongoing adversary, negating the need to create new, independent enemies each week. This presence gave the series an epic scope, establishing a war that didn't end and created a contrast with the stories of innocent civilians who found themselves having to contend with a world beyond their normal, domestic experiences (Magee 1986a, 12).

As the series progressed, THRUSH became an international power without real estate or allegiance to any country or political philosophy. It had endless numbers of pawns and knights alike, numerous ruthless scientists on its payroll, and an eye for any innovative new technology it could put to its own uses. One Harlan Ellison–penned episode claimed the organization had more than $1.6 billion in assets. In the series, THRUSH Central, relying on a mysterious device called the Ultimate Computer, governed the organization. THRUSH Central never stayed in one location, making it difficult to search for the masters behind the minions. Each of its branch offices were called "satraps." In one second-season episode, viewers got an idea of THRUSH's size, with the Ultimate Computer claiming over 2,000 female agents were on the Pacific Coast alone. We learn that THRUSH had a long history, raising some agents, now in their twenties, from childhood. In another episode, we learn THRUSH was established by a group of businessmen after World War II. Although television viewers learned little more about the evildoers than these bare facts, *U.N.C.L.E.* fans gained other insights from the Ace novels, which yielded valuable information for the truly devoted. For example, in the fourth novel by David McDaniel, *The Dagger Affair,* we hear the full history of THRUSH and the meaning of its acronym— the Technological Hierarchy for the Removal of Undesirables and the Subjugation of Humanity.

Oddly, NBC objected to the use of THRUSH as a name, fearing it was too similar to SMERSH, a real and deadly Russian organization battled in fiction by James Bond. In the pilot, WASP was substituted, but producers fought for THRUSH because of its sinister ring, evoking quiet danger. Ultimately, according to Heitland, sixty-eight of *U.N.C.L.E.*'s 105 episodes dealt with THRUSH, accounting for two of the three major plot lines. The first was battling THRUSH when it invented, stole, or was on the verge of capturing some new technological weapon to conquer the world. The second plot line was U.N.C.L.E.'s and THRUSH's attempts to destroy each other. A third category included opponents unrelated to THRUSH. As an in-joke, these adversaries had bird names including Dr. Egret, Simon Sparrow, and various characters named Raven or Partridge.

SPYING AS POP CULTURE

I have no particular desire to be bigger than Herman and the Hermits.
—Illya Kuryakin

On November 20, 1963, filming of the pilot began. It was two days before Vaughn's thirty-first birthday and the day U.S. president John F. Kennedy was assassinated. In the original version, entitled "Solo," Carroll hadn't yet been cast, and the chief of U.N.C.L.E. was a humorless Mr. Alison (Will Kuluva). For the most part, the network liked what they saw, although they weren't sure how to define it. U.N.C.L.E. was so new and different that it defied easy categorizing. Despite the go-ahead, NBC didn't budget the future filming to be in color as opposed to black and white, despite Felton's protests. He knew color shows would have more residual value in the re-run market.

Despite this problem, in years to come, all U.N.C.L.E. aficionados would agree the first season beginning on September 22, 1964, was by far the best. It established the characters and environment in a unique way. For one thing, there was the distinctive logo of the word U.N.C.L.E. under a globe surrounded by concentric circles and a man with a gun. For another, each section of the show opened with act headings with humorous quotes or lines from that act, a clever innovation at the time that emulated titles of old-time movie serials. At first, the production team was unsure about the role of humor in U.N.C.L.E. Network executives feared humor would destroy suspense, so Felton held back the lighter episodes to appease NBC, which thought it had bought a straightforward dramatic series.

"The Never, Never Affair" was the turning point, establishing the blend of adventure and humor that became the ideal U.N.C.L.E. formula. In that episode, Barbara Feldon, later Get Smart's 99, played the role of the innocent, in this case an underling in U.N.C.L.E. headquarters in the Portuguese translation department. She craved the excitement of fieldwork, but after being captured by THRUSH, she learned it's best to enjoy the comforts of normal life. Other first season adventures worked off this theme, usually casting an attractive young woman as a housewife, secretary, or schoolteacher. One exception was "The Strigas Affair," which guest starred William Shatner as an innocent bug exterminator with Leonard Nimoy as the villain—two years before the two rose together to fame in Star Trek.

U.N.C.L.E. didn't do well during its first thirteen weeks, and it was precariously close to cancellation. As Heitland reports, ratings improved with a publicity blitz and a move to a Monday-night slot (Heitland 1988). But a meteoric rise in popularity occurred when college audiences adopted the new show over the Christmas holiday, and an informal word-of-mouth campaign began. Equally important, Illya Kuryakin became "the blond Beatle," as beloved as John, Paul, George, and Ringo. Five months after the death bells were warming up, *The Man from U.N.C.L.E.* was not only a consistent top ten show, it was a phenomenon with over 10,000 fan letters pouring in each week. All later commentators would agree *U.N.C.L.E.* was the first television series to become an international sensation on this level, the second being Gene Roddenberry's *Star Trek*. No series would achieve a similar level of interest until *The X-Files* in the 1990s.

> Casting a lead character as a Russian then, at the height of the Cold War, would be like casting an Arab today. The big question is whether Kuryakin was a communist. They never say one way or another, and I think it must've pissed [J. Edgar] Hoover off.
> —Cynthia Walker (quoted in Pringle 2000)

In 1994, critic Rick Worland saw a subtext to the sudden and unique acceptance of a Russian spy on American television. According to Worland, as Illya Kuryakin captured women's hearts (admittedly the best-dressed Communist on television) intentionally or not, *U.N.C.L.E.* represented the decreasing bipolarization of the Cold War as other nations were claiming a place in the evening news. East-West differences were fragmenting, as smaller countries battled with terrorists, insurgents, and dictators. In Worland's view, *U.N.C.L.E.*'s weekly international escapades in Latin America, Africa, Asia, and any number of fictional countries mirrored America's views, which had changed since the 1950s (Worland 1994, 23).

Such thinking was in the eye of critical beholders, not the producers of the show. In various interviews, Robert Vaughn repeatedly noted there were no Cold War aspects to *U.N.C.L.E.*—it was for him pure escapism. "The Cold War was all around us at the time and very real, and the plots of [*U.N.C.L.E.*] and the Bond pictures were very unreal," he told TV Guide in 1997."We did high-tech warfare, tongue-in-cheek fashion, as opposed to being blown up by the real atom bomb" (Johnson 1997 23). Some observers were unhappy about this fantasy, as in archconservative Ayn Rand's 1965 article, "Bootleg Romanticism," in which she complained that Illya and Solo were almost subversive travesties of standard thriller-fiction heroes like James Bond and Mike Hammer. In her view, Bond and Hammer were dead serious against the forces of evil, whereas the men from U.N.C.L.E. were campy mockers of the "righteous causes to which they declare nominal allegiance" (Wolfe 1965). Still, Worland pointed to an important shift in American thought that perhaps helps account for the phenomenon of *U.N.C.L.E.* In Worland's view, Solo and Kuryakin, unlike Herbert Philbrick, led two lives—as secret agents and superstars.

Worland was certainly correct on the latter point. Whether allegory for the Cold War or not, *U.N.C.L.E.* wasn't just an hour drama, it quickly permeated popular culture. During this period of popularity, the program was broadcast in over sixty countries, and critical acclaim joined the applause. The philosophy expressed in the 1966 "Writer's Guide" for the show demonstrated why the series had a wide appeal. For youngsters, the guide stated, *U.N.C.L.E.* was simply an exciting adventure. For discerning adults, it could be considered a spoof, a satire, and a sly commentary on manners and the times (Walker 1999, 187). Because of the appeal to young audiences, Vaughn and McCallum were suddenly elevated to a status more akin to rock stars than actors. Personal appearances more resembled Beatlemania than autograph signings. Many were canceled because the number of fans exceeded what security could handle. Vaughn couldn't make it through a crowd without losing hair and clothes. McCallum was equally traumatized. In an auditorium in LaGrange, Illinois, teenagers wearing *U.N.C.L.E.* T-shirts became so threatening, a riot squad had to spirit the star away. In Baton Rouge, Louisiana, an overzealous grandmother pursued him into a ladies' washroom. On such occasions, McCallum noted, "I was bleeding profusely. From such multiple embraces, multiple contusions" (Wolfe 1965).

U.N.C.L.E.'s presence was so pervasive that other TV shows from all three networks referred to the show in their titles, as in *The Avengers* episode called "Girl from A.U.N.T.I.E." In 1966, Hanna-Barbara joined the chorus with *The Man Called F.L.I.N.T.S.T.O.N.E.* In commercials, housewives were saved from the dangers of spoiling food by the "Man From G.L.A.D." who offered them name-brand sandwich bags and plastic wrap. Solo and Kuryakin appeared in one episode of the series *Please Don't Eat the Daises*, and Napoleon Solo walked into Doris Day's film comedy, *The Glass Bottom Boat* (1966). Illya Kuryakin hosted the rock show *Hullabaloo* on September 25, 1965, introducing rock acts with his *U.N.C.L.E.* pen communicator and bringing *U.N.C.L.E.*'s trademark "Open Channel D" into the musical media.

Before the show had even aired, Norman Felton knew his revenue would depend on more than advertising and began plans for tie-in merchandising. *U.N.C.L.E.* generated so many toys, books, trading cards, cars, games, and other items that a 144-page catalog, *The Toys from U.N.C.L.E.: Memorabilia and Collectors Guide*, appeared in 1990. Beyond the novels that expanded the world of *U.N.C.L.E.*'s adventures, a digest magazine appeared each month with stories reportedly written by Roger Hart Davis, a pseudonym for many writers. The Davis name also appeared on a series of hardcover stories crafted for young readers (Peel and Magee 1985, 78). For girls, there were teen magazines with kissable pinups of Illya; for boys, there were books like The Man from U.N.C.L.E.*'s ABC's of Espionage* (Signet, 1966), in which Solo and Kuryakin opened up U.N.C.L.E.'s files for future secret agents.

Perhaps most notably, Felton designed a five-piece U.N.C.L.E. gun his agents were seen assembling in the series but rarely used. For Rolfe, who had created the TV Western *Have Gun Will Travel* based on the concept of a roaming frontier knight, the U.N.C.L.E. Special was the modern equivalent to King Arthur's Excalibur, a dangerous weapon used on the side of the angels. This gun, surprisingly, evoked many unusual responses. The Treasury Department sent agents to the production facilities, saying the guns used on the set were illegal, as the prop crew was building firearms without a license. They fined MGM $10,000 for the infraction. The U.S. Army sent representatives to explore any real-world viability for the extended silencer, arm stock, gun scope, and bipod attachments. Oddest of all, the U.N.C.L.E. gun got its own fan mail, reportedly 500 pieces in one week. A number of U.N.C.L.E. guns and gadgets were highlighted in December 1965 *Popular Science* article, and thirty years after the series' demise, Cynthia Walker gave the U.N.C.L.E. Special the academic treatment in an article published in the 1999 *Bang Bang, Shoot Shoot: Essays on Guns in Popular Culture*.

According to a televised interview with Vaughn, the Beatles themselves were fans of the show. During their second trip to Los Angeles, the group was asked what they'd like to do, and all four requested a meeting with Vaughn. As both the actor and the group shared the same press agent, the rendezvous was easily arranged. To accommodate the request, a Brinks truck was rented to move the group from Capitol Records to their hotel on Vine Street. This summit of cultural icons was emblematic of the times—the Beatles were serving up American rock 'n' roll with their Liverpool flavor, and *U.N.C.L.E.* returned the favor by giving the British their James Bond in the living room. As Vaughn later recalled, the movies based on *U.N.C.L.E.* were, on one level, more successful in England than the Bond series, considering the relatively low costs involved in producing them.

The eight movies were yet another of Felton's means to generate revenue. From the beginning, Felton envisioned the advantages to selling *U.N.C.L.E.* films overseas by expanding television episodes with extra footage. In his opinion, such plans would allow for better production values, more character development, and would attract marquee-value guest stars that would enhance both the series and the films. Two episodes from the first season, including the pilot, "The Vulcan Affair," and "The Double Affair" became *To Trap a Spy* and *The Spy with My Face*. In both cases, extra footage was shot that was more racy than what was acceptable on television, putting Napoleon Solo into the bedroom. *The Spy with My Face*, ironically, included two scenes repeated almost shot for shot in Bond's next film, *Thunderball*. In both films, we see a man whose face is covered in bandages watching his prey. Later we see this man—an exact double for Solo in the *U.N.C.L.E.*

version, a NATO pilot in *Thunderball*—greet his duplicate in a doorway and then gas him.

From that point on, a number of *U.N.C.L.E.* episodes were shown as two-parters on American television and then reassembled as movies, including *One Spy Too Many*, *The Karate Killers*, *The Helicopter Spies*, *The Spy in the Green Hat*, and *How to Steal the World*. One scene in an episode entitled "The Bat Cave Affair" capitalized on the movies for an in-joke. When Solo watches an in-flight film on his way to Europe, TV viewers see the movie is *One Spy Too Many*. Solo is asked what he thinks of spy movies. He replies, "Well, they're all right if you like light entertainment. I just think they're pretty far-fetched."

Such ventures did attract many well-known stars for both the films and regular episodes, including Joan Crawford, Ricardo Montalban, Nancy Sinatra, and football player Roosevelt Grier. Future Bond bad guys Telly Savalas and Richard Kiel also appeared on *U.N.C.L.E.* Veteran actor Jack Palance starred in Vaughn's favorite episode, "The Concrete Overcoat Affair," which was remade into *The Spy in the Green Hat*.

One of the two-part episodes filmed for movie release, "The Alexander the Greater Affair," introduced *U.N.C.L.E.*'s second season on September 17, 1965. Now in color, the explanatory narration was no longer needed, so teasers introduced viewers to the new episodes. In addition, *U.N.C.L.E.* was now accompanied by a bevy of imitators that cumulatively became known as "The Year of the Spy." Although all observers recognized that James Bond was the leader of the pack on the silver screen, the TV spies were clearly equally modeled after *U.N.C.L.E.* In September 1965, *The Wild Wild West* and *I Spy* debuted, both buddy series in the same formula as *U.N.C.L.E. I Spy*'s Scott and Kelly were white and black as Solo and Kuryakin were American and Russian. *The Wild Wild West* had James West taking Solo's sophistication and womanizing wiles to the Old West, while his partner, Artemus Gordon, emulated Kuryakin's intellectual and disguise-making capabilities. *Get Smart* was unveiled the same month, as much a parody of *U.N.C.L.E.* as Bond, as demonstrated by the title sequence in which Maxwell Smart enters a secret headquarters by way of a disguised phone booth, a clear reference to *U.N.C.L.E.*'s Del Floria's Tailor Shop.

U.N.C.L.E. entered its second year no longer worrying about ratings. Now, the major concern was the budget. NBC expected the series to remain a high-flying international sensation with a budget equal to that of the producer's, Arena's, other hit, *Dr. Kildare*, a hospital drama that was much cheaper to produce. So inventive ways had to be found to keep the show costs low. Fortunately, the *U.N.C.L.E.* team was filming on the MGM lot, which had one of the most extensive back lots and set locations in the industry. Hence, when the *U.N.C.L.E.* crew needed a jungle, for example, they had the jungle created for earlier Tarzan epics. Innovation also helped keep costs down. To indicate transitions in time and place, the *U.N.C.L.E.* team invented the "whip pan," a short blur of fast-speed visuals accompanied by equally fast-paced music. To indicate setting, they used stock footage of international landmarks like the Eiffel Tower or Golden Gate Bridge with the captions "Somewhere in France," "Somewhere in San Francisco," and so forth. As a result of this creativity, the *U.N.C.L.E.* team won a Golden Globe, and the show was nominated for ten Emmys. Most notably, the prop team was nominated for a special Emmy for their work, the only time such an award has been given.

But some episodes of *U.N.C.L.E.*'s second season were alarming harbingers of things to come. Whereas some of the episodes retained the flavor intended by Rolfe, others were overblown nonsense. This trend from humor into overt comedy indicated a loss of continuity. According to Heitland (1988), a noticeable shift away from agent ingenuity toward more gadgets showed that Sam Rolfe was no longer in charge. With the second season underway, the program's creator felt his job was done, that all else would simply be adding bricks to his foundation. He wanted new challenges. So, one new producer issued a new "Writers Guide" indicating his philosophy—U.N.C.L.E. was now a "preposterous organization," a concept far removed from Felton's and Rolfe's concepts.

Still, some writers kept the spirit alive. Dean Hargrove, writer of the "Never, Never Affair," later said the *U.N.C.L.E.* writers were very free to do what they liked, especially to make extraordinary things happen in ordinary places, which was one of the show's appeals. Another important writer was Alan Caillou, an actual former spy turned writer and actor. He brought his four-year experience from British Intelligence in World War II to his scripts and is credited with helping develop and shape the character of Illya Kuryakin. Such writers walked the tightrope of plausibility—not realism—versus make-believe. Some writers were less successful, and one of the most famous was SF author Harlan Ellison. While he later praised *U.N.C.L.E.*'s creative team, his own contributions, unlike his scripts for *Star Trek*, are among those that pushed *U.N.C.L.E.* far from the plausible range. For example, his "Sort of Do It Yourself Dreadful Affair" was a yarn about sexy female bulletproof robots, a device more successful in the intentionally comic first Austin Powers movie.

THE UNMAKING OF A PHENOMENON

> I can't help but think, Mr. Solo, that your days on this earth are numbered.
>
> —Mr. Waverly, from *The Double Affair*

This new brand of silliness defined *U.N.C.L.E.*'s third season, a year in which huge success gave way to excess on two fronts. Jon Heitland's chapter on this season is entitled "The Unmaking of a Series," a phrase that sums it up (1988). Because of the success of the campy *Batman* on ABC, NBC pressured *U.N.C.L.E.* to go forth and do likewise. The results were not mixed. In one episode, Rome firefighters ran around like the Keystone Cops accompanied by old-time silent movie piano rolls. In another, Solo danced the Watusi with a man in a gorilla suit. One episode was based on THRUSH's manufacture of exploding apples, and in another, bad guys threw Popsicle grenades. Some silliness turned out to be prophetic. In the third season's "The Jingle Bells Affair," a grandfatherly Soviet leader came to New York preaching peace on earth and donned a Santa Claus outfit to show his human concern. Twenty-two years later, Russian premier Mikhail Gorbachev made a similar New York trip, although without wearing the red and white suit. Similarly, the "Pieces of Fate Affair" opened with a Jerry Springer–like talk show host who berated his guests and gloated over increased ratings after a guest was shot.

One episode, "The Caps and Gowns Affair," was part of an ongoing trend that may have contributed to the ultimate demise of the 1960s spy boom as a whole. In that story, antiwar protestors were treated with obvious derision as they first put up signs saying "Down with U.N.C.L.E." before switching sides after learning they'd been duped by THRUSH. Like other spy shows, this casting of peace protestors as dupes of international conspiracies was a recurring concept. For example, in one episode of *Amos Burke, Secret Agent*, peace demonstrators were unwitting carriers of chemical destruction. *Mission: Impossible* also used this concept, as seen in 1971's "Take Over," which had American criminals manipulating the peace movement. In 1970's "The Martyr," *Mission: Impossible* used stock footage of student protests along with a folk singer performing Bob Dylan's "The Times They Are A-Changin'" in an episode about the potential exploitation of a youth congress in a Third World country. *Get Smart* featured a rock trio promoted by the "Groovy Guru" called "Sacred Cows," which sent subliminal messages to America's youth with lyrics like "Make a scene, knock off the dean." The message to the young in America from all these shows was so uncomplimentary that it seemed the networks were deliberately biting the hands that fed them.

It is true that the *U.N.C.L.E.* episodes in question were aired several years before anti-Vietnam protests began in earnest and media reports revealed the CIA was in fact engaged in questionable activities at American universities. Although the fictional story lines were clearly more exploitation than the propaganda that characterized 1950s television spies, such approaches mirrored the philosophies of the FBI and CIA, which kept watchdog lists in an operation dubbed "Minaret" that focused on performers like John Lennon, Jane Fonda, and Joan Baez (Bamford 2001, 431). Still, considering that college students had saved *U.N.C.L.E.* from cancellation in 1964, portraying campus rebels as empty-headed malcontents or foolishly immature and easily led pretty bimbos showed an attitude markedly out of touch with the show's primary supporters.

When comic Bill Dana, one of *Get Smart*'s influences, made a guest appearance on *U.N.C.L.E.* as that week's innocent, he asked Kuryakin who he was. "I'm Illya," McCallum replied. Dana responded, "I'm not feeling that well myself." Many viewers echoed that sentiment. When Sam Rolfe saw the episode in which Kuryakin rode a stink bomb to earth, he turned to his wife and said not to expect many more royalty checks if this is what his show had become. He stopped watching the series and later said he couldn't understand why Vaughn and McCallum hadn't insisted on better scripts (Magee 1986b, 28). Writer Alan Caillou felt the same and was stunned by the direction he saw as more musical farce than the program he'd helped shape. He quit writing for the show.

In addition, the *U.N.C.L.E.* franchise had sprouted a spin-off. During the second season, writer Dean Hargrove was given the task of creating *The Girl from U.N.C.L.E.*, a concept introduced in one episode called "The Moonglow Affair." In what was essentially a pilot for the new show, Mary Ann Mobley was cast as April Dancer, a name Hargrove found on one of the unused telegraph notes left by Ian Fleming. In "Moonglow," Dancer was a young, vulnerable agent mentored by an elderly Mark Slate (Norman Fell) who reluctantly left retirement to watch over her. But Mobley's Dancer was so elegant that the producers worried she might be considered a weak imitation of Solo. By the fall of 1966, Stephanie Powers, the producer's first choice to begin with, replaced Mobley.

At the time, Powers was grateful for the role, feeling she'd been trapped in B movies and had been labeled as one of Hollywood's "faceless wonders," the actresses who worked often, dated well-known stars, and were financially well-off (Ephron 1967, 104). The vulnerability and conservative style of Mobley were dropped in favor of mod fashions and go-go boots, and Dancer was portrayed as being as capable as her partner. For the new series, Mark Slate was no longer an elder statesman but rather Dancer's contemporary played by singer Noel Harrison. Harrison was cast for the role when *Girl* producer Douglas Benton saw him singing his hit single, "A Young Girl," on the *Tonight Show*. If *U.N.C.L.E.* agents were to be treated like rock stars, why not cast a singer to begin with, especially one with a pronounced British accent?

As it happened, *Girl* didn't set sail with the full blessings of the parent show's originators. Rolfe was extremely unhappy that he received neither credit nor royalties for the use of his concepts and format. Felton was unsure that the NBC Standards and Practices Board would accept a series featuring a female involved in physical action, and he also thought the show should be restricted to a thirty-minute format (Anderson 1993, 91). Network executives were especially vigilant in reviewing action scenes involving female characters and had sent explicit directives to the parent show about women guest stars and what they could do and couldn't have done to them. For *Girl*, one means to work around these restrictions was to substitute humor for action whenever possible. In one scene, the agents were trapped in a giant toaster; in another, a car chase was filmed using go-carts. Because of network constraints, according to some critics, Dancer wasn't allowed to become a fully developed lead character, instead spraying adversaries with atomizers rather than fighting them. In some episodes, she screamed; in others, she scratched and clawed like a cat.

Questions about Dancer as a female action-adventure role also led to confusion about handling guest stars. Having a female lead made the *U.N.C.L.E.* device of using a fetching innocent in each episode less workable. Dancer's male guest stars tended to be either leering potential rapists or mere bumblers. Still, although many complained about *Girl*'s choices in mixing feminism with femininity, it should be noted that, for decades to come, the same issues would arise time and time again. Before April Dancer, Emma Peel, Honey West, and women in adventure shows, such as Connie Stevens (*Hawaiian Eye*) and Dorothy Provine (*Naked City*), were largely decorative admirers of male superiority, sex objects who merely offered young women romantic glimpses into exciting worlds beyond domestic duties or minor office jobs (Douglas 1993, 210). Hollywood's uncertainty about women leads continued into the 1980s when CBS worried that Cagney and Lacey were too hard-bitten and not feminine enough. More often, producers preferred series like ABC's *Charlie's Angels*, programs focused on posterqueen eye candy. As many have noted, fully developed women action-adventure stars are few and far between. Despite its shortcomings, however, *Girl* joined *Man* in breaking new ground in television history. April Dancer was the first female lead in an hour-long drama, opening the door for her subsequent sisters in espionage. In addition, Leo G. Carroll's portrayal of Mr. Waverly in both series was a new innovation, repeated only by Richard Anderson as Oscar Goldman in the later *Six Million Dollar Man* and *Bionic Woman* series.

Beyond these matters, the over-the-top comic aspects of both *U.N.C.L.E.* series simply didn't work. Both Benton and McCallum approached Harrison, telling him he had to take his role more seriously or he could take both shows down. In Harrison's opinion, how could anyone take this stuff seriously? On one occasion, he and Powers fell into a fit of giggles so uncontrollable that they were sent home. In an interview for *The Girl from U.N.C.L.E. Digest*, Powers told Nora Ephron that "Noel Harrison and I play to characters who are hopefully as real as they can be in ludicrous situations" (Ephron 1967, 104). More ludicrous than real, *Girl* wasn't renewed for a second season.

As plans began for *U.N.C.L.E.*'s fourth season, it was clear the show was in trouble. New producer Anthony Spinner issued a revised "Writer's Guide," saying it was time to return to the flavor of the original concept, more James Bond and less *Get Smart*. A new theme was recorded, and, to underline the new get-back-to-basics approach, the background music returned to the Jerry Goldsmith themes of the first season. But sixteen episodes later, the network made it clear the changes were too late. Without warning, in November 1967 the show was canceled. One weekend, the cast and crew were simply told not to return to work. McCallum had to call the office to learn if what he was reading in the papers was true. In the last episode, in the last scene, Waverly, Solo, and Kuryakin watched a coffin being loaded into a plane while a narrator spoke of the war between justice and evil. The symbolism was obvious. The next week, *Rowan and Martin's Laugh-In* debuted with its new hit-and-run breed of comedy. In one sketch, quips were exchanged at a party, and a busboy pushed in a cart. He turned out to be Leo G. Carroll. Pulling out an *U.N.C.L.E.* communicator he said, "Mr. Solo, Mr. Kuryakin, come quick. I've found THRUSH headquarters at last." With that joke, *The Man from U.N.C.L.E.* became television history.

AFTERMATH OF A PHENOMENON

> I don't think *U.N.C.L.E.* is anything to put in a cathedral. I don't think it was earth shaking. It didn't cure cancer. What it was, was a very special kind of show in the annals of television. It was an entertainment piece. Underlying it might have been something saying we really should try to work together as nations so we don't blow ourselves apart. This was subliminal.
>
> Sam Rolfe (quoted in Magee 1986a, 12)

Despite being the center of the 1960s television spy universe, *The Man from U.N.C.L.E.* had a surprisingly limited afterlife. The merchandising bonanza quickly fizzled as only the Ace novels continued to be issued after the series cancellation. What would have been the twenty-fourth of these stories, David McDaniel's unpublished "The Final Affair," would have tied up the loose ends with THRUSH destroyed, Waverly killed, and Illya returning to the Russian Navy. In "The Final Affair," Solo would have become the head of U.N.C.L.E., after learning his wife, Joan, believed to be long dead, was actually alive and now a defector from THRUSH. But few would know of these developments. For the viewing public, both U.N.C.L.E. and THRUSH seemed to disappear without a trace.

In large part, this sudden disappearance resulted from a fifteen-year absence from the small screen. During the 1970s, *U.N.C.L.E.* was rarely seen in reruns. Fans were limited to occasional weekend airings of *U.N.C.L.E.* movies. In 1977, Sam Rolfe wrote a two-hour movie script, "The Malthusian Affair," but learned that making television adventures now cost too much to interest studios. As Rolfe told Glenn Magee in 1986, gone were the days when he could bicycle around the vast MGM back lots looking for locations with the only studio cost being lighting (Magee 1986b, 29). By the dawn of the video and DVD era, a generation had passed that knew nothing about Napoleon Solo or Illya Kuryakin, so only those who'd watched the original programs had any interest in the show. Further, when video sets of forty-four adventures were released, they were overpriced, taken from chopped-up syndication copies, and were primarily shows featuring name guest stars rather then the better episodes. These few offerings quickly became unavailable after low sales.

In the middle of the 1980s, a brief revival delighted fans of old, especially the 1983 reunion of Vaughn and McCallum in *The Return of the Man from U.N.C.L.E.*, which was produced by Michael Sloan, creator of *The Equalizer* and the first scriptwriter for *The Six Million Dollar Man*. In a number of ways, this made-for-TV movie was the ultimate old spy reunion, although many would complain about the results. The most noted critic was Sam Rolfe, who said he was both disgusted and frustrated by Sloan's film (Magee 1986b, 29). As Leo G. Carroll had died at the age of eighty on October 16, 1972, the lead Avenger, Patrick Macnee, was cast as Sir John Raleigh, the new head of U.N.C.L.E. In one scene, with a revised version of John Barry's 007 musical theme, George Lazenby reprised his version of James Bond, aiding Solo with his gimmick-laden Aston Martin. When the girl Solo had rescued saw Lazenby's car and license plate, she cried, "Just like *On Her Majesty's Secret Service!*" As Roger Moore was filming *Octopussy* and Sean Connery was working on his *Thunderball* remake, *Never Say Never Again*, at the same time, 1983 was the year that all the actors who'd starred as Bond up to that point were doing so again simultaneously. Other Bond references in *Return* included Z, U.N.C.L.E.'s new armorer reminiscent of Bond's Q. When Solo is first seen, he was sitting in a casino in a scene identical to James Bond's first appearance in *Dr. No*.

In "The Fifteen Years Later Affair," Solo was unhappily selling computers, residing in an inherited New York penthouse in the Alexandria Park Hotel. Judging from his luck and worries in the casino scene, the business wasn't lucrative. He was reactivated when the new THRUSH head (Anthony Zerbe) insisted Solo deliver ransom money to avoid a nuclear detonation, as the new breed of U.N.C.L.E. agents were beneath THRUSH's contempt. Illya was doing considerably better in terms of finance as owner of Uncle Varnia's fashion designing. In nearly every way, times had changed. THRUSH had been out of business for fifteen years and was suddenly reorganizing. Del Floria's was now an actual tailor shop, and Z tells Solo the old U.N.C.L.E. Special gun was now housed in the special *U.N.C.L.E.* wing of the Smithsonian Institution. The new headquarters was elegant but not filled with oversize computers. Agent Benjamin Kowalski (Tom Mason) represented the new breed of U.N.C.L.E. agent: brash, unsophisticated, and abrasive. Gone also were the fantasy elements. In this adventure, THRUSH had become a nuclear power, stealing an atomic bomb that Solo and Kuryakin had to find and disarm. The old humor was limited to in-jokes, as in the scene in which the new head of THRUSH asked Solo how he continued to look so young. "Good makeup man," Solo quipped. The film was well made and won its time slot, but because of its production costs, no plans were made for new movies. Vaughn and McCallum were willing, but the odds remain that this was the last meeting of the spies who started it all.

During the 1980s, *U.N.C.L.E.* reruns also enjoyed a revival first on the cable channel CBN and later on the then-new Ted Turner network, TNT, which broadcast the original series during the afternoons and as part of its "Totally Weird" afternoon feature. On New Year's Eve 1989, TNT ran back-to-back episodes of both *Man* and *Girl* episodes for ten hours, including interviews and short features to help launch a new generation's interest. In addition, two comic book companies attempted to bring back the show in new illustrated stories, notably the short-lived series by the independent TE Comics. Millennium Comics issued a two-part set, "The Birds of Prey Affair," in the new glossy format favored by collectors. In 1985 and 1986, John Peel issued a series of *U.N.C.L.E. Files* magazines, containing both episode guides and technical information about U.N.C.L.E. headquarters. But interest again waned.

By 1990, the *U.N.C.L.E.* revival too was history. Occasional publications continued to surface, including Robert Anderson's 1994 *The U.N.C.L.E. Tribute Book*. While continuing to work on new *U.N.C.L.E.* projects, Sam Rolfe died July 10, 1993, at the age of sixty-nine. Any future remake would not include the writer Kathleen Crighton dubbed "The Real Man from U.N.C.L.E" (Crighton 1993). Still, plans to make an *U.N.C.L.E.* feature film were announced that year when John Davis first optioned the rights. Since 1993, various writers have worked on scripts, but, as of January 2003, none of these scripts was scheduled to be produced. If such a movie is ever made, clearly new actors would take over the roles created by Robert Vaughn and David McCallum.

One obvious legacy of *U.N.C.L.E.* was the career of Robert Vaughn. Immediately after the series was canceled, he moved to Europe as a response to the American political climate. While in England, he starred as Harry Rule, the leader of the British crime-fighting *Protectors* (1972–1973), a fashionable nod to *The Avengers*, with the Contessa Caroline di Contini (Nyree Dawn Porter). Lew Grade, then the head of all commercial television in Britain, called Vaughn's agent in England and asked if Vaughn would be interested in doing a spy show there. "I said I wasn't very interested," Vaughn told me in 2002, "and then they said, 'Well it's only a half-hour show, you'd only be here one year,' and they offered a pretty good deal. I didn't realize that in England, it took them five to six to seven days to shoot a half-hour show, whereas in America it would take only three days. I wound up doing a second season, so I was there almost three years."[3] Vaughn disliked the thin stories and violence of the thirty-minute syndicated project. Its producer was Gerry Anderson, who was known for puppet shows like *Supercar* and *The Thunderbirds*. (See Note 1, Chapter 11.) Thirty-minute dramas had seen their day, and quick duels with bogus religious cults and protecting potential defectors were no longer ideas that fostered much viewer interest. "I wasn't too happy with the quality of the stories," Vaughn said, "but I had a wonderful time . . . We did a lot of filming on the Continent in Spain, Italy, Germany, Denmark, and just about every country available in Europe." After a respectable run of fifty-two episodes in *The Protectors*, Vaughn vowed to do no further series. Still, Harry Rule and his globe-trotting team had their own flavor, and the little program is worth keeping a place in the rerun market. Its theme, with lyrics sung by Tom Jones in the end credits, is also worthy of an honorable mention. In summer 2002, episodes of *The Protectors* were issued on DVD sets for European markets.

Vaughn changed his mind in 1986 when he joined the already-established series, *The A-Team*, after producer-friend John Ashley, who'd been a young actor with Vaughn when both were in their twenties, asked him to come help out a show with sagging ratings. In one fourth-season episode of that series, "The Say U.N.C.L.E. Affair" (first broadcast on October 31, 1986), Vaughn costarred with David McCallum, who played Vaughn's ex-partner, Ivan Tregorin, now a traitor working for the Chinese. *U.N.C.L.E.* elements were added to the script, including using "Channel D," quick camera pans, and chapter titles for sections of the episode.

Vaughn worked with Avenger Patrick Macnee several times after the *U.N.C.L.E.* reunion film. Both starred in two episodes of *Kung Fu: The Legend Continues* as elder statesmen of spycraft. In November 1997, Vaughn and Macnee teamed up with *I Spy* alumni Robert Culp and *Mission: Impossible*'s Barbara Bain in one episode of Dick Van Dyke's *Diagnosis: Murder* again as secret agents with interesting pasts. Likely, this reunion was the last spy hurrah for Vaughn (sixty-four years old at the time), Culp (sixty-seven), Bain (sixty-three), and Macnee (seventy-five). Still, Vaughn continued to appear in television dramas, including a recurring role as a vengeful power broker butting heads with District Attorney Adam Schiff (*Mission: Impossible* veteran Steven Hill) on NBC's *Law and Order*.

McCallum also continued a successful acting career, including work as a TV spy. After his short-lived 1975 *The Invisible Man* (see Chapter 11), he continued his sci-fi investigations in *Sapphire and Steel* (1979–1982), co-starring ex-*New Avengers* Joanna Lumley. In the 1990s, McCallum was part of a mysterious government alliance in the SF series *VR.5*. He played a character named Ian Felton in one appearance in the spy show *Mr. and Mrs. Smith* (1996) in an episode entitled "The Impossible Mission" with several *U.N.C.L.E.* references. By this time, McCallum was well known for his reluctance to discuss his *U.N.C.L.E.* days. For him, the series was long ago and far away, and he was tired of repeated questions regarding Illya

Kuryakin. Still, he was able to joke about starring in shows with acronym titles when he joined the cast of *NCIS: Naval Criminal Investigative Service*, playing "Duckie" Mallard, a lecherous lab technician in the *JAG* spinoff.

Robert Vaughn had different feelings. By 2001, the once-politically-active liberal had become curious about how his days as Napoleon Solo had influenced the generation who had watched his show. Vaughn learned that he had made an important impact on the lives of many devotees, who continued their interest in the show long after it ceased airing, as demonstrated by ongoing discussions on the Internet. Grenada Television credited online fan pressure for its decision to rebroadcast *U.N.C.L.E.* in May 2002. After September 11, 2001, online interest in *U.N.C.L.E.* grew as many observers pointed to the organization's international scope as a fictional blueprint for the new war against terror—thirty-five years after the demise of the series. So what is the show's place in our social consciousness, once so prevalent it often out-Bonded 007?

On one level, *U.N.C.L.E.*, and the 1960s spy genre as a whole, broke new ground in television, as it, and other series like it, reflected social shifts during that decade. A few comparisons with fellow-1960s-phenomenon *Star Trek* illustrate some of these contributions. For example, it has often been stated that the two most popular figures in 1960s television were Illya Kuryakin and Leonard Nimoy's Mr. Spock. Both characters were cool, aloof aliens in a strange world, traits that appealed to adolescents who felt a similar sense of disenfranchisement from an adult world that became known as "The Establishment" when college students began their revolt against the Vietnam War. Kuryakin and Spock appealed to a growing trend championing nonconformity and an interest in fictional figures that were different from previous media heroes and role models. The freshness of this trend can be demonstrated by the fact that both characters were nearly killed off by the networks, as executives feared they would be too unusual to be accepted on American television. Ironically, NBC was later less worried about the African American lead of Bill Cosby in *I Spy* than they were about starring a Russian in the earlier *U.N.C.L.E.* As it turned out, with one eye on Kuryakin and one on *The Monkees*, *Star Trek* introduced its own Russian long-hair in its second season, the young Ensign Chekov (Walter Koenig) precisely to appeal to the audience created by *U.N.C.L.E.*

Star Trek is known for featuring an intelligent African American woman, Nichelle Nichols, a casting choice reflecting the then-new-and-rare opportunities given to African Americans such as Greg Morris (*Mission: Impossible*) and Bill Cosby (*I Spy*). Unlike the pervasive Westerns, in which the roles of women and minorities were frozen in nineteenth-century values, SF and secret agent shows fostered new and futuristic qualities for new kinds of heroes and heroines. In the 1960s, female leads like April Dancer, Agent 99, and Emma Peel joined in the physical action, out-thought their partners, and didn't totally rely on serving as temptresses. Spy shows like *Mission: Impossible* and *U.N.C.L.E.* deserve equal credit, alongside *Star Trek*, for these accomplishments.

In addition, *Star Trek* has often been described as an optimistic window into the future. According to *U.N.C.L.E.* expert Bill Koenig, both Felton and Rolfe were political liberals, believing in "the viability and necessity of concepts such as the United Nations . . . Clearly, *U.N.C.L.E.* was a kind of 'optimistic' spy show, with people of different nations uniting against common foes" (Koenig 1997). As secret agent yarns borrowed much from science fiction, science fiction in turn took on many aspects of Fleming-flavored espionage. As we shall see, by the twenty-first century, the merging of these two genres often made fantasy television series as much one genre as the other, and many could trace their frameworks to both *Star Trek* and *U.N.C.L.E.*

On another level, the formula and success of *U.N.C.L.E.* influenced a wide variety of subsequent television series. Comparisons in reviews of later shows often pointed to minor and superficial connections. For example, it was noted that the 1970s police drama *Starsky and Hutch* starred a black-haired extrovert and a blond-haired introvert, a formula established by *U.N.C.L.E.* More obvious influences were seen in series often better remembered for their gimmicks than their story lines. But a few examples from the 1970s include *The Delphi Bureau, Assignment: Vienna, Search,* and *A Man Called Sloane.* In the 1980s, other aspects of *U.N.C.L.E.* reappeared in new approaches. In 1983, *Scarecrow and Mrs. King* took to a new level the concept of an innocent being dragged into the secret world, with Kate Jackson's Mrs. King becoming a permanent innocent under the guidance of professional agent "Scarecrow." In 1997, comic writer Lowell Cunningham admitted his *Men in Black* projects were inspired by *U.N.C.L.E.* because of its humorous approach and the fact that the agents wore business suits (Solomon 1997, 68). Andre Norton and Rosemary Edgehill's 1999 fantasy novel, *Shadow of Albion*, featured a spy named Wessex working in 1805. He entered his organization's secret headquarters through the back of a tailor shop run by a man named Flowers, and Wessex's partner was Illya Koscuisko. (To make the 1960s homage even more apparent, the butler at headquarters was named Charteris, and Wessex's horse was called Hironpel, the fictional maker of the Saint's famous car.) The 2001 incarnation of *The Invisible Man* also reached into television's past to create its technological enemy, Chrysalis. As discussed in my overview of that series in Chapter 13, Chrysalis was the THRUSH of the twenty-first century.

In short, *The Man from U.N.C.L.E.* must be considered one of the most important television action-adventure series, despite its seemingly low profile in the twenty-first century. Although imitators looked to the gadgetry and gimmicks in various attempts to recapture the spirit of the show, most successors missed the point. Sophistication and style, elegance and gentlemanly behavior were what distinguished the men from U.N.C.L.E. They operated with cool and flair in the midst of comic mayhem. As products of their time, Solo and Kuryakin were not alone in presenting these attributes on the small screen. Certainly they had their rivals, but few American rivals equaled them in elegance. Truer compatriots in the gentlemanly arts were most often found on the English stage, and topping the list would certainly be the very model of an English gentlemen, Major John Steed of *The Avengers*.

CHAPTER 4

More British Than Bond: John Steed, *The Avengers,* and Feminist Role-Playing

THE ORIGINS OF AN EPIC

> Extraordinary crimes against the people and the state have to be avenged by agents extraordinary. Two such people are John Steed, top professional, and his partner, Emma Peel, talented amateur, otherwise known as The Avengers.
> —Opening narration to the first American season of *The Avengers*, 1966

O f all the English imports in the television spy milieu, no series was more British than *The Avengers*. Most of the team's adventures took place on English soil, all the villains were enemies of the British state or way of life, and no character on television could be more traditionally upper-crust English than Major John Steed. Adorned with a bowler hat, armed with an umbrella, impeccably tailored, and genteel as a lord, Patrick Macnee's urbane John Steed was often described as a throwback to a long-past romantic age. Like one Leslie Charteris description of Simon Templar, Steed was a walking anachronism who would have worn a sword by his side, a feather in his cap, and spurs on his heels in earlier times.

Although debuting in 1961 before *Dr. No* (1962), no other television series had as many overt connections to the world of James Bond. Lois Maxwell, Sean Connery's Miss Moneypenny, appeared in one episode. Another, entitled "From Venus with Love," echoed the title of Bond's second film adventure. In *Goldfinger*, Oddjob used a razor-tipped bowler, and John Steed too would find his hat a useful weapon. The first Avenger, Ian Hendry, briefly appeared in *Casino Royale*. Few Americans witnessed Honor Blackman's adventures playing Cathy Gale until the 1990s. But when Blackman costarred with Sean Connery in *Goldfinger*, her role in *The Avengers* was part of the publicity for that film. Three Bond films later, Blackman's successor, Diana Rigg, became 007's only married consort in *On Her Majesty's Secret Service*. In the same outing, moviegoers were introduced to Joanna Lumley playing the smallest of bit parts. But she joined the ranks of *Avengers* girls when she took on the role of Purdey in *The New Avengers* (1976). The one Avenger to appear in all its incarnations, Patrick Macnee, took his turn in the world of Bond when he appeared as Sir Godfrey Tibbett in Roger Moore's sendoff escapade, *A View to a Kill*. Finally, Sean Connery himself returned the favor, starring as the villain in the ill-conceived and disastrous film version of *The Avengers* in 1998.

Through it all, *The Avengers* ultimately became the most successful of all the televised spy shows, at least in terms of being seen and appreciated by successive generations of viewers. By 2001, *The Avengers* had been established as England's most successful television export, seen in over one hundred twenty countries. Largely due to the wildly successful pairing of Macnee with Diana Rigg as Mrs. Emma Peel, the two seasons showcasing this team remained in the rerun circuit into the twenty-first century. *The Avengers* was the first non-*Star Trek* television series to join the DVD market in 1998, and it has taken its place as one of the best classic series in television history. But the story of *The Avengers* goes well beyond the adventures of Steed and Peel, Diana Rigg being only one of Steed's avenging partners. Before her were Dr. David Keel (Ian Hendry) and Blackman's Cathy Gale. After her were the winsome Tara King (Linda Thorson), Lumley's Purdey, and Gareth Hunt as Mike Gambit. Forgotten Avengers include Dr. Martin King (John Rollason) and singer Venus Smith (Julie Stevens). Long after these characters stopped appearing in original television dramas, novelists including Macnee himself gave readers thirteen new adventures for literary enjoyment. Steed and his partners appeared on the stage, on radio, and in comic books. More collectibles tied in with *The Avengers* appeared after its demise than while it was on the air. Numerous articles have analyzed the importance of the series, and a number of full-length books on the show have been published, ranging from Dave Rogers's behind-the-scenes revelations (1989) to Toby Miller's 1998 study of the show as pop culture and as an example of postmodern techniques.[1] Laurie Johnson's theme music is still one of the most recognized spy tunes in the genre, appearing on as many CD collections as any Bond title song. Clearly, something beyond nostalgia must account for this ongoing presence.

In the beginning, John Steed was almost an afterthought. In December 1960, the short-lived British series *Police Surgeon* starring Ian Hendry as Dr. Geoffrey Brent was coming to a close. Canadian-born producer Sydney Newman was on the lookout for a new project in which he could feature Hendry in a similar way. In 1959, *Police Surgeon* had been the lucky hybrid of two genres—cops and doctors—and likewise the spin-off, *The Avengers*, would link doctors and a British undercover agent named Steed. According to some reports, Newman created the title and is reputed to have said, "We're calling it *The Avengers*. I don't know what it means, but it's a hell of a good title." In one interview, Newman said he didn't like the title, feeling revenge wasn't a particularly biblical approach to crime fighting (Caruba 1985, 18). Whatever the case, *The Avengers* began seeking Hendry's counterpart.

Newman's new partner, former Canadian television producer Leonard White, approached thirty-eight-year-old Patrick Macnee to be Steed. He told Macnee to read the Ian Fleming books to get an idea of what the producers were after. Mostly, they wanted Hendry to be the idealistic, extremely moral, and somewhat naive avenger of his fiancée's murder. He would then be brought into the seamy underworld of Steed, who was immoral, sophisticated, and mysterious. The first Avengers team was to work together out of necessity, with some mutual respect but with much personal disagreement. Dr. David Keel was the series focal point, and Keel saw Steed as reprehensible, nearly as evil as the opponents they battled. During the preproduction process, Hendry had the easier job. His character was essentially the same as his role in *Police Surgeon* but with a different name. His innocence was to provide humor in the new series, the Cary Grant figure taken out of *North by Northwest*—another instance in which Hitchcock was a clear influence on television spies.

Macnee, on the other hand, had been given a copy of *Casino Royale* and one script with one line of character description: "Steed stands there." In his memoir of his *Avengers* years, *The Avengers and Me* (Macnee and Rogers, 1997), the actor recalled the sadism and torture in the Bond novel and decided to create a different character entirely. He used his father as one model—a man who loved horses, tailored clothes, and kept a carnation in his buttonhole. Macnee also thought of the Scarlet Pimpernel, a foppish character who was therefore not a visible or likely threat to his enemies. He claimed other models were his commanding officer in the Royal Navy and Ralph Richardson's character in the film, *Q Planes* (1939). He decided Steed would never carry a gun and would instead find ways to use his trademark umbrella. In short, the actor created his own character with little input from writers or production chiefs.

Macnee enjoyed wide latitude partly because Newman and White wished to keep Steed as shadowy as possible, never making it overtly clear for which agency or department he worked. In the first season, Steed reported to a mysterious One-Ten, working ostensibly for British intelligence. Through subsequent years, Steed's back story was never fully fleshed out and was often contradictory. In one third-season story, Steed was said to be the younger son of a younger son of a noble family, a black sheep who attended Eton. In that episode, he allegedly commanded a navy torpedo boat during World War II and had been an economic adviser to a Middle Eastern sheik.

In an episode aired just months later, Major Steed's war service was said to have been a 1945 stint in the army based in Munich. In the seventh season, we learned he'd briefly been a prisoner of war in Germany. As *The Avengers* stories were rarely set outside of England, and then only in the early seasons, such references gave Steed his credentials as an experienced international agent. In the final year of the original series, for example, we learned Steed shot an enemy agent in Berlin in 1963, an adventure not part of the filmed *Avengers* canon. Viewers learned little more until the second season of *The New Avengers* in 1977. In one episode, Steed revealed he earned a medal for charging a machine-gun post, and that the youthful athlete had earned club cricket honors in 1957.

Despite the minimal details about his past, as time progressed, the character became more clearly defined, neither spy nor counterspy. Instead, he was an investigating agent sent out on cases too sensitive, too bizarre, or beyond the understanding of ordinary agents. He was never sent out to save the world, but rather portions of the British Isles threatened by both local and international adversaries of every stripe. Steed's first three partners were amateurs he himself chose—Keel, Gale, and Peel. As the seasons and costars changed, Steed evolved into an unflappable agent who enjoyed himself and had many interests and tastes. Demonstrating his breeding and respect for tradition, he continued to give his female partners titles long after there would seem to be need, Mrs. Gale, Mrs. Peel, Miss King. Beyond his bowler, brolly, and buttonhole carnation, he typically held a glass of champagne in his hand. As a horse lover, his apartment was appropriately located in Stable Mews. His garage housed a succession of vintage Bentleys and Rolls Royce Silver Ghosts.

As the evolving leading man, Steed was unique. As writer John Peel noted in his 1980s *Files* magazines on the series, it was Steed's partners, especially his leading ladies, who fulfilled much of the action, stunt, and fight duties expected of the hero. He was the professional who worked in the most quirky world of any secret agent, but as he observed, studied, analyzed, and occasionally hit an opponent with his steel-rimmed bowler, Steed allowed his partners to shine and the costars to stand out. In John Peel's opinion, by standing back, Steed became the most beloved character in the genre and certainly the one most recognizable anywhere in the globe.

But before these developments, in 1961 the man in the shadows and the grieving doctor opened their first season in England with "Hot Snow," in which drug smugglers killed Keel's fiancée, Peggy. In that first year, the sense of fashion that would characterize later seasons wasn't yet evident; Macnee recalled the two lead characters lurking around in seedy raincoats. At that time, Steed's Edwardian garb was underplayed. Hendry warned Macnee that too much affectation would create high camp, something Hendry wanted to avoid. Champagne wasn't yet a series trademark, with Steed preferring scotch bourbon. The pair dealt with forgers, smugglers, petty gangsters, and blackmailing strippers.

On the set, working conditions made the job time-consuming. The actors learned sixty pages of dialogue per week, working ten hours a day. It became impossible to attribute just who scripted the early episodes, as Hendry was known to tear up scripts and work with Macnee to change dialogue and action. In one interview for the British program "Avenging the Avengers," Macnee recalled the writers for the show "were very considerable, but Ian Hendry treated them as hacks, which was a brilliant idea because it stirred them up. It made them furious. So everybody came in with their creative juices very highly developed." As the series was taped live, on-camera errors were retained. If someone accidentally wandered into the set, they became an extra on the spot. And because of budgetary constraints, shooting was limited to narrow views such as stairwells. Camera operators avoided wide-angle establishing shots to save money on set design. Outside of two fully developed sets per episode, most situations were "suggested." For example, to suggest a bank, cameras focused on a teller window and stacks of money. Even the furniture was minimal, with one couch being moved from scene to scene in the first year. Unlike later seasons, the characters occasionally left the country, with Keel working once in Mexico and Steed once in the Caribbean.

Many British viewers never saw these efforts as many regional stations didn't pick up on the series until the first ten episodes had been broadcast in other areas. (In the 1980s, only one Keel kinescope, "The Frighteners," was known to survive. In 2001, a second Keel outing was discovered, "Girl on a Trapeze.") In 1960, ITV was the only independent British network, and local producers sold their products to other areas of the country, where these "imports" were broadcast in random schedules. For years, ratings for *The Avengers* had no meaning as even episodes in the later seasons appeared on different nights and times throughout England. Later, writer Brian Clemens claimed the first incarnation of the show was "on a par with other series that were on at the time" (Sutcliffe 1984, 29). The series developed a large enough following that, after twenty-six adventures, it was renewed for 1962, but production halted for five months because of a lengthy Actors Guild strike. When the dust settled, *The Avengers* was back but the leading man was gone. Hendry had decided to pursue a film career instead.

Turning misfortune into advantage, the producers opted to give Steed a female partner who would take Keel's disapproval of Steed to a new level. This new zest in the series was actually something that had been in the planning stages the first year. There were several attempts to bring women into the spotlight, beginning with Dr. Keel's receptionist, Carol Wilson (Ingrid Hafner). Although she was never considered a partner, she was often kidnapped and held hostage. She helped bail out both Steed and Keel and was the most regular supporting character of the first year. In some episodes, she worked with Keel without Steed, and vice versa. Before the third year, when Gale became Steed's full-time partner, some unused Keel scripts were given to another doctor character, Martin King (John Rollason), as a stop-gap. Planning to alternate Steed with other Avengers in the second season, the producers introduced a nightclub singer, Venus Smith (Julie Stevens). (Ironically, future *Goldfinger* girl Shirley Eaton was also considered for the part.) Smith appeared in a number of adventures, but she was dropped, as using the singer meant Steed had to run across her accidentally to involve her, and the producers decided this would result in too many coincidences. Not much of a detective to begin with, Smith's primary contributions to the show were her musical numbers, which spiced up her appearances. So the second season featured Steed as the new star with a rotating cast, as concepts and ideas evolved in a transitional year.

Without question, Honor Blackman's Cathy Gale, Leonard White's creation, became Ian Hendry's true successor. Her arrival inspired a new approach to the series, despite the fact her first appearances used rewrites of scripts intended for Hendry. Gale could not only rebuff Steed on intellectual and moral grounds, but she continually pushed back his sexual advances as well. As she was to be the physically active fighter of the team, thirty-five-year-old Blackman took judo lessons to prepare for the role. As the show was still being taped as live action, there were no retakes nor opportunities to insert stunt doubles. Blackman was responsible for all her own fights, although many were recorded the night before the actual taping. "The fights," Blackman later told "Avenging the Avengers," "really put some iron in my soul. Having been the first woman to ever have fought, and having to do it on the studio floor on the cement, it was really tough going." To deal with any wardrobe problems that might result live and on camera, the Cathy Gale green-leather outfits were created and quickly became a British sensation. (Green was the chosen color as black clothes didn't film well.) Style was very much at the heart of such decisions, establishing a new dimension to the show that helped define its later success in the pop 1960s. British designer Michael Whittaker created Gale's clothes to keep her ahead of fashion trends. In turn, Macnee was asked to develop his own wardrobe, becoming even more the dandified Edwardian man about town. Gale was the one to throw her enemies; Steed tripped his opponents, showing little physical exertion. Steed continued to be immoral; Gale repeatedly said the ends don't justify the means. Gale found Steed lazy and seemingly always taking the easy road, but she ardently defended his patriotism and supported her partner when the chips were down.

Unlike Steed, great thought went into creating a back story for Gale. In the 1962 season, Steed found his new partner as a working anthropologist in the British Museum. He learned that her husband, a farmer in Kenya, and two children had been killed in a political coup, during which Gale gained her prowess with firearms. These were characteristics taken from two women admired by Newman and White, anthropologist Margaret Mead and *Life Magazine* photographer Margaret Bourke-White (Eramo 1998, 24–28). Thus, Gale was a blend of colonialism and the modern England. As the partnership developed, viewers learned that Gale was trained in the martial arts and had an extensive knowledge of science, photography, criminology, and other fields. Whereas the other Avenger women's tastes were reflected in their cars, Gale preferred motorcycles. In Blackman's opinion, Gale was "wonderfully pure and proper, yet saucy and feminist." At the time, network executives were unhappy that Gale and Steed were not romantically in-volved—a strong departure from tradition—and they unsuccessfully pushed for a closer pairing. In years to come, some critics complained the bicker-ing partners feminized the Steed character, and others sought a lesbian subtext to Gale's independence and lack of interest in Steed, a perspective fueled by the obvious similarities between Gale and the lesbian Pussy Galore in *Goldfinger*. Blackman herself simply like the "kinky" aspects of her cos-tumes, and the series is sometimes credited with making that term popu-lar in modern parlance.

Originally, Gale was supposed to defend herself with several small pistols concealed in her handbag. But her armory extended to include a garter holster, miniature swords, daggers, and a Kongo stick. As her forte was judo, Blackman went with Macnee to learn hand-to-hand combat from Rene Burdet, former chief of the French Resistance in Marseilles during World War II. Blackman became a Brown Belt and published a book on martial arts self-defense. Later, she praised photographer Peter Hammond, who used strange mirror shots and unusual keyhole shots and in general made the fight scenes so successful that they tried to have at least two fights per show. In "Avenging the Avengers," Blackman claimed this creativity resulted from the very young team working on the show, with nearly everyone involved in their twenties and thirties, all working together collaboratively. Her role, in particular, forced the writers to "jolt their prejudices," as no one had written for a character like Cathy Gale before. She recalled that Macnee kept her on her toes by "winging" his dialogue, often improving scenes with his improvisations.

This new Avengers team debuted on September 29, 1962, in "Mr. Teddy Bear." Like later American critics of the first Macnee-Rigg season, early British reviewers noted the series was incredibly well made but many were puzzled by the content. Later, Bond novelist Kingsley Amis replied to dubi-ous reviewers by saying that those who scrutinized Cathy Gale and couldn't figure out who her employer was missed the point by looking for realistic details that didn't matter. For Amis, *The Avengers* had style with modern fig-ures "who knock off a couple of world-wide conspiracies in the intervals of choosing their spring wardrobe. All this, so to speak, a wink at the au-dience, a joke shared with them. This kind of game is impossible unless the producers have confidence in their audience who must have the mental agility to appreciate the odd satirical nudge and still believe in the story as a thriller" (Buxton 1990, 102).

For the next two years, Blackman recalled, the cast and crew rehearsed every day for two weeks. They then shot the episodes straight through with only one commercial break, during which the actors changed clothes while running to the next set. The two most important sets were the apartments of the leads, as visits on the home turf became a staple of all successive Avenger interactions. By this means, viewers were given glimpses into the private lives of the characters through meetings in their various apartments. Gale lived on Primrose Hill surrounded by avant-garde art. At that time, Steed lived at 5 Westminster Mews in an apartment decorated with heirlooms and antiques. Steed would always represent England's past, and his partners, England's future.

During these two seasons, Steed and Gale defeated ivory smugglers, radar jammers, and spies who hid microdots on wine lists. A mysterious boss, known only as Charles (Paul Whitsun-Jones), now gave Steed his missions. This team occasionally worked overseas, once in Switzerland, once on the French Riviera. Hints of the humor to come occasionally brightened some episodes. One adventure featured two elderly women who used a top secret electronics jamming machine simply to ensure peace and quiet in the area surrounding their rural home. In one episode, a deranged general determined that Gale was a living descendant of the Stuart royal house and schemed to place her on the English throne. Some Gale episodes were later retaped to feature Mrs. Peel, such as the virtually identical versions of "The Death of a Great Dane." Both Gale and Peel were threatened by madmen who sent them cut-up pieces of photographs of their target. In another Gale adventure, Steed and Gale uncovered an academy for gentlemen that turned out to be a school for killers, an episode also revised for the Steed-Peel pairing. That episode was a harbinger of plots to come for Gale, Peel, and King, when the Avengers met a continuing series of schools for nannies, secretaries, and butlers, all of which turned out to be covers for wild new breeds of assassins. In years to come, Steed and his partners would find such cutthroats in the guises of window washers, dating services, dance schools, fitness classes, midget circus clowns, and those certain that life exists on Venus.

This version of *The Avengers* was more successful than the original, earning the 1963 Variety Club Award, the British equivalent of the American Emmy. Blackman's Gale was credited for most of the success, as the plot lines were largely conventional undercover stories. Blackman, signed for nine months, agreed to extend her stay for two years. In England, her presence was so famous that ITV canceled one episode on an election night because Blackman had appeared in a commercial for the Liberal Party. The network feared voters might mistake Gale's heroism as a political endorsement. In another adventure, she actually knocked one of her opponents unconscious for seven minutes, a feat reported throughout the British press the following day. But in December 1963, after her two-season contract expired, Blackman announced her retirement as Cathy Gale, turning in her green leather and going on to wrestle James Bond as the immortal Pussy Galore. Later, Macnee learned Blackman could have done both *Goldfinger* and the series, but she decided the pace, low pay, and treatment *The Avengers* actors were subjected to weren't worth it. Two-week rehearsals on top of hours of clothing and costume fittings on top of judo classes had simply become too much. In addition, Blackman worried about scripts becoming repetitious and the very real possibility of her own role as an actor becoming typecast. Macnee would hear this story again. Later, Blackman claimed great pride for her Cathy Gale role, saying in "Avenging the Avengers," "It was the first women's lib part. Certainly, the first woman who was an intellectual equal to the man. And, by far and away, the very first woman who ever defended herself physically." These two Avengers parted on a whimsical note in Blackman's last episode entitled "Lobster Quadrille." Steed told Blackman "You'll be pussyfooting around on some beach." Everyone in Britain understood that in-joke. (Another unintentional prefigurement of Blackman's role in *Goldfinger* occurred in one *Avengers* episode in which Gale led a gang of happy crooks into a gold vault after gassing the guards, both elements in the later Bond story.)

PASSING THE TORCH

> Don't fight it, Mrs. Peel. We're inseparable.
>
> —John Steed

As would become usual with *The Avengers*, with each new face came a new production team, and Brian Clemens and Albert Fennell were now at the helm. Clemens, who'd written the pilot and supervised scripts for the first season of *Danger Man*, came to *The Avengers* with clear ideas for the direction he wanted the show to take. No women would be killed, although they could be bound and gagged. To create the strange world that gave the characters their unique presence, no extras would be used. No overt realism would destroy the magical ambiance he had in mind. There would be no dealing with realistic issues such as drugs or race. References to the Cold War or British politics would be satirical and humorous (Carraze and Putheaud 1987, 169–72). But how could they replace one of the Britain's favorite leading ladies? All they had was a name: Emma Peel, a twist on the descriptive hoped-for characteristic—"Man appeal" (m-a-ppeal).

At first, actress Elizabeth Shepherd was cast for the role. She taped two episodes before producers decided she was unsuitable for the part. Auburn-haired Shakespearean veteran Diana Rigg, seventeen years Macnee's junior, triumphed despite an abortive screen test. Born in 1938 and raised for her first eight years in India, the classically trained Rigg had never seen the program and went to the audition on a lark, not especially concerned with whether or not she got the part. Later, she recalled the actresses called to audition were "told to turn up in black polo necks and black slacks, looking like an army of junior Nazis" (Lane 1997).

With Rigg came composer Laurie Johnson. He replaced Johnny Dankworth's short theme of the Keel-Gale seasons with not only one of the best-loved title tunes in the spy genre, but a new sense of style and humor for the incidental and background music. Johnson later recalled the series music was memorable because each episode was orchestrated individually like little movies rather than relying on stock recordings. Stunt coordinator Ray Austin joined the team, creating a more choreographed, ballet-fashioned fighting style for Peel—more karate than judo. A humorous exit scene in each episode's tag had Steed and Peel leave in a different type of conveyance before the end credits. With two new principal writers, Clemens and Philip Levene, who introduced the sci-fi elements that would define the revamped show, the world of *The Avengers* now became as imaginative as any series produced for television. (Both Clemens and Levene had earlier worked on the first British "Spy-Fi" series, 1958's *Invisible Man*.)

In September 1966, Emma Peel entered the stage without a nod to Cathy Gale, who was rarely mentioned again except in one episode, "Too Many Christmas Trees." In one scene, Steed told Peel he had a Christmas card from Gale but couldn't understand why the return address is "Fort Knox." This was another comic reference to Blackman's role in *Goldfinger*. (In 1967's "The Hidden Tiger," Peel came across Steed in a room full of cats and exclaimed, "Pussies galore!") It was never explained how Peel and Steed became the new team, although in "Death's Door," the two recalled meeting when Steed ran his Bentley into the rear bumper of Peel's car. Like Steed, viewers learned few details about her past. In "The House That Jack Built," we see a photograph of Emma's father and learn she took control of his company when he died. In Macnee's *Avengers* novels, we learn Emma Peel was educated on the Continent and in South America. Her father, Sir John Knight, was a rich shipping magnate. Her late husband, Peter Peel, was an ace test pilot who had supposedly crashed in South America. Her flat was in Hampstead and was adorned with abstract paintings.

In a sense, Emma Peel out-Galed Gale. Peel was proficient in the art of combat, knowledgeable on any number of subjects, irreverent, charming, and graceful. Like Steed, she enjoyed the life of danger, and like Cathy Gale, she kept Steed's amorous attentions at bay, although the two clearly enjoyed each other's company during and between bouts with evil. Like Gale, Emma Peel's tight-fitting leather fighting outfit became a sensation, as did her cat suit, dubbed by the press as the "Emma Peeler," which was created for the color season. Knowing the power of merchandising, John Bates designed a specialty line of clothes for Rigg to wear on screen and to be sold in retail stores, the first time fashions were designed for this purpose. Another trademark was Peel's powder blue Lotus Elan, a modern counterpart to Steed's trusty Bentleys. Steed too became a fashion statement, helping make designer Pierre Cardin a household name. His bowler and brolly were now international trademarks with Bondian connections. His umbrella became a swordstick, gas gun, and camera. After serving as a steel-rimmed weapon in the original series, for *The New Avengers* Steed's bowler contained a telescopic antenna and a two-way radio.

As with *U.N.C.L.E.*, *Avengers* producers found a special blend of humor and realism, each episode beginning with at least one murder but never any visible blood. The typical *Avengers* attitude can be summarized by one brief scene in "The Girl from A.U.N.T.I.E.," in which Steed chased clues with a stand-in for Mrs. Peel. Steed says to his new partner, "Six bodies in an hour and twenty minutes. What do you call that?" "It's a good first act," replied the lady. After such good first acts, subsequent investigations uncovered eccentric experts on any number of subjects, bizarre organizations, murderous clergymen, armies of hypnotized assassins, supercharged killer kittens, efficiency experts, boarding-school astronauts, deadly alien plants, and villains as unlikely as Henrietta, the macabre puppet. Characters often had strange names, such as B. Bumble, a honey merchant, and J. J. Hooter, a perfume manufacturer. Numerous plays on *The Man from U.N.C.L.E.* included strange organizations like P.U.R.R.R. (Philanthropic Union for the Rescue, Relief, and Recuperation of Cats).

If the supernatural was involved, then Emma would run into agents of both F.O.G. (Friends of Ghosts) and their nemesis, S.M.O.G. (Scientific Measurement of Ghosts). If their adventures didn't begin with a murder, the pair began in cemeteries with a touch of the bizarre. In one episode, an antenna poked up through the dirt of a fresh grave. In others, characters walked out of them. In *The Avengers*, graveyards were doorways to subterranean worlds where spies worked literally underground. Nods to the Gothic were frequent, as in the stylized castles and moors emulating the look of Hammer Films, the producers of numerous horror movies starring Peter Cushing and Christopher Lee, both of whom guest-starred on the series as diabolical madmen. The program's attitude toward death was always portrayed with black humor. In "The Interrogators," for example, one character is shot while alive and kicking. A football, that is.

Because ABC (Associated British Corporation) wanted to appeal to the American market, they knew they needed an element American shows couldn't offer. So, they decided to stress the Britishness of every aspect of the characters and settings. Most adventures took place in quaint little country and seacoast villages, seemingly worlds unto themselves. Numerous supporting characters came from various branches of the British military, many of them as anachronistic as Steed. The team tracked down spies on derelict airfields and abandoned army bases. These settings and characters became a signature hallmark of the series, giving it the classic selective reality and sense of timelessness it still enjoys. These hamlets and London back alleys were worlds of myth and legend, always keeping *The Avengers* in a realm fanciful and fantastic. As Steed represented England's romantic past and his partners symbolized the modern Britain, these settings allowed the criminal plots to be technological invasions into the rustic English way of life that needed the protection of sophisticated agents from both sides of English consciousness. The sci-fi elements worked because viewers knew realism was only a cover for the unexpected and highly imaginative countryside of an England that never was.

Another frequently cited reason for the popularity of the Peel episodes is that Emma Peel was also seen as a new kind of role model for women. As Maria Alvarez recalled in a 1998 *New Statesman* article, Peel came to represent what was later dubbed "post-feminism," that is, Peel took feminism for granted (Alvarez 1998, 17–18). In one episode, coming across the villainess tied to a pillar, Peel asked her, "Didn't we get the vote?" Peel was indispensable, and Steed knew it. She was versatile, adaptable, and personable. One minute, Peel was dancing in a harem, the next in pseudo-Restoration England. According to Alvarez, the black outfits were more than sex appeal. They "evoked the pitiless dominatrix, the machine age's version of Venus in Furs—Venus in Leathers" (Alvarez 1998, 18). Her smooth, dark, helmet-shaped hair and sleek outlines harkened back to archetypes of female warriors such as Joan of Arc. These types, in Alverez's opinion, suggest the woman who becomes erotic through "masculinisation." Peel was the femme fatale as pure calculator, the epitome of the rational brain working efficiently under pressure. Even when she was overtly sexy, as in the famous "Touch of Brimstone" outfit of a black corset, thigh-high leather boots, and a choker adorned with lethal prongs, there was an unyielding hardness in her facial expression rather than feminine softness. (Rigg herself designed the costume, including chains and a boa constrictor.) In Alvarez's opinion, Steed was subtly feminized by his Regency dandy persona and was noticeably inferior to his partner when she helped him cheat on a test to join a Mensa-like society, a test that Emma had no trouble passing. In this view, Peel kick-boxed with exuberant energy and irony; she was no nurturing Earth Mother. Other views see Emma Peel as more multidimensional. Macnee, for example, stated in a 2001 Mystery Channel interview that even in fight scenes, Peel showed vulnerability. The actor pointed to scenes where Peel defeated enemies only to show a facial expression after the fight that said, "I did that?"

The biggest success of the series came in 1966 when British ABC became only the second British company to sell an English series to an American network. The American Broadcasting Company was eager for its own spy series, having none of its own against the offerings on competing networks. At first, American critics weren't sure what to make of this import, seeing it as yet another mix of mystery, mayhem, and humor already well ensconced in American versions of the same formula. Some found the first screened episodes to be brutal, and American ABC banned the aforementioned "A Touch of Brimstone" episode. (British censors complained about Peel being whipped while wearing the sado-masochistic costume, and shortened the whipping scene.) Macnee recalled that Peel was the first televised character to wear a miniskirt, and the American network was none too happy about it. But the British producers decided to stick with their vision, as it were, and not worry about the consequences (Carraze and Putheaud 1987, 7). But American viewers took to these Avengers. One reviewer claimed the series was one means to take "pop culture" out of the hands of teenagers to appeal to adult audiences (Miller 1998, 37). Steed and Peel were poised to ride into American immortality.

But the zenith of the series almost didn't happen. Like Honor Blackman before her, Diana Rigg became disgusted with the treatment given her and felt conditions were bad enough to leave the show. After working on her first twelve episodes, she discovered that she was paid less than the cameraman. Feeling exploited, she felt moved to put a stop to this problem and renegotiated her contract (Lane 1997). After receiving a raise and getting time off to continue her stage work, and after some encouragement from Macnee, she agreed to star for one more year. That was the year of the first color version, and it marked the culmination of all the best elements of the series.

The new title sequence included the long drum solo with the gunshot and glass-clinking champagne toast to introduce the Laurie Johnson theme. Each episode now began with a short teaser. Publicity subtitles formerly only used in print *TV Times* advertisements were now seen on-screen. (For example, under the title for "Escape in Time," the legend read "Steed visits a barber. Emma has a close shave.") Now Steed's costar was called to action each week by receiving a note—delivered in numerous clever ways—saying, "Mrs. Peel, we're needed." This was the 1967 season, which gave the series its only two Emmy nominations, for best dramatic series and for Diana Rigg's performance. Ironically, *Mission: Impossible* beat *The Avengers* in both categories, Barbara Bain's Cinnamon Carter besting Emma Peel.

This was the season *The Avengers* spoofed the spoofs, as in "The Winged Avenger" which took on Batman and costumed superheroes. This was the season Steed and Peel were copied into robots, defeated the cybernauts (remote-controlled machine men) a second time, and had their bodies switched, shrunk, and zapped by a human electrode. Viewers speculated on the nonprofessional relationship between the leads. Although Macnee later claimed Steed certainly slept with each of his female partners, Peel told Steed in "Escape in Time," "Our relationship hasn't exactly been domestic." But despite its number-one rating on two sides of the ocean, Rigg finally bowed out from her role, to the consternation of fans internationally.

Like Honor Blackman before her, Rigg found the pressures more than the series was worth. She was uncomfortable with the demands of interviews, publicity and photography sessions, and with the overwhelming recognition the series brought her. "It was frightening," she said later. "I was used to strolling in the street without a second thought. And suddenly everyone was looking at you wherever you went, nudging, winking." After reading some of her odd fan mail, Rigg handed the chore of dealing with it over to her mother, who wrote replies typically advising "take a cold shower," or "run around the block" (Lane 1997). According to some sources, Rigg had already decided the one color season would be her last, but Macnee claimed that if he'd been forceful with the producers and more supportive of Rigg, she might have stayed on. Reportedly, she told him they could have done two more years together if he hadn't let his own personal problems distract him from the show. As it happened, the network had ten unaired Peel episodes to begin a new season, but little clue as to what to do next.

THE FINAL SEASON

> Always keep your bowler on in times of stress. Watch out for diabolical masterminds. Good-bye, Steed.
>
> —Emma Peel

Out with the old—producers as well—and in with the new. In the sixth season, Toronto-born Linda Thorson debuted as Tara King, Steed's first official partner assigned by the new chief of British intelligence known as "Mother" (Patrick Newell). In years to come, many would complain about the casting of the new *Avengers* girl, who, like Diana Rigg before her, hadn't owned a television set and had never seen the series. Thorson came to the show by way of a recommendation from director John Huston. He'd wanted her in a film role but discovered she was too tall for the part. In an "Avenging the Avengers" interview, Thorson recalled competing for the part of Tara King by spending a day creating a nine-minute film in which she rode a horse and a motorbike, climbed a tree, swam in freezing water, and danced in a discotheque. When she learned she had the part, she fainted. As it happened, she was living with John Bryce, who had worked on the Gale seasons. He'd just been hired as the new producer for the series, as the British ABC felt Clemens and Fennell had taken the eccentric to the extreme. The network wanted the show to return to its more grounded Galelike era. Still, studio executives worried about Thorson's age, especially a young unmarried woman hanging around Steed's apartment. Thorson convinced them it was more inappropriate for married women in the same circumstance (Olexa 1998, 28–29). She created her own character's name based on her love of *Gone with the Wind* and her idea that "Tara" worked for "King and Country."

At first, Macnee was among the critics of his new partner. For one thing, Thorson seemed too young and inexperienced for the role, never having appeared before a camera. Macnee's alter-ego was equally uncertain, saying in one episode that Tara was, oddly, too female and vulnerable to go on assignments alone. "It's all a game to her," he told Mother, certain she would blunder into trouble. Which she did. In one early episode, she had difficulty playing Steed's fictional wife, too young to be the mother of the son Steed ostensibly wanted to enter in a bogus military school.

In the first episodes, Tara was too pudgy for the part. In the scripts, she lost more fights than she won, combating her opponents with bricks in her handbag or with metal chairs rather than martial arts. When captured, she screamed and moaned. Tara King rarely showed Peel-like grace under pressure. When tortured, she whimpered. Often, she was handicapped by having her ankles or legs in casts from both real and faked falls. In her second adventure, she held up a mission by having to do her nails, hair, and makeup, telling Steed he could hurry the process if he did her hair. Miss King was clearly more feminine than feminist.

In turn, Macnee felt out of contact with his own character, and he wasn't sure how to relate to the new supporting cast. Because the American network now called most of the shots, the series moved into an assembly-line approach, taping unrelated scenes from various episodes each week. John Bryce seemed unable to keep any schedule going, and the series began falling behind in production. It became apparent that Bryce was unaware of the changes in filming techniques since his days with live action video. Thinking Tara King would make a bigger impression if she were blond, Thorson was asked to dye her hair to help distinguish her from Mrs. Peel. Her natural hair was ruined, so she was forced to wear wigs for her early outings.

After the first episodes were completed, Clemens and Fennell were restored to the production helm, bringing with them new executive producer Gordon L. Scott. They quickly upgraded standards. Although they felt Thorson was miscast, they relied on the writers to work with what they had. As Thorson was still Bryce's girlfriend, emotions on the set were at first uncomfortable. The actress left production meetings in tears, feeling her treatment was extremely unkind. Later, she credited Macnee as her knight errant, coming to her aid on the set. The PR department, knowing they had a hard sell with viewers after Diana Rigg, promoted Thorson as a lookalike for Shirley Maclaine, developing her fashions to emphasize her somewhat more curvaceous figure than her predecessors. Both Thorson and Macnee lost weight, and all soon noticed Thorson had her own charms when dressed in mod miniskirts.

Clemens and Fennell quickly realized most of the Bryce footage was unusable, so writers cobbled together quick scripts using pieces from three episodes. One Bryce episode was considered so bad that Clemens turned it into a joke, having Mother tell it as a story to his aunts in "Arsenic and Old Lace." They brought back Diana Rigg for one transitional episode, "Forget-Me-Not," which introduced the audience to Tara King and allowed Mrs. Peel to say her good-byes to Steed in a poignant, humorous sendoff. In a past episode, viewers had seen a photo of Emma's father wearing a bowler and looking very much like Steed. When Peter Peel, Emma's believed-to-be-dead husband returns, he picks her up driving a Bentley and also looks very much like Steed. This wasn't surprising, as Macnee played the short part himself. Emma's last look at Steed from her husband's car shows she had this joke in her mind all along. Her brief words of advice to Tara King as the two women pass on Steed's stairwell are, "He likes his tea stirred anti-clockwise." Perhaps the relationship was more domestic than Peel admitted in "Escape in Time." (In "Avenging the Avengers," Clemens claimed he wrote the episode to avoid the usual trap of killing off a main character, which would inevitably become an episode hated by fans. His story, he said, allowed Steed to both lose the girl and win the girl simultaneously.)

Many of finest *Avengers* hours were in the Steed-King season, although it would take years for many to admit this. Macnee himself said that decades after the show had been off the air, he saw some of the Thorson episodes with new eyes and appreciated more fully what she contributed. Critics like Graham Williams later wrote that Tara King was more human and three-dimensional than the more stylized Emma Peel (Williams 1986, 92). Instead of being an amateur, King was a trained agent in Steed's department with the interesting code number, sixty-nine. Unlike Gale and Peel, she was clearly enamored with Steed. She had her own quirky sense of humor and an oddball fashion sense, notably a series of wigs used to disguise her growing hair during the first episodes. Beside her, for some, Steed seemed breezier and more carefree (Williams 1986, 32). As Tara saw Steed as her knight in shining armor, for some observers, he finally came to the fore as the series' central figure. Steed's role was now a far, cry from the mysterious supporting character to a grieving doctor.

Many of the Steed-King scripts are now acknowledged to be among the best, including "Game" and "Super-Secret-Cipher-Snatch." Many of the finest writers for the Peel adventures wrote the best of the thirty-three King adventures, including Dennis Spooner, Philip Levene, and Brian Clemens. The Steed-King season, according to some sources, commanded higher ratings than previous years, especially in France, where viewers preferred King to Peel. Thorson herself can hardly be blamed for being expected to replace a television icon. As she put it, her role was like being the second wife when all the friends liked the original spouse. After two independent, spirited, and irrepressible women closer to Steed's generation, the producers needed someone distinctive. Casting a younger figure made a measure of sense, especially with the show's appeal to a young audience. Still, Thorson was more like April Dancer than Gale or Peel, and critics still maintain her role eroded the status of women obtained by Blackman and Rigg (Cornell, Day, and Topping 1998, 347).

Despite Macnee's misgivings, the addition of secondary characters helped the final *Avengers* season, especially Patrick Newell's Mother, who helped take some of the weight off of the new girl's shoulders. At first, Mother was only intended for the "Forget-Me-Not" episode. But the American network liked the oafish boss, and the Brits were happy to make him a permanent chief. He helped give the show an *U.N.C.L.E.* touch by being the British counterpart to Mr. Waverly. Patrick Newell's Mother was an appropriate name for the character as he acted like a fussing mother hen looking after his agents, complaining about too much reliance on gadgets and gizmos. Paralyzed from the waist down, he rode in a wheelchair accompanied by his six-foot statuesque bodyguard, Rhonda (Rhonda Parker), an Amazon who never speaks. Their inclusion added a new dimension of humor to the permanent cast, especially Mother's many strange headquarters, which included the second deck of a British double-decker bus, the middle of a deserted field of buttercups, floating in pools, or in submarines in shallow rivers.

However, the magic was gone, for whatever reason. Both Macnee and Thorson thought the secret agent boom was coming to an end and suspected *The Avengers* was running on its last legs. Ironically, it was *Rowan and Martin's Laugh-In*, the show that had replaced *The Man from U.N.C.L.E.*, that finally knocked *The Avengers* out of the ratings in the United States. In an appropriate sendoff in the last scene, Steed and King are sent off into space on a rocket as Mother tells the audience, "They will be back. You can depend on it." Well, he was partly right. The Macnee-Thorson pairing reunited for a 1975 French champagne commercial. *The Avengers* themselves had many lives yet, but not Steed and King.

AFTERLIFE OF THE AVENGERS

> Sorry Steed, I'm needed elsewhere.
>
> —Emma Peel

Small productions of *The Avengers* began in 1971. The first recast of *The Avengers* was as a stage play starring Simon Oates, who'd appeared in various roles in the series, as Steed. Sue Lloyd starred as new *Avengers* girl, Hannah Wilde, a character based on the crack shot Hannah from the 1967 "Superlative Seven" episode. Despite a script by Brian Clemens and Terence Field, Steed's battle against invisible girls didn't work on stage and the production was short-lived. The following year, *The Avengers* appeared as a South African radio series with fifteen-minute episodes each day drawn from television scripts. Most notoriously, or infamously, was the short-lived *New Avengers* in which a semiretired Steed was teamed up with two younger agents, Purdey (Joanna Lumley) and Mike Gambit (Gareth Hunt).

From the beginning, problems were rooted in the unstable group of investors who financed the show, urging Clemens and Fennell to target the production for American tastes and with a 1970s flavor. French backers supported the first season, and hoping Linda Thorson would reappear as Tara King was the prime interest for French audiences. But after the original episodes of *The New Avengers* weren't aired on American prime time, the French group sold the series to Canadian investors, who also contributed minimal production funds. Macnee felt the formula didn't work as a threesome. He would have preferred reuniting with Thorson or staring with Lumley. Alternatively, he thought that Hunt and Lumley would have had a chance if they'd set off on their own without the Steed father figure. In addition, Macnee felt the scripts were largely dull and the villains uninteresting. In the first episodes, Steed wasn't Steed, and the actor knew it. He was now a member of the landed gentry, an important figure in upper echelons, a stable owner, and womanizer extraordinaire. All this could have been handled well enough, but the sight of Steed driving a Jaguar signaled the old eccentricities had been drained off in favor of simple respectability. Macnee too had lost touch with the character until, he claimed, he saw a Benny Hill parody of Steed in one of Hill's comedy sketches. As Macnee watched Hill playing Steed on the phone talking nonchalantly while destruction went on around him, the light of inspiration reached the fifty-five-year-old actor. Steed was back.

In retrospect, there was nothing wrong with the casting of the younger actors. According to Brian Clemens, the original Avengers were cardboard characters; the new Avengers were made of thicker cardboard (Sutcliffe 1984, 30). Twenty-nine-year-old Lumley's Purdey, in particular, was the ideal *Avengers* girl, as independent as her predecessors were, with a personality all her own. A former fashion model, Lumley had lived in India, Hong Kong, and London, and brought her own world-wise sense to Purdey. Like Lumley, Purdey was allegedly raised in a respectable family with an international background. Originally, her character's name was Charley, until the producer's learned a new line of perfume was being introduced with that name. Lumley herself chose the name Purdey, after a line of expensive shotguns. In her 1989 memoir, *Stare Back and Smile*, Lumley recalled her thoughts on Purdey, saying she'd wanted to create a character who was self-confident and who went to bed by 11:00—alone. In the first episode, shot in Scotland, we learn Purdey loves chess, fashions, and French-style kick-fighting. Later, we learn her stepfather was a bishop and that her father had been shot as a spy.

Lumley's two years as Purdey demonstrated that, for TV producers, little had changed since the 1960s regarding media thoughts on the role of women. Fennell advised Lumley that heroines didn't wear short hair, so she had a designer create the Purdey "mushroom" cut, which became a popular fashion in Europe. Hoping to play up Purdey's independence, Lumley showed up for the first press conference for *The New Avengers* wearing tights. But after pressure from Fennell and media photographers who'd been promised shots of "suspenders and stockings," Lumley was forced to trade clothes with a production staffer to show off her thighs (Lumley 1989, 146). After the publicity blitz for the series, viewers expected many glimpses of these thighs, but in the series viewers were disappointed on that front. Instead, Purdey seemed a perfect mixture of the sophistication of Gale and Peel, with Tara's youth and clear desire for Steed's affections. There are fans who see her as the best *Avengers* girl of all.

It was Mike Gambit who seemed the third wheel, clearly intended to take on the fisticuffs Steed was no longer likely to engage in considering his age, energy, and fashion sense. According to Lumley, Gambit was to represent "flinty-toughness in a high-tech package" (Lumley 1989, 150). Actor Gareth Hunt, born in February 1943, was a veteran of the British Merchant Navy and, like Rigg, had played at the Royal Shakespeare Company. He came to Brian Clemens's attention when he starred as Frederick on the popular series *Upstairs, Downstairs* and was as capable an actor as the series could wish. To be fair, it was the role given him on *The New Avengers* that didn't stand out. Gambit dressed conservatively to underline his essential stillness and quietness, which was to blur into action when the fights began. His apartment was barren, as he claimed he hadn't had time to unpack since leaving the navy. Thus, Gambit's low-key style didn't provide him much of a personality. Some described Gambit as an emasculated James Bond, as he clearly fancied Purdey but was continually rebuffed, a return to the Gale-Steed sparrings of old. He had a bit of a past; he was supposedly a major in the paratroopers and a former mercenary in the Congo. He lived just around the corner from Purdey and was thus able to literally dump her out of bed when she didn't respond to phone summons. Again, in retrospect, there was nothing wrong with thirty-three-year-old Hunt's casting. *The New Avengers* had other problems.

For one thing, the feel of the show had lost most of the elements that gave the original series its flavor. Gone were the surreal, over-the-top bad guys. Gone were the quaint backwater British villages. In the original series, Steed's garb and cars were anachronistic, and Peel and King wore and drove their own unconventional fashions and stylized sports cars. But the realism of the new team would ultimately make this series look more dated than its predecessor. Its emphasis on topical issues such as drugs also dates the series in an era not fondly remembered for its fashions or artistic milieu. By design, the opponents were far too believable, at least by 1970s standards. The adventures now took place in vividly realistic settings, as in a number of episodes shot in Canada and France to appease the Canadian and French backers of the series. To a large extent, the original show had drawn viewers into a mythological England, which is precisely the element giving those episodes the timelessness they continue to enjoy. With the loss of quirky local color and surprising supporting characters, the Avengers were out of sync with what had made them unique. Producer Clemens, with the help of original *Avengers* scriptwriter Dennis Spooner, felt these changes were needed as audiences had become more sophisticated. He saw no sense in repeating what had already been done. Had the series been given a fair chance, he might have been proved right.

Certainly, considerable planning had gone into the much-awaited new series. Both Hunt and Lumley spent three weeks in an Olympic crash course to build up stamina and suppleness. So many crew members returned from the original series that Lumley became accustomed to being called "Diana." When the series debuted in September 1976, some scripts had interesting twists, as in the third appearance of the cybernauts, and one episode, "Target," set on a shooting range where intelligence agents were mysteriously infected with a deadly disease. Some guest appearances were memorable, as in the return of Peter Cushing to the series in the first episode, "Eagle's Nest." Two missed opportunities included guest star Ian Hendry in "To Catch a Rat," which didn't capitalize on his own *Avengers* past. He played a different character Steed once knew, which allowed Steed to say, "I know I'm seventeen years too late, but welcome back." A two-parter, "K Is for Kill," wasted a cameo by Diana Rigg, who briefly talked with Steed over the phone, revealing Mrs. Peel was no longer her name. (The cameo was achieved using footage from the 1967 series.) Connections with the old were sparse. In the cybernauts episode, Gambit chided Purdey for never mentioning Emma Peel. In "Eagle's Nest," Purdey noticed three framed photos of Gale, Peel, and King in Steed's country home. But outside of such small moments, *The New Avengers* wasn't especially new and owed little to the old. Instead of making trends, *The New Avengers* followed in the wakes of popular 1970s private eye shows, complete with funky *Shaft*-inspired music.

More to the point, perhaps, *The New Avengers* was never seen in prime time in America, the major target for the investors. Instead, CBS aired it late night on Fridays after local news and alongside episodes of *Return of the Saint*. When funds from the French investors didn't meet expectations, the second season relied on new Canadian backers, who insisted a goodly percentage of the show be filmed in Canada. As a result, Canadian crews were responsible for many of the shows produced in 1977, with little input or direction from the English home base. Oddly, "*The New Avengers* in Canada," as these programs were collectively labeled, dealt with Cold War themes in a setting that couldn't mesh this concept with the provincial environment. Consequently, revenues were low and the series was canceled.

To be fair, *The New Avengers* enjoyed a measure of success in Europe, especially Holland, Italy, Germany, and France. After the first season, merchandisers issued Purdey sheets, Purdey stockings, Purdey look-alike competitions, and an ill-conceived perfume called "Purdey" that wasn't sanctioned and so quickly disappeared. However, Sweden, Denmark, and Norway deemed the show too violent and opted not to broadcast it.

After *The New Avengers*, Brian Clemens tried still more ways to resurrect the series. He wrote a pilot script for *The Avengers U.S.A.*, which resulted in the TV movie *Escapade* for Quinn Martin Productions in 1980. Later, Clemens and Dennis Spooner tried again with a script for CBS, hoping *Monty Python* veteran John Cleese would be cast as the villain. A final attempt was made in 1985, but this was the last shot until the 1998 movie (Cornell, Day, and Topping 1998, 2).

Still, *The Avengers* saga was far from complete. In 1973, Macnee and Rigg enjoyed a brief reunion on the short-lived comedy, *Diana*. Produced by *Get Smart*'s Leonard Stern, one episode guest starred Macnee and used many *Avengers* trademarks for laughs. In the opening, the Rigg character received a window display card saying, "Diana Smythe, you're needed." She told her colleagues the "ghost of London past has come back to haunt me." Rigg found Macnee in her office, who told her she was nine years late for their meeting. According to Macnee, plans were underway to introduce him as a long-term love interest, but the series was canceled before more could develop.

During the 1980s, several fans kept the flame going by publishing a variety of books and magazines, which were essentially officially sanctioned episode guides with commentary. American John Peel, writing a series of *Files* magazines for Bond movies and *U.N.C.L.E.*, published seven issues devoted to *The Avengers*. *Avengers* fan extraordinaire Dave Rogers did the same in England, expanding his "On Target" and "Stay Tuned" episode guides into full-length oversize books, culminating in *The Complete Avengers* in 1989.

In 1990, Peel and Rogers collaborated on one of the most interesting literary incarnations of any secret agent venture, *Too Many Targets*. This well-done novel pits all five original Avengers against one new enemy and one old, the creator of the cybernauts, Dr. Armstrong. Both Charles and Mother are called into action, and we are told the stories of Steed's ex-partners after they had moved on. Keel joined the World Health Organization, and Gale returned to her life as an anthropologist in Africa. By adventure's end, they have been working together, are mutually attracted, and go to Africa to deal with a crisis as a team. Emma Peel's husband, thought dead until Rigg's last episode in the series, does die in the novel. She takes command of her father's company, Knight Industries, specializing in electronics and computers. It is at Knight Industries that the villains make their headquarters, drawing in the various Avengers for revenge on one account or another. Set in the period when King was Steed's partner, the young agent shows jealousy toward Peel. But in the end Emma returns to industry and Tara keeps her man.

Other *Avengers* projects included Macnee's first autobiography, *Blind in One Ear* (1989). This book said little about the actor's most famous role, leaving the way clear for his second book, *The Avengers and Me* (1997), written with the help of erstwhile coauthor Dave Rogers. Titan Books reissued Macnee's *Avengers* novels in 1994, coinciding with ongoing efforts to have the series broadcast, on the A&E cable network, from first to last for the first time on American television. Macnee had long noted that syndicated reruns tended to cut bits and pieces from the show and noticed many bootleg videos weren't paying him any royalties. Beyond working on seeing that all participants began receiving payments for their past labors, he helped oversee the remastering of the Blackman episodes to preserve them for new generations (Sabo 2000). He appreciated the fact that he earned more money from the first two months of the A&E airings than he'd received the entire nine years of the first broadcasts. On interview shows like *Late Night with Conan O'Brien*, he supported the network's release of new video sets of the Blackman and Rigg episodes, which began brisk sales internationally. Few other secret agent series have earned the care and effort of this project, and these are the visions of the 1960s that will likely carry on the tradition well into the twenty-first century.

Beyond the TV projects Macnee shared with Robert Vaughn (discussed in Chapter Three), from 1982 to 1983 he costarred with the late Robert Urich in the spy-oriented *Gavilan*. Later, Macnee narrated the behind-the-scenes documentaries for the James Bond DVD special editions in 2000 and 2001. Before his death on December 24, 1984, Ian Hendry guest starred on series including *Danger Man*, *The Protectors*, *The Persuaders*, *The New Avengers*, and *Return of the Saint*. Another *Avengers* alumnus to appear on *Return of the Saint* was Linda Thorson, who played Diamond, a bodyguard for a female rock star. After a long distinguished career on British television and the stage, Honor Blackman, along with Robert Wagner and four other Bond girls, cohosted ABC's "James Bond Picture Show" airing of *Goldfinger* on February 9, 2002.

After costarring with George Lazenby and Telly Savalas in *On Her Majesty's Secret Service*, Rigg worked again with Savalas in the 1969 action-adventure comedy, *The Assassination Bureau*. For years afterward, she steered clear of roles that involved guns to avoid comparisons with Emma Peel. In 1989, Dame Diana Rigg (she was given the title in 1994) became the host for the long-running PBS anthology *Mystery* series, which aired her 1990 BBC production *Mother Love*, costarring David McCallum. From 1979 to 1982, Joanna Lumley also costarred with McCallum in the SF British serial, *Sapphire and Steel*. In April 1999, Lumley and Macnee reunited in the British television film Rosamunde Pilcher's *Nancherrow*. In May 2000 she won the BAFTA Special Award for her role in *The Avengers*. She shared this with the three other women who played alongside Macnee—Honor Blackman, Diana Rigg, and Linda Thorson.

As noted earlier, one film remake of *The Avengers* was released in 1998, but the less said about it the better, except to note Macnee played a cameo as "Invisible Jones" to assist the new Steed (Ralph Fiennes). Allegedly "saving the world in style," the film was more a pastiche of old *Avengers* concepts than a well-realized movie. Emma Peel (Uma Thurman), now Dr. Peel, a jujitsu expert and specialist in meteorology, battled a clone duplicate of herself, a nod to the perennial *Avenger* adversaries, the cybernauts. Sean Connery's Sir August De Wynter invented a weather-controlling machine based on one *Avengers* episode, "A Surfeit of H_2O," in which a rain-making machine threatened England. Whatever quibbles critics might have had with the casting, the most important problem for the project was the cumbersome plot, which didn't work even in a novelization that didn't depend on acting, direction, or big-budget values to tell a convoluted story. Someone else may have been wearing the bowler and brolly, but the voice of Patrick Macnee was all that carried over from the original to the fake.

It is problematic to trace the influence of *The Avengers* on subsequent series, as virtually every pairing of male and female agents has been reviewed with at least a passing reference to Steed and Peel. *Scarecrow and Mrs. King* (1983–1987), starring Bruce Boxleitner and Kate Jackson, was clearly connected to shows of the past, although it more resembled *The Man from U.N.C.L.E.* There was *Mr. and Mrs. Smith* (1996), which featured an unusual relationship between series regulars Scott Bakula and Maria Bello. Later, Lucy Lawless, star of the 1996 syndicated *Xena, Warrior Princess*, claimed she based her performance on Diana Rigg's Emma Peel. Another series unquestionably influenced by *The Avengers* was the 1997 TV comedy *Spy Game*, featuring characters Lorne Cash (Linden Ashby) and Max Landon (Allison Smith). These agents of E.C.H.O. were first seen in *Avengers*-like opening titles, and Patrick Macnee played a brief cameo in the first episode. Equally obvious was the casting of Francesca Hunt as Rebecca Fogg for the 2001 *Secret Adventures of Jules Verne*, in which Hunt used her real-life sword-fighting skills, wore Emma Peel-like leather outfits, and engaged in the fights her male costars avoided. Similarly, Sydney Bristow (Jennifer Garner) wore skin-tight outfits and fought with "smash mouth" kickboxing in the 2001 *Alias*. The most discussed show connected to *The Avengers* remains the 1990s phenomenon, *The X-Files*. The comparisons have as much to do with the series mix of espionage and science fiction as the relationship between FBI agents Fox Mulder and Dana Scully. (See extended description in Chapter 13 including Chris Carter's comments on *The Avengers*.) Even the perennial adversaries, the cybernauts, have been credited with influencing later films, from *The Terminator* to *Robocop*. Simple pairings of a man and woman do not an *Avengers* make, but the prevalence of spy/sci-fi series on independent stations do owe much to *The Avengers*, and this will be a subject for a lengthy discussion in Chapter 13. In short, like *U.N.C.L.E.*, *The Avengers* was a seminal show

CHAPTER 5

Cold War Sports and Games: *I Spy* and Racial Politics

BREAKING NEW GROUND

If you're going to fly through the jungle like Superman, someone has to be there to carry your phone booth.

—Alexander Scott

A t the end of the first episode of *I Spy*, Alexander Scott (Bill Cosby) asked his partner Kelly Robinson (Robert Culp) to join him and a young friend at a matinee as a reward for a job well done. "What picture?" Robinson asked. Scott replied, "It's an English picture. Wonderful cast, many of your favorite stars." "It's *The Adventures of 007*," exclaimed the youngster. "Oh no," Robinson protests, as Scott urges, "Now listen, don't knock the competition. You may learn something."

This brand of humor helped define *I Spy*, something more than a mere copycat effort by pioneer television producer Sheldon Leonard. When it debuted on NBC in September 1965, critics disagreed wildly on its merits. While *Variety* panned the new show, *Newsweek* claimed the series was a most adept attempt to capitalize on the James Bond mania. On one level, what most contributed to *I Spy*'s success was the presence of standup comic Bill Cosby, who was then making a name for himself in his widely popular comedy albums on Warner Brothers Records. On one album, Cosby even kidded about Leonard and the success of the show. In that routine, Cosby said that Leonard interviewed him for the part of Scott, hired him, and that "it was a hit." After a brief pause, Cosby simply added, "I don't complicate anything." But *I Spy* was far from a comedy, and each episode contained considerably fewer light touches than *The Avengers* or *The Man from U.N.C.L.E.* Instead, the humor was in the dialogue between the lead characters, who were more cynical and sarcastic than their television brethren, especially when questioning the motives of their superiors. This attitude served *I Spy* well, appealing to the new "counterculture" of youthful viewers who responded to rebellious, authority-questioning characters.

This is not to minimize the role of then thirty-five-year-old Robert Culp in the series, an actor once considered for the role of Napoleon Solo. Culp had come to Sheldon Leonard's partner, Carl Reiner, with a script he'd written for a comedy series he wanted to create. As a result of this meeting, Reiner recommended Culp to Leonard. Both Culp and Leonard agreed Culp's comedy series ideas weren't quite as good as the *I Spy* concept, so Culp joined the *I Spy* project as both actor and writer. Culp wrote the first aired episode of the series, "So Long, Patrick Henry." He later wrote six other adventures, wrote and directed "Court of the Lions," and choreographed his own stunts. Culp was nominated for Emmys for acting for all three years, and received one nomination for writing "The Warlord," in which he played a dual role. Culp believed he was the only one who could properly capture the flavor of the agents' friendship in their dialogues. Culp, in a Tom Snyder interview in the early 1990s, described his interaction with Cosby on the show as "blowin' jazz with words."

As Cosby, seven years Culp's junior, was primarily a stand-up comic when he took the role of Alexander Scott, he relied heavily on Culp's coaching to help with his acting duties. In the beginning, Cosby was wooden, not listening to other actors nor responding to their lines. Cosby instead merely heard the words as cues for his own parts (Cohen 1969, 21). Cosby ended up winning three consecutive Emmys for his acting, telling the audience for his first win that Culp didn't win because he'd helped out his partner so much.

According to Leonard's autobiography, *And the Show Goes On* (1995), before cast considerations began, Leonard approached NBC executives Mort Werner and Herb Schlosser to sell his idea of leaving closed sets to film location shots.[1] In Leonard's opinion, getting away from studio back lots would create new interest in television action adventure. He claimed the spy genre was the ideal medium to use new technology, having his agents go around the world and be filmed in exotic settings not ordinarily seen on television or in films. At that time, Leonard was becoming aware of the "cinemobile," a portable camera and movable soundstage developed by Egyptian pioneer cinematographer, Fouad Said. After much persistent salesmanship from Fouad and getting the go-ahead from NBC, Leonard gave his concept to Mort Fine and Dave Friedkin, two writers with radio experience in high-adventure shows. Fine and Friedkin ultimately wrote over fourteen of the show's scripts. Meanwhile, Leonard contacted composer Earle Hagen—who'd written the themes for *Perry Mason, Andy Griffith, The Dick*

Van Dyke Show, and later *The Mod Squad*—to write *I Spy*'s title track. Hagan worked with Herbert Klynn of Format Productions to create the first synchronized mix of theme music with the multiple use of graphic art, animation, and live action in the title sequence.[2]

Leonard wanted a cast that was athletic and able to move credibly from serious to lighter moments. After signing Culp, Leonard saw Cosby on *The Tonight Show*, when it was hosted by Jack Paar, and knew he had his man. But African Americans were not yet accepted on network television, and Leonard knew he had a hard sell. Before *I Spy*, black leads in television action-adventure series were limited to local programs, notably 1954's *Harlem Detective* seen only in New York City, or in stereotyped guest roles or one-shot episodes for then-popular anthology series. Critics praised such efforts, but American television was geared for entertainment, which made money, not social commentary, which didn't (Bogle 2001, 112–21).

Leonard was well aware of sponsor unease regarding black themes or actors. His *Danny Thomas Show* received bags of hate mail when the series lead made physical or emotional contact with Amanda Randolph, the actress playing the family housekeeper. Ironically, *Mission: Impossible*'s Greg Morris had guest starred on an episode of Leonard's *Dick Van Dyke* Show, an appearance that concerned network executives, particularly regarding southern stations, which typically banned episodes they considered integration propaganda. In that program, Rob Petrie (Van Dyke) worried that his newborn son might have been exchanged with another family's son at the hospital. In the final scene, he learns the other family was African American. Leonard told the network that if he didn't get a great response from the in-studio audience, he'd pay for a reshoot out of his own pocket. The audience gave *The Dick Van Dyke Show* one of its longest-running sustained laughs for this appearance. After the broadcast, out of 1,960 letters, over 1,700 were positive. Leonard was armed with these facts when he went in to sell the idea of casting Cosby. To its credit, NBC didn't balk at having a black star, as they were under governmental pressure to make such moves in their programming. However, the executives worried about casting Cosby after seeing the November 1964 pilot. Clearly, Cosby's acting was amateurish, and he was in need of considerable coaching. NBC felt a black lead could be dealt with, but said there must be someone better to cast for the Scott character. Leonard fought for his choice, and his instincts proved to be on target.

From the beginning, Leonard was a hands-on producer. When Cosby's job was threatened, Leonard put his own position on the line. He fielded sponsors' questions regarding race. Would Culp and Cosby ride in the front seat or would Culp ride in the back? If they checked into a hotel room, what would happen if the clerk refused to register Scott? Would they share the same room? Many of these questions were easily dealt with when Leonard explained most episodes would occur overseas where such problems didn't exist. He fostered Cosby's first steps, invested his own money into the series, and even acted in three episodes, including one appearance as himself. Leonard also appeared in the background in several other episodes, sitting at a table in a restaurant, riding in a car, and the like. For his troubles, Leonard happily noted the only problems he had with sponsors was that he was getting more than he could use. And Cosby, according to one 1966 survey, was that year's favorite actor among children twelve to seventeen, third among those eighteen to twenty-four, and tying for eighth among the total viewing public (MacDonald 1983, 118–20).

What gave *I Spy* its flavor was neither the often-serious plot lines nor the milieu in which the team operated, but the relationship between the two lead characters. Unlike all the other secret agents in the genre, Culp's character was vulnerable, emotional, and introspective. No other secret agent was seen to be broken, beaten, and psychologically damaged by enemy torture as was Culp in "A Room with a Rack." With a twist of Cold War ethics, Culp's Kelly Robinson learned his sacrifice had been unnecessary. His department had wanted him to leak the misinformation to confuse the opposition. In "A Cup of Kindness," Robinson suffered pangs of guilt when he was ordered to kill his mentor, Russ Conley (played by writer Friedkin), who had become a double agent. Before his death, the former instructor reminded Kelly that, to face evil, agents must face the evil within themselves and accept a measure of corruption. This side of the secret agent was also seen in the November 13, 1997, *Diagnosis: Murder* spy reunion, "Discards," in which the Culp character, sounding very much like Kelly Robinson, confessed his doubts about any contributions he may have made in the undercover world. He mourned the death of his ex-partner and told his son he regretted neglecting his family all those years. In an interview about this *Diagnosis: Murder* appearance, Culp was asked what Kelly Robinson would be doing in the 1990s. He replied, "Kelly would be dead of alcoholism somehow. Either that or he might be a kept man. But they'd have to lock him up to keep the booze away from him" (Johnson 1997, 24). This human side of the secret agent is what distinguished *I Spy*'s eighty-two filmed episodes. It was a show closer to the realities of Cold War espionage than its other American counterparts, with more complex character flaws. In addition, a realistic flavor was evident in the visuals due to Leonard's choice of location shots, which he often directed, rather than back lots. Such locations added their own set of problems, however, as in the pilot episode that had to be filmed in only seven days before an oncoming monsoon hit Hong Kong. Fouad Said added to this realism, taking physical risks by shooting camera angles hanging over rooftops. According to Said, the six months of preproduction were unique, as international action adventure requires a great many editorial cuts and is much more demanding than a straight dramatic TV series. Authenticity included dealing with crowds, underwater and sea sequences, and the aforementioned typhoon in a tight production schedule.

Said noted that "we developed, created, engineered, improvised, or built special equipment to fulfill the needs of filming abroad" (Said 1966, 180–83). Shooting eight to twelve pages of script per day with four to five major changes of locale required portable cameras easy to hold by hand or set up on the top of a truck, a building, or a cliff. Filming was as covert as the plots, as Said hid cameras in coats, in windows, and on balconies. As crews included foreign-language speakers, communication was difficult, so Said attempted to use the smallest crews possible. Smaller crews also attracted less attention from onlookers. In addition, Said created an innovative radio microphone, eliminating the need for coordinated sound and sight cables, the first use of such technology in television. By means of "electronic zooms," passersby didn't know they were being filmed. "We have shot Robert Culp and Bill Cosby in complete isolation and in the middle of the tightest crowd congestion possible—all without detection" (Said 1966, 181).

In a 2001 personal e-mail to this author, composer Earle Hagen recalled other memories regarding the process of creating *I Spy*:

The original pilot was done the year before the series went into production. What amazes me is that I've seen it written that the show interiors were done here [southern California] and the exteriors shot on location. With the exception of six shows that were shot in the US, the entire series was shot on location. There were doubles when pickups [scenes requiring reshooting] were necessary and the star had gone back to the US. Occasionally, when scenes were re-written or cuts made that had to be patched before dubbing and shipping, the sets would be matched and re-shot in Hollywood. (See Note 2 to this chapter.)

During the first season, Asia was the primary setting, with Associate Producer Ron Jacobs and Said using shots from their own staff, along with footage from NBC news film crews. Similar techniques were used in the second and third seasons in Spain, Morocco, Japan, Mexico, Greece, and Italy. While not shot on location, the agents went to Vietnam in Culp's "The Tiger," a setting most entertainment series found too topical for prime-time adventure. Leonard wanted to film in the People's Republic of China, but the government insisted the film would have to be edited on Chinese equipment, which would have resulted in an inferior product by American standards.

However, the team's cover belied true realism in the series. The two agents pretended to be a pair of sportsmen, Robinson the tennis pro, and Scott his trainer. Robinson was something of a celebrity, well known for his winnings in various Davis Cup tournaments. Like other fictional spies, these characters were given detailed backgrounds, although subsequent writers often had problems keeping the continuity interconnected. Alexander Scott, a Philadelphian, graduated from Temple University and went to Oxford as a Rhodes scholar. He was a Phi Beta Kappa football star who spoke fifteen languages. In "A Cup of Kindness," Scott revealed the department recruited him after he translated Sanskrit for a university professor. In addition, he knew a great deal about nuclear reactors and New Orleans jazz. On the surface, he seemed softer and more cerebral than his partner. He could act the buffoon, quote the Koran, or erect a booby trap with equal ease.

Robinson's background was less firmly established. Apparently, he hailed from Akron, Ohio. But in one episode, we learn his mother died when he was young. In another, he received a watch from her sent to Kelly through his orthodontist. His troublesome old friends showed up in the series so often that Scott complained he was sick of seeing them. One story, ostensibly about the pair recovering a lost planeload of gold, spent most of the hour with Robinson reconnecting with the girlfriend he'd left behind when he joined the department. At adventure's end, he planned to leave the agency to be with her and gave Scott his letter of resignation. But, while Robinson was apparently leaving, Scott sat nonchalantly reading a newspaper until his friend returned. Scotty had already torn up the letter, knowing Kelly wouldn't resign.

When novelist John Tiger received his contract to create *I Spy* novels, he got little such information and repeatedly claimed Robinson was an elegant Californian who played the dilettante. Tiger described Robinson as a former law student at Princeton, a detail also noted in one TV script. In the televised series, Robinson enjoyed drinking, smoking, and womanizing. His partner preferred the company of books, enjoyed photography, and often called his mother. Scott never drank, a theme often touched on throughout the series.

Because both men knew serious relationships were impossible, Robinson had many brief encounters, but Scott had very few. According to some sources, this was one area Cosby was unhappy about. The African American community agreed. The message seemed to be a continuation of the old emasculated, nonsexual presence of black males in the media. Other sources claim the opposite, that the producers didn't want Scott to convey the stereotypical sex-crazed black male. According to Ronald L. Smith, "Scott was going to be a hero, not the smirking macho fantasy that James Bond was" (1997, 57). Instead, in keeping with the dignified character Cosby had shaped, for the first time, young black actresses would have more to do than play the part of personable maids or demure secretaries. Oddly, some wondered why Cosby didn't bed white women. In a *London Times* article headlined "Why Cosby Never Gets a White Girl," Cosby said, "As long as I'm on the screen, whether television or films, I will never hold or kiss a white woman. Hey, our black women have just nothing to look forward to in films, nothing to identify with" (Smith 1997, 57).

Still, even these relationships were few on *I Spy*. In the sixth episode, Eartha Kitt was featured as a near-romantic partner for Scott. The first episode, in which Culp took a notable backseat, had Scott hooking up with a

Canadian agronomist. In one episode called "Lori," jazz singer Nancy Wilson was brought in to provide Scott a love interest, an event so important that *Ebony* magazine ran a cover story on it. Wilson played a Las Vegas singer suspected of aiding her brother (the ubiquitous Greg Morris), and she gave Scott a parting kiss in the last scene. A small moment by later standards, and a brief one in *I Spy*'s run, but notable in the then-testier racial climate.

These agents lived in a violent world of psychopaths and professional killers, not mythological madmen and evil geniuses. The Cold War themes were not subtle, with the partnership seeing its battleground as a world of ghosts, men without true identities fighting men with equally false identification papers. The pair didn't travel in gadget-laden Aston Martins, and they rarely used any technology of the Bondian flavor. On one occasion, they used a tape recorder for a decoded message. On another, they used a tracking system in their car, and twice they used a stimulant that was kept in their belts.

Just whom the agents worked for was a mystery, with most assignments given by a variety of contacts. In the second season, Ken Tobey appeared in "Magic Mirror" as a hard-nosed superior named "Gabe." But when he became a recurring cast member, he became "Conway," then "Russ Conway," and finally "Russell Gabriel Conway." Continuity problems were evident in one episode in which the character in the script was Russ Conway, but in the credits he was called "Jeff." The agency all three worked for was never defined. It was clearly not the CIA, usually called "the department," and described in one episode as "more military than the CIA but less publicized." In some episodes, it was evident Robinson and Scott could be loaned out to the army, navy, and State Department.

> You know what I always say. Lose the skirmish, call the maid.
> —Alexander Scott

I Spy continued for three years, the first two on Wednesday nights at 10:00, the third on Mondays at the same time. According to some sources, it was never a high-flying success, never entering the top ten, hence the change in the third season. According to others, the show did well in the first two years but fell after the time and day shift that NBC had hoped would help its faltering Monday night lineup. While nominated for a number of Emmys, outside of Cosby's three awards, the only other Emmy win was Earle Hagen's musical score for the episode entitled "Laya." In the opinion of some aficionados of the show, *I Spy* began to decline in the second season and was noticeably gasping for creativity in the third year. Some reviewers complained that although ad-libs had been a feature of the acting styles, these off-the-cuff remarks ruined suspense. These few critics point to the one occasion when Leonard reshot a scene because of what he considered an inappropriate ad-lib by Culp. Most fans disagree with this assessment, feeling the show declined because of production budget cuts, resulting in cheaper sets, more use of stock footage, and less location shooting with more scenes filmed on the studio lot, especially in hotel rooms. For these viewers, suspense was never the point to begin with, but rather the banter of the characters. Good scripts, supporters point out, were filmed in the third year such as Culp's "Home to Judgment." Whatever viewers felt, *I Spy* was probably most seriously hurt when its time slot changed to Mondays and had to compete with the popular *Carol Burnett Show*. Whatever the reason, *I Spy* ended a good three-year run and joined the other 1960s spy shows in the vaults of TV history.

Ironically, it was Cosby's career in comedy that helped keep the show alive long after its cancellation. Any new interest was often due to Cosby's other projects. When *The Cosby Show* became a hit in the 1980s, *I Spy* briefly returned, puzzling many viewers of PBS stations, which used the drama to boost ratings. In the opinion of some reviewers, *I Spy* had no place on public television. In 1984, Culp guest starred on Cosby's sitcom as Dr. Huxtable's Navy buddy Scott Kelly in an episode entitled "The Bald and the Beautiful." In 1999, the season premiere of Cosby's third sitcom, simply titled *Cosby*, had Cosby's character Hilton Lucas dreaming that he was Alexander Scott after watching an *I Spy* marathon on TV. Culp guest starred as Kelly Robinson, who, in the dream, came to ask for Scotty's help after thirty years of Scotty being "undercover" as Hilton Lucas. When Cosby is hot, all his various films and series are offered anew. But when his visibility is low, so too is that of *I Spy*. However, beginning in 2001, Image Entertainment began issuing all of the *I Spy* episodes on DVD. In August of that year, they released a two-disc DVD set called the "Culp Collection," with the seven episodes Culp wrote and his commentary. These new releases were not tied to any Cosby project as he didn't have a series on the air, an unusual situation for the prolific actor.

Still, on an important level, the connection between actor and series indicates how much American culture has changed since 1965. When *I Spy* debuted, NBC stations in Birmingham, Alabama; Daytona Beach, Florida; and the Georgia cities of Albany and Savannah refused to air the premiere. But the network stuck to its guns for a change, and 180 other network affiliates made television history, breaking a color barrier for later characters in *Mission: Impossible*, *Star Trek*, and the increasing number of African American stars in later decades.

Cosby has always played down this aspect of the show, seeing his opportunity as a door opening through the color line, but insisting other African Americans found and will find success on their own merits. According to one *Ebony* interview, Cosby vetoed racial content in the series, as he was building his reputation in comedy with nonracial material. His choice was to deal with the color line by being an acceptable, nonthreatening figure.

In 1982, Culp stated the two actors had agreed to make *I Spy* a nonstatement on race, thereby making it a statement. The theme of the show was the friendship of the partners, and by casting both characters as friends and equals, the actors felt, any other overt commentary was unnecessary. At first, Scott had been conceived to be largely a bodyguard for Robinson, but Culp and Cosby together persuaded Leonard and the writers to make them equals. They decided not to discuss race on the show and keep racial jokes, as it were, on the light side (MacDonald 1983, 119). A source of both praise and criticism from black viewers was that an actor of any racial group could have played Alexander Scott.

For the most part, within the show itself, being "color-blind" allowed other African American actors, such as Barbara MacNair and Godfrey Cambridge, to play friends or foes without calling attention to skin color. Whereas other series used black actors in supporting roles, *I Spy* was the first show to present them in a context where they matched wits and wiles with a black series star. One interesting story, "Tonia," was the only episode that dealt directly with racism. In that adventure, Leslie Uggams worked for an anti-American propagandist who wanted to destroy Scott and Kelly's friendship because he saw them as "the picture of racial harmony." Further, many of these guest stars played nontraditional roles for black actors. Diana Sands played a Canadian agronomist, and Cicely Tyson played African royalty, with Ivan Dixon as the American athlete to whom she was engaged. Leslie Uggams's character was active in a Communist plot in Italy. In subsequent decades, the pairing of Cosby and Culp would be compared to other interracial teams that contributed to new careers for younger black actors. Of note were Philip Michael Thomas and Don Johnson in *Miami Vice*, Avery Brooks and Robert Urich in *Spencer for Hire*, and Howard Robbins and Carroll O'Connor on *In the Heat of the Night*.

Still, reactions to the race issue were mixed. Special criticism was aimed at actors like Cosby, Harry Belafonte, and Sammy Davis Jr., as their presence in 1960s television inspired high expectations. High visibility stars were asked to be all things to all areas of African American consciousness, something no single actor or show could possibly accomplish. Some African Americans noted that as Scott was the trainer and not a tennis pro himself, he was merely extending the traditional service function of previous dramatic roles of black actors playing maids, servants, and doormen. Had the roles been reversed, one presumes similar complaints would be that Scott would have served as the stereotypical black athlete. On the other hand, as MacDonald noted, the scene in which Cosby walked among the ruins of the Greek Parthenon, a symbol of the roots of Western democracy, was a powerful testament to the nature of the series. This moment showed white viewers a black star operating constructively abroad in the service of the United States. For MacDonald, the Scott character compared well with the black exploitation figures of the 1970s like Shaft and Superfly, as Scott was a mature, grounded, realistic man and not myth. He was able to show emotions historically forbidden to black characters (MacDonald 1983, 120).

However, others were less happy. The first episode, in particular, raised certain issues. In the story, China wanted political influence in Africa by ostensibly seeking contracts to fund Afro-Asian games. In one emotional scene, Scott told the African American protagonist planning to defect to China, "The whole world is trying to keep bloody fools like you from sellin' themselves back into slavery. But you did it, Elroy." *Variety* responded to the episode noting the courage to cast Cosby, but added the Chinese were portrayed in stereotypical Charlie Chan fashion. Although Cosby said he walked numerous fine lines—not speaking in dialect that would sound dated, not speaking too well that it sounded threatening—most black viewers were glad to see an African American presence. But some wished Scott would demonstrate rage alongside his obvious talents. Many felt the actor who played him was obligated to attend integration marches in the South. These were the times that called for such thinking, but stars from Dianne Carroll—bitterly criticized for her light, nonracial middle-class humor in *Julia*—to Cosby noted overt commentary rarely entertains and rarely lasted long on the tube. So the show was what it was and the actors made their speeches in other settings. These cultural dimensions give *I Spy* an important role in changing values beyond the historic choice of Cosby as the first African American lead in a successful series.

AFTERLIFE OF *I SPY*

> I'll have a shower and a shave, and then once again I'll be your alert,
> clean-cut, clear-eyed government issue Captain Marvel.
>
> —Kelly Robinson

While Robert Culp primarily became known in later decades for his directing, his continuing and varied career included spy roles reminiscent of Kelly Robinson. In addition to the *Diagnosis: Murder* reunion, he played Mark Bishop on one episode of television's *Viper* (1997) as a member of S.E.N.I.O.R., the Special Executive Network of Intelligence Officers Retired. In 1978, Cosby and Leonard reunited for the made-for-TV movie *Top Secret*. In 1994, Cosby served as executive producer of the made-for-TV movie *I Spy Returns*, again with Leonard. After a long and distinguished career in entertainment, this project was one of Leonard's last as he died in 1997 at the age of 90.

In this update, Kelly was the director of an unnamed intelligence agency, and his former partner, a Romance languages professor, returned to protest his daughter's new career as a field agent. This film was one of the more successful reunion remakes, although purists disliked many aspects of the character interactions. The old partners teamed up to tail and assist their offspring, Nicole Scott (Salli Richardson) and Bennett Robinson (George Newbern). Both teams demonstrated their various strengths and weaknesses, rescuing each other from missteps and bumbles, showing the humanity of the characters. At the end of the film, Cosby returned to his private life assuring his wife he doesn't miss the life of a secret agent. In private, he looked at mementos of his former days and quietly admitted, "I just miss him." Friendship was the theme of *I Spy*, the world of espionage only the setting for this message.

This theme resulted in one of the most devoted fan bases in the spy realm, although *I Spy* didn't generate the volume of printed homages in the 1980s enjoyed by other shows. However, with the advent of the Internet, a number of web pages and discussion groups sprang up, although not to the extent of other series. A number of foreign-language sites are online in French, German, and Italian. In 1999, Dave Cole and Bob Mitsch created the *I Spy—The Definitive Site* and the *I Spy* Forum, where fans discuss the show on nearly a daily basis. These two venues, with several online episode guides, collections of interviews and essays, photos, and links to related pages, are but a few access points for those interested in the series. *I Spy* may come and go from broadcast television, but it's presence lingers in new technology. Naturally, devoted fans showed considerable interest when word came out in January 2001 that a film version of *I Spy* was in development, starring Eddie Murphy and Owen Wilson. However, the Columbia Pictures production, released in November 2002, reversed the racial makeup of the team and made other major changes in the characters. Murphy played Robinson—now a boxer—and Wilson played Scott. To the surprise of many, director Betty Thomas, a former *Hill Street Blues* star, didn't offer the now traditional cameo appearances to the originators of the roles. *TV Guide* speculated in March 2002 that no one involved with the remake thought the fan appeal was worth the trouble of dealing with either Culp or Cosby. Judging from commentary on the DVD version of the film, the creative team was more influenced by *Get Smart* and other parodies of the spy genre than the show from whence the film got it's title. It remains to be seen what impact, if any, the film will have on the milieu of Sheldon Leonard's significant, and often underrated, contribution to TV spies in particular and American culture in general.

CHAPTER 6

The Cold War and Existential Fables: *Danger Man, Secret Agent,* and *The Prisoner*

ROOTED IN REALITY

> Every government has its Secret Service branch, America its CIA, France, the Deuxieme Bureau, England, MI-5. NATO, too, has its secret service. A messy job? Well, that's when they usually call on me, or someone like me. Oh yes, my name is Drake. John Drake.
> —Opening narration to the original thirty-minute *Danger Man*

During the 1960s, British television had a very different sensibility from the creators of *U.N.C.L.E., The Wild Wild West,* or *Get Smart.* The three spy adventures starring Patrick McGoohan—*Danger Man, Secret Agent,* and *The Prisoner*—made no attempt to distance themselves from the Cold War nor the proxy battles of the East and West in Third World countries. For many English producers, it was difficult to distance themselves from Cold War interactions, as the British Isles were historically the front line defense both geographically and ideologically for the West. During World War II, the Nazis had targeted England much more directly than the United States, and England had the scars to show for it. According to Bond director Peter Hunt, members of his then over-thirty generation who helped shape the early Connery films had "all been on nodding terms with danger and the prospect of imminent annihilation whether as children of the Blitz or . . . a member of the Armed Forces." It was such experiences that "helped us so closely identify with Fleming's creation" (Giblin 2001, 9). In a 1997 interview, Patrick Macnee stated the primary reason Steed carried an umbrella and not a gun was "because I've been through five years of the Second World War and have seen most of my friends blown to bits" (Johnson 1997,

24). Even as late as 1985, British actor Edward Woodward said he found the inner anger he needed for his character, Robert McCall in *The Equalizer*, from growing up during the Nazi blitz when his school was bombed several times.

Like the Nazis, postwar Communist opponents to England were not an ocean away but a mere ferry ride across the English Channel. When England became a nuclear power in 1952, the government was keenly aware that the British Isles would be first to face Soviet wrath in any atomic showdown. Twentieth-century battles were literally fought in their own backyard, within their own intelligence services. The most notorious traitors were British, notably the famous Cambridge Spy Ring led by Kim Philby. For many observers, Philby's betrayal ended the illusion of "decency and civility" in the British intelligence community, which led to a climate of paranoia that changed spy fiction (Hoffman 2001, 101). Without question, the best spy literature was British, including the novels of John Buchan, Somerset Maugham, Frederick Forsyte, Graham Greene, Len Deighton, John le Carré, and Ian Fleming. Not surprisingly, then, British TV spies had a very different flavor from the American varieties that went far beyond local color and quaint Old World eccentricities.

Whereas *The Avengers* used the Cold War to provide a loose foundation for its unique brand of fantasy, *Danger Man* and *Secret Agent* were more literary, more televised novels than visually oriented high adventure. In *Danger Man*, the settings were gritty, the opponents cold and brutal, and the dilemmas reflected situations seen on evening BBC broadcasts and not far-fetched imagination. In *Danger Man*, the gadgets and technology were simple and underplayed. The adversaries were very human opposite numbers to John Drake, agents of "The Opposition," or leaders of small postcolonial countries in danger of being overthrown from within or without. The show reflected the decline of colonial power in the British Empire, as political control was now largely a matter of gathering information, stirring up matters with undercover provocateurs, and often illegal covert action rather than military incursions. For some, as in the novels of John le Carré, *Danger Man* represented a shadow government in England known for using the BBC to broadcast misinformation to the Russians. For example, one episode of *Danger Man*, "Not So Jolly Roger," found Drake playing a disc jockey on a pirate radio station broadcasting secrets along with pop hits at a time when such stations were a controversial subject in the British press and government.

Another reason agent John Drake was without frills and more hard-edged than his Bondian counterparts was that the show began production in 1959 and appeared on British television in 1960 before the Bond boom began. The first British spy series, *The Invisible Man*, was the direct precursor to *Danger Man*, as both were created by ITV studio director Lew Grade, former scriptwriter-turned-producer Ralph Smart, and Associate Director David

Tomlin. After fusing H. G. Wells with Ian Fleming in *The Invisible Man*, Grade and Smart decided to look to Fleming and Hitchcock to create a new series. They had a premise in mind and found their secret agent when Patrick McGoohan was voted in a British poll the best actor of the year for a 1959 film. In one of the best ironies of the secret agent genre, the man who became known as the quintessential British spy had been born from Irish parents in Queens, New York, in 1928.

Their new half-hour drama, *Danger Man*, premiered September 11, 1960, in a pilot written by script editor Brian Clemens, later the leading producer of *The Avengers*, which debuted four months after *Danger Man*. The British *TV Times* introduced the new show saying, "As he winds his knightly way around the world seeking out villainy, his fists will be as virtuous as his cause. Those who fall before him will have been clobbered with a fairness which will make the Queensbury Rules look almost criminal" (Buxton 1990, 39). At first, Clemens's scripts had Drake as an American agent assigned to a secret organization associated with NATO and based in Washington, D.C.—a loner sent out on assignments of international importance. As Grade always had one eye on American sales, he based Drake in Washington specifically to attract American viewers before James Bond made the British Secret Service a subject of international fascination. Before Bond, actors Lois Maxwell (Miss Moneypenny), Robert Shaw (Red Grant in *From Russia with Love*), and Charles Gray (Ernst Stavro Blofeld in *Diamonds Are Forever*) made their first forays into the world of secret agents as guest stars on *Danger Man*. Other featured actors included Ian Hendry, after he completed his stint as an Avenger.

Five years before Sheldon Leonard convinced NBC executives that location filming in exotic settings would add interest in TV action adventure, the creators of *Danger Man* used picturesque international settings occasionally filmed on location to give the series almost a travel-documentary look and feel. In the first thirty-minute episodes, John Drake was no 007. Unlike Bond, Drake wasn't permitted to enjoy expensive luxuries. When a colleague complained that he never gets to meet a Russian spy in a sleeping car of a train, Drake responded that if he did, "the treasury would send you a memo afterwards asking why it was necessary for you to travel first class."

McGoohan had considerable input into his character, and he wanted to distance himself from the excesses of the Fleming books and be a more intellectual, unpredictable, and enigmatic secret agent. His ability to portray many roles allowed Drake to be a true undercover agent, using acting skills more than physical disguises. He was able to move up in class, disguised as a major or diplomat, and move down, often as a servant. He was cultured one minute, angry working-class the next, a travel agent, teacher, journalist, writer, photographer, engineer, businessman, disc jockey, and civil servant. He had to know each type's skills, attitudes, and behavior (Buxton 1990, 92).

As McGoohan was aware that children would be a large part of the show's audience, he decided that, to discourage any notions of promiscuity, Drake would never kiss a woman. He insisted one scene planned for the pilot, in which Drake made out with a woman in a hotel bedroom, be cut. (According to an interview with McGoohan for the British DVD sets of *Danger Man*, Drake's attitude regarding romance changed in the later seasons. He said Drake began looking at the opposite sex differently because he felt it had come time for the character to settle down and marry.) In addition, Drake carried a gun, but he rarely used it and showed considerable distaste for any violence. There was always a dramatic brawl scene near the end of each episode, but the series was noted for its lack of gratuitous violence. Unlike 007, Drake fought clean and left few corpses behind. There were gadgets, but they were always in the realm of likelihood, not implausible sci-fi possibilities. Limited to thirty minutes, the first shows were essentially fast-paced action adventure, although character development and well-crafted plot lines characterized the program. Only once did the original series come close to a Bond story with "Dead Man Walks," in which a highly contagious bacteria is introduced that could kill plant life in a matter of hours.

Beginning in April 1961, *Danger Man* aired briefly on the American CBS network, but in both England and the States, the show disappeared after completing the original thirty-nine episodes. It was an international success, but because the Americans didn't take to the thirty-minute adventures, Grade closed down the shop. McGoohan moved on and was the first actor approached by producers Robert Baker and Monty Berman when they sought their first TV Simon Templar. Roger Moore took the role instead, as McGoohan wanted nothing to do with the frequent relationships with women planned for the first *Saint* series, and the producers felt McGoohan lacked the sense of humor they needed.

Danger Man returned in 1964 as an hour-long drama after ITC studios found success with the Saint and because the international market was still interested in the first-run half-hour series. The Bond boom had taken hold, and Ralph Smart took note. John Drake was recalled into the auspices of Her Majesty's Secret Service rather than NATO as a special agent for M-9 who reported to the bureaucratic chief, Hobbs (Peter Madden). Under the cover of the World Travel Agency, Drake's now extended adventures allowed for more complicated story lines and more character development. Drake's wry humor and sense of decency were more evident in the hour shows. With a larger budget, reportedly paying McGoohan the highest salary of any British television actor, the series had more gadgets, with one new offering per show, but again they seemed in keeping with the times. Drake had tape recorders in electric razors, knockout gas guns hidden in tobacco pipes, pocket telescopes, and a briefcase full of wire cutters. One memorable gadget in the "Time to Kill" episode was a rifle assembled from innocent looking car parts. There were now rare Bondian flashes of humor as in "Battle of the Cameras," in which Hobbs told an agent sent out to assist Drake that he would no doubt find him with "his nose to the grindstone." The setting quickly switched to a scene where Drake sat in a casino eyeing a beautiful woman.

In its extended format, *Danger Man* explored moral concerns and made social commentary that was impossible in the earlier run. One theme of the series was exploring the life of a loner who was always in the service of others. Questions about loyalty and just outcomes can be seen in episodes like "It's Up to the Lady," in which Drake convinced a defector on the run to return home promising no charges would be filed against him. But when the defector followed Drake back into friendly territory, he was arrested, much to Drake's distress. An additional irony to the situation was that the defector had been forced to flee England because he'd been unjustly suspected and hounded by British intelligence for treason he hadn't committed. M-9 often deceived Drake. In one story, Hobbs assured Drake that he would have the full support and backup of M-9's Iraqi station, only to discover this unit consisted of two people and one was an injured agent. In "A Room in the Basement," Drake was told, "There is no room for personal loyalty in this business" when a colleague's friend asked Drake to help her get her husband out of a Romanian embassy. Drake quickly assembled a team of agents who valued friendship enough to join him in a *Mission: Impossible*–like rescue not sanctioned by the British government.

In one way or another, each hour-long *Danger Man* commented on the morals and values within the covert world. In one episode, Drake commented that government surveillance was simply a euphemism for violating the rights of private citizens. Drake took the opposite stance in another episode when a colleague told him that imperialistic interference can do more harm than good. Drake responded that it isn't an agent's job to question policy, but to follow the credo of every good soldier: "Ours is but to do or die." In "Colony 3," Drake escaped from a Communist training camp and was forced to leave behind an innocent English girl who had been kidnapped. His government wouldn't help him get her out—in their eyes, she no longer existed.

With new line producer Sidney Cole, Smart again looked to America and sold the new series to CBS. However, to appeal to the American audience, the show was retitled *Secret Agent*. American singer Johnny Rivers was hired to sing a new title song written by American hitmakers P. F. Sloan and Steve Barri. "Secret Agent Man," with its distinctive guitar hook, became the definitive spy theme, reaching number three in the charts in March 1966 for Rivers and later as a minor instrumental hit for The Ventures. In years to come, the melody would appear in commercials, be redone by groups such as Devo, be used in films such as *Austin Powers, International Man of Mystery,* and reworked thirty years later as the theme for a new *Secret Agent* series. In England, *Danger Man* had a different theme, "High Wire" written by Edwin Astley, who was responsible for music in *The Saint* and *The Champions*. American viewers heard "High Wire" as the music behind episode titles when the new show debuted on April 3, 1965. Airing on Saturday evenings at 9:00, the show ran until September 10, 1966. Largely due to the popularity of the theme song, *Secret Agent* had an immediate following, although beyond the obligatory board game and Gold Key comic books, it didn't spin off the merchandising tie-ins associated with other series. (An unlicensed "Secret Agent" lunchbox appeared without images from the series, and any connections to John Drake are unknown.) Oddly, the one arena that should have been successful for this carefully thought out series were the novelizations of the show, and MacFadden Publishing indeed quickly issued a number of books throughout 1966. But, for some reason, the almost literary aspects of the show didn't translate well into the novels. Ironically, it was spy-spoof *Get Smart* that knocked *Secret Agent* out of the American ratings. The series, never in the top ten in America, was canceled long before the television industry felt the spy boom had run its course. As it happened, after thirty-nine episodes of *Danger Man* and forty-seven of *Secret Agent*, McGoohan wanted to move on, and he had an interesting idea. Still, *Secret Agent* had one more appearance, a two-part episode shot in color in 1967, "Koroshi" and "Shinda Shima," which were broadcast in June. These episodes were intended to be the first in a new season of color *Danger Man* outings, as Lew Grade wanted *Danger Man* to continue despite its failure in America. But McGoohan was simply too enthralled with his new project to continue with a role he felt was exhausted.

FROM REALITY TO PARABLE

> I've always been obsessed with the idea of prisons in a liberal, democratic society. I believe in democracy, but the inherent danger is that, with an excess of freedom in all directions, we will eventually destroy ourselves.
>
> —Patrick McGoohan (quoted in Gerani 1977, 124)

McGoohan's idea for a new spy show created both one of the most memorable series in television history and one of the most hotly debated continuous discussions among spy buffs and SF fans alike. In one episode of *Danger Man*, the above discussed "Colony 3," Drake encountered a re-created British town called "the village" somewhere behind Communist boundaries. Based on actual training schools, kidnapped British citizens populated this village to interact with Russian spies being trained to live in England. To encourage compliance, those who didn't collaborate were ostracized. This concept sounded like the obvious inspiration for the setting for *The Prisoner*, a mysterious town called "the Village," in which McGoohan cannot tell friend from foe, spy from innocent, keeper from kept. In one line of the "Secret Agent Man" theme, Rivers sang that a number had replaced the agent's name, an idea that was central to *The Prisoner*'s world of dehumanized drones. British observers quickly noted the production team for *The Prisoner* included many *Danger Man* veterans, notably director David Tomlin and writer George Markstein. The distinctive set at Portmeirion had been used in three *Danger Man* episodes. But was Number Six, McGoohan's character, actually John Drake himself?

McGoohan has never stated his position one way or the other, although at the time of *The Prisoner*'s inception, he was trying to distance himself from Drake. This stance resulted in Number Six never having a given name, even when the adventures went back into his secret agent past. Most telling is the fact that legally, McGoohan's own Everyman Productions couldn't have used the John Drake name as it belonged to Ralph Smart and would have involved spending extra cash for the privilege. To ask would have been bad form, as Smart had just lost his most successful show due to McGoohan's refusal to renew his contract. We do not know who Number Six was, and connections to John Drake are in the eyes of the viewers and not necessarily of *The Prisoner*'s creative team.

In 1966, McGoohan approached the head of ITV, Lew Grade, and pitched his idea. According to some stories, the concept came from writer George Markstein, a former agent of British intelligence. Allegedly, he mentioned the idea of rest homes for retired spies that actually existed. In particular, his research into material for *Danger Man* unearthed information about a site called Inverlair Lodge in Glenspean, Scotland. There, old secret agents could freely discuss their past without worries about revenge or kidnappings from their enemies. What would happen, Markstein speculated, if someone was placed in one of these retirement villages by force (Carraze and Putheaud 1987, 209)? According to some sources, Markstein had long wanted to expose the dark secrets of such camps, which used brainwashing and social control of British soldiers, although he wanted to emphasize fact over McGoohan's fantasy. Other sources claim McGoohan himself created the idea for the show after reading a book about retired agents that inspired him to speculate about what might happen to John Drake (Phillips and Garcia 1996, 223).

Whoever originated the concept, Grade pondered over the proposed series, worrying that viewers would reject the idea of a hero unable to escape from a prison, week after week. After the globe-trotting of *Danger Man*, Grade wondered how viewers would respond to a series limited to one location. Finally, he reportedly answered, "It's so crazy, it might work." Although Grade wasn't certain what the show's direction would be, he wanted to retain McGoohan as part of the ITV success. Because of McGoohan's star status, overseas sales were guaranteed, especially since McGoohan was going to serve as actor, writer, director, and executive producer of the new project. Also contributing to the foundation of *The Prisoner* was that the team retained about half the *Danger Man* crew, the other half moving over to another new Lew Grade production, *Man in a Suitcase*. (See Chapter 11.)

If Ian Rakoff's interviews with production participants are to be trusted, the show's creation was part brilliance, part ongoing evolution, and part luck. According to ex-production manager Bernie Williams, the first part of the creative process was a nightmare because most of the concepts were not on paper but in McGoohan's head, and he told the others what he wanted as he went along.[1] It's clear that George Markstein and David Tomlin deserve considerable credit for helping shape the series, with both men collaborating on the pilot, "Arrival." (Markstein can be seen in each episode as the man behind the desk in the opening sequence and in the same setting in "Many Happy Returns.")

Choosing former *Avengers* Don Chaffey as principal director was another case of brilliant planning. He was asked to do "Arrival" to set the tone for all subsequent episodes and to direct the opening sequence used in sixteen of the seventeen outings. He shot all the Portmeirion footage as a library for all future shows, and directed five other episodes to give the show a continuity in look and approach. Another example of good decision making was the idea of casting a new Number Two each week to keep audiences interested in a variety of adversaries. In a later interview, David Tomlin said originally they had planned to use only one Number Two, but he recommended changing the character each week because one motif of "the Village" was that no relationships could be established. "You never had security, you could never hatch plots, you could never escape because you could never trust anybody." New Number Twos kept people apart from each other (Phillips and Garcia 1996, 223). Still, two Number Twos did make returning appearances. Colin Gordon was Number Two in two back-to-back episodes, "The General" and "AB and C"; Leo McKern starred in three episodes.

Finding the North Wales setting of Portmeirion was a bit of good luck, as it was surrounded by sea and mountains that helped keep the Village enclosed by natural boundaries. The actual town, designed for tourists, contained a number of buildings of varying styles of architecture, giving no distinctive connections to any particular place. One section looked Italian, another looked Austrian. The unusual mix of styles, combined with the fashions and cars used in the series, gave the show a timeless look that helps keep it from appearing dated. As Bernie Williams later noted in commentary for the DVD series, the setting also made location shooting extremely expensive. Actors and crews were transported 300 miles into the Welsh mountains, including a nine-mile train ride, which was both time-consuming and costly.

Another example of luck was the creation of the balloonish guard, "Rover." In one version of Rover's origins, the machine-guard had been a specially designed hovercraft that could cross sea and land and climb buildings. But on the first day of shooting, it sank into the water and was never seen again. In another version, according to Bernie Williams, the production team was given a Rover that looked so ludicrous, like a cake on wheels, that it couldn't be used. Looking for something to replace it, Williams pointed to a meteorological balloon. While McGoohan shot scenes without Rover, Williams rushed off and returned with 100 balloons. Whether either of these tales are apocryphal or fact, throughout the series, the team filled these six-foot-diameter balloons with water, oxygen, or helium, depending on what they wanted. Before the series was completed, the crew reportedly had used 6,000 different balloons. The image of the roaring, deadly Rover became one of the series' most memorable elements.

Filming of the series began on December 1966, with several crews working simultaneously. One was on location, while permanent sets were being constructed in the MGM studios in London. During production, director Stanley Kubrick was filming 2001: A Space Odyssey in the same studios, and Prisoner designers asked to use some of Kubrick's hand-painted sky mats. Although each episode was shot in about two weeks, producing the seventeen episodes dragged out to nearly a year. One of the questions many viewers had regarding the two-part conclusion to the series was that actor Leo McKern's Number Two had a beard in the first episode, but not the finale. This discrepancy occurred because a year went by between the filming of the two hours, and McKern refused to regrow his beard for the show. Through it all, postproduction became something of a nightmare for the crew, as the perfectionist boss, McGoohan, micromanaged each aspect of the process, delegating less and less and becoming conspicuously exhausted.

During postproduction, McGoohan pioneered a fast editing style that came to characterize shows in the 1980s, when movement from one set to another was kept to a minimum. One notable example was the opening sequence, which showed how the Prisoner resigned, was kidnapped, and became aware of his new home in but a few minutes. As the pace of each episode accelerated, it was clear that the show's avant-garde music, originally commissioned by Robert Farnon, was no longer appropriate. Ron Grainer, composer for Doctor Who and Man in a Suitcase, crafted the memorable guitar-driven instrumental title music, possibly based on a melody McGoohan whistled for him.

In the first episode, "Arrival," the viewer was introduced to an unknown agent who drove his Lotus into a secret headquarters where he loudly resigned from his position.[2] He returned home and began to pack furiously, but outside his house, a hearse pulled up and a Victorian-dressed undertaker walked to the agent's door. The soon-to-be prisoner looked up as he heard the sound of gas coming into his room and then passed out. When he awakened, he found himself in a cottage that was a duplicate of his actual home, but this cottage was not what it seemed. Opening his window, the former secret agent learned he was in a strange resortlike town with unusual, baroque architecture.

Exploring his new home under the guidance of his tour guide, the first Number Two, Number Six discovered this Village was on the sea surrounded by mountains that served as natural boundaries helping keep the inmates confined. All doors opened automatically. No matter the emergency, doctors or police arrived within seconds. One guard for the Village was a roaring, gelatinous, large ball called "Rover" (discussed above), which could overcome any person on water or land. The Village was self-contained with its own shops, recreation centers, and heavily censored public broadcasting system and newspaper, *Tally ho*.

In the Village, childlike innocence was demonstrated in the candy-stripe trim of the buildings and the nursery-rhyme music coming from the broadcast speakers. Alcoholic-flavored beverages were available, but alcohol itself was strictly controlled. Pets were forbidden, although a mysterious black cat made occasional appearances. The inhabitants wore stylish suits and badges with numbers. Six himself took to wearing the trademark black blazer with the white trim, but he pointedly refused to put on his number badge. Six could buy a map, but its boundaries ended at the outskirts of the Village. Many citizens, it seemed, saw such envelopment as a haven and a comfortable home to reside in. With all needs met and many leisure pursuits available, most citizens acted like sheep being herded into any situation the mysterious keepers shaped. Six began hearing the oft-repeated maxims that characterized the Village keepers' viewpoint, such as "Questions are a burden to others, answers a prison for oneself." Most ominous of all was the mandatory parting phrase accompanied by a strange hand salute, "Be seeing you,"—a clear reference to the ever-present human and electronic watchers. Even the statues were eavesdropping devices that fed information to an ultrasophisticated room with maps of the globe and heavens adorning the walls.

Six learned the center of power was under a green dome where, each week, a new Number Two presented him with a new puzzle designed to get Six to reveal why he resigned. It was never clear who wanted this information, the opposition or his own government. Six's repeated inquiry, "Who is Number One?" invariably got a hearty laugh from each new Number Two, who replied, "That would be telling." One recurring character was a dwarfish, nameless, silent butler (Angelo Muscat) who represented the little man in society, willing to shift loyalty and obedience to whomever was in command, as does Peter Swanwick as the nameless Supervisor in seven episodes. (According to *The Prisoner Video Companion* (2003) the butler's silence reflected the ideas of writer Henry David Thoreau, who said human-kind lived in a state of "quiet desperation.") The setting was replete with such symbols, as in the ever-present image of a penny-farthing bicycle representing the slowing down of technological progress.

In each episode, one kind of mind game or another was tried on *The Prisoner*, sometimes quite fantastic, sometimes overt attempts at brainwashing. In all circumstances, he endured continuing pressures to comply, conform, and cooperate while making it repeatedly clear his goal was to first escape and then return to obliterate the Village. As the keepers valued Six, they could not use ordinary methods to break him, despite their philosophy that "Humanity must be humanized by force." So a series of techniques were used to get the information they wanted "by hook or by crook." All efforts were keyed to manipulating, tricking, or coercing his compliance with so-called "democratic values," in which the majority is always right.

In the first episodes, broadcast in England in 1967 after a summer run in Canada, Six explored this bizarre new setting, learning the limited perimeters of his prison. Escape and communication with the outside continually tempted him, only to have hope pulled out from under him time and time again. Simultaneously, the Prisoner learned that his keepers pushed a public image of false democracy, allowing the captive citizens a sham election in "Free for All." This McGoohan-penned script emphasized that elections gave comfort and encouraged conformity, but the real power was hidden behind the walls of city hall. Similarly, in "A Change of Mind," Number Two tried to force Six into compliance by having a community committee brand Six a disharmonious "unmutual" ostracized from all others. When enforced loneliness failed, Six underwent a bogus operation that allegedly destroyed his aggressive tendencies. Discovering the ploy, Six turned the tables by having Number Two branded as "unmutual" instead.

In "Chimes of Big Ben," Six was nearly tricked into revealing why he resigned when an elaborate hoax convinced him he'd escaped and arrived back in his old headquarters. He discovered the trick by checking his watch and noticing he hadn't left the village's time zone, said to be sixty miles from the Polish border in Lithuania. It was implied that the Prisoner's own department was behind the mystery, or perhaps the seeming enemies of the Cold War were either collaborators or more alike than they might appear. The Number Two in this story stated the two sides of the Cold War were mirror opposites of each other, becoming identical with the passing of time. The Village was thus a blueprint for a new world order in which such distinctions no longer mattered, another important theme in *The Prisoner*.

In "Many Happy Returns," *The Prisoner* awakened to find himself in a deserted Village from which escape is easy. This especially well-done episode had *The Prisoner* traveling across the sea and Europe, ostensibly for twenty-five days, with very little dialogue in the first thirty minutes. In this adventure, the Village was discovered to be apparently somewhere on the coast of Spain or Portugal, or perhaps in Morocco. Whatever the case, Six returned to his English home and found his Lotus and house were now owned by a seemingly kind and helpful lady named Mrs. Butterworth. After his department had him join a pilot to locate the Village, Six was suddenly ejected from the plane as he heard the pilot say, "Be seeing you." Parachuting into an apparently still Village, when Six entered his cottage, the water started flowing, his teakettle began singing, and Mrs. Butterworth appeared with a birthday cake saying "Many happy returns." His bogus escape hadn't led to freedom or, more important, the truth about the Village.

The early episodes reveal much about McGoohan's thoughts on modern society. Inflexible rules were challenged in "The Dance of the Dead," in which Six was sentenced to death for possession of a radio, the premise being no individual should have privileges denied others. In "Checkmate," he learned a means to tell jailer from prisoners. Prisoners will unflinchingly accept orders, while the keepers are arrogant. But when Six tried to organize an escape attempt, his partner foiled him because he assumed Six must be a keeper. Number Two told him, "I was sure you'd recognize the jailers by their subconscious arrogance. But you forgot one thing. The way you directed the escape operation with such authority persuaded the others you were one of ours." Individualism is a double bind—to be free, one must impose his will on others.

But the arrogance of power could be used against the captors. In "Hammer into Anvil," Six took on a personal dislike for a psychopathic Number Two. In a twist of the usual formula, Six played mind games with this Number Two by performing a series of seemingly random, pointless, erratic, and eccentric acts that led Number Two into thinking all around him were conspiring against him. Playing on this paranoia, Six convinced this Number Two that the Prisoner is the one working for the keepers, and he instructed the town leader to turn himself in as a security risk. In this story, those in power do themselves in by seeing treachery that isn't there.

When clever subterfuge failed to yield results, the captors resorted to brainwashing techniques, beginning with a speed-learning device in "The General." The keepers imply technology will improve the world until Six demonstrated even the ultimate computer cannot answer the simple question, "Why?" This episode illustrated a key theme of the series, that knowledge is not wisdom. The captors then attacked the Prisoner's mind and identity in "AB and C," in which a returning Number Two (Colin Gordon) was convinced Six resigned because he planned to sell out.

Six was hooked up to a device that not only projected his dreams onto a viewscreen, Number Two could insert films of people he thought might be the contacts Six planned to sell himself to. Six discovered the plan, took control, and revealed what Number Two should have known—he wasn't selling out to anyone.

In "Schizoid Man," an exact duplicate for Six was introduced to take his place, challenging his very identity. Six was brainwashed into thinking he was really Number Twelve, left-handed, and himself the duplicate until he uncovered the plot.

In several episodes, the keepers manipulated Six into assisting them with plans unrelated to his resignation. In "It's Your Funeral," a prospective Number Two tricked the Prisoner into working with a group of saboteurs called "the Jammers." In the past, this group had attempted to disrupt the Village with phony plots and escape plans to the point where no one believed anything they said. Number Two and the powers behind the Village maneuvered one Jammer into building a bomb to blow up a retiring Number Two, so he could appear to be killed by the villagers and not the controlling watchers. Six discovered the plan and helped the retiring Number Two escape, although the nervous elder spy admitted he would be killed sometime and somewhere else. Six turned to the new Number Two and told him his turn would also come—the keepers are as much prisoners as the kept. Another such outing, "Do Not Forsake Me, Oh My Darling," was the only episode with a pretitle teaser. In it, the keepers wondered how to find a missing scientist who had invented a mind-switching machine and decide to use Six as their unwitting agent to find him. First, they brainwashed him into thinking he had had amnesia for a year. Then they transferred his mind into the body of a colonel, an agent of the Village. In this other body, Six awakened in his old home, returned to his old headquarters, and found no one believed his story. After locating the doctor, the keepers kidnap the scientist and Six in order to force the doctor into demonstrating how the process can be reversed. Foiling the masters, the doctor returned Six to his old body but transferred his own mind into that of the colonel. He escaped, leaving the keepers without the process they desired.

Before the two-part grand finale, fantasy distinguished two episodes. "Living in Harmony" was another example in which the keepers found themselves more involved in their fantasies than Number Six. This episode had the Prisoner wake up in the Old West in circumstances similar to his real predicament. Throughout this adventure, Six played a man forced to be a sheriff against his will and who is befriended by a woman who was apparently killed at episode's end. In the keeper's plan, this loss of love would unhinge Six, especially after he had his identity challenged in two different times and worlds. But when Six discovered the ploy, he frustrated the keepers by quickly distinguishing fantasy from fact, foiling their attempt to disorient his mind.[3]

In "The Girl Who Was Death," the Prisoner chased Lady Death in a ploy designed to see if he would slip up telling Village children a haunting bedtime story. Perhaps the lightest episode of the series, the adventure paid homage to *Mission: Impossible* by having Six receive orders from a tape in a record store. He chased an eccentric assassin from one life-threatening situation to another, with apparent nods to *The Avengers*. For example, the girl's father dressed like Napoleon and commanded his own little army in a rocket disguised as a lighthouse.

This use of fantasy finished off the series in a two-part episode. In "Once Upon a Time," an earlier Number Two (Leo McKern) returned to reach into the Prisoner's childhood for one final showdown in a contest of wills. In a process called "Degree Absolute," McKern's Number Two put his own life on the line, taking Six into a basement room for one week where the agent was drugged and brought through the seven stages of life, but he ultimately killed Number Two with sheer willpower. He has triumphed, and is escorted to meet Number One.

In the final episode, "Fallout," perhaps the most surreal hour in television history, the Prisoner was freed, but no plot lines were tied up in any normal sense of the term. In a macabre courtroom, Six became the "Ultimate Leader," encouraged to take over the Village and inspire all to be like him. Depending on one's interpretation of this hour, "Fallout" is a play touching on themes of rebellious youth, the role of the independent man in a world that tends to either worship or demonize such freethinkers, and the uselessness of seeking any "Number One." Number Six, now simply called "Sir," was described as representing the best kind of rebellion, being iron-willed and pure of spirit. In a trial of two Villagers, he was compared to a young man, Number 48, who was described as "rebellion without purpose." After being resurrected from the dead, Leo McKern's Number Two, confessing he too was brought to the Village against his will, was portrayed as an Establishment figure who turned on his own principles. Therefore, according to *The Prisoner Video Companion*, Six's rebellion made him a prophet on a level beyond youthful cynicism or remorse of elder statesmen. Other interpreters note that although the courtroom participants seemed to worship Six, their main purpose wasn't hidden—they wanted him to sacrifice his freedom to rule the Village. As the president told him, "Lead us . . . or go."

The meaning of "Number One" was central to the episode. When Six finally encountered Number One, he pulled off a series of masks, including one of an ape, beneath which was the face of the Prisoner himself. The viewer thus learns that our jailers are within ourselves. In the view of some, the two faces showed McGoohan's interest in the dual nature of humanity. The ape face represented the animal side of humans, and the face of Number Six our intellectual side. This scene also, for some, cast new light on the opening dialogue between each Number Two and Number Six. When the Prisoner asked, "Who is Number One?" he was told, "You are Number Six." With the insert of a comma, the answer is, "You are, Number Six." According to Gary Gerani, this means:

He quit his intelligence post, therefore, for two reasons. First, to protest the repression fostered by the intelligence community as represented by the Rovers and the omnipresent bugs. And second, to imprison himself thereby demonstrating that each man is his own warden, conforming to society's design only by his own commands. His continual escape attempts demonstrate even though they were continually thwarted, that society's, i.e., his own, repression must be matched by individual steadfastness if freedom and democracy will ever be safe from the conspiracies of Number One, i.e., himself. (Gerani 1977, 124)

In the end, a rocket destroyed the Village in a scene of carnage as the music of the Beatles's "All You Need Is Love" was played as a soundtrack. The little butler accompanied Six back to his home, which oddly now had automatic doors just like his apartment in the Village. The final moments show the Prisoner riding off in his Lotus, the same scene with which the series began. If Gerani's interpretation is close to McGoohan's intention, the final moments show the cycle is about to repeat, although Six is no longer in the Village. He is still a Prisoner in the naturalistic sense; that is, he is still forced to operate in deterministic cycles of continuing obstacles to true freedom.

INFLUENCE OF THE PRISONER

Like the stubbornly independent Number Six in the classic British television series, *The Prisoner*, Pym resolutely keeps part of himself free . . . Sometimes our actions are questions, not answers. Espionage is existential expression. Sometimes a thing is done and still its reasons are a mystery.
—From Todd Hoffman's 2001 analysis of the novel *A Perfect Spy*, in *John le Carré's Landscape*, 178)

At first, viewer reaction to the show, especially its ending, was so negative that McGoohan left England in exile. The broadcaster's phone lines were deluged with angry complaints about nothing being neatly tied up. The production crew was equally unhappy, as McGoohan had defied the wishes of Markstein and others who, in McGoohan's opinion, had wanted to turn the grand finale into a version of *Goldfinger*. He preferred to shock everyone instead (Walters). For a time, McGoohan's commercial clout plummeted. The actor found his old backer Lew Grade less willing to invest in his new projects. But the show quickly grew in popularity as a cult classic, particularly among college students who were at the time chanting, "I am an individual—do not fold, spindle, or mutilate"—a call echoed in the Prisoner's defiant "I will not be pushed, briefed, debriefed, stamped, indexed, or numbered." Ex-Beatle George Harrison recalled in 2000 that his first 1966 trip to India was enlightening because he broke through the world of social security numbers that he associated with, like many others, Number Six.

The plots, acting, and the stylized settings distinguished *The Prisoner*, giving it a timelessness that continues to earn new respect and studied interest from new generations. The North Wales Portmeirion setting where the series exteriors were filmed became so famous that its owners finally banned annual conventions of *Prisoner* fans to keep the town a tourist attraction for the general public. Still, one souvenir shop still sells Number Six merchandise. For many, it has become the site of an annual pilgrimage, where devotees absorb the atmosphere and try to capture something of the myth from the still unusual architectural ambiance. All of these devotees bring much of themselves into the realm of Number Six, some seeing parallels in political realities, others seeking the transcendence of the show, which gave it the timelessness that keeps it relevant long after its original airing.

In some ways, *The Prisoner* was the last classic secret agent series of the 1960s. It is ironic that, of all its peers, it has had the longest shelf life of any series outside of *The Avengers*. This endurance is especially surprising considering it was a show with only seventeen episodes. Since the series conclusion, various novelists have tried their hand at new stories, set both before and after "Fallout," including Hank Stein, Thomas Disch, and *U.N.C.L.E.* author David McDaniel. *In the Village*, a quarterly magazine published by The Prisoner Appreciation Society, is mailed out with many extras for members, including *Prisoner* buttons, posters, and maps of "the Village." In January 1984, eight-hundred thousand watchers saw the one-hour documentary, "Six into One: The Prisoner File" on WTVA (BBC-2) (26). (Unfortunately, this documentary was aired only once and never issued on video or DVD.) Books about the show include *Inside* The Prisoner: *Radical Television and Film in the 1960s* by Ian Rakoff (1998) and Alain Carraze and Helene Oswald's *The Prisoner: A Televisionary Masterpiece* (1995). Such books are part insider looks into the series, part personal reaction to the show, and part speculation about what the sequel should be. Responses vary from the hyperintellectual (Was Rover an ideological weather balloon?) to the absurd (What sex was Rover?). The literary works of George Orwell, G. K. Chesterson, Lewis Carroll, John Fowles, John le Carré, and especially Franz Kafka have all been compared to the show. In one odd magazine article, an author decided there was a conspiracy connecting *The Prisoner* with *The Avengers*. In that writer's view, Six was actually Peter Peel, Emma's long-lost husband. Tara King was an agent for the Village's keepers, and we can know this by the penny-farthing symbol on her apartment wall (Miller 1998, 153). There are better connections between the two series: preceding *The Prisoner* was one 1966 *Avengers* episode, "Room without a View," in which people entering a hotel disappeared and were never seen again. In 1967's "Epic," Mrs. Peel was gassed in her apartment and woke up in a duplicate of her home. Both series employed mind-switching machines and both had their leads fight duplicates of themselves.

Continuing interest in *The Prisoner* can also be seen in television series created long after 1967. Nods to *The Prisoner* are evident in sci-fi shows such as *Babylon 5*. One episode of note was "Mind War," which dealt with the mysterious PsiCorps manipulating governments with brainwashing and mind games. One character, Bestor, says, "Let me pass on to you one thing I've learned about this place. No one here is exactly what he appears." To make the connection apparent, producers offered the role of Bestor to McGoohan who was interested but happened to be out of the country while the episode was being filmed. In the closing scene, Bestor, played by *Star Trek*'s Walter Koenig, leaves Commander Sinclair with a prisoner hand salute with the trademark phrase, "Be seeing you." In another episode, an alien force took over the B5 computer. Careful viewers can see the words quickly scrolling on the computer screen include a sequence of phrases from *The Prisoner*.

Other direct influences were apparent in the 1995 Fox drama *VR.5*, which fused mind games, tinkering with the subconsciousness, and complex relationships between a reluctant secret agent and the secret world. In one episode, the lead character was given a piece of paper that read, "Just call this number and ask for the Prisoner, no names." Not surprisingly, *The Prisoner* is often seen in reruns on the SciFi Channel, where more adult-oriented fantasy distinguishes what the channel offers. Bringing a show partially about the dangers of technology into the postmodern world, the SciFi Channel aired *The Prisoner* in June 1995 in tandem with New York online conclave ECHO, as part of the then experimental interactive broadcasting media. As host for the marathon, author Harlan Ellison provided brief commentary and analysis for each hour.

On September 6, 2001, the SciFi Channel aired another homage to *The Prisoner* in one episode of its original series, *The Invisible Man*. Investigating the "Agency of Sequestered Seclusion," Darien Fawkes and Bobby Hobbs found themselves unwilling prisoners in a resort for spies who'd been apparently murdered so they could retire into a secret "Community." Told they can never leave, Fawkes and Hobbs find their apartments have been duplicated in the "Community," and that they are under constant surveillance by "Minders," small helicopters reminiscent of Rover. The agents are under constant pressure from the residents to conform to life in the Community and are threatened with death if they disturb the happy balance of secret retirement. In the end, of course, the agents kick "A.S.S." after making other humorous nods to several TV spies. One agent, looking very much like John Steed, walks past them and both seem to recognize the figure. ("Isn't that the guy?" "No, he's the one they based the show on.")

As to *The Prisoner*'s creator, Patrick McGoohan never reclaimed his 1960s superstar status, but he continued to appear on the large and small screen in the following decades. He played a spy on *Columbo* in 1975's "Identity Crisis," which he also directed. In this episode, he played top government agent Nelson Brenner, who killed a former partner. At one point, McGoohan's character told Columbo, "Be seeing you," an obvious Prisoner-ism. *Secret Agent* had a kind of second life in the year 2000 when UPN offered *Secret Agent Man*, a slickly produced series using an updated version of the ubiquitous Sloan-Barri theme song. All other similarities to 1960s secret agents were with *U.N.C.L.E.* and *The Avengers*.

Although *The Prisoner* enjoys an ongoing cult status, it remains surprising that, except for the repeated use of the theme song, *Secret Agent* and *Danger Man* never gained much of a following after the 1960s. Part of this lack of interest certainly goes back to *Secret Agent*'s low ratings when it originally aired in the United States. What discussion there is about the show usually portrays it as a mere precursor to *The Prisoner*. Because of its use of topical issues and its lack of fantasy, the series perhaps didn't, and still doesn't, reach viewers less interested in gritty stories than escapist adventure. It is also possible that the buddy series like *U.N.C.L.E.* and *The Wild Wild West* enjoy continued interest because many spy aficionados are interested in the relationships and friendships between the lead characters. Unlike another buddy series, *I Spy*, which had special interest for Americans largely due to its racial dimension, perhaps *Secret Agent* is too British for U.S. tastes as it lacked the comforting quirky eccentricities of series like *The Avengers*. This might account for the fact that British DVD versions of the show contain many extra features not on U.S. collections, which offer limited filmographies and a short bio of McGoohan—not the interviews English audiences are rewarded with. However, on a variety of levels, *Secret Agent* was one of the best-crafted series in the genre and is, in many ways, one of the best televised time capsules of the Cold War in the 1960s. With more character development and less reliance on gimmickry, *Danger Man* may look dated, but the literary dramas still contain themes and subtexts any thoughtful viewer can still enjoy. Had the series been shot in color, it undoubtedly would have a stronger presence in the rerun market. And, were it not for *The Prisoner*'s shadow, the series could be appreciated for its own merits. It is, however, worthy of rediscovery and should maintain a long shelf life.

CHAPTER 7

The Page and the Screen: *The Saint* and Robin Hood Spies

OUTLAW SPIES

The low-down shocker is a decent and clean and honest to God form of literature. It does deal with things that have a right to occupy a man's mind. Of primitive chivalry, and damsels in distress, and virtue triumphant, and a wholesale slaughter of villains at the end, and a real fight running through it all. It mayn't be true to life as we know it, but it ought to be true. And that's why it's the best stuff for people to read if they must read about things instead of doing them. Only I prefer to do them.

—Simon Templar in *The Saint: Knight Templar*, 1930

Strictly speaking, Simon Templar, the "Robin Hood of Modern Crime," was only occasionally a secret agent in the spirit of 007 and his contemporaries. For one thing, Templar's first appearance in creator Leslie Charteris's novels was 1928's *Meet the Tiger*. For most observers, Simon Templar is most often seen as a continuation of earlier French and English eighteenth- and nineteenth-century fictional and real-life adventurers who played both sides of the law. According to a Turner Movie Classic documentary, the Saint novels appeared during a period of British literary "gentlemen outlaws" dominated by roguish heroes with names like "Raffles, the Falcon, and the Black Shirt." For other observers, the televised Saint had more in common with the private investigators of old-time radio and television's early years such as Richard Diamond and Peter Gunn. But the variety of the Saint's adventures and the longevity of his career defy easy categorizing. In his afterword to *The Fantastic Saint* (1982), Leslie Charteris admitted the Saint literary canon was deliberately varied to avoid monotony and the formulas Charteris felt other writers fell prey to. He listed his chosen formats as whodunits, what-was-its, straight adventure, espionage, and big and little swindles. Ironically, it was to keep the Saint out of legal trouble that Sir Hamilton Dorn had Templar join the British Secret Service in *The Saint Meets His Match* (also known as *Angels of Doom*) in 1930.

Long before Roger Moore put the Saint on television, connections between the literary worlds of Leslie Charteris and Ian Fleming were hard to miss. One weakness in O. F. Snelling's *James Bond 007: A Report* (1964) is that the author felt Bond's predecessors were primarily hard-boiled pulp fiction detectives like Bulldog Drummond and Dornford Yates. Still, Snelling admitted Bond would probably prefer the company of Simon Templar. In turn, Charteris once labeled Bond "Mickey Spillane in an old Etonian tie,"—a bureaucrat with a gun (Donovan 1983, 91). But, beyond the dual roles of the Saint and Bond portrayed by Roger Moore, it is clear that they are but two branches of the same family tree.

For example, as chronicled in the opening pages of *The Saint in New York* (1934), the Saint's first adventures included thwarting political assassinations and destroying mad scientists who had created diabolical weapons that Templar feared would instigate rather than deter war. Long before *The Avengers* and the spies of the 1960s fused sci-fi with espionage, Simon Templar defeated giant ants, voodoo zombies, and the Loch Ness monster. In 1935's *The Saint Overboard*, the Saint fought an underwater battle thirty years before Sean Connery repeated the scene in *Thunderball*. In 1930's *The Saint: Knight Templar*, the Saint foiled financiers who tried to create wars for profit, fifty years before Bond did the same in *Tomorrow Never Dies*. In the same novel, Simon Templar crawled down a makeshift rope ladder from a plane to a moving train, climbing inside to persuade the engineer to stop before hitting a bomb. He wasn't the only hero to perform such feats, but the Saint and his literary, film, and radio compatriots did such things long before viewers first saw these escapades in the 1960s.

Before Bond, Templar often aided his country's secret services. In *The Saint in Miami* (1940), he rescued secret agent Karen Leith. Short espionage yarns included "Miracle Tea Party" (1938) and the unsold story, "Missing in Action," which dealt with a sneak attack by the Japanese on California before the outbreak of World War II. In *The Saint Steps In* (1944), Templar worked for the U.S. government fighting American businessmen prone to fascism. In *The Saint Sees It Through* (1946), Templar temporarily worked for Sir Hamilton Dorn a second time. In 1956's "The Inescapable Word," Templar was asked to ferret out a murder on a secret installation, uncovering a Soviet spy in the process. Even when not on official duty, the Saint didn't mind pretending he was a spy. In 1930, when The Saint needed to impersonate a secret agent and persuade a police officer he worked for the government, he flashed the back page of his pilot's license, which read, "The

Civil, Naval, and Military Authorities, including the police, are respectfully requested to aid and assist the holder of this certificate."

Charteris's spy yarns, alongside many written by TV scriptwriters, became part of Roger Moore's TV Saint legacy. For example, in one episode, Moore's Templar pretended to be a Russian secret police chief, and in "When Spring Is Sprung," he rescued a Russian spy victimized by the British. In "The Helpful Pirate," he worked for British intelligence and was identified repeatedly throughout the episode as a British agent. In other adventures with clear Cold War themes, he battled spy rings, recovered secret plans and formulas, nailed a defector, and saved government officials from blackmail. He fought terrorists and helped out in political revolutions as in "The Wonderful War," using tape recorders, loudspeakers, and the smallest of all possible armies to save a Middle Eastern government. The Saint became even more involved with espionage when Ian Ogilvy took over the part in the 1970s. In short, no discussion of TV spies is complete without a careful look into the story of Simon Templar.

FROM THE PAGE TO THE SCREEN

> Don't you know? it was in all this morning's papers. Listen, "Brian Ufalets, the prominent film producer, plans to make a picture based on the true life story of the famous Simon Templar."
> —Young fan to Roger Moore's Saint

Before Ian Fleming's milieu came to the screen, the Saint had long been a mainstay in popular media, first as one of many detectives during the Golden Age of old-time radio. In 1939, the Saint joined other independent-minded characters on radio, including Lone Wolf, Boston Blackie, and Michael Shane. The BBC broadcast the first six adventures in 1939, starring Terence DeMarney.

In 1945, the first American series starred Edgar Barrier and later Brian Aherne (Charteris's favorite actor to portray the Saint), with script supervision by Charteris. In 1947, CBS brought Vincent Price to the role, who later reprised his portrayal in 1949. Three years later, Barry Sullivan filled in for Price before actor Tom Conway took the role to the end of the series in 1951. Demonstrating his unique versatility, Leslie Charteris himself composed the signature whistled title melody for *The Saint*, the same tune later expanded by Edwin Astley, Brain Dee, Irving Martin, and Orbital in television and film versions of the theme. During this era, Charteris converted his Saint radio dramas into short stories anthologized in various collections. He also took a turn at penning stories for the King Features comic strip "Secret Agent X-9."

Before *Dr. No*, a series of Saint movies came to the screen, beginning with *The Saint in New York* (1938), starring Louis Hayward. George Saunders played the role from 1939 to 1941 in six films. For many, Saunders defined the role in his witty, bemused, and mischievous style, introducing each adventure with the trademark whistle composed by Charteris. In 1941, Hugh Sinclair took over the role for two films before Louis Hayward returned in 1954 in a film alternately titled *The Saint's Girl Friday* and *The Saint Returns*. Two French actors also took a turn, Felix Martin and Jean Maris, but the results were so poor that Charteris refused to let the films be aired outside of France. If any fictional character was destined to have a life on television, then Simon Templar, star of radio, the silver screen, and the page, seemed preordained to be the candidate in the late 1950s—even before the spy boom began.

FROM SILVER SCREEN TO SMALL SCREEN

> The TV shows themselves I'm afraid I can't do much about. I have nothing to do with the production. It is very astute of you to realize that the taboos of TV make it impossible to show *The Saint* as he really is, and for him to do exactly the same things that he does in the books. But to make matters worse, you also have to contend with the incurable mentality of all film producers whether it is for the big or little screen.
> —From a letter by Leslie Charteris (quoted in Barer 1993, 116)

> Simon Templar was an impossibly interfering Boy Scout of a character. A world overrun with Simon Templars would be exceptionally trying. I don't believe in heroes like that. A man who behaves like *The Saint* is an idiot.
> —Roger Moore (quoted in Donovan 1983, 110)

The idea of bringing the Saint to television began in the 1950s, when various producers wanted to film episodes for then popular anthology series. Burned by the film versions of his character, Charteris held off such offers, fearing any live actor wouldn't meet his or his readers' expectations. However, by 1961, newcomers Robert Baker and Monty Berman obtained the rights for the first TV effort. Baker impressed Charteris with his independent films and his wartime background as a cameraman (Donovan 1983, 98). After talking with Charteris, Baker approached Lew Grade, who was immediately excited by the prospect and quickly agreed to back the project. The producers, wanting to give *The Saint* a modern touch, contacted several European sports car manufacturers seeking a Saint trademark. Volvo was so interested in having its P-1800 line on British television, the company flew in a white model from Sweden for the show, as no other white Volvos were yet available in England. The Volvo with its license plate reading "ST-1," alongside Charteris's haloed stick figure, became a signature icon for *The Saint*. The Volvo turned out to be a precursor to the similar uses of signature cars in *The Avengers* and the Bond films, an early indication of the trend-identifying fictional characters and the growing interest in pop culture symbolism.

The first actor interviewed for the role was Patrick McGoohan, after he had finished his initial run in *Danger Man*. As usual, McGoohan wouldn't have anything to do with women, a decidedly non-Saint approach. The producers felt he didn't have the sense of humor needed (Barer 1993, 122). As Baker and Berman looked for their lead, they read Charteris's books and chose the characterization of the Saint after World War II, when he was a loner and known as "the famous Simon Templar." All scripts for the first season were contractually based on Charteris stories. The author reviewed each of the scripts, and at first was relatively happy. He agreed with the need to expand his stories to fit the hour format, which usually meant writers adding subplots and secondary characters not in the original stories, usually including beautiful women. Some scripts, as in the first televised Roger Moore story, "The Talented Husband," required little alteration.

Sir Roger Moore (the actor was knighted in 2003) was born the son of a south London police constable on October 14, 1927. Throughout his career, Moore has repeatedly admitted his acting talent was minimal, characterized by two facial expressions punctuated with his trademark raised eyebrows. He became known for playing himself—a cavalier, slightly cynical, debonair, light-hearted man of the world with an eye for the ladies (Donovan 1983, 90–91). His prior film career hadn't been especially notable, one effort being *The King's Feast*, starring former Saint George Saunders. One 1961 Western was memorable only for the prophetic title, *Gold of the Seven Saints*. Under contract to Warner Brothers, Moore unhappily played Bo Maverick in nineteen episodes of the wildly popular *Maverick*, after series star James Garner departed in 1960.

Moore's time with Warner did give him two decided advantages when he was approached to play Simon Templar. As *Maverick* was a show then currently being broadcast on Lew Grade's British network, no screen test was deemed necessary. In addition, his days in the Warner Brothers gymnasium prepared him for on-screen stunt fights. Moore later said Grade had gotten him for half price because Moore thought the series would be half-hour adventures like *Danger Man*. One-hour series were not yet common in England, but Grade had his sights on America. At first, *The Saint* was filmed in black and white, as there were few color sets in England. America too was only slowly making plans to move to color. Moore thought he had a six-month project in front of him. His run in *The Saint* turned out to be six years.

After the first rushes of *Saint* clips were aired in the production room, all involved quickly realized Simon Templar had finally been perfectly cast for the screen, particularly due to Moore's sense of timing and humor. As it happened, when Moore showed up for these initial filmings in June 1962, former radio Saint, Vincent Price, looked on while working on a film project. Like most viewers, both then and now, Price felt Moore was perfect for the role. Price tried to pass on some of his ideas about the character to Moore, but after being rebuffed, Price decided never to mention the Saint to the new actor again. Moore had his own ideas about Simon Templar, having read Charteris's stories as a child in the 1930s, and he'd thought about buying the TV rights himself. Unlike Charteris, Moore was attracted to the British television codes, which inevitably would drain off the more violent and sadistic aspects of the print stories, leaving a character more suited to the actor's light touch. He liked the fact that his Saint couldn't maim, kill, or disfigure; he had to adhere to the Marquis of Queensbury Rules and fight clean. He couldn't pick locks because small boys might imitate what they saw on TV. He had to return all stolen money. Off screen, Moore endeared himself to the production crew with his self-effacing approach and willingness to put in hard work during the two-week shooting schedule for each episode. Reportedly, he was on time each day for the entire run of *The Saint*.

From the beginning, *The Saint* was a hit in its homeland, rising to number two in popularity among male viewers. The American reception, at first, was somewhat different. After eight episodes had been filmed, Grade chose two and flew to New York in 1963 to show the episodes to NBC vice president of programming Mort Werner. After viewing the first episode, Werner reportedly walked out proclaiming, "I've never seen so much crap in all my life" (Barer 1993, 128). CBS and ABC had similar reactions, claiming the show was too old-fashioned and too British. However, *The Saint* became one of the most successful dramas ever offered in American syndication. The New York NBC affiliate found the show won in ratings against its competitors' movies on Saturday nights, and similar success followed in Los Angeles and Chicago. Until the advent of independent cable stations, *The Saint* was the only series aired coast to coast in syndication in prime-time broadcasting.

Like Charteris's books, there was considerable variety in Roger Moore's adventures. By giving the character an air of sophistication brought into vogue by Bond and *The Avengers*, Moore in a sense validated the literary Saint, which had often been dismissed as vulgar pulp fiction. Each of the first *Saint* television hours began with Moore giving the audience a brief on-camera lecture on one point of law, crime, or the tribulations of the lives of the rich and famous. These on-camera monologues were intended to draw viewers into the world of Simon Templar, inviting them to participate in his soon-to-begin escapade. Invariably, someone identifying Moore as "the famous Simon Templar" followed the commentary insights, which prompted the first bars of the title theme as a halo appeared over Moore's head.

In each story, although the violence and gunplay of Charteris was toned down, the verbal repartee and surprising plot twists were retained, keeping the character recognizable to the reading public as Moore gallivanted in his Volvo P-1800. The Saint's longtime nemesis, Inspector Teal, was on hand, usually played by the capable Ivor Dean, who was the very embodiment of the pot-bellied, long-suffering policeman. Although other actors had played Teal before Dean, he was the most available and suitable for the part. During the initial run of *The Saint*, Moore directed four black-and-white episodes, featuring stars such as *Goldfinger* girl Shirley Eaton. Future TV spies included William Gaunt, later of *The Champions*, and Edward Woodward, later star of *The Equalizer*.

On at least one level, the Saint's creator saw the series in the same light as he viewed the earlier films, and he became something of a nuisance to the producers. By the second season, Charteris felt the show was deviating too far from his plots and the spirit of the character, and he began writing a series of irritable letters to the show's producers while publicly distancing himself from the show. He felt particularly proprietary, accusing the television industry of being deliberately mediocre and emasculating his show with pointless taboos (Barer 1993, 131). He was unhappy that the Saint was seen to be independently wealthy and not allowed to make any money. In his increasingly sarcastic notes, Charteris repeatedly claimed that producers felt they must improve on any writer's work and transform "it practically out of all recognition . . . I can find precious little on television worth wasting my time on" (Barer 1993, 156). According to Toby Miller, as the success of ITV's other project, *The Avengers*, made it a phenomenon, the story lines of *The Saint* began to emulate the adventures of Steed and Peel (1998, 17). Such moves didn't please Charteris. When he reviewed one script, he complained the story disintegrated into another TV stereotype, "which, with minor changes, could fit any series from *The Man From U.N.C.L.E.* to *Danger Man*" (Barer 1993, 156).

Despite all his bile, after his own stock of short stories had been used up, Charteris found ways to capitalize on the TV scripts written by others. In 1967, to keep his *Saint* magazine alive, Charteris reversed the process of story-to-script by adapting TV scripts into short stories with collaborator Fleming Lee. In turn, these stories were reprinted in "new" Saint books, including the Doubleday hardbacks *The Saint on TV* and *The Saint Abroad*. Old Saint paperback books were reissued with Roger Moore photographs on the cover, while Moore promoted the show by appearing on *The Today Show*, *The Tonight Show*, *Merv Griffin*, and *The Match Game*. Although Charteris might have disliked what he saw on screen, the popularity of Roger Moore helped keep Saint books on the paperback racks.

Because *The Saint* had already enjoyed a modest measure of success in the movie house, it seemed natural enough to expand *Saint* TV episodes into films. These quickly produced stories too showed the range of the character. *Vendetta for the Saint* (book, 1964; film, 1969) was a straightforward adventure with the Saint taking on the Mafia in Italy. In *The Fiction Makers* (1966), a decided nod to James Bond, *The Saint* took on a fictional crime organization called S.W.O.R.D. (Supreme World Organization for Retaliation and Destruction). *Vendetta* was distinguished by the fact that ex-*Avengers* Ian Hendry costarred with Moore as the principal heavy. These films set the stage for Moore as the 1970s version of 007. In one episode of *The Saint*, Moore even pretended to be Bond to earn the trust of a doting landlady, a harbinger of fantasies to come.

CHANGING FACES

> If I had been writing for TV from the beginning instead of books, I don't
> know how *The Saint* would have progressed, if at all.
> —From a letter by Charteris (quoted in Barer 1993, 120)

From October 1962 to August 1965, Moore starred in seventy-one black-and-white adventures, followed by forty-seven color episodes, which aired from September 1966 to February 1969. Before the color episodes went into production, Moore formed his own company in a partnership with Robert Baker, Bamoore Productions, and purchased the rights to the color episodes himself. NBC now made *The Saint* part of its regular programming, and the new production company happily made the color programs glossier for American networks by doing more location shooting, notably in Italy.

Had a new company not become involved, it was possible Charteris would have pulled the plug. When he negotiated the television rights with Bamoore, Charteris insisted recurring characters had to be recognizable to readers of his books. He continued the process of reviewing each new script and quickly became disenchanted with the color shows, although he found one writer he championed, John Kruse. But *The Saint*'s creator was slowing down, setting in the 1950s what new stories he wrote, as he realized Simon Templar's chronological age, according to the books, would place him in his seventies. Although not much of a problem for the page, other issues arose after the summer of 1968, when Roger Moore announced he felt he had done all he could do with the character.

Unlike the search for Moore, finding his replacement in 1977 was a relatively easy chore. Only one actor was considered for *Return of The Saint*, Moore look-alike Ian Ogilvy, a former *Avengers* guest star. At first, Ogilvy was to be the son of the original Simon Templar. The initial plans were to feature a gray-haired Roger Moore introducing each episode before sending his offspring into the fray. These plans were dropped in favor of the Bondlike suspension of age. The baggy-trousered 1970s Saint was instead designed to capitalize on trends of the period.

Ian Ogilvy made his debut on CBS in 1978 in adventures broadcast late on Friday nights after *The New Avengers*. Simultaneously, the network aired original Moore reruns on other evenings. But, like *The New Avengers*, the new Saint didn't make much of a splash. The biggest change was that this Saint

was no longer an independent Robin Hood. He typically represented repu-
table firms like Lloyds of London, often acting as an insurance investigator.
The new Templar worked for the CIA, the Ministry of Defense, and the SAS
(Special Air Services), and he helped M16 after they put him through surreptitious testing in the Alps to measure his skills. Story lines implied he'd
been something of a commando in his past. In three adventures, he foiled
assassinations. He orchestrated a prison break to save a girl framed for espionage, and in another episode he worked to keep a secret formula's inventor from defecting. In stories taken from news events, Templar assisted
Israeli agents and took on PLO terrorists. He helped a disabled agent who'd
worked with him in Yemen, and he aided a young woman pursued by the
secret police of a Cambodian-like country when England could do nothing
to help her. In the most typical spy plot of all, Templar saved London from
a hidden bomb.

This series kept close connections with the Moore production team, one
principal writer being Terence Feeley, who'd written for *The Saint*, *The
Persuaders*, *The Prisoner*, and *The New Avengers*. Another TV spy connection
was one appearance by ex-Avenger Linda Thorson. Each episode of the
original *Saint* cost $75,000; the *Return* outings cost $300,000 to accommodate the lavish production values and location shootings. Nine of the twenty-
four episodes were shot in Italy, the rest in the studio. The new Saint now
drove a Jaguar XJS, which became the model for a collectible toy in 2001.

As might be expected, Charteris had many opinions about the show.
Kindly, he sympathized with Ogilvy, writing him in September 1977, "It has
always been a big worry that the great natural niceness which is your own
personality would dominate your portrayal of *The Saint* and weaken him.
The Saint has all that charm but isn't always so very nice." Further, Charteris
thought the show couldn't be a hit under the weight of all the "wishy washy
taboos" (Barer 1993, 199). But Charteris wasn't discouraged from issuing
tie-in books with Ogilvy's picture to capitalize on the new series. In 1978,
he published *Send for the Saint*, which was another collection of adapted TV
scripts from the 1968 season. Charteris made one brief cameo appearance
in the series two-part opener, "Salvage for The Saint." Available on video
as *The Saint and the Brave Goose*, Charteris can be seen walking behind Ogilvy
and Gail Hunicutt in a scene filmed on the docks (Barer 1993, 216).

Two further attempts to recapture the magic of the Saint came under the
direction of producer D. L. Taffner. The first was a 1987 pilot called *The Saint
in Manhattan*. Robert Baker spent three years looking for a new Saint and
unearthed, surprisingly, Australian actor Andrew Clark. Reportedly, Clark
had been on the short list to replace Roger Moore as 007, but he looked
more like Tom Selleck than the first TV Saint. It was quickly apparent Clark's
Saint was more a Thomas Magnum–Matt Houston type of detective than
international playboy, which fit the network's desire for character and setting that were as American as possible. CBS insisted *The Saint* move from

London to New York, so the one-hour pilot was filmed in famous New York locations, including the Waldorf-Astoria, Lincoln Center, and Little Italy. George Rose was cast to be the Saint's trusted valet and friend, Woods.

In the spirit of the times, gimmicks replaced character, as in Templar's small, ostentatious Lamborghini Countach, which made his claim to be hiding from the law a bit unbelievable. In the summer of 1987, this pilot was aired with viewers asked to call the network and vote on whether the show should be a series or not. While the phone vote was ten to one in favor, the hour placed third in the ratings. Clark, certain of stardom, was disappointed, as this version of *The Saint* quickly disappeared.

Taffner's second attempt came in the form of six two-hour movies in 1987 and 1988 made for the coproducers of Saint Productions in association with London Weekend Television. Starring Simon Dutton, these TV movies were alternated once a month with other shows as part of the syndicated "Mystery Wheel of Adventure," which was intended to be a trial run for prospective series. Taffner was encouraged by the success of the syndicated *Star Trek: The Next Generation*, which indicated new, independent stations could do as well as established networks. Promoting the new series, Taffner's sales and marketing director said the audience for mystery shows was wider than that for science fiction, so *The Saint* had as good a chance as *Star Trek*. Original orders for the new Saint adventures included over 70 percent of America's independent stations, indicating U.S. broadcasters agreed with this assessment.

Simon Dutton, chosen out of 250 actors, was a perfect choice. Charteris approved of the casting, telling Dutton he looked much like the character he'd written. Dutton noted the differences between older versions and his series, especially the fact that the new plots came from newspaper stories of current events. "We're actually going back to the books in that we allude to *The Saint*'s dark side. In the '60s he was some sort of playboy-private detective but he is actually a crook who lives on both sides of the law" (Barer 1993, 227). Ironically, Dutton's mother had named him after the Saint, as she was a great fan of Simon Templar.

With a hefty budget, the production values for the new *Saint* were excellent. A cadre of international investors allowed *The Saint* to be produced by independent crews in France, Germany, Italy, and Australia. To appeal to an international audience, local stars from each country were billed with one American guest star per episode to reach that all-important central market. Considerable thought had gone into shaping the world of this Saint, such as the decision, against the wishes of dubious superiors, to cast Teal as a reluctant ally of Templar. Spy adventures included the German-set "Wrong Number," in which Templar worked with a beautiful, retired secret agent. Templar helped Interpol foil corporate intrigue, and in "The Software Murders," a typical espionage plot revolved around three murdered scientists. But the scripts were below par and story lines tended to meander. The six scripts were obviously rushed to meet deadlines and some scenes were clearly improvised. But the primary reason this series went no further was due to a team of film producers who wanted the movie rights and negotiated a deal with Taffner. To bring the Saint to the big screen, the TV show had to stop. Rights to the Dutton films reverted to the various countries of origin, and these efforts are not yet available on commercial video.

DOUBLE O SAINT

Immediately after the first Saint TV series finished production in 1968, Roger Moore and partner Robert Baker planned to create a series of films, one being *Crossplot*, a poor espionage outing deemed a low-grade version of *North by Northwest*. Somewhat more successful was their new television series, *The Persuaders*, which Lew Grade sold to America's ABC before a script had been written or a scene filmed.

Baker conceived the new series, originally titled "The Friendly Persuaders," with the now obligatory international market in mind (Brooks and Marsh 1999, 800). This series juxtaposed a British crime fighter (Moore) with an American counterpart (Tony Curtis). Baker liked the idea of using the head-butting tradition of films like *Boom Town*, which starred Clark Gable and Spencer Tracy, and *Butch Cassidy and the Sundance Kid* starring Paul Newman and Robert Redford. So two characters were developed. One was feminine, foppish Lord Brett Sinclair—a wealthy, idle, blasé aristocrat who smoked cigars and drank champagne. Obtaining film star Tony Curtis to play Bronx native Danny Wilde was quite a coup, although Moore had to accept second billing under Curtis's name. Wilde was a self-made millionaire who drove a Ferrari, but was equally as idle as Sinclair. From 1971 to 1972, Sinclair and Wilde sought out adventures using extremely contrasting styles. Judge Fulton (Laurence Naismith), a former judge at the Nuremberg trials, had tricked them at a party on the Riviera into becoming secret agents, convincing them they were wasting their lives, talents, and money.

Under the script guidance of Terry Nation, who'd contributed some of the best Steed-King *Avengers* story lines, the show had a good shot. *The Persuaders* was the most expensive series made by ITV in England, making Moore the first British star to be a multimillionaire actor based on TV rather than film work. Planned to go for five years, *The Persuaders* sold to even more countries than *The Saint* and earned huge sums for all concerned even before it was filmed. The show even boasted a John Barry theme.

Moore directed two of the episodes, and one of these, "Long Goodbye," included a small role for his daughter, seven-year-old Deborah. His son Jeffrey was seen as the young version of Brett Sinclair in the opening credit montage. Adopting techniques successful in other series, Moore and Curtis were encouraged to ad-lib freely to give the team an *I Spy* personality. However, this supposed combination of the best of the two English-speaking perspectives just didn't jell. The series couldn't compete in its time slot against the reinvigorated *Mission: Impossible*. The show is now primarily recalled as the reason Moore didn't become James Bond sooner.

Moore also tried his hand at playing in *Sherlock Holmes in New York* (1975), an NBC television movie costarring *Avengers* alumnus Patrick Macnee. In subsequent decades, Moore's television appearances were most often as a narrator for espionage-related documentary series. He reprised his role as James Bond in the May 1987 ABC "Happy Anniversary 007" celebration, and he hosted the March 7, 2002, broadcast of *Live and Let Die* for the ABC "James Bond Picture Show." The following day, he made his first network television acting appearance in over twenty years on the ABC spy series *Alias*.

When the Saint returned to the cinema in 1997 starring Val Kilmer, the new Saint was largely unrecognizable to fans of old. In the years leading up to the creation of the film, producers wondered how to bring the story up to date. Early scripts had Simon Holme, son of Simon Templar and his longtime girlfriend Patricia Holme, seeking out his father in order to become the inheritor of the family myth. According to director Philip Noyce's commentary for the DVD edition of the film, he wanted to provide a back story for Simon Templar not explored by Charteris. Noyce drafted a plot line in which viewers saw the development of how and why a sinner became a saint in "a journey from the selfish to the selfless." For this reason, strains of the *Saint* signature tune were only hinted at throughout the film, as in Simon's car alarm. The full theme was only heard when the thief had earned his title. According to Noyce, elements for his version of Simon Templar came from clues in the Charteris stories alongside an account of a real-life crook-turned-British-secret-agent he compared to the character in *La Femme Nikita*.

By the time the final script had been hammered out, in the pretitle sequence we see a young orphan with an unknown name being forced by priests to accept an identity chosen by the church. Escaping from his tormentors, the boy created his own name based on a fusion of Simon Magus, the early Christian magician, and the Knights Templar. (In the Charteris novels, Simon Templar was the Saint's given name, and he took on his trademark appellation when he was nineteen.)

In the film we then see the grown Saint in action, a greedy burglar seeking to make a million-dollar payoff to retire. We learn he has used clever disguises to carry out his criminal activity, using the names of Catholic saints in his nefarious robberies. This wasn't Charteris's Saint—in both the novels and television series, The Saint would use aliases, most usually that of "Sebastian Tombs," but not canonized saints. Unlike Charteris's secure, confident, arrogant Simon Templar, Kilmer's version is tortured, psychologically damaged by his youth. Ultimately, his love interest, Dr. Emma Russell, reformed the thief who performed three miracles to save the new Russian government. As we hear the strains of the original *Saint* theme for the first time, and as Roger Moore provided a cameo narration as a newscaster in the closing minutes, we see a disguised Saint seated by Inspector Teal and adorned with a little Saint stick-figure pin. Thus the legend began anew.

As always with the Saint, all things old are new again. With the release of the Kilmer film, Saint expert Barer wrote a novelization of the film based on the story by Jonathan Hensleigh and Philip Noyce. Thus, Simon Templar returned to the printed page. In the same decade, Charteris himself became a fictionalized character in Max Allan Collins's *The Hindenburg Murders*. After surviving nearly a century in nearly every available popular media, it seems unlikely the Saint will be off camera for very long, whether large or small screen. Certainly, the Moore series of the 1960s remains the zenith of the character's popularity to date, as shown by the 2001 release of the first two Moore DVD boxed sets of *Saint* adventures. But the books of Leslie Charteris still attract new readers and keep appearing in one publisher's hands or another, and the sort of independence and freewheeling spirit of Simon Templar make him a character suitable for new editions for each generation. Like James Bond, the actor who portrays him is but one face in the legend, one link in a chain that still entertains new audiences. In the Saint's own words, we learn one key reason for such immortality. "Isn't the outlaw one of the most popular figures in fiction?" he asked. "Isn't Robin Hood every schoolboy's idol? There's a reason for everything people love, and there must be a reason for that. It must be the response of one of the most fundamental impulses of humanity . . . for the same reason Adam fell for the apple, because it's in the nature of man to break laws." For the Saint, there was no real difference between the thrill of overthrowing a legitimate obstacle and the thrill of overthrowing a legitimate biblical commandment (*The Saint: Knight Templar*, 1930). Whenever the lines between legalities and justice blur, and whenever official sanctions preclude vengeance, lone wolves like the Saint will be around to irritate law enforcement and the criminal mind alike. In other cases, teams of "Saints" will appear on the side of the angels, as in the officially disavowed spies from *Mission: Impossible*.

The "Pop Star" spies: from left, Leo G. Carroll, David McCallum, and Robert Vaughn in *The Man from U.N.C.L.E.* (Courtesy Remember When Shop, Dallas, TX)

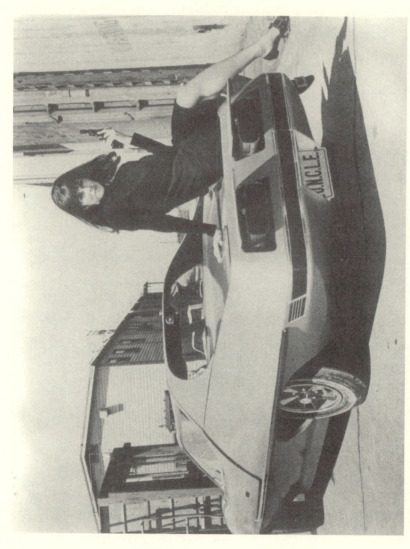

Gams, guns, and hot wheels: Stephanie Powers shows off her secret agent charms in *The Girl from U.N.C.L.E.* (Courtesy Remember When Shop, Dallas, TX)

The most successful pairing in TV spy history: Patrick Macnee and Diana Rigg in *The Avengers*. (Courtesy Remember When Shop, Dallas, TX)

The best-known faces from *Mission: Impossible*. In back, from left, Barbara Bain and Peter Graves. In front, from left, Peter Lupis, Greg Morris, and Martin Landau. (Courtesy Remember When Shop, Dallas, TX)

Master spoofs: Don Adams and Barbara Feldon in *Get Smart*. (Courtesy Remember When Shop, Dallas, TX)

A dandy and his disguise expert: from left, Ross Martin and Robert Conrad in *The Wild Wild West*. (Courtesy Remember When Shop, Dallas, TX)

The quintessential British secret agent: Patrick McGoohan in *The Prisoner*. (Courtesy Remember When Shop, Dallas, TX)

"You want me to steal?" Robert Wagner and Malachi Throne in *It Takes a Thief*. (Courtesy Remember When Shop, Dallas, TX)

Roger Moore lookalike Ian Ogilvy brought Simon Templar back to TV in *Return of The Saint*. (Courtesy Ian Dickerson and "The Saint Club")

The super-spy of the 1970s: Lee Majors with Richard Anderson in *The Six Million Dollar Man*. (Courtesy Remember When Shop, Dallas, TX)

The spy with bullet-bouncing bracelets: Lynda Carter in *Wonder Woman*. (Courtesy Remember When Shop, Dallas, TX)

Spies without names: from left, Maria Bello and Scott Bakula in *Mr. and Mrs. Smith*. (Courtesy Remember When Shop, Dallas, TX)

Spies in the sky: from left, Ernest Borgnine and Jan-Michael Vincent in *Airwolf*. (Courtesy Remember When Shop, Dallas, TX)

Mission: Impossible turned upside-down. The cast of the original *A-Team*. In back, Dwight Schultz and Dirk Benedict. In foreground, Mr. T and George Peppard. (Courtesy Remember When Shop, Dallas, TX)

Kate Jackson (left) and Bruce Boxleitner on their home turf: the professional and amateur spies of *Scarecrow and Mrs. King*. (Courtesy Remember When Shop, Dallas, TX)

Guest star Lori Loughlin (left) with Edward Woodward in *The Equalizer*. (Courtesy Remember When Shop, Dallas, TX)

The squeaky-clean spy: Richard Dean Anderson as *MacGyver*. (Courtesy Remember When Shop, Dallas, TX)

"The truth is out there": from left, David Duchovny and Gillian Anderson in *The X-Files*. (Courtesy Remember When Shop, Dallas, TX)

Undercover in the twenty-first century: The first case of *24*. From left: Penny Johnson Jerald, Dennis Haysbert, Sarah Clarke, Leslie Hope, Kiefer Sutherland, and Elisha Cuthbert. (Courtesy Remember When Shop, Dallas, TX)

CHAPTER 8

Interchangeable Parts: Missions: Impossible

THE SECRET OF TEAMWORK

> Don't you talk to me about rights. They're for decent people, not jerks like you. I will fight you with your own methods, Frank. I'm going to work you over and sweat you until you tell me everything I want to know.
>
> —Jim Phelps

At the beginning of most episodes of *Mission: Impossible* (MI), the camera revealed an ordinary location, say a playground or camera shop. Then a quiet stranger entered the scene. At some point, an ordinary-looking clerk or secretary presented the stranger with a key or package, which the stranger then took to some private corner or room. There, he discovered a file of photos and a tape recorder. He pressed the play button and was greeted with a message describing a potential world calamity that law enforcement agencies were powerless to do anything about. After describing the dilemma, the taped voice would end the message saying, "As always, if you choose to accept this mission and any member of your Impossible Mission Force is caught or killed, the secretary will disavow any knowledge of your actions. Good luck. This tape will self destruct in five seconds." Invariably, five seconds later, smoke emerged from the player. The viewer then sees a match being struck, a fuse lit, and hears the opening strains of the signature *Mission: Impossible* theme.[1]

In the first season which began on September 17, 1966, it was the affable, chunky Dan Briggs (Hill) who retired to his black-and-white decorated apartment to scan over a pile of dossiers, choosing which team members of the Impossible Mission Force (IMF) would join him in the operation. From the second season on, it was Jim Phelps (Peter Graves) who tossed down the photo of each member so the audience could see whom from the IMF was included in the team for the new assignment. In the first three seasons, four faces turned up time and time again.

Rollin Hand (Martin Landau), the master of disguises and deceit, was often first on the pile. Landau, a Brooklyn, New York, native, was *Mission*'s most visible connection to Alfred Hitchcock. He'd starred alongside Cary Grant and Leo G. Carroll in 1959's *North by Northwest*. He'd been on the short list for both Illya Kuryakin and Mr. Spock, roles he turned down to be free to pursue his motion picture career. Still, *Mission: Impossible* executive producer Bruce Geller had created Rollin Hand with Landau in mind, as Geller admired both Landau's acting ability and the acting classes he taught to such talents as Robert Blake and Jack Nicholson.

When *Mission: Impossible* debuted, Landau was billed as a guest star, and it took some doing to get him under contract. Later, Landau described Hand as a night club performer who was liked, loyal, an adventurer, and a soldier of fortune wanting to enliven his life. Landau's character considered that the ultimate performance was when his life was on the line, his talent always being tested. A master of bluff and bluster, Hand would play everything from a clergyman to Adolph Hitler.[2]

The next photo on the pile was often that of Cinnamon Carter, played by Landau's wife, Barbara Bain. Bain had earlier starred as Karen Wells, the girlfriend of TV detective Richard Diamond. According to Bain, Geller wrote the part of Carter especially for her. But when Desilu owner Lucille Ball learned Bain was married to Landau, Ball apparently worried that something funny might be going on with the casting choices. Bain was told to go to Ball's bungalow on the Paramount lot and to bring along the latest piece of film she'd done. "The latest at the time was a comedy," Bain said, "And I wasn't about to walk into her bungalow with a comedy. I couldn't do it. I was just going to walk in with me. So I did. And she just looked me up and down and said, 'Looks OK to me.' That was it" (Johnson 1997).

Bain's Carter was a throaty-voiced actress who played many roles, most often as perfumed bait or as an international playgirl, using feminine wiles to gain the attention of her prey. She was thus effective in situations where a man couldn't do the same things. "My job's simply doing what comes naturally," Carter said in the series pilot. For three years, she played a cabaret singer, career woman, princess, floozy, model, astrologer, plastic surgeon, stewardess, drug addict, and mind reader.

As each mission involved some electronic trickery, scientific wizard Barney Collier (Greg Morris) was needed. Morris had starred in an earlier unsold pilot for Geller, who remembered him when the *MI* project got network approval. Geller was primarily interested in Morris's athletic build, not his race. According to Don Bogle, Geller claimed if Morris hadn't accepted the role, his next choice was a blue-eyed, blond Scandinavian (Bogle 2001, 128–30). Like *I Spy*'s Bill Cosby, Morris played a new kind of African American hero, an intellectual and forceful presence on the team. On one level, Morris's role was the serious side to fellow African American actor Ivan Dixon's portrayal of Sgt. James Kinchloe in the 1965-to-1971 program *Hogan's Heroes*. In that comedy series, Dixon's character was a precursor to Barney Collier, an intelligent electronics and demolitions expert, a savvy co-equal underground operative with the rest of Hogan's team.

Ironically, it was Morris's appearance on another comedy series, *The Dick Van Dyke* Show, that gave Sheldon Leonard the ammunition he needed to convince NBC that casting Bill Cosby would work for *I Spy*. Like Cosby's Alexander Scott, Morris's Barney Collier was always cool under pressure, despite being shot three times, beaten, blinded, brainwashed, poisoned, and stranded in a live minefield. Collier shared his *MI* teammates' tendency to never question their mission, unlike Scott in *I Spy*.

Rounding out the original team was gentle strongman and utility player Willy Armitage played by Peter "Lup" Lupus, a six-foot four-inch, 250-pound ex-bodybuilding champion. Lupus had starred in various Italian gladiator films before joining the IMF. In the beginning, his strongman persona was important to the show's format, but after the first episodes, this need quickly disappeared. Thereafter, he became the team's driver and assistant to Collier. He had few lines, and he learned young viewers counted them in each episode, reporting their findings to him in their fan mail. While he seemed the most dispensable member of the team, alongside Greg Morris, he was one of the two original cast members to survive *Mission: Impossible*'s entire run. The only other participant to "appear" until the end was Bob Johnson, the voice of all those self-destructing tapes.

Although these four players were the nucleus of one of the most successful concepts in television, none of them was ever developed into charismatic stars as were leads in other shows. The IMF was rarely a character-driven team. It was, at first, an ensemble cast with all actors being equal. The show developed no relationships among the characters nor did it provide much background into their past until the final years, when three original cast members had departed. In each mission, the dialogue was limited to the technical and the expository. The music provided the narrative continuity while the team set up its equipment or moved from set to set. As the point of the show was the team's elaborate sting operations, its stars were as much writers and backstage crew as they were actors, as they invented new ways to coax a dictator out of his country, trick a financier into moving ill-gotten gains out of impenetrable vaults, or deceive an arms merchant into tipping his hand and opening himself up to legal prosecution. The two essential story lines were to retrieve an object or person from the clutches of evildoers and/or eliminating or discrediting criminals or corrupted government officials. The point wasn't so much who pulled these feats off but how they pulled them off. The story of *Mission: Impossible*, then, is a history of interchangeable parts, both on and off screen, and the creation of a formula that came to dominate many spy shows to follow.

GOOD MORNING, MR. BRIGGS

Mission: Impossible was the brainchild of Desilu producer Bruce Geller, the man who struck the match seen in the moments before the opening strains of Lalo Schifrin's title theme. Geller created a show critically acclaimed enough to win a number of Golden Globes and Emmys, besting even *The Avengers*. It was distinguished by one of the most recognized title themes in history, resulting in two hit albums for composer Schifrin. In a recorded interview for *The Best of Mission: Impossible* CD, Peter Graves claimed this theme elevated a "pretty good show" by "about 70%."

But the series didn't rise to its creative heights easily. Before *MI*, Bruce Geller had a lengthy writing résumé, including scripts for *Flash Gordon*, *Rocky King*, *Detective*, and various Westerns. In the beginning, *Mission: Impossible* was entitled "Briggs's Squad," a show intended to be a thirty-minute drama. When the network told Geller they were no longer interested in half-hour adventure shows, he expanded the plan for his pilot. Because of the plot's complexity, he put his ideas on index cards and called the script a "Rube Goldberg crossword puzzle" (White 1991, 34). As the script progressed, he decided the idea would have to be a movie, as it would never work as a sustained series. He thought the stories would all have to be two-part or three-part serials, an idea that didn't come to fruition until the fourth season. (During *Mission*'s first run, only one two-parter, "The Council," was made into a 1968 movie released in Europe, *Mission: Impossible vs. the Mob*.)

At first, "Briggs's Squad" was a former special forces group performing hazardous, unrewarded work because the United States had to disavow their actions. Lt. Col. David Briggs's Squad consisted of Albert Nay, a wheeler-dealer; Jack Smith, the womanizer; Barney Collier, the ballistics expert and chemical engineer; and Willy Armitage, the "grunt" who was ill-educated, inept, and probably the strongest man on earth. The squad also included Little Terry Targo, the mild-mannered martial arts expert, and master of disguise Martin Land, the pickpocket who was fluent in fifteen languages. Land could hold his breath for eight minutes and was a master magician. ("Martin Land" became "Rollin Hand" because the original name was too similar to that of the actor who played him, and "Rollin Hand" was easy to substitute in the already typed scripts.) After the war, Briggs turned this team into crooks because ordinary life bored them. Briggs had to find work that was fascinating and interesting and usually on the wrong side of the law. To make the team acceptable for TV, Geller knew they would need some sort of semiofficial status. With the success of secret agent shows, Geller decided they too would work as secret agents, although Geller conceived the group as a private team that would work for anyone, but was most often hired for action the government couldn't legally take on.

In another draft, only three characters were involved—Briggs, Collier, and Carter. In each of these versions, Geller provided no back stories, as he intended the characters to jump into their weekly disguises within the first five minutes. He included an apartment scene at the beginning of the pilot where the characters could assemble, discuss the mission, and quickly demonstrate the devices they'd use. The apartment scenes were to be set in black and white, with the characters wearing black or gray as a contrast to the colorful world they would be quickly involved in. These notions suggest a series with novel approaches, but it's a matter of some debate how much of the concept was original with Geller. As described in Chapter 2, NBC had aired thirteen episodes of *21 Beacon Street*, a 1959 series set around the Dennis Chase Detective Agency. In 1968, Filmways sued Geller claiming *MI*'s concept was plagiarism. Writer Laurence Heath, who worked for both shows and wrote more *MI* episodes than anyone, said Geller claimed to have never seen *21 Beacon Street*. Ironically, after the demise of *MI*, Geller saw numerous shows imitating his creation, but he could do nothing about it except assume imitation is unremunerated flattery.

Despite the minor *21 Beacon Street* controversy, it is clear that Geller created the premise for *Mission: Impossible* and directed the casting of the original characters. But it is also well established that many hands developed the series' direction after the pilot, in which Geller had wanted to emulate the style of *The Ipcress File*, the Michael Caine spy venture popular that year. Geller enjoyed good fortune, as he was working for Lucille Ball's powerful and independent Desilu Studios. Unlike other series of the era, Geller thus had little network influence until after CBS had bought the series. As it happened, Desilu was somewhat desperate and needed to sell shows beyond the flagship *Here's Lucy*, starring the studio owner. As *MI* went into production, so did *Star Trek*, another Desilu project, which would have some influence on the direction of *MI*.

Although not ordinarily a hands-on studio executive, Ball had much to do with the launching of *MI*. Beyond her involvement with casting choices, when CBS balked at purchasing *MI*, Ball threw her powerful weight behind the project. CBS admired the pilot so much, they feared no subsequent episodes could equal it without worrisome high budgets, a fear that proved to have considerable merit. Although Ball later claimed she didn't understand the pilot or the subsequent plots, she knew she had a quality product. One story was that Ball called up CBS chair William Paley and insisted *MI* was the best pilot of the year, and he agreed. Another story has it that Ball threatened to cancel her own series if the network didn't purchase *MI*. They came to terms and signed a $12 million long-term contract, the largest such commitment of the decade.[3]

After the series was sold, producer Joseph Gantman essentially took over the show because Geller wanted only supervisory duties. Gantman quickly noted Geller had prepared no "bible" for the series, had no scripts prepared beyond the pilot, and had no direction in mind. Gantman had been an associate producer for the *U.N.C.L.E.* pilot, one the *MI* production crew admired. (Sam Rolfe complimented Geller for the *MI* pilot, saying it was the best he had seen, a high compliment indeed, as Geller felt the same about "Solo.") As Geller and Gantman knew their series would be measured against *U.N.C.L.E.*, they kept humor out so the plots would be more realistic and credible, a policy that won the show considerable critical praise. Gantman began pulling together his team, which became a logistical nightmare. It didn't take long for the show to gain a reputation as a director killer because of the prep time involved and the number of fast cuts and edits— twice as many as any other show—that gave the show its staccato pace. Director Gerald Mayer said the show was not fun to work on, with the crew invariably behind schedule before filming began. To keep the pace in constant motion, the crew employed a number of camera tricks, including the overuse of the optical zoom lens. Another frequent trick was "rack focusing," which blurred the background so the camera could focus on something interesting in the foreground. Most important, the crew relied on "insert shots," those that didn't require the principal actors. Inserts were normally shots of hands holding or working with tools or objects, fingers pushing buttons, and the obligatory views of watch or clock faces ticking away. Like *Star Trek*, *MI* relied on weekly creations by the special effects team, led in *MI*'s case by Johnny Burke, a veteran of Dean Martin's *The Silencers* spy spoof. To establish the realism *MI* demanded, Burke studied many technical journals, bringing together elements from separate fields of study and drawing from what was possible. In one instance, Hughes Aircraft demanded an investigation of the show's use of a fictional hydrofoil machine, as the company had one in the works. Burke had to prove his device didn't work and was pulled with wires.

Because of the precise timing involved, directors had no flexibility in crafting their assignments and were required to invest extra effort in the post-production editing process. To help save time, despite union rules, a second unit was formed to handle the inserts. By the final years, four separate crews were filming different scenes simultaneously. The taped message sequences were filmed en masse to help in scheduling.

During the first year, viewers looked for clues into the characters' motivations and histories and many sought further details in the John Tiger novelizations, which were published by Popular Library and similar to his *I Spy* efforts. Unlike the *I Spy* books, which were largely unrelated to the show on which they capitalized, the *Mission* books showed some awareness of Bruce Geller's ideas and the backgrounds of the actors portraying the IMF team. For example, according to Tiger, it was Dan Briggs who had recruited the four other primary agents, a concept reflecting Geller's original "Briggs's Squad" idea. Briggs had been a high school football coach before doing intelligence work in Korea, an idea later repeated in Peter Graves's back story for Jim Phelps. Briggs's wife and two children had been killed in a California automobile accident. He was a two-year student of psychology and games theory, a chess champion, an expert on foreign armies and military equipment, and a master glider and glide plane pilot (Tiger 1967, 5–7). All these descriptions did, in fact, tie in with Geller's view of Briggs as a master strategist who was an effective planner skilled in reading the psychology of his prey.

According to Tiger, the others knew none of this, as each knew little about their teammates' lives before joining the IMF. Each agent clearly had a life outside of the IMF, but they apparently dropped whatever they were doing to rush to the call of their chief. In Tiger's realm, Briggs, intimately familiar with their dossiers, knew Willy Armitage had won medals in the Olympics, was a son of a Pennsylvania coal miner, and was the youngest of five boys. Rollin Hand had run his own Florida acting company and was the son of a Park Avenue doctor's daughter and a genuine Gypsy prince (Tiger 1967, 9). In truth, Peter Lupus had won a number of weight-lifting competitions, and Martin Landau had indeed run his own acting school. In Tiger's outline, Barney Collier had been third in his class at Caltech, was an expert water-skier, and had joined the most secret of secret agencies to avoid difficulties with lady friends desirous of his attention. Maybe, maybe not. According to Don Bogle, the few facts known about Barney were that his parents were teachers, and that he was independently wealthy as president of his own Collier Electronics. In the 1970 to 1971 season, we learn Collier had a brother, Larry, who was murdered. According to Tiger, in Briggs's opinion, Carter, a former cover girl for *Vogue* and *Harper's Bazaar* and a Chicago banker's daughter, was the one team member who saw him as something more than a father figure (Tiger 1967, 10). In the series, however, there was never a clue of a romance between Carter and Briggs. The closest we see to any such interaction was in the episode "A Spool There Was," a unique story that featured Carter and Hand working as a couple without the rest of the team.

However anyone viewed Dan Briggs, the actor who played him bore no relationship to his thoughtful character. Steven Hill was an actor with a deserved reputation for being both brilliant and brash. He kept the show's production in turmoil due to his temper and his demand he be allowed to leave early on Fridays to observe the Sabbath. CBS and Desilu didn't like him because he didn't have the star power they felt was needed to carry the series. But Geller felt Hill was perfect for the role and had been an admirer of his acting since the two met on an episode Geller had written for the Western hit *Rawhide*. In particular, Geller liked Hill's ability to shift from quiet, cerebral dialogues to menacing, ruthless confrontations with adversaries. Geller stuck by Hill even as it became more and more evident that the series had to work around the actor's unwillingness to work long hours. On many episodes, he only appeared in the opening sequences, and producers resented paying him full salary when he wasn't available for work. Landau began taking over the scenes intended for Hill, and Geller finally convinced Landau to sign a contract as a regular cast member. Although Geller had thought many guest stars would be involved in the IMF team, it became apparent few were needed, as Landau could handle any type of character offered to him.

Before the first season ended, Geller finally gave up on Hill, after the actor retreated to his trailer and refused to work. Hill brought the production to a halt by refusing to run up a set of stairs in one scene, an action hardly atypical of his normal duties. Producer Herb Solo put him on suspension, brought in a replacement actor, and two days of filming became unusable. For that episode, Geller had the taped message scene filmed around Cinnamon in a beauty salon. Briggs didn't appear, and no mention was made of his absence. In another episode, "The Imposter," Briggs was the main character, but as he was in disguise and played by a different actor, Hill wasn't needed for most of the shots. Later, Hill claimed, "The work got to be mechanical week after week," which was why he left the series (Lipton and Schnaufer 1995, 46). However, according to Patrick White, Hill was upset when he learned from an article in *Variety Magazine* that he had been replaced. Without fanfare or any on-screen explanation, Peter Graves became Jim Phelps at the onset of the second season, and his presence transformed the show.

GOOD MORNING, MR. PHELPS

At the end of the first season, *Mission: Impossible* was a show in trouble. It rated at number fifty-one and seemed doomed to certain cancellation. But CBS thought the show was too classy to kill, so the series was moved from Saturdays to Sundays. All involved basked in the glow of six Emmy nominations. *MI* won four: best dramatic series and best actress, editing, and writing. In addition, it picked up two Grammys and two Golden Globes for best series and best actor for Martin Landau. These awards helped widen audience appeal in the spring reruns.

Simultaneously, the search was on for a replacement for Steven Hill. Geller thought of Peter Graves, who had starred in one of his unsold pilots, "Call to Danger." At that time, Graves was no stranger to network TV, having been a star of 1955's *Fury*. Graves was also known for being the younger brother of James Arness, the star of the popular Western, *Gunsmoke*.

Quickly getting into the spirit of the show, Graves and Geller began crafting the new character, and Graves wrote his own back story for Phelps. He described Phelps as a young man leaving college, going into the Korean War, and having a career with Pan Am airlines before coming home to receive a recorded message that changed his life. Geller approved, feeling that Phelps was much like Briggs. For one thing, both Briggs and Phelps apparently liked black-and-white apartments, and both preferred using the same four agents. But Phelps was more involved in the assignments. Where Briggs was the strategist who set things in motion, Phelps was equally cerebral but also athletic. He appeared most often as authority figures like doctors, scientists, and investigators, but also as hustlers, spies, and gangsters. He appeared often as a middle-American salesman, a role especially suited to Graves's vocal delivery. Graves became a welcome addition to the cast, a willing worker who brought a new sense of looseness to the set. With its most famous cast now in place, *Mission: Impossible* moved into its most praised years, the second to fourth seasons.

According to series writer James Buchanan, the scripts for *MI* were heavily influenced by English professor David W. Moore's *The Big Con* (1940), a detailed study of the methods of confidence artists. According to Moore's ideas, "grifters" had to have dishonest prey so they could work on fatal flaws and hoist the villain on his or her own petard. While the prey is cheating someone else, he or she is unaware of also being cheated. In *The Big Con*, victims are often lured into a phony "big store," a fully equipped betting hall, telegraph office, or brokerage firm operated solely for the mark or victim (White 1991, 47). *MI* created many such "big stores," including artificial prison cells, hospital rooms, submarines, trains, and ocean freighters. Such settings made for unique adventures, as in the episode shot in a bogus airline cabin from which no one could escape or maneuver if the situation went wrong. In "The Execution," a bogus gas chamber was used in a deliberately brutal story intended to be an antideath sentence penalty statement. Often, the team revealed the false walls after the mission was completed to show the mark the evidence of his or her downfall.

Other tricks included having the mark think he or she has had amnesia for months or years. The team used the old swindler's technique of creating "dream machines" to make their prey think they can make diamonds, heroin, counterfeit cash, or mind-controlling drugs. When dealing with a gambler, they naturally rigged games. If they were unable to catch the bad guy for the actual crime, they'd frame him or her or ensnare the prey in something the IMF team set up just before they disappeared, leaving no witness or evidence to support the victim's story.

The writers felt it was important to have the IMF's adversaries be worthy opponents, stronger on their own terms than any one member of the team. Otherwise, viewers might feel sympathy for the out-maneuvered victim. When guest stars turned out performances of effective and strong bad guys, they were invited back repeatedly to star in the show. Other guest stars drew from the ranks of TV spies, including Noel Harrison, Mary Ann Mobley, Anne Francis, and Robert Conrad. The original movie "Saint," George Saunders, made one of his last acting appearances on *MI*.

During its early years, *Mission: Impossible* held wide audience appeal. As it wasn't originally targeted to the young, the program yielded little in collectible tie-in merchandise. There were the inevitable Gold Key Comics and novels published by Popular Library, including the first in the series by John Tiger, which explained the format of each mission. Phase 1: Infiltrate the target area and establish your agent's bona fides in their disguises. Phase 2: Reconnoiter the target area and make surreptitious contact with the target. Phase 3: Execute the usually complex and detailed sting, always having a backup plan. Phase 4: Complete the mission and extricate the team safely and triumphantly (Tiger 1967, 24).

According to academic Bruce Beatie, this pattern closely followed similar story lines of medieval legends (Beatie 1983, 46). For example, in tales of old, the temptress typically was a test for all heroes. In ancient legends, magical devices aided the hero, and in the modern world the magician is the scientist who makes gold out of lead. In *MI*'s case, it was Barney Collier who constructed false walls and fake machines, counterfeited documents, created special effects, cracked safes, picked locks, and broke codes. The world of magic often meant excursions into the supernatural. *MI* often used paranormal settings for its "big stores," as in "Phantoms," which was based on writings of Russian novelist Alexander Solzhenitsyn. For this episode, writers noted a passage describing Soviet dictator Joseph Stalin seeing ghosts. In such setups, superstitious opponents found their fears preyed on as a host of ghosts invaded their homes and spoke to them from the grave.

In old legends, some kind of transfiguration occurred, an animal into human, beast into prince, witch into princess (Beatie 1983, 48). In the first three years of *MI*, this magician was disguise master Rollin Hand. Landau's Rollin Hand built his disguises around facial latex life-masks. One cliché of the show was having these camouflaging masks pulled off an agent's face to reveal the agent beneath. As the show relied on cliffhangers at the end of each act, typically one agent was in danger of being revealed just before the commercial break.

All teammates played roles to confuse and maneuver their prey into the intended trap. Sometimes they played opposing sides of the law in separate teams to make victims think some of the IMF was on their side, the others against them. In other situations, the IMF used the "divide and conquer" ploy of having one bad guy discover, usually incorrectly, that one of his aides or superiors was working against him, so the team's target ended up killing one of his own. The IMF worked in tunnels, elevator shafts, on rafters, and in basements. They worked both behind the scenes and coyly sitting beside their target in luxurious penthouses. They pulled off the unusual as in "The Seal," in which the IMF's most surprising agent, Rusty the cat, used its feline teeth to rescue a government seal from a purse.

But no plot line, old or new, can entertain without a series of tests and obstacles thwarting the best-laid plans of mice and *MI*. Split-second timing and happy coincidences were of paramount importance for the IMF, providing much of the show's suspense. Typically, in the third act something would go wrong with the original plan, and the team would be forced to improvise and create last-minute solutions. One classic, and romantic, example occurred both on and off screen during the filming of "The Falcon." Like a medieval play, the story dealt with a princess forced to marry against her will. But such a simple premise ended up inspiring one dilemma after another, to the point where the story became *MI*'s only three-part episode, fulfilling Geller's original idea of creating an old-fashioned serial. In the end, like knights of old who earned their magical, or romantic, reward, the last scenes of each *MI* episode showed the team bundled into a car, plane, or helicopter to the beat of Lalo Schifrin's "Mission: Impossible March."

Many characteristics of *Mission: Impossible* distinguished it from the rest of the secret agent shows still flourishing when *MI* debuted. There were few car chases and not much stunt work in *MI*. The plots were cerebral, not action adventure, which helped keep the show out of the antiviolence backlash against the industry after the Robert Kennedy assassination. Still, there was danger on and off screen. In one 1967 episode, a bomb was placed in Phelps's car. As Graves went to look at it, "someone accidentally threw the switch, and the car blew up when I was only 15 feet away. A fender went whizzing past my ear" (Lipton and Schnaufer 1995, 47). Lupus nearly drowned filming one episode, and he was thrown over thirty feet in one motorcycle accident, saved by the helmet he had not wanted to wear. The humor was also largely off screen. In 1969, knowing Bain was claustrophobic, the producers built one episode around her fear of enclosed spaces. In "The Exchange," a departure from the usual format in that an IMF agent was captured, Cinnamon Carter was tortured by the "other side" and locked up in a series of smaller and smaller rooms. The actress survived the scripted practical joke because there were only three walls to each room, one always open for the cameras.

Warm personal interactions were not hallmarks of the series, but the producers made it clear that the team had a strong bond of loyalty alongside their professionalism. They wanted viewers to know if one member was injured on a mission, the rest of the team would complete the task but would always make a point of taking any wounded partner with them in the final reel. When the audience got glimpses into the lives of the characters, these typically occurred in episodes that strayed from the usual mold. For example, in "The Condemned," Phelps asked the team to help him on a personal mission to save a friend accused of a murder he didn't commit. Vulnerability was rarely seen, but in one clever outing, "The Town," we see a helpless Phelps when he ran across a small town that turned out to be a village of assassins. In an adventure reminiscent of the *Avengers* 1967 episode "Murdersville," Phelps was shot with curare and was bedridden, unable to speak, relying on Barney and the rest to both foil the villains and cure him.

One aspect of the series that reflected an important trend in the espionage genre was the diverse casting of its leads, particularly the casting and performances of Greg Morris. Like *I Spy*, *Mission: Impossible* was deliberately color-blind, which led some African American viewers to wonder how a black American could successfully pretend to disguise himself as an East European security guard without anyone noticing. Like Bill Cosby's interactions with other black actors in *I Spy*, African American viewers were equally interested in Morris's relationships with guest stars like Brock Peters, George Stanford Brown, and Barbara McNair. Such focused interest was partly due to some commentators dubbing 1966 the "Year of the Negro" in television because of the new black leads in *MI*, *Star Trek*, *Daktari*, and characters or performers in some two dozen shows (MacDonald 1983, 120).

Despite Morris's important place in the team, some African American viewers complained most of his activities were behind-the-scenes projects and rarely as a visible figure in the foreground of character interaction. The first episode featuring Collier didn't occur until the 1969 to 1970 season. In "Death Squad," Collier and Phelps were on vacation in the Caribbean where Barney accidentally killed his girlfriend's (Cicely Tyson) attacker. He was imprisoned, the team was called in to rescue him, and viewers got a brief glimpse into the Collier character. (This script would be revised for an episode of the *MI* revival in 1988, discussed below.) In another episode, "The Contender," Collier pretended to be a boxer aided by guest star, real-life champion Sugar Ray Robinson. Although one might think the role was more suited to Peter Lupus, the weight lifter claimed he knew nothing about boxing, so Morris volunteered despite his equal lack of knowledge. In this story, he was beaten in the ring while the team successfully pulled off its anti-gambling sting. As it turned out, Morris starred in more *MI* episodes than any other actor and played many foreground roles as the seasons progressed.

Equally ironic was the amount of mail that opposed any relationship between Collier and Carter. Producers had staff go through Morris's mail to remove any hate letters. Odd samples of such racism appeared in network communications, however. One memo from CBS asked that Bain and Morris be filmed as far apart as possible, ostensibly for "contrast." *MI*'s production team didn't miss the meaning of this memo, and from that point forward, filmed the two together as often as possible. This was certainly appropriate, as the two characters were both faces of changing times. Like

Morris's Collier, Barbara Bain's Cinnamon Carter demonstrated dignity, brains, and beauty like fellow women leads in *The Avengers* and *Get Smart*, who were the equals of, or often superior to, their leading men. As discussed earlier, the spy genre in general was an ideal setting to show the resourcefulness of cooperation among nationalities, cultures, and genders, and this was even more evident in a series in which teamwork was the point of the adventures.

Still, the series clearly demonstrated the cultural smugness America seemed to feel in the 1960s, and its intrusion into other countries' affairs would become a source of controversy in the Watergate era. For example, we'd see a corrupt Third World leader crush a child's toy under his boot before the setting changed to a smiling Phelps playing golf. The IMF clearly was intended to show the superiority of American values in a dangerous world. In most taped instructions, the parties to be saved were always "friendly to the West." Some commentators noted that IMF also stood for the International Monetary Fund, feeling *MI* too represented American commercial interests as much as good versus evil battles.

GOOD MORNING, MR. SPOCK

Although *MI*'s emphasis on teamwork meant the players involved were easily replaceable, this wasn't part of the original concept, but rather a result of behind-the-scenes squabbles with network and studio executives. In the beginning, each *MI* episode cost $225,000, for which CBS paid $170,000. Geller shot up to 50,000 feet of film per screen hour, more than twice the average. Special effects and writing costs also went above studio policy to create the feature-film look Geller sought. As the show moved into its third season, the team and series format began to fall apart largely due to budgetary concerns. As the opening sequence had been parodied on shows from *Get Smart* and *Carol Burnett*, to *The Tonight Show*, the now pointless review of file dossiers was often skipped or cut short, as the team was invariably the same. The show's primary developers, former *Playboy* photographer William Woodfield and his partner Alan Balter, briefly took the production helm when Paramount Studios bought Desilu in July 1967. Despite *MI*'s eleven Emmy nominations for its second season, when the third year began, Paramount executive Douglas J. Cramer became the budget master at the studio, starting the wars that eventually drove Bruce Geller literally off the lot. Before the third year had filmed its first seven episodes, Woodfield and Balter stormed out of the studio, never to return.

Feeling Graves was indispensable but Landau was not, Cramer immediately became embroiled in a salary dispute with the latter. The feud spilled over onto Bain, who was fired from the series hours before she accepted her third Emmy nomination. Although she later claimed she was happy before the firing, Bain publicly denounced Cramer when she accepted her

1969 Emmy—a stark contrast to her 1968 acceptance speech in which she'd warmly thanked writers Woodfield and Balter for helping shape Cinnamon Carter. After Bain's announcement that she was leaving the show, Landau followed suit, and the network branded the husband-and-wife team trouble-makers in the industry.

In 1969, the first replacement for Martin Landau's role was Leonard Nimoy as Paris the magician; Nimoy was an actor beginning to rise to cult status as Mr. Spock on another Desilu production, *Star Trek*. As the two shows were sister projects in many ways, the choice of Nimoy seemed natural enough, a mere walk across the studio lot for the actor after *Star Trek*'s demise. George Takai, *Star Trek*'s Ensign Sulu, and Mark Leonard, Spock's father Sarak, had already guest starred on *MI*. William Shatner would later do villain duties, and Bob Justman, one of *MI*'s original producers, had moved over to *Star Trek* after *Mission*'s first season. While Robert Vaughn and Ross Martin had each been considered as a new IMF team player, Nimoy liked the idea of having a fresh role to break his Mr. Spock image and felt *MI* would give him a variety of characters to play. A personal friend of Landau, Nimoy made a point of calling him to ensure that he wasn't forc-ing him out of his role. Remaining with the *MI* cast until 1971, it continues to be surprising that Nimoy's Paris was quickly forgotten in television his-tory, especially in light of his ongoing popularity in subsequent decades. He later noted that in all his press conferences and public appearances, he got few questions about his role as Paris.

At the beginning of his stint as Paris, little was done with already writ-ten scripts, as the character was virtually identical to Rollin Hand, although Nimoy portrayed Paris with a more low-key, less melodramatic flair. In the first year, Paris tended to repeat unsuccessful love affairs and play a wide range of characters from a Latin American revolutionary to a Chinese gen-eral to a Middle Eastern police officer. But in his second season, Nimoy became unhappy with the lack of substantial characters in his parts, which even included a robot. During that year, he slowly became aware he wanted out of the series.

Another new IMF agent was Sam Elliot as Dr. Roberts (1970–1971). Elliot had been intended as a replacement for Peter Lupus when former *Wild Wild West* producer Bruce Lansbury took over the increasingly battle-worn *MI* staff. Lansbury sought to slowly phase Elliott in, giving him various names, including Roberts and Lang, as a way to introduce a younger actor. But fan response persuaded the studio to retain Lupus. Elliott, with little to do, lasted only one season. His character was apparently a doctor, with no specialty the IMF required. In most of his appearances, he served as a chauffeur, or as a doctor when agents were wounded.

Similarly, when Lesley Ann Warren, then known for her singing role in a 1966 production of *Cinderella*, was named Barbara Bain's successor, re-sponse wasn't what she might have hoped for. Before her arrival, a variety of actresses had trial runs, but it was quickly evident that different women playing roles wasn't the same thing as having one key player in a variety of guises. The show's producers decided to appeal to younger viewers and bring in a youthful agent, Warren's Dana Lambert, in the same spirit *The Avengers* had followed with the hiring of Linda Thorson.

Immediately, it was clear no one was happy with the choice. Geller, whose presence at Paramount was being reduced in a move to force him out, had nothing to do with the casting and thought she was very wrong for the series. Warren later recalled they battled over her freckles. She wanted to display them, he wanted her to look older. In the spirit of the times, she wanted to work braless and forced studio executives into a compromise over the issue. Warren was too young to be believable as an international trade representative or a hardened bank robber, and her age was even more apparent when surrounded by the rest of the cast, who didn't enjoy the comparison. And although she'd been hired partly due to her talents as a singer and dancer, the show rarely employed Warren's gifts in these arenas. She was the first character for which an official introduction to the team was written, but this scene in a recording studio was cut when producers weren't sure in what order the episodes would be aired. Of the two songs Warren sang for the series, only one was used. She quickly became unhappy and left after her first year.

Many of the episodes during these seasons showed the need to stretch the formula, and some changes were more successful than others. Producer Bruce Lansbury brought with him notions from his *Wild Wild West* days, including an emphasis on fantastic gadgets, multiple story lines, and sense of surprise, which helped new Mission scripts. New writers were sought out, resulting in work from Jerry Ludwig and British writer Leigh Vance who'd worked on *The Saint* and *The Avengers*. Another British contributor was Donald James, who had written for *The Champions* and *The Persuaders*. The lack of character development, long a source of criticism, was modified in some episodes. For example, "Homecoming" was set in Phelps's hometown, where he nostalgically gazed at his homestead and his father's old business sign advertising the now defunct boat and lakeside equipment shop.

In addition, the characters began to question their activities, as in "Fair Play," in which an innocent was forced to assist the IMF against his will. In a reversal of the lighter *U.N.C.L.E.* format, "Fair Play" forced the agents to consider what right they had to pressure others into their schemes. In a similar episode, Greg Morris pretended to be in love with actress Abby Lincoln to trick her into helping him. At the end of the mission when he confessed his ploy, he got a well deserved "drop dead" from Lincoln. More playing with the format included a greater emphasis on improvisation, often having the plan fouled earlier in the episodes to have the IMF think more on its feet. "The Killing" was especially clever, featuring Robert Conrad as Lorca, an assassin who worked randomly, making it impossible for the IMF to preplan their assignment to stop him. Topical subjects in latter adventures included South African apartheid, in which a white racist got his comeuppance by having his skin color changed to that of the race he despised.

Because of such scripts, the series rebounded in the fifth year, assuring *MI* another season despite Paramount's desire to kill the show. The studio wanted to make its money in the syndicated rerun market, but CBS didn't want to lose a hit show that was apparently getting its second wind. Still, the days of Emmy glory were gone. In the final years, two nominations for each season were only in the technical categories. Yet another new producer, Laurence Heath, again began casting around for new ideas and characters, and ironically, the creativity of Bruce Geller once more came into play.

In the 1970 to 1971 television season, Geller had produced The *Silent Force* for ABC, a half-hour crime show featuring three federal undercover agents in a south California strike force fighting organized crime. Ward Fuller (Ed Nelson), Jason Hart (Percy Rodriguez), and Amelia Cole (Lynda Day, soon to be Lynda Day George) exposed operations that preyed on innocent citizens, as in the first episode during which the team revealed that a candidate for governor was a member of "the Syndicate." *Silent Force* influenced *Mission: Impossible* in two important ways. First, Heath decided to combine the femme fatale with the disguise expert into one character, hiring *Silent Force*'s Lynda Day George as Casey. A former model, George described her *MI* years as "*The Silent Force* for grown-ups" (White 1991, 124). Although only two years older than Warren, George was more believable in her roles as a murderer, psychopath, mental patient, blackmailer, and mail-order bride. Like Nimoy, her 1971 to 1973 seasons with *MI* were forgotten in later decades, despite her quality performances and the high regard the cast and producers had for her. Of course, by that time, the series itself was finding new ideas hard to come by. George played a space alien in one outing and a 140-year-old woman in another, as fake time-travel episodes, set both in the past and future, became part of the IMF repertoire of "big stores."

In 1971, Lynda's husband, Christopher George, star of TV's *Rat Patrol*, guest starred on one *Mission*. A year later, the couple announced Lynda's pregnancy, so the producers began seeking ways to accommodate her. In some episodes, the sets were built to hide her growing weight. In others, they had her in disguise most of the episode so another actress could play the role ostensibly as Agent Casey. When George finally went on maternity leave, Barbara Anderson joined the show in the fall of 1972 as Mimi Davis. Well known for her role as Eve Whitfield, Raymond Burr's detective aide on *Ironside* (1967–1971), Anderson only appeared in seven episodes, as she wanted part-time work and fit the bill perfectly for *MI* until George's return in the final episodes of 1973.

By the final year, the IMF was focused on criminal activity alone, very much in the mold of *Silent Force*. This change resulted from both budget cuts and worries that viewers might associate the IMF with the growing Watergate scandal, in which government agents were, in fact, doing nasty things that were disavowed by higher-ups. In 1997, Barbara Bain stated, "*Mission* was a fantasy. People saw it as a fantasy. And that's how it was geared. Nobody for a minute at that time thought any of that stuff was going on" (Johnson 1997, 24). However, according to the Museum of Broadcasting Communications, *MI*'s overseas sales in sixty-nine countries led some to worry that other nations were in fact getting an exaggerated idea of the CIA's abilities and predilection for involving itself into other nations' affairs. So the scope of the show was limited to U.S. settings, and the filmings were reduced to studio back lots, which resulted in a look of sameness and less expensive production values. However, regarding the old plots, according to Peter Graves, others had a lighter view. "You do it better than we do," two CIA agents reportedly once told Graves. "You ought to have our writers," Graves replied (Lipton and Schnaufer 1995, 47). Still, despite Barbara Bain's protests, according to a December 2001 American Movie Channel documentary, "Into the Shadows: the CIA in Hollywood," the real-world intelligence community was, in fact, paying attention. It was to the *MI* set that disguise expert Tony Mendez came in 1970 when he sought professional help in creating disguise kits for his agents. In the documentary, Mendez observed, "We used to have to assign one of our officers to watch *Mission: Impossible* every week. We'd always get the phone calls the next morning, 'Can you guys do that?'"

However, by this point, the creative team of *MI* was noticeably grasping for ideas, weeding through unfilmed scripts to salvage starting points from rejected plot lines. There was more violence, with more injuries to the agents, and usually one killing in the new teasers at the beginning of each hour. Still, some ideas worked, but tricking homegrown gangsters didn't have the force or colorful settings of the old international confrontations. On February 9, 1973, the show was canceled under uncertain circumstances, apparently part of a network dispute that had nothing to do with ratings, program quality, or studio squabbles. Paramount was relieved, finally free to begin syndication sales. The cast was neither surprised nor disappointed, feeling the show had outlasted its creative possibilities. Scripts were available for the next season, but Laurence Heath admitted they were not likely to have done much for the series' reputation.

When the plethora of revivals and renewals of old TV shows began in the mid-1970s, *Mission: Impossible* was among those fueling speculation and interest. But for a variety of reasons, it would take over fifteen years for the show to be reborn. In the meantime, a succession of scripts came and went, one of the most interesting surfacing in 1980. In it, the law has caught up with the IMF and the story opened with Phelps emerging from prison after a six-year sentence for burglary, conspiracy, wiretapping, and refusing to testify before Congress. Phelps bristled when a TV reporter called him the last of the Watergate generation and defends the IMF saying, "It was different times." Then, spies could do more radical things for the good of the country despite any obvious civil rights violations. In this script, Phelps is recruited to undo damage he understands was committed by Hand and Carter, and he calls on Collier, now a teacher. However, Armitage, now a television personality and gymnasium entrepreneur, refuses to help. It turns out this mission was a deception, with Hand and Carter not involved in the heist Phelps felt responsible for. To no one's regret, this script died at NBC. Another such script was shown to Leonard Nimoy after he directed *Star Trek III: The Search for Spock*. Producers wondered if he would direct a *Mission: Impossible* feature film. He refused, saying his heart wasn't in it.

Meanwhile, for the original cast, there was some afterlife to the success of *MI*, although one tragedy affected all of them. In May 1978, Bruce Geller died in an airplane crash, ending any role he might have had in future revivals. After a period away from acting, Steven Hill played cranky Manhattan district attorney Adam Schiff, the longest running original player on NBC's *Law and Order*. Then husband-and-wife team Martin Landau and Barbara Bain found cult status in their imaginative SF opus, *Space 1999* (1974–1976), working with former *Prisoner* producer, David Tomlin. Landau had appeared as a vampirish villain, Count Zarg, in *The Man from U.N.C.L.E.*, a role ironically foreshadowing his part as Bela Lugosi in 1994's *Ed Wood*, for which he won an Oscar for best supporting actor. He appeared in the second *Six Million Dollar Man* TV movie and *The X-Files: Fight the Future* film (1998).

Bain reprised her role as Cinnamon Carter in the November 13, 1997, episode of *Diagnosis: Murder*, in which Carter, a retired agent, meets up with old friends played by fellow 1960s alumni Robert Vaughn, Patrick Macnee, and Robert Culp. (In the episode entitled "Discards," Carter revealed she received a special commendation from Ronald Reagan and George Bush on April 20, 1981, in a private ceremony.) At the end of the episode, the CIA reactivated Culp and Bain, demonstrating that even old spies can have second lives. In 1993, she and Landau divorced after being separated for the last decade of their thirty-six-year marriage.

After *MI*, Peter Lupus turned to comic roles, including Leslie Nielsen's underling on TV's *Police Squad*. He tried out for the 1988 film spin-off, *The Naked Gun*, but lost out to O. J. Simpson. In 1997, the veteran fitness enthusiast set a world record for strength and endurance by lifting thirty-eight tons in thirty minutes (Lipton and Schnaufer 1995, 46–47). In a three-part 1983 comedy outing on *The Jeffersons*, Greg Morris spoofed his Barney Collier past as an unnamed electronics genius who convinced two con men the world was coming to an end. After guest starring on shows like *Wonder Woman*, *The Six Million Dollar Man*, and playing a secondary role in Robert Urich's *Vega$* (1979), Morris died on August 27, 1996. In 1988, he'd reprised his role as Barney Collier in two episodes of the 1988 to 1990 *Mission: Impossible* return to network television.

As it happened, a threatened Writers Guild strike brought *MI* back to life when Paramount decided it could bypass writers and restructure *Mission: Impossible* using old scripts. With no apologies for the ploy, seven stories were chosen for their apolitical nature, and casting began. With the exception of Graves reprising his role as Jim Phelps, the cast of *Mission: Impossible '88* was entirely new, although retired actor Bob Johnson still recorded the assignment tapes. (Johnson died in 1993, at age seventy-three.) In the premise to this revival, Phelps was called out of retirement after the death of his successor and protégé. Now, it was Phelps seen striking the match before the title sequence. His apartment was gray rather than black and white, and his portfolio was in a computer hidden in his coffee table. The self-destructing tapes were now self-destructing laser discs, which only Phelps could open with his computerized thumb print. Now, the agents wore more colorful clothes during the apartment scene, even though most of the set was dark. And in this version, there were fewer guest team members.

At one point, the new cast members were to take over the character names of the first team, but the producers wisely decided to give them new identities, if not exactly very different roles on the team. The new cast consisted of Nicholas Black (Thaao Penghlis) the Martin Landau actor, and Max Harte (Tony Hamilton) as the successor to Willy Armitage. The casting of Penghlis was one indication of the process new *MI* actors went through to earn their roles. In two days of testing for Paramount and ABC, he was asked to play an accountant, a Gestapo officer, a seventy-year-old man, and a man on death row. In addition, other actors were tested in both Hollywood and Australia. In a much-publicized move, Greg Morris's son, Phil, played Collier's son, Grant, as the electronics expert in the new cast. In the fifth episode, the young Morris/Collier joined the new team to rescue his imprisoned father falsely accused of murder in Turkey, a story line reworked from an episode in the original series. Like Robert Culp's character in the *Diagnosis: Murder* spy reunion, the elder Collier showed remorse for neglecting his family during his *MI* days, but was comforted by his son, who clearly admired him.

Keeping with the spirit of changeable agents, the first female lead, Casey Randall (Terry Markwell), was killed off after twelve episodes and was replaced by Shannon Reed, an ex-Olympic athlete, cop, and broadcaster (Jane Badler). Unlike the original show, when an agent was killed on the new version, it was explained. When the plot called for details about the team's backgrounds, these agents, especially Reed, were versatile, experienced, and seemingly more developed than their predecessors. For example, in one outing, Reid showed her fear of small planes after she lost her memory in a plane crash. These players' roles were less defined, as in Black, Harte, and Collier sharing the acting duties that would have gone to Rollin Hand or Paris in the original series. There were nods to the old, as in one episode featuring Lynda Day George as Casey, called Lisa Casey to distinguish her from the murdered agent.

For its two-year production, most filming was done in Australia to avoid problems with the Hollywood writers strike and to allow for cheaper production values, although filming in Australia provided diverse and distinctive scenery that wasn't possible on a Paramount back lot. According to Peter Graves, the new series was long overdue, as he felt the show had as much of a cult following as *Star Trek*, then also enjoying a new life with a new cast. However, critics complained the new version had little of the flavor or style of the original. ABC moved it from time slot to time slot, but much of its success came in syndication when it was aired after prime time.

After the demise of this version of *MI*, Peter Graves spoofed his leading man image in *Airplane II* (1982), in which pilot Graves attempted to shut down a computer only to have it self-destruct to the musical strains of the *MI* theme. In 1984, Graves played a comic secret agent in *Mad Mission III*, in which he boarded a rickshaw to get instructions from a self-destructing tape.

> This isn't Mission: Difficult, Mr. Hunt. It's Mission: Impossible.
> —Ethan Hunt's supervisor in *Mission: Impossible 2*

Oddly, the theme of teamwork is what disappeared from the highly successful *Mission: Impossible* films starring Tom Cruise. The first of these efforts in 1996 was clearly not a reunion film, with a new team led by a new Jim Phelps (Jon Voight) and his wife of two years, Claire (Emmanuelle Beart). In one of the most unexpected plot twists of the remake genre, Phelps became the villain of the film, with agent Ethan Hunt (Cruise) becoming the leader of the new IMF made up of formerly disaffected agents Krieger (Jean Reno) and Luther (Ving Rhames). According to Peter Barsocchini's well-written novelization of the David Koepp's script, the IMF had always been part of the CIA, but after the Aldrich Ames scandal, the agency took direct control over the operations to clean up covert actions. One of the most unusual tie-ins to the movie was the May 1996 Marvel Comics version of the film's IMF, introducing the new team in two adventures. By the time comic readers had met the new IMF, the movie, in which all the new characters but one were killed off or vilified, was released.

Although this film was a well-made, if oddly constructed, action adventure directed by Brian De Palma, the only connections to the original series were the highly recognizable theme music (performed by Larry Mullen and Adam Clayton of U2), the use of latex face masks, and the opening device of recorded assignments for Phelps. We hear the phrase "Good morning, Mr. Phelps" twice, but the second time is to show the agency has learned of the former team leader's duplicity and murder of his wife. Fans of the original series criticized these moves, especially the turning of the show's most recognizable face into a traitor. Reportedly, Greg Morris walked out of the film after the first forty minutes, saying the movie was a travesty. In a 1997 interview, Barbara Bain said she intended to see the film but changed her mind after learning it was only a vehicle for Cruise. According to various CNN reports, Graves too was dissatisfied, saying some other name than Phelps should have been given to the traitorous leader of the new IMF.

The controversial changes showed something about what the filmmakers thought audience response would be. Unlike other, more character-driven shows, the original *Mission: Impossible* had emphasized teamwork over personality, replaced team members with little change in the format, and few viewers can remember the stars or their roles from the original broadcasts. In the new films, teamwork became less important than the high-tech gadgetry typical of all action-adventure movies of the era. The stunts and car chases avoided in the original series were what these films were built on. On one level, the new *MI* production team miscalculated audience reception to the new ideas, thinking the TV show had earned respect and admiration, but not affection. The formula sold the series, not the players, and so the new formula would sell the films as well.

The last hurrah for the IMF was probably *Mission: Impossible* 2 bringing back Tom Cruise with a cleaner slate after the Phelps controversy had dissipated. In the second movie, one theme is stated in the first minutes and is repeated throughout—a hero must be sought out, and a hero can only be found when there is a villain. The emphasis on the singular could not be missed. The format again shifted, with Cruise getting initial orders in the old way, but he was told he could choose only two team members and had to involve a new civilian partner he hadn't met. She turned out to be Nyah Hall (Thandie Newton), an untrained but crafty burglar as much love interest for both hero and villain as superspy. The adversary was an ex-IMF agent, Sean Ambrose (Dougray Scott) who had come into possession of a deadly virus. According to commentary on the DVD version of the film, Ambrose was motivated by his dislike of Hunt, always feeling number two to his nemesis. The plot was typically modern—a pharmaceutical company planned to unleash this virus to sell its own antidote. The film had yet another version of the famous theme, this time performed by Limp Bizkit, but with a subdued tone as if to underline the distance of the project from its namesake. In the first hour, the film was clearly far removed from the context of the television series, seeking to establish new ground for itself in relationships and characters, especially in the romantic triangle. As Cruise's boss only uses tape messages to make initial contact and is thereafter not a faceless voice, Cruise can question the means and ends and get lectured on what needs to be done.

After setting up these characters, the second half of the film disintegrated into de rigueur motorcycle chases and karate fights that made *Mission: Impossible* 2 watchable if forgettable. Again, according to DVD commentary by the participants, this outcome was by design. Director John Woo had created the action sequences before the scriptwriters were brought in, so the plot was crafted around the motorcycle, helicopter, and car chases. With this project, *Mission: Impossible* moved too far and too fast from what Bruce Geller wrought, and the original concept is likely now a series relegated to the nostalgia of cult status.

Still, the concept of the IMF was one of the most influential formulas for subsequent television series. Although there had been ensemble casts before *MI*, all post-1960s spy programs couldn't escape comparison to *Mission: Impossible*. In the 1980s, *The A-Team* was seen overall as *Mission: Impossible* turned upside down, with a cast of misfits and rebels always difficult to mold into a professional, organized unit. When *Avengers* producer Brian Clemens and composer turned producer Laurie Johnson unleashed *The New Avengers* in 1976, they also backed a sister project, *The Professionals*, a more action-adventure version featuring a British IMF. These highly trained agents of CE5 (Criminal Investigators) were designed to go beyond the limits of other police activities. In 2001, *The Agency* included a cast of experts, featuring a disguise master who created latex masks and counterfeit documents (see Conclusion).

In short, *Mission: Impossible* established a formula open to many possibilities—create one charming con artist with a knack for disguise and petty theft; one sexy, leggy seductress; one technological wizard; and one strong-man, preferably with arms and explosive experience—and then shake, stir, and bring to a simmering boil. Toss in other ingredients to taste, say a rip-roaring good theme tune, or use ingredients from yet other formulas, and *Mission: Impossible* will rise again. Only the viewers will decide if they will accept these new missions.

CHAPTER 9

James Bond on the Prairie: From *The Wild Wild West* to the *Secret Adventures of Jules Verne*

FUSING GENRES

> We need you again. You're the finest underground intelligence officer we have. And I'm going to lay it right on the line for you, boy. This nation's in a pot of trouble. Inflation eating the South alive. Washington crawling with carpetbaggers. Jackals just gathering for the kill, and now . . . now new trouble.
>
> —President Grant to James West in the opening moments of the first episode of *The Wild Wild West*, 1965

In 1965, *The Wild Wild West* was almost an inevitability. Since the 1950s, and dating back to earlier radio dramas like *The Lone Ranger* and *Gunsmoke*, the Western was the most prevalent form of action adventure. A few radio serials were clear precursors for *WWW* (or *W3*), including ABC's *Tennessee Jed* (1945–1947), starring Johnny Thomas as Tennessee Jed Sloane, a squirrel-gun marksman. Jed was a "Lone Ranger" type who reported directly to President Grant as his personal Western agent. From 1951 to 1955, a hero named Jim West (Jim Ameche) roamed the Northwest for the Royal Canadian Mounted Police in *Silver Eagle*. During World War II, Western film and radio star Tom Mix did his share of defeating invisible agents and other SF-oriented Axis spies. On television, *Cowboy G-Men* (1953) had been director Leslie Celander's low-budget thirty-nine episode series featuring nineteenth-century government agents Pat Gallagher (Russell Hayden) and Stoney Crockett (Jackie Coogan). However, beginning with *U.N.C.L.E.* in 1964, the dominance of more straightforward "horse operas" was challenged by secret agent programs. A logical response was to bring the two genres together in one double-barreled project.

The creator of *WWW* was Michael Garrison, who'd once owned the rights to Ian Fleming's *Casino Royale*. At first, CBS executives were eager for Garrison's concept, but almost immediately, behind-the-scenes problems almost derailed the series. Throughout the process of creating the series, nothing ever seemed certain, which turned out to be a harbinger of tensions to come. For example, during the early stages of preproduction, CBS went through a complete administrative shake-up. By the time the first episode aired, most of the men who'd shaped the concept were gone. Thereafter, a succession of eight producers constantly changed the direction of the show. To the alarm of CBS, Garrison had little concept of budget constraints, spending $35,000 on the second "Wanderer" train set, consisting of a coach car with the trademark trick pool table, kitchen, laboratory, and gun room decorated in green and gold. Guns were hidden in every nook and cranny, and a telegraph machine was hidden to receive messages from the president. The costumes were new as well, with James West's (Robert Conrad) look based on flamenco dancer–styled suits. Immediately, tensions over the budget made for uneasy relations between Garrison and the network, and for the next two years, Garrison's involvement was limited, as were many of the concepts he wanted in his creation.

According to Susan Kesler's in-depth *The Wild Wild West: The Series* (1988), even the two leads, Robert Conrad and Ross Martin, were not always simpatico. Both had come to a measure of television prominence in 1959 in roles that were clear precursors to their *WWW* characters. Conrad had starred in *Hawaiian Eye*, a fusion of two detective romps, *77 Sunset Strip* and *Adventures in Paradise*. Until the series cancellation in 1963, Conrad enjoyed fun-in-the-sun adventures with nightclub singer Cricket Blake, played by sex symbol Connie Stevens. In 1959, Polish-American character actor Ross Martin was a master of disguises as a costar in the popular *Mr. Lucky*, a New York based police drama. Very much in the spirit of Artemus Gordon, Martin used his special knack for dialects and disguises to get his friends out of trouble, leaving the tough action for the other leads.

A radio and film actor since 1955, Martin signed to *WWW* with the understanding he was a costar with Conrad. The first concept of the Gordon character had been to provide West with a traveling peddler who would give West messages and gadgets. But before signing Martin, Garrison's production team decided the show needed contrasting leads. West was to be a straightforward action-oriented square assigned by President Grant to play a dandified rich Easterner able to afford his own private train. As Conrad was a relatively short leading man, the sets were arranged to deemphasize his stature. Camera angles were designed to keep West in the foreground and all other actors set back. As Susan Kesler noted, before the fantasy aspects of the series took hold, the producers thought Conrad would be in the saddle most of the time anyway (Kesler 1988, 33). Gordon was planned to be a colorful, personable foil in the spirit of *U.N.C.L.E.* Gordon carried his wagon and horses on the train called "The Wanderer," able to transform his identity at a moment's notice. But the first season came and went before Conrad, the seventeenth actor to try out for the role, allowed Martin to have romantic relationships, as Conrad felt that was his province. Conrad wanted more action, less dialogue. Martin wanted variety and a more visible place at the center of the stage, saying he was the actor, Conrad a glorified stuntman.[1]

However, other accounts cast a very different light on the costars' relationship. In 2002, Conrad told me:

> There was nothing which Ross Martin, in his personality, for me not to get along with. We were totally different. He was educated, spoke several languages, he'd gone to law school. He was a bright guy, I dropped out of high school, my second language is "street." It was a great relationship because he gave me things I wasn't exposed to and I think I gave him things. He would go to the opera or ballet, theater on weekends, and I would go Thursday nights to the Olympic auditorium to the fights. It was a perfect relationship, perfect, 'cause we weren't in conflict and didn't have the same interests. But when we worked together as actors, it just worked. Well, obviously, I mean it's one of the most successful syndicated shows in the history of the film, and we're still talking about it. I didn't know in sixty-four when I did the pilot that in 2002 I'd be talking about that show. I'm real plum-proud to have that in my biography.[2]

One clear difference between the two actors was that, at that point in his career, Conrad was young (twenty-nine when signed), wild, and more involved with the stunt team than his costars. One of his contributions turned out to be some of the best action sequences on television because of his interaction, interplay, and planning with the only continuous, returning team of stuntmen in the industry. As it happened, CBS wasn't happy with this concept, feeling viewers would come to recognize recurring extras. But Conrad claimed an experienced team could prevent costly errors. According to Conrad's stand-in, Richard Cangey, the regular team resulted in the show hiring guest stars based on their resemblance to stuntmen rather than the other way around (Cangey 1996, 23). In addition, to keep costs down, Conrad wished to do his own stunts. Interested in the martial arts since 1957, Conrad later claimed he fused his background in Kajukenbo and Shotokan fighting styles with "flamenco dancing into a choreographed fluidity for the show" (Smith). CBS was considering canceling the show when Conrad made the request, and he won this battle as the network then felt it had nothing to lose. Looking back on it in 1996, Conrad said the success of the show was due to the "esprit de corps" established among these men, along with certain writers and one producer, Bruce Lansbury (Cangey 1996, i).

With their leads in place, the original producers ultimately found the style they were looking for, which was exemplified by the animated title sequence designed by the Pink Panther artists of Consolidated Film. The concept had four squares surrounding the hero in the middle. In each square, a separate figure represented one element of the show, a bank robber, a card cheat reaching for an ace in his boot, a hand reaching for a gun, and a knife-wielding woman. The animated hero in the center defeats each of the villains, and the theme music then begins in earnest. CBS decided to expand on this concept and use the squares for break art. In the last moment before each commercial break, a live action freeze frame dissolved into an animation cell replacing one of the figures in the blocks. Like *U.N.C.L.E.*, which had the word *"Affair"* in each episode title, *WWW*'s episodes usually began with *"The Night of . . ."* With this imagery, *The Wild Wild West* had a look all its own and went forward to do battle with the forces of evil and the competitors on other networks.

MASTERMINDS ON THE RESERVATION

> I love to make beautiful things, Mr. West. With my voice, with my hands, with my brain. Someday I'll show you some of them in my laboratory if you're still around.
> —Miguelito Loveless in "The Night the Wizard Shook the Earth"

In September 1965, *The Wild Wild West* survived its birth pangs and its opening night, but not yet its identity crisis. In black and white, the first four episodes were essentially Westerns with secret agents, a format the series reluctantly returned to three seasons later. From the beginning, former U.S. Calvary Officer Capt. James West, Artemus Gordon, and their adversaries were equipped with interesting weapons, from guns constructed from parts hidden in boot heels and belt buckles to exploding garter belts. In the first episode, West used his trademark "sleeve derringer" that sprang into his hands, a gadget inspiring the first tie-in toy associated with the series.

But the show took on a new flair with the introduction of three-foot ten-inch genius Miguelito Loveless, played by the charismatic Michael Dunn. Dunn had played similar roles in *Amos Burke, Secret Agent* and *Voyage to the Bottom of the Sea* and as the first villain in *Get Smart*. Considerable time was put into developing Loveless, seen as an existential devil angry with God for making him small. Born to a landed California family of Spanish descent and a father who lost his land to some exploitative plunderer, the "little Napoleon" hated everyone. His first name was the Spanish version of

Michael, a nod to Michael Garrison. Loveless was clearly a name that said much about his personality. First appearing in "The Night the Wizard Shook the Earth," Loveless was ultimately featured ten times in the series, his popularity rivaling that of the two leads. As Dunn had an excellent singing voice, real-life-singing partner Phoebe Dorin was cast as Loveless's long-legged assistant, Antoinette. The pair offered this musical dimension to their characters in each of their appearances. In addition, seven-foot giant Richard Kiel, later the "Jaws" in two Bond films, was Voltaire, Loveless's mute strongman. Later, Kiel said his role as Voltaire prepared him to portray the lurking, silent nemesis of James Bond (Kiel 2002, 55).

For two seasons, while moving from black and white to color, *WWW* became characterized by sci-fi/Western/secret agent adventures. This merging of genres began in season one with "The Night of the Burning Diamond," one of six episodes produced by *Star Trek* alumni Gene L. Coon. (Sound effects for this adventure included the *Star Trek* communicators.) The enemies of the U.S. Secret Service now included magicians, blind pirates, counterfeiters, foreign potentates, evil puppets, disembodied brains, bogus space aliens, and ex-Confederate generals (the Wild West's counterpart to the ex-Nazis prevalent in other series). Anachronisms were a staple of the show, including the electric chair, robots, aqualungs, and film itself. In one episode, a short kinescope of President Grant signing a treaty with an unsavory nation is used for blackmail. In the tag Gordon tells West someday longer movies could be made and tickets sold for a profit. "It'll never catch on," West replies. Other devices echoed the SF of *U.N.C.L.E.* In one episode, people became invisible by moving faster than the speed of light after drinking a special potion made from diamond dust. Nods to 007 were obvious, as in West's carriage with an ejector seat à la Bond's famous Aston Martin. In one story, a governor's secretary is "Miss Piecemeal," a clear nod to Fleming's odd choices for character names. *WWW* producers were delighted when, in *Diamonds Are Forever*, Bond used a gun that shot a dart attached to a long line, allowing 007 to swing across Los Vegas like Spiderman—*WWW* had already used this gimmick.

Like most action adventure shows, *WWW* wasn't known for its social commentary, although issues regarding women, the environment, and Native Americans arose from time to time. However, *WWW* was rarely ahead of its time or politically correct in such matters. Perhaps Spanish American viewers could well sympathize with the various Mexican adversaries who wished to restore the American Southwest to its pre-English-speaking culture. For feminists, "Night of the Red-Eyed Madman" had a terrorist group that wanted to overthrow the government, with an army of both women—treated as equals—and men. The show's tag had Gordon and West laughing at the idea of women being soldiers. In another adventure, a scientist created tidal waves to strike back at those who were polluting the ocean, and "The Night of Sudden Death" concerned an animal activist. Villains were thus often portrayed as social extremists who carried their concerns over the edge.

Not surprisingly, the role of Native Americans could not be missed in *WWW*. In one episode, a Cheyenne chief named American Knife, a graduate of Dartmouth College, was described as ungrateful because he left white missionaries to rejoin his own people. When American Knife tells West that someday the latter can say, "Some of my best friends are Cheyenne," it was a gentle jab at white liberalism. In another episode, President Grant worried about a political competitor named General Baldwin, who stirred up Indian uprisings so he could lead massacres and gain public support. On one hand, the script pointed to the network's desire to emphasize negotiated peace; on the other, a behind-the-scenes event pointed to television's way of revising history. Producer Bruce Lansbury asked one actor to speak in an authentic Sioux dialect, but then opted to use gibberish instead because the actual language didn't sound "Sioux enough" for entertainment purposes. Such momentary interests in realism seem especially odd in a show in which Martin could regularly join in small groups of American Indians, East Indians, and any number of small enclaves without generating any suspicion for his sudden appearance as one of the gang.

Like *U.N.C.L.E.*, the show began featuring famous guest stars, including the young Richard Pryor, Carroll O'Connor, Boris Karloff, and Agnes Moorehead, who won an Emmy for her appearance. In one episode, Las Vegas Rat Pack buddies Sammy Davis Jr. and Peter Lawford enjoyed themselves so much, they asked *WWW* director Richard Donner, who'd been one of the more successful and respected directors for *U.N.C.L.E.*, to direct their own 1968 feature-length spy project, *Salt and Pepper*. Later, after directing for *Get Smart* and *The Six Million Dollar Man*, Donner said his *Salt and Pepper* experience led to his Hollywood career, including films like *Superman* and the *Lethal Weapon* movies.

But as time progressed, the network decided to downplay the fantasy aspects in *WWW*, especially after 1967 when industry insiders believed the spy boom was over. In the fall season that year, few new spy shows were offered. CBS felt *WWW* could survive if it became more Western than fantasy. In addition, Westerns were considerably easier to keep under budget. After the assassinations of Robert Kennedy and Martin Luther King Jr., the networks also began toning down television violence, ordering limits on fistfights, stunt violence, and gunplay. In 1997, Robert Vaughn recalled NBC sending down two dictums to the *U.N.C.L.E.* producers. The creative team was told to begin using sleep darts rather than bullets and said the shooter and the person being fired on couldn't be filmed in the same screen. Similarly, CBS specifically banned stunts using chairs, guns, and kicks in *WWW*. After the National Association for Better Broadcasts targeted *WWW* for containing "some of the most frightening and sadistic scenes ever made for television," West was asked to attempt negotiating with bad guys before resorting to any fisticuffs. He stopped carrying guns altogether (Phillips and Garcia 1996, 488). Sound effects of connecting punches were replaced with music. Networks began keeping statistics of television violence, with West totaling 393 fights against 940 opponents in four years, according to Susan Kesler. Kesler believed network politics also affected the cast, as when many of Conrad's cronies were fired specifically to keep Conrad in his place (Kesler 1988, 84). Health problems kept Michael Dunn out of the scripts, appearing only once in the third season. Still, continuing success was evident for WWW, especially for Martin, who received considerable popular acclaim in Mexico and Europe. He was nominated for an Emmy in the same year as fellow secret agents Peter Graves and Martin Landau from Mission: Impossible.

The dark cloud of disasters, both in and out of scripts, continually plagued the series. The numerous stunts resulted in injuries for both leads. Gordon occasionally wore casts when Martin broke limbs in stunt accidents. After boxing expert Richard Cangey became Conrad's stand-in, Conrad became passionate about boxing, and he moved from using karate to using fistfights in the series. Unlike other TV actors who only learned enough about fighting to look good on screen, Conrad put in a boxing ring for after-hours training and bought the contract of a title contender. Because of his desire to be involved in fights and stunts, he suffered numerous on-camera wounds, including one shoulder injury that gave him continual pain for years. After nearly being killed in a missed leap to a chandelier in the third season, which resulted in two episodes being canceled, CBS forbade him to do any further stunt work in the fourth season (Cangey 1996, 68–69). Phoebe Dorin, Michael Dunn's accomplice, nearly died in one shooting when her dress was trapped in an underwater accident.

In August 1968, Martin suffered a heart attack, forcing producer Bruce Lansbury to supply new costars to fill in while Martin recuperated. Most notably, Charles Aidman stepped in as a Gordon-like Jeremy Pike for four episodes, earning both audience and critical respect. But the producers wanted to retain Martin, so they used other guest fill-ins for three episodes, including William Schallert as Frank Harper in the series first two-part episode, "The Night of the Winged Terror." In another attempt to retain audience interest during Martin's absence, WWW ran one episode with a Gilligan's Island tie in. West's partner was Alan Hale Jr., the skipper from Gilligan's Island and the former Biff Baker. Jim Backus, the millionaire from Gilligan's Island, played a bit part. At the end of the episode, the Hale character rode off into the sunset claiming he wishes to find a desert island, while in the background the Gilligan's Island theme music was playing. (Trivia buffs can easily spot sets in *WWW* that look suspiciously like the other show's lagoon, both series using the same set for aquatic locations.)

In September 1968, Martin returned from intensive care. CBS intermingled his new episodes with those shot with guest stars so the audience wouldn't notice a long lapse between Gordon's appearances. But in March 1969, citing excessive violence, CBS canceled the series, despite its ratings, in an attempt to placate pressure groups in Washington. According to Kesler, Conrad heard the news during one of his in-person rodeo appearances and agreed with many insiders that the violence claim was exaggerated. After all, the higher-rated and much more violent *Mannix* remained on the air (Kesler 1988, 89). Still, the show had enjoyed a good run.

AFTERLIFE OF *WWW*

> Am I to understand, sir, that you're going to bring a couple of overaged, out-of-shape, ex-agents out of retirement to handle this case? When the service is full of young deserving agents who've just been spoiling for a chance to prove themselves?
> —Hugo Kaughman in *The Wild Wild West Revisited*, 1979

After CBS reran specially selected episodes during the summer of 1970 with much of the "objectionable" violence cut, *The Wild Wild West* found an immediate and lasting place in the syndicated rerun market. In 1979, responding to a new wave of nostalgia, *The Wild Wild West Revisited* appeared with singer Paul Williams starring as Miguelito Quixote Loveless Jr., who was seeking revenge for the death of his father.

In the made-for-TV film written by William Bowers and directed by Burt Kennedy, West was retired and was living in Mexico with four wives and numerous children. Lucky in love, he was also clearly rusty with fisticuffs. Gordon had returned to a life as an actor, working in a traveling tent show called "The Deadwood Shakespearean Strolling Players." Both characters were older—Grover Cleveland is now president—and both were reluctant to leave retirement. The aging spies had to deal with secret agents from Britain, Russia, and Spain, as Miguelito Loveless Jr. had substituted doubles for the kidnapped leaders of these countries. In addition, Loveless had created pseudobionic robots he called the "$600 People," a comic reference to the then-popular *Six Million Dollar Man*. Loveless's sister, Carmenita, had eyes for West, turned out to be on the side of the good guys, and at the end of the film, revealed her brother had five duplicates of himself not yet destroyed. West and Gordon said one Loveless was enough for them, and returned to their private lives, despite their fear Loveless had tricked them into placing duplicates of monarchs on thrones that might have been held by the true leaders.

In the film, Harry Morgan was introduced as new Secret Service Chief Robert T. "Skinny" Malone, a role he reprised in 1980's *More Wild Wild West*, a two-part television movie. In the slow-paced, meandering plot, the agents were again reluctantly pulled into public service. Gordon told a young agent he wouldn't return unless West did, certain his partner would turn the request down. Instead, as an angry woman and her band of outlaws were chasing West, he willingly took the opportunity to escape her wrath. Jonathan Winters played Albert Paradine the Second, the last villain to challenge the original actors. The character was a mad genius who could turn himself invisible and used his skill to upset a peace conference set up by Dr. Messenger (Victor Buono), a clear parody of the former secretary of state, Henry Kissinger. Both films were considered more satire than homage, created by new teams of producers and directors, as CBS wanted input from directors with movie rather than television experience. With a mix of location shots in Tucson, Arizona, and sets based on original designs, the reunion films were and are not well regarded by fans, who justly blast the latter film for its padding and relatively limited screen time for Conrad and Martin. The TV movies largely disappeared from circulation until Encore cable "Westerns" stations began rebroadcasting the adventures in the 1990s. Reflecting back in 2002, Robert Conrad himself, however, saw the films in a kinder light:

> I thought they were fun. I don't think they ever came up to the level of what we were doing before when we were on a roll. We didn't even know it, I mean, everything was working . . . we didn't know how good we were and what our rapport was as actors. When we came back to try to re-create it, you know, it was kind of like visiting the ex-wife. And she was still the wife, so it wasn't so bad.

More Wild Wild West was the last outing of the original cast, and new films became impossible after Ross Martin died on July 3, 1981, at the age of sixty-one. This event was the final tragedy for a show marked by adversity. Series creator Michael Garrison had died in August 1966 while the show was still on the air, a victim of a fall down marble stairs in his home. Michael Dunn died in 1973 at the age of thirty-nine from complications due to his dwarfism—not from a much-rumored suicide. Robert Conrad continued a successful small-screen career in the highly acclaimed miniseries *Centennial*, and he was the popular Pappy Boyington in *Black Sheep Squadron* (1976–1978). As discussed in Chapter 11, he also starred in two other secret agent series, *Assignment: Vienna* and *A Man Called Sloane*. As time passed, he made it clear his days as James T. West were long since past. By 2000, Conrad had been parodied on *Saturday Night Live* for his macho "I dare you" commercials for Ever-Ready batteries and had become a spokesman for conservative values in appearances on Bill Maher's *Politically Incorrect* discussion show.

Before his death, Martin guest starred in the 1975 version of *The Invisible Man*, its follow-up *The Gemini Man*, and, like his comrade Robert Conrad, guest starred on *Columbo*. He appeared as Chinese detective Charlie Chan in the 1975 TV movie, *Happiness Is a Warm Clue* filmed at Universal Studios. Intended as a pilot for a new series, the acting and tone were indeed warm, but, as usual, network executives didn't have a clue. Long after his death, Martin's role as Artemus Gordon turned out to be an inspiration for at least one actor in a new generation. *Saturday Night Live*'s Dana Carvey reportedly became a master of impressions because of his love of Martin's acting work (Phillips and Garcia 1996, 488). Obviously, if any new attempt to re-create *WWW*'s quirky world were to be made, it would have to be done by a new generation with new ideas and new faces.

In 1998, such new ideas disappointed everyone who viewed African American rap singer and actor Will Smith's portrayal of James West in director Barry Sonnenfeld's update of *WWW*. Robert Conrad, for one, read the script and refused to play a cameo as President Grant. Similarly, *WWW* fans were irritated when actor Kevin Kline, signed to play the new Artemus Gordon, stated he'd never watched the original series because he felt it was silly. The new film was clearly as much a sequel to *Men in Black* (1996) as *WWW*, with lead actor Smith and most of *Men*'s production crew the same. According to Sonnenfeld, he chose Smith primarily because the singer/actor understood the impulsive, action-oriented nature of the West character. In his commentary for the DVD release of the film, Sonnenfeld said he decided casting Smith would make *The Wild Wild West* "hip and smart." For him, a black lead allowed him to do something different to distinguish the movie from the series. For others, Smith's race was beside the point. For them, James T. West should have remained a Western straight shooter, without comic lines.

Robert Conrad had rarely played for laughs. Even Smith later admitted the film was a disappointment. Outside of this 1998 Smith and Kline vehicle, *WWW* fans had little to remember the show by beyond the increasingly spotty reruns. During its heyday, *WWW* had spun off little in the way of tie-in merchandise beyond the obligatory lunchbox, board game, and seven Gold Key Comics. Unlike other shows, only one *WWW* paperback was issued while the show was on the air, and it wasn't an original story. Richard Wormser's 1966 *The Wild Wild West* was nothing more than an expansion of "The Night of the Double-Edged Knife" episode from the first season. It is neither rare nor treasured in the collector's market. Outside of this novel, fans wrote the only new adventures for privately published fanzines. By 2001, Columbia House had issued twenty-five videos of *WWW* adventures through subscriptions, but copies are now hard to come by. These tapes are considered the best versions available on the collector's market, as opposed to the two boxed sets issued at the time of the film's release, which offered only one episode on each of the six tapes.

The Wild Wild West has not been credited with influencing many subsequent films or TV series, although its use of anachronisms has been repeated in a number of projects. Some films borrowed the device of placing secret agents in the Old West, as in Charles Bronson's 1975 *Breakheart Pass*, which told the story of a train heading for a fort whose occupants allegedly were suffering from a diphtheria epidemic. But unknown to the passengers bringing a serum for the disease, there was no epidemic, only a takeover by an outlaw band in collusion with Indians. The film featured music by the erstwhile Jerry Goldsmith and a script by Alistair MacLean. Similarly, 2003's *League of Extraordinary Gentlemen* had Sean Connery leading a team of nineteenth century fictional characters in a fantastic adventure. This odd team included H. G. Wells's Invisible Man, Bram Stoker's Nina Harker, Jules Verne's Captain Nemo, and Mark Twain's Tom Sawyer as an agent of the United States Secret Service.

NEW TV VISIONS

The first television series to be widely described as a takeoff of *WWW* was ABC's *Barbary Coast* starring Captain Kirk himself, William Shatner. In a television movie aired in the spring of 1975, Shatner played Jeff Cable, an agent during the 1880s for the governor of California in the San Francisco square mile called the Barbary Coast. Dennis Cole played "Golden Gate" casino owner Cash Conover, Cable's reluctant partner in stopping a national disaster. At first titled "Cash and Cable," Shatner played an Artemus Gordon–like disguise artist who was to be the sidekick in the adventures. But by the time the series debuted in September, several changes beyond the program's title were evident. Doug McClure, who'd been slated to play the lead, had the Cash role, and Richard Kiel, a former villain for *WWW*, was now Moose Moran, the casino's bouncer. Shatner was now a fusion of West and Gordon drawing costumes from a large wardrobe behind a hidden door in the casino. Not for the first time, this series had a good premise and a good cast, but little else. Critics noted the series was locked into one localized setting and the sets were clearly back lots (McNeil 1996, 74). In 2002, Richard Kiel claimed the show suffered when new producers for the series replaced the original TV film's creators. He also felt that, unlike Ross Martin in *WWW*, Shatner's disguises were so real, viewers didn't know when he was on screen and were often confused (Kiel 2002, 105). So *Barbary Coast* sank. For Kiel, however, the series changed his career. Bond producer Albert Broccoli saw Kiel as Moose Moran, which inspired him to ask the actor to play Jaws in *The Spy Who Loved Me* (Kiel 2002, 111).

In 1979, producer Kenneth Johnson created *Cliffhangers*, a clever attempt to update the matinee serials of the 1940s. With a million-dollar budget per episode, Johnson envisioned three continuing stories with seventeen minutes each per hour. One adventure was a vampire story; another was "Stop

Susan Williams," a spy spoof starring Susan Anton; and the third serial was "Secret Empire," starring Jeffrey Scott as U.S. Marshall Jim Donner. In the 1880s, he discovered an underground alien city in the Old West. Each 17-minute segment ended with a cliffhanger, as with Susan Williams stranded on a river raft surrounded by crocodiles, or Jim Donner locked in combat with a giant spider. NBC worried about the big budgets and the three separate working crews, but no worthwhile concept could compare with ABC's competition, *Happy Days* and *Laverne and Shirley*.

Two shows starring comic actor Bruce Campbell clearly owed much to *WWW*. Fox's *Adventures of Brisco County, Jr.* employed the device of crashing a alien spacecraft in the Old West. Set in 1893, this lighthearted 1993 to 1994 series featured Campbell as the title character, a Harvard-educated lawyer who became a bounty hunter because he had no taste for practicing law (Brooks and Marsh 1999, 13). His Artemus Gordon–like partner was James Lonefeather (Julius Carry), a black bounty hunter who went by the name of Lord Bowler. Most of their assignments came from Socrates Poole (Christian Clemenson), an attorney for the Westerfield Club, the San Francisco organization that had hired Brisco to look after its interests in the West. Throughout the first season, Brisco tracked ruthless criminal John Bly (Billy Drago), who sought the powers of fragments from the mysterious alien craft. While critics hailed the show's style, scripts, and fresh approach, viewers didn't respond.

In 2000, Campbell returned in *Jack of All Trades* (USA Network), another anachronistic secret agent series in which Jack Stiles (Campbell) was commissioned by U.S. president Thomas Jefferson to frustrate Napoleon's desires to expand his empire in the East Indies. For twenty-two episodes, Stiles, a reluctant adventurer and rogue, was forced to play manservant to Emilia Rothschild (Angela Marie Dotchin), an agent of the English Crown. Primarily filmed in New Zealand, the out-of-time characteristics were largely the show's premise, characterizations, and dialogue. For example, Jefferson likely would never have uttered sentences like, "Touch my knee again, and George Washington will cut down your cherry tree." *Jack of All Trades* was a thirty-minute show paired with *Cleopatra 2525* and had its charms. For example, Stiles adopted the role of a local folk hero, "the Daring Dragon," which gave him a means to carry out his missions. As with *Brisco County, Jr.*, critics' responses to *Jack* ranged from kind to enthralled; however, audiences didn't agree.

The most imaginative of such shows to date was the SciFi Channel's *Secret Adventures of Jules Verne* created by Gavin Scott in 1999. Set in the 1860s, the young Bohemian writer Jules Verne (Chris Demetral) was drawn into the war against the League of Darkness, an aristocratic organization wishing to retain power for the rich and nobly born by stirring up wars to prevent peace, which promotes democracy. Verne's compatriots included the cynical gambler Phileas Fogg (Michael Praed), the son of the deceased creator of the British Secret Service. His cousin was Rebecca Fogg (Francesca Hunt), the very Emma Peel–like leather-clad first female secret agent for the service. Rebecca idolized her late uncle, Sir Barnabus Fogg, while Phileas remained angry that his father sent his brother, Erasmus, to his death on a secret mission. Thus, Rebecca was the earnest spy while Phileas was the reluctant secret agent. Phileas's multi-talented manservant, Passepartout (Michel Courtemanche), brought Verne's scientific ideas to life in inspirational and aggravating ways in his lab on the fantastic airship *Aurora*, a "Wanderer"-like craft Fogg won in a Montreal card game.

Producer Gavin Scott's premise was that Verne's classic tales were not created out of whole cloth from the writer's imagination, but were instead inspired by his own wild adventures as a youth, later fictionalized as stories (Olexa 2001a, 70). At first, there were worries no American outlet would pick up the Montreal-based production. After the first twenty-two episodes were filmed, however, the SciFi Channel took note. Although the concept seemed unworkable on paper, the final product was fresh, unique in format and execution, and of high quality. Scott and his team created one of the world's largest production facilities to house the project. Called Angus Yards, it was a former train depot (Freeman 1999, 44) equipped with complete costume, prop, and set design shops; computer graphics facilities; and the world's largest green screen. As *Secret Adventures* was the first all digitally produced television series, costs were maintained by housing production and postproduction in the same building, allowing for quick integration of special effects with live action (Olexa 2001b, 57).

Although all involved with the series emphasized its SF aspects, connections to the secret agent genre were evident on many levels. According to one producer, the show was "like *The X-Files* style of fantasy, where you believe it and it did really happen to those guys, only with the higher production values" (Olexa 2001b, 56). One connection to *The Wild Wild West* was the recurring adversary Count Gregory (Rick Overton), the armor-clad, half-metal leader of an ageless cult. He evoked villains similar to *WWW*'s television and movie incarnations, while representing the dark side of the nineteenth-century Industrial Age.

Francesca Hunt's Rebecca Fogg, in particular, evoked *The Avengers* spirit, alternating between coy and demure and aggressive fighting, as she was the central action figure in the series. Also like *The Avengers*, according to Hunt, a key element of the series was the ironic British sense of humor (Olexa 2001b, 56–59). She noted the difficulty of modern action-adventure acting with new special effects, claiming it takes a special ability to gawk at and speak to rockets or people that aren't there until the digital experts work with the film. Like Honor Blackman, whose judo skills from her *Avengers* days made her the leading candidate to play Pussy Galore, Hunt performed her own stunts and employed her four years of training in dancing and swordplay, the latter a skill she never expected to use in her career.

Like previous efforts, *The Secret Adventures of Jules Verne* didn't catch on, but the series will hopefully return in video and DVD releases at some later date. As of 2002, it was in syndication on late nights on UPN and CBS stations.

Beyond setting the stage for later historical spies, the circumstances surrounding the demise of *WWW* tell us much about America's response to its problems with violence. The most famous antiviolence statement of the era came from John F. Kennedy's appointed head of the Federal Communications Commission, Newton Minnow. In May 1961, he told the National Association of Broadcasters that television was "a vast wasteland of violence, boredom, and banality." In the wake of the Robert Kennedy assassination, network TV again came under close scrutiny, many echoing attorney Maurice L. Ernst's comments on the *Merv Griffin* show that "we're being murdered by TV, not by the guns" (Barnouw 1990, 415). Scheduled hours of *The Avengers* were canceled. *Get Smart* and *It Takes a Thief* scripts were blue-pencilled before going into production. But, by and large, Eric Barnouw claimed most spy shows were not violent "in the primitive fashion of Westerns or gangster films. The means were more discreet and arcane, and seldom noisy" (Barnouw 1990, 373). To appease congressional committees, he noted, most killings of foreign agents on *Mission: Impossible* were seen to happen by accident. Although critics complained about violence and formulaic scripts, the networks pointed out that good versus evil shows were what sold. In addition, action adventure had become a bonanza in the international market because, unlike comedies, there were fewer problems in translation or dubbing. Extended fight sequences needed no dubbing and the terse dialogue of detectives and spies was more manageable than longer personal interactions (Barnouw 1990, 231).

Nonetheless, in the 1970s, the police drama *SWAT* was pulled off the air for being too violent, and reportedly reruns of *The Man from U.N.C.L.E.* were kept off the air due to PTA antiviolence advocacy. Similarly, pressure was put on the long-running hit *Hawaii Five-O* to reduce its on-screen death toll. One watchdog group counted forty-three weapons in one hour, with an average of more than twenty an episode. In one program, the group counted seven deaths and three injuries (Meyers 1989, 144). Senator John Pasteur condemned the figures, but a representative to the U.S. Congress of Mayors, Jon J. Gunther, claimed the opposite. He believed television gunplay was becoming antiseptic. For him, the trauma of violence was numbed in the public consciousness to the point that it no longer mattered. Still others felt canceling shows like *WWW* was merely a case of scapegoating, tarring the media for problems legislators refused to deal with on other levels. In 2002, Robert Conrad told me two of his series, *WWW* and *Black Sheep Squadron*, were canceled because of so-called violence. "I must be a violent guy," he said. "I keep getting canceled because of my violence." After these experiences, Conrad was no longer concerned about such attacks. "Bureaucrats," he told me, "have no business in creative stuff. Bureaucrats should work on issues that are much more important."

Calls for similar censorship have continued into the twenty-first century, as new leaders repeatedly point to the media as cause for rather than a mirror of violent behavior. Network hypocrisy too remains clearly at work. A telling example of this was the controversial November 21, 1988, ABC episode of *MacGyver*. "Blood Brother" was intended to both explain why MacGyver never carried a gun and to be a statement against youthful gun violence. The show's producers planned to post facts and data about hand-gun violence at the end of the episode, but the network bowed to pressure from the National Rifle Association and deleted this material. For some, fictional bullets are worrisome, real killings are less so. Later, television writer Larry Gelbart observed that, for all the hand-wringing over media violence, the true victim is simple originality. Creativity cannot flourish in an arena of offending no one and therefore pleasing no one (Gelbart 1997, 108).

This issue cannot be adequately described here, and these brief notes only point to spy shows as but one example of the blurring of fiction and fact in the modern world. We might assume most viewers know the difference between the evil of Miguelito Loveless from a Timothy McVeigh, but, then again, the *Man from U.N.C.L.E* gun received its own fan mail. As the new century opened, television had moved from the days when fantasy was meant to be separate from realism into a new TV environment of so-called "reality shows," including *Hill Street Blues*, *Law and Order*, and *CSI*. Such shows deliberately blur the distinction between fictional entertainment and supposed reality. We may not see the violence, but we are given graphic details about its aftermath. At some point, complaints about these shows will result in new censorship, and the cycle of protest and appeasement will begin anew.

In short, the *WWW* cancellation was but one blip on the continuum of our social seesaw regarding media violence, and perhaps we will never reach the point where we can distinguish the weather report from the lightning. In the meantime, *The Wild Wild West* remains both a classic example of the creativity of 1960s TV spy producers and a historic example of the dialogue between the public, Hollywood, and the government regarding the responsibility of what appears on America's airways.

CHAPTER 10

From Tongues in Cheek to Tongues Sticking Out: *Get Smart* and the Spoofing of a Genre

CONTINUING A TRADITION

> We have to be able to kill, maim, and destroy, 99. We stand for the forces of goodness, virtue, and justice.
>
> —Maxwell Smart

> Everybody recognized the comedy of authority. Everybody hates authority. Everybody hates bureaucracy. And to be able to expose it so fiercely with so much insanity and anger liberated people's fears about authority. That's why I think it was very successful.
>
> —Mel Brooks commenting on *Get Smart*
> (quoted in Green 1993, 14)

In 1996, a PBS special reunited the creative team of the 1950s radio classic *The Sid Caesar Hour*. The participants included producer Carl Reiner, *M*A*S*H* creator Larry Gelbart, playwright Neil Simon, and *Get Smart* (GS) writer Mel Brooks. In the get-together, Reiner recalled one favorite sketch written by Gelbart and Simon about a comic master spy. In the sketch, Reiner told Caesar:

> You will go to Istanbul. Because a diamond is not expected to be in a brown paper bag, you will carry this cumbersome diamond in a brown paper bag. . . . When you come to Istanbul and get off the train, a man will come up to you and say, "Give me the diamond." Don't give it to him. He asks everybody for the diamond. However, however, however, a beautiful, beautiful blonde woman dressed in a satin dress, a tight-fitting satin dress with a gorgeous body wearing two large earrings will come up to you and she will say, "Give me

the diamond." You will give it to her. That woman will be me. And Sid said, "You'll be in disguise?" I said, "No, I'm in disguise now."[1]

This brand of what was known as "Borscht Belt" comedy, written twenty years before the Bond boom, had much to do with the humor of *Get Smart*. Drawing from a wide range of comic backgrounds, the principal creative team of Daniel Melnick, Leonard Stern, Buck Henry, and *Sid Caesar* alumnus Mel Brooks created a satire that was both groundbreaking and unique in television history. Premiering on September 18, 1965, *Get Smart* combined slapstick, black comedy, social commentary, and wit served up by some of the best talents in the business. As detailed in Donna McCrohan's exhaustive *The Life and Times of Maxwell Smart* (1988) and Joey Green's *The Get Smart Handbook* (1993), former radio producer Stern brought together a team combining writing experience from satirical efforts like *Your Show of Shows*, *That Was the Week That Was*, and *The Steve Allen Show* alongside writers with traditional situation comedy backgrounds.

The result was a cooperative effort unmatched at that time. Stern created the title sequence, including the many doors Agent 86 passed through on his way to the phone booth, the secret entrance to Control headquarters at 123 Main Street, Washington, D.C. Buck Henry named Agent 99 and invented the Cone of Silence, the transparent dome supposedly designed to keep conversations secret. Using the cone inevitably backfired, a typical situation for *Get Smart*'s comic gadgetry. Among other contributions, Mel Brooks created Smart's signature gimmick, the shoe phone, after allegedly speaking into his own shoe on a day when all the office phones seemed to never stop ringing. Many other gags resulted from similar behind-the-scenes problems with props. On one such occasion, one prop man worried about a stunt, saying, "Don't tell me that won't work." "It won't," replied a coworker. "I asked you not to tell me that," said the first prop man. This impromptu line became one of the many catch phrases that characterized *Get Smart*.

Smart himself, actor Don Adams, came to the role of Agent 86 with contributions from his own career. In a comic routine developed with former partner Bill Dana, Adams had a stand-up act full of inside showbiz references. In one routine, "The Defense Attorney," Adams adopted the clipped speech cadence of actor William Powell. This imitation became widely known when Adams was a regular on the early 1960s *Perry Como Show*, despite the fact that Adams himself didn't think the voice was especially funny. Adams also used this voice for the cartoon character of Tennessee Tuxedo in 1963. In the same year, he expanded on the impression in the role of inept house detective Byron Glick on *The Bill Dana Show*. Adams then refined the Byron Glick character into the self-confident but monumentally inept secret agent, Maxwell Smart.

It was from one of Adams's stand-up routines that the inevitable and oft repeated "Would you believe . . ." jokes originated. ("Would you believe I have this building surrounded by 100 Bengal Lancers?" "No." "Would you believe Gunga Din on a donkey?") Another line he added to the pilot was, "You really know how to hurt a guy," which he'd used during his days on the *Perry Como Show*. When Smart heard the descriptions of the tortures KAOS intended for him, his response was always, "And loving it." Throughout America, *Get Smart*'s popularity was reflected in both conversational and commercial repetitions of such catch phrases. "Sorry about that, Chief" and "missed it by that much" were uttered by more Adams impersonators than Adams himself.

But in the beginning, *Get Smart* was an idea looking for a creative team. Daniel Melnick had scripted the pilot for ABC, which asked that Smart be given a mother and a dog. In his script, Melnick reluctantly provided Fang the dog, but refused to have Smart explaining himself to an unneeded mother. Melnick brought in Leonard Stern to work on the project, who brought in Brooks and Henry. After reading their revised script for the pilot, ABC rejected the series saying it was too un-American (Green 1993, 5). Stern approached NBC's Grant Tinker, who loved the script. He took it to Vice President Mort Werner, even though NBC had already spent their development money for the fall season. For *GS*, Werner made an exception. The pilot, the only episode shot in black and white, immediately went into production. Immediately, the censors objected to the use of rubber garbage on a scow, as they feared viewers would complain if they happened to be dining while watching the series. According to McCrohan, the producers responded that they'd only use nice garbage such as fruit (McCrohan 1988, 21). Ironically, Michael Dunn, shortly to become the equally maniacal Miguelito Loveless on *The Wild Wild West*, played the bad guy for the pilot, Mr. Big.

COMIC CHEMISTRY

> Well, 99, we are what we are. I'm a secret agent trained to be cold, vicious, and savage. Not enough to be a businessman.
> —Maxwell Smart

For trivia buffs, the origins of the agents' code numbers were not random. 86, named by Melnick, came from the bartender's phrase for throwing someone out: "86 that guy." Don Adams came to this role by luck, being already under contract with NBC as a supporting character on the then ending *Bill Dana Show*. Early contenders for the part included Mel Brooks himself, comic Orson Bean, and actor Tom Poston. When Adams was chosen, he was given the choice of a large salary or a smaller stipend with a piece of the show. Wisely, he took the second option, which resulted in an annuity for the rest of his life. His character, of course, could never be described as wise. Agent 86 was a corporal in the army in Korea, and Control recruited him immediately after he graduated from an unnamed college. He failed Torture three years in a row in spy school. His ego was noted by his wearing his code number on his bathrobe and pajamas. His apartment number was 86, despite the fact he lived on the second floor of his building.

Barbara Feldon was the producers' choice from the beginning for Agent 99, due partly to her work on the Talent Associates drama *East Side/West Side* and her role as an industrial spy in *Mr. Broadway*. She was well known for her sexy Revlon commercials, especially for Top Brass men's cologne. In those spots, she purred and growled to the "tigers" in the viewing audience with a sultry come-hither look. A former drama student at Carnegie Tech, Feldon's TV debut was as a winning contestant on *The $64,000 Question* as a Shakespeare expert. In the opinion of *Get Smart*'s creators, she really was a 99, only one number short of perfect. The missing 1 percent was that Feldon was noticeably taller than Adams. In some scenes, he had to stand on inclined planes beside her, and Feldon herself was forced to find ways to seem shorter on camera.

In subsequent decades, trivia buffs pointed to one episode in which 99 claimed her true name was Susan Hilton, although the episode later revealed this was a cover name. According to McCrohan, creator Buck Henry denied Agent 99 was ever given a name. It was part of the comedy, he said, for Max to be so oblivious to his partner-turned-love interest that he never knew her name, even after their marriage in 1968. At her wedding, when the minister pronounced her name, the Admiral snored so loudly no one heard it. Even her mother never said her name, only using euphemisms like "honey" and "darling."

An important ingredient in the show was the Feldon-Adams chemistry. Much of the show's humor came from the fact that 99 wanted a relationship with Smart, while he was too dumb to notice. In the pilot, the episode was half over before Smart realized his partner was female. As Adams noted in a 2001 TV Land documentary on *GS*, Smart always saw 99 as his partner, just one of the guys. Throughout the series, Feldon allowed Adams to have center stage with the comic lines. She supported him with silent physical humor, especially her trademark eye roll employed to finish off scenes and show her gentle forbearance for her partner's bumbling.

To provide these characters a measure of believability, the producers developed short back stories, although Agent 86's background was much less detailed than 99's. 99 was a fashion model before joining Control where she earned three Lamont Cranston Awards, a nod to radio's *The Shadow*. She was raised forty miles north of Twin Falls, Idaho. Her mother (Jane Dulo), a recurring character on the show, was unaware of her profession, thinking she and Max worked for the Chief at Potomac Greeting Cards. Mom's attempts to romance the Chief were unrequited, and she was so hard-bitten that she was the only one able to resist the charms of KAOS's irresistible agent, Simon the Likeable. In one episode, 99 learned her father too was a spy. All we learn of Agent 86's family, however, is that his mother was apparently a widow to whom Max sent $15 a week. In Max's "Little Black Book," we hear 86's father didn't take him to ball games and apparently didn't speak much to him while he was growing up.

Beyond the 86-99 pairing, much of the show's success was due to the cast of supporting characters, including the Chief of Control played by former singer Edward Platt, who was best-known for his role in *Rebel without a Cause* (1955). He had also appeared in Hitchcock's 1959 *North by Northwest*. Platt came to his role at the last minute, signed the day before shooting began. The producers weren't certain this serious actor could do comedy until he broke into a rendition of "Old Man River" at his audition. They decided anyone with that much courage could take on a role that demanded showing courage and forbearance. The Chief was never given a full name, but trivia experts remember that, for comic purposes, Smart drew out the Chief's first name in one episode—the Chief was reluctant to admit his first name was Thaddeus. The Chief was clearly a symbol of frustration and forgiveness, as his best agent continually tried his patience but always came out on top despite himself.

86's comic world included other Control agents, such as the depressed, claustrophobic Agent 13 (Dave Ketchum). He was often hidden in cramped, uncomfortable, and odd places like washing machines or airport lockers. Other characters included actor Dick Gautier as Hymie, the gentle robot that once worked for KAOS. A doctor on the side of good had invented Hymie, but sold him to KAOS when he discovered there was no money in being benevolent. Rewired by Smart, the robot became the agent's best friend, a comic foil for the all-too-human 86. Overly literal, when Hymie was told to "kill the lights," he shot out the lightbulbs. Other agents included the dog K-13, or Fang, who graduated from the same spy class as 86. In one episode, Fang saved the lives of Smart and 99, who were tied up and unable to blow out a deadly exploding candle. By singing "Happy Birthday" to Fang, the Control agents inspired Fang to blow out the candle. When the Chief retired Fang from active duty, he promoted him to an important senior desk job—burying evidence. Adams's cousin Robert Karvelas played Larrabee, the one agent who made Smart look smart. In the three-part "A Man Called Smart," Admiral Harold Hargrave (William Schallert) was introduced as the ninety-one-year-old original head of Control, a man so senile his hobbies were chess and burying old friends.

The opposite of Control, in religion, philosophy, and the war of niceness versus rottenness was KAOS. KAOS, with its symbol of a vulture sitting on an egg-shaped earth, was created as an international terror organization in order to avoid any connections to Cold War metaphors. It paid its agents better than Control and provided a better health and dental plan. KAOS agents laughed at their Control counterparts, who once threatened to go on strike and were twice reduced to being part-time agents due to budgetary cutbacks. Control's picket signs, of course, were in code.

Smart's most frequent adversary was the ex-Nazi Conrad Siegfried (Bernie Kopell), KAOS's vice president for public relations and terror. An agent for KAOS for twenty years, Siegfried had risen in the ranks from being an office boy and part-time assassin. He was the sort of villain who sent death-threat telegrams collect and was known for saying, "Ve don't shush people here." He was the sort of villain who sold out his own sister to Control to earn a modest bounty. His assistant, KAOS's answer to Larrabee, was Shtarker (King Moody, a friend of Kopell's). According to Siegfried, KAOS agents were all "former grease monkeys, disc jockeys, used car salesmen, TV repairmen, and politicians." At first, Siegfried was intended for one guest shot, but Bernie Kopell's portrayal of an angry adversary worked well. In the 2001 TV Land documentary on the series, Kopell claimed he drew from his own personal anger to give Siegfried his personality. This acting choice resulted in one of the most memorable, and beloved, villains in television.

With this mix of characters, *Get Smart* became a comic realm touching a variety of bases in the sitcom ballpark. Most noticeably, the show targeted its television secret agent competitors, as in the title sequence, in which Agent 86 walked past a series of giant doors before entering a phone booth and dropping into Control headquarters. This sequence clearly referred to the secret entrance to U.N.C.L.E. headquarters at the back of a tailor shop. Similarly, the opening narration of *Get Smart*'s pilot poked fun at *U.N.C.L.E.*'s voice-over introducing the agents and the organization. In the first outing of *GS*, the narrator explained that Control is a secret organization located somewhere in Washington, D.C., and Max Smart, seen sitting in a symphony hall, is a secret agent trained *to never reveal that he is a spy*. Then, as the orchestra plays, Max's shoe phone rings.

Other parodies included one episode entitled "The Impossible Mission," in which 86 pressed a button on a tape recorder expecting it to explode, as in the opening sequence of *Mission: Impossible*. In Maxwell Smart's world, the tape doesn't self-destruct—everything else in the room does. Imitating Jim Phelps's perusal of a portfolio to choose his IMF agents for a mission, 86 examined a portfolio of his own and considered photos of TV personality David Susskind, Leonardo da Vinci's "Mona Lisa," *Mad Magazine*'s Alfred E. Newman, and singer Tiny Tim, whose picture Max tears to pieces. (Three *Mission: Impossible* veterans, Martin Landau, Barbara Bain, and Leonard

Nimoy guest starred on *Get Smart*.) In another send-up, "Die Spy," Smart joined an African American partner to win a ping-pong championship, a clear parody of *I Spy*, including Earle Hagen's distinctive theme music. In that episode, Robert Culp played a cameo as a waiter, and impressionist Stu Gilliam played a credible, and on-target, parody of Bill Cosby. In "Run, Robot, Run," 86 battled two KAOS agents named Donald Sneed and Mrs. Emily Neel, operatives of KAOS's Contrived Accident Division. Clearly, the agents' names were a nod to *The Avengers*.

But, in Mel Brooks's opinion, *Get Smart* also spoke to a more general feeling of disbelief in a government that was less than honest about Vietnam and other actions and created the "credibility gap" in President Lyndon Johnson's administration. For Brooks, one of the points of *Get Smart* was to make fun of government boondoggles and propaganda. According to Buck Henry, viewers could "see government espionage for what it really is, an idiotic enterprise glamorized by Hollywood" (Green 1993, 5). Dick Gautier agreed, saying, "I guess Maxwell Smart is like a lot of government officials. People who are filled with self-importance, feeling that they know a great deal and in a position they don't really belong in are incapable of functioning properly . . . It's the Peter principle at work, failing upwards until you get into a position of authority except that you looked at Max kindly" (Green 1993, 29). William Schallert (the Admiral) had similar views. "I especially liked the scene where the Admiral decided to go on television and tell the people everything was O.K. when, in fact, the country was headed for disaster. That's a nutty satire on government cover-ups that seems remarkably prescient in light of what we know today" (Green 1993, 143). One comment on government secrecy was the scene in which Max was given a certificate of merit, but was instructed to read it once and destroy it to preserve Control's secrecy. Similarly, when Max and 99 give the Chief a birthday cake, "Happy Birthday, Chief" was written with invisible icing for the same reason.

As if to underline these perspectives, later revelations about the show's connections to the real espionage community were as humorous as the intentional comedy. In August 1966, the U.S. Army Counter Intelligence Corps invited *Get Smart* cast members to entertain at its nineteenth Annual Convention Banquet. According to McCrohan, network publicists asked that photos be cleared for public release, and real spies posed with Adams and Feldon for gag shots (McCrohan 1988, 89–91). But the earlier clearance was revoked, and the photos could never be used. Agents demanded the negatives of the film and a letter stating the negatives had been given over. The letter was written with a carbon, but the carbon had been reversed. One operative confiscated the carbon paper and burned it in an ashtray. Equally unusual was a revelation by a former CIA operative that his agency was concerned that *Get Smart*'s writers occasionally came too close to reality, especially the Cone of Silence, which they in fact had created. The agency considered sending the producers a list of areas to avoid, but elected not to as they feared such a list would result in a parody of their effort.

The primary objective of *GS* was entertainment, and any brand of humor that fit into the mix was incorporated into the scripts. In his interview for the TV Land special on *GS*, Adams claimed there were often too many cooks working on the show, which led to many battles over what was deemed funny. According to Buck Henry, the sight gags were for the children, the dialogue for adults. Thus, those who liked physical comedy and those who enjoyed sophisticated writing could sit side by side on the same couch. Any idea could be incorporated into scripts at the last minute. When Adams's friend Don Rickles appeared for one guest appearance, the two cracked so many ad-lib jokes that the episode was expanded into a two-parter. Other notable guests included talk show hosts Steve Allen, Johnny Carson, and Joey Bishop. Bishop's announcer, the young Regis Philbin, also appeared in one episode. Guest stars on *GS* tended to be drawn from the ranks of nightclub entertainers and actors with a light touch, including Caesar Romero, Milton Berle, Bob Hope, and Carol Burnett.

Each episode of *GS* was produced in three days under one of the lowest budgets of the era. Despite these limitations, the show earned seven Emmys, including three for Adams, and the show reached number twelve in its first season. But despite its four-year success at NBC, knocking CBS's competitor *Secret Agent* off the air, the network canceled the show after the 1969 season. They felt everything that could be pilloried had been pilloried, and that spy humor was now best relegated to Saturday morning children's shows. *Get Smart* had outlived other imitators such as the obvious clone, ABC's *The Double Life of Henry Phyfe*.

In this 1966 mid-season replacement sitcom, comedian Red Buttons played Henry Wadsworth Phyfe, an exact duplicate of a recently deceased CIS government agent who was code-named U-31. Predictably, the mild-mannered accountant resembled the agent in facial features alone, U-31 having been a Don Juan, master linguist, and crack shot. Using premises avoided by *Get Smart*'s creators, Phyfe's life was centered on his fiancée Judy Kimball (Zeme North), his future mother-in-law and landlady Florence Kimball (Marge Redmond), and his boss, none of whom knew about his other life. Only Gerald B. Hannahan (Fred Clark), the bombastic, balding CIS director, linked him to undercover work. Judy and her mother were phased out quickly from the series, but Henry soon followed suit.

But this wasn't the case for *Get Smart*, which quickly enjoyed its first of many double lives. In its last NBC season, the show attempted to renew interest by having Agents 86 and 99 marry. Buck Henry, who'd left the series to work on his film *The Graduate*, later said he would have fought this move like a tiger. "What sort of conceivable sex life would those two have?"

he asked in the TV Land special. This move changed the relationships in the series too much for viewers, and the show slipped out of the top thirty. After 112 NBC episodes, the network said enough. One day after its NBC cancellation, however, GS was picked up by CBS so quickly that, for most viewers, the switch was barely noticeable.

Some changes were evident in the title sequence, which now included quick shots of the Capitol, the White House, and the Lincoln Memorial to the strains of the slightly revamped theme music. In the first moments of the new season, Smart, 99, and the Chief met on the moon, the most clandestine site they could find before NASA astronauts landed and ruined the secrecy. 86 now drove a gold Opel GTE, and Adams was now the series' most frequent director. To attract lost viewers, the CBS debut showcased the birth of twins to 86 and 99. For a time, the Smarts juggled secret missions with finding baby-sitters, forcing even the Chief and Larrabee to help out while Max and 99 battled KAOS. Realizing the babies were more distraction than attraction, as Feldon put it in the TV Land documentary, "We quickly got rid of them." Other problems were evident, as in one episode in which Adams refused to participate. In his opinion, the script to "Ice Station Siegfried" was identical to a third-season show, the setting transplanted from South America to the Arctic. For that episode, Bill Dana stepped in for his one appearance on the show as Control Agent Quigley. (Fans have attempted to determine which episode Adams felt was similar to "Siegfried," and some guess "Swartz's Island" may be the one, although the similarities seemed more obvious to Adams than to his most loyal viewers.) When 99 became jealous as the married Max seduced KAOS temptresses, the uniqueness of *Get Smart* had clearly given way to the humor more appropriate for *The Dick Van Dyke Show* or *I Love Lucy*. In one story, 99 even became jealous of herself when KAOS planted a double of her in the Smart's apartment. In the final episode, we saw the last bit of satire on the spy genre when 86 was brainwashed into not being himself; that is, he becomes wise, insightful, and sophisticated. For one brief moment, Agent 86 was everything he pretended to be and 99 liked the change. But the moment quickly passed, and the final moments had Max return to his old self, saving the world in his own unsophisticated style.

AFTERLIFE OF *GET SMART*

In terms of life after cancellation, *Get Smart* enjoyed considerable success in subsequent decades, as its one hundred thirty-eight episodes continued in reruns long after the shows it parodied largely disappeared from the air. Because it was a comedy with a thirty-minute format, it easily fit between other sitcoms in any schedule. GS is still a mainstay in the syndication market, although fans continue to complain that up to three minutes are cut from each episode. In 2001, *GS* played in Argentina, Brazil, Australia, Estonia, New Zealand, and South Africa. While its "workplace humor" format was set in the world of covert actions, its general themes are still relevant and funny, and *Get Smart*'s antics continue to be fresh for new audiences who do not need to understand some of the topical jokes to be entertained. Of course, some things never change. Modern audiences should easily recognize who is being parodied when they see a white-mustached southern gentleman who owns Colonel Kirby's Tennessee Fricasseed Froglegs.

According to the Museum of Broadcasting Communications, alongside series like *Hogan's Heroes*, *McHale's Navy* and *F-Troop*, *Get Smart* is credited with opening up the situation-comedy format, allowing later series to break away from other more domestic settings. In fact, *GS* went further as it had nothing to do with "service comedy," which uses gags to complain about military life. Unlike other situation comedies, before and after, that are typically locked into particular settings of a home or office, *GS*'s vista was international, which gives each episode the feeling of a miniature movie. If Mel Brooks is correct, *Get Smart*'s themes of poking fun at a government many distrust make Agents 86 and 99 the comic counterparts to agents Scully and Mulder, the voices of a cynical age in *The X-Files*. On many levels, there is good reason to suspect *Get Smart* will have a long afterlife. As of 2003, it was part of the evening fare on cable network's TV Land channel. Surprisingly, as of 2003, no *GS* episodes have been released on video or DVD. And, as of this writing, there are no plans to release such.

99's place in television history has become an interesting case study in defining feminism in the 1960s. For some observers, 99 can be seen as a prefeminist who still deferred to men, unlike April Dancer, Honey West, or Emma Peel, all of whom made their TV debuts after 99. Always jealous of other women, 99 fed Max his best ideas in a way that let him think he came up with them. Far from being a model of women's liberation, 99 seemed to be embarrassed to out-think Max, being very aware of his ego. Invariably, he took advantage of his alleged seniority over 99—he joined Control two weeks before her—to force her to do most of the heavy labor, including lugging heavy equipment or blazing jungle trails with a machete. Virtually apologizing for being smarter than Smart, her sweet, self-effacing nature, which placed men first, was typical of the times.

Still, Feldon recalled many women told her that 99 was a role model, one of the first intelligent women they'd seen on TV (Green 1993, 40). 99 has been seen as a transitional figure like Elizabeth Montgomery's Samantha Stevens in *Bewitched*, in which the female lead was more capable than her partner but who was obliged to be the deferential power behind the throne. In this view, like her less lovelorn sister spies, 99 represented a shift in cultural expectations of women in the workplace largely because she operated in a profession that took her out of the kitchen and the secretarial pool.

However, portraying 99 as a role model points to one interesting gap in how the genders view fictional characters. After all, who would claim Agent 86 as a model for young boys?

Get Smart remains central in the careers of Don Adams and Barbara Feldon. For example, Adams continued to earn paychecks for reprising Smart-like caricatures in commercials for Chief Auto Parts and Coors Light Beer, in which he was besieged by annoying Maxwell Smart impersonators. Among other projects, reflecting her real-life troubles as a typecast TV secret agent, Feldon appeared on one episode of the 1990s comedy *Mad About You*, starring as an older actress whom everyone remembers from a fictional TV series called *Spy Girl*.

In 1979, Universal Pictures announced *The Return of Maxwell Smart* for a budget of eight million dollars. As it happened, one earlier attempt to produce a *GS* film had been suggested in 1966, but Paramount had decided not to make the attempt in the wake of the disastrous *Munster Go Home* theatrical release. Instead, the Leonard-Stern scripted "The Man Called Smart" was made into a three-part television outing. In 1978, original members of the show's creative team worked on a script for an effort geared for foreign markets, with the American debut intended as a television movie. But public demand caused Universal to decide to make the film more of a major motion picture effort, reducing the input of Leonard Stern and his collaborators. (Stern was ultimately banned from the set.) Adams disliked the script, but signed on, as he'd just remarried and needed the money.

When the film appeared as *The Nude Bomb* in 1980, only Max Smart and Larrabee reprised their TV roles. A clear loss was the lack of the 99-86 chemistry. 86 was now an agent for P.I.T.S. (Provisional Intelligence Tactical Service). Some updated gags connected to the original series, as in 86's refurbished shoe phone now equipped with an answering machine. The plot was typical *GS*: KAOS threatened the world with a bomb that would destroy all known fabrics, leaving civilization at the mercy of a KAOS fashion designer, who had the only fabric not susceptible to the "Nude Bomb." Critics quickly pointed out that most of the flavor of the series didn't make it to the screen, and that the lengthy car chase in the Universal Pictures back lot was no less than a commercial to promote tours of that attraction. Ticket sales were attributed to what once was, not what was being offered in the new decade. When *The Nude Bomb* regained its original title for airing on television, it won the ratings for its night, but again the success was attributed rightfully to nostalgia, not new creativity.

More successful, at least in creative terms, was *Get Smart Again*, a 1989 made-for-TV movie produced by Burt Nodella and directed by Gary Nelson, a veteran director from the original series. Unlike *The Nude Bomb*, *Get Smart Again* reunited all the original cast members with the exception of the deceased Edward Platt, to whom the film was dedicated. In this story, viewers learn Control had been phased out twenty years earlier after the demise of KAOS, as the agency had been created by the U.S. Intelligence Agency especially to battle KAOS. Control's headquarters was now empty except for Larrabee, who was told by President Nixon to maintain his post, and no one had rescinded the memo. Hymie was now literally a crash test dummy, and Agent 13 was working part time. Max was a protocol officer for the State Department, and 99 was writing her memoirs. Reflecting the times, KAOS was reinvigorated by a corporate raider's takeover.

Nods to the old were evident in new uses for the catch phrases, with many recycled bits of dialogue taken from old scripts. We learn KAOS lost its top assassin in a trade with THRUSH. Siegfried turned out to be one of triplets, his brother taking his place in the scheme to force Americans to read when a weather machine is planned to destroy TV broadcasts. Such satirical touches made *Get Smart Again* one of the best remakes in the reunion genre, tapping into what made the show a success, while updating the topical references for new audiences.

In 1995, a short-lived sequel to the series was aired on the Fox network, starring Adams as the new Chief of Control with his son, Zack (Andy Dick), now the bumbling field agent. Originally intended as a vehicle for Dick, Adams and Feldon were brought in at the last minute to attract viewers. Oddly, producers wanted the Smarts to be divorced, but this concept was nixed by an irate Feldon. For a mere seven episodes, KAOS had become a corporation bent on world domination, 99 had been elected to Congress, and the new entrance to Control headquarters was through a soft drink machine in the waiting room of a car wash. Zack Smart was paired with the beautiful and smarter Agent 66 (Elaine Hendrix), who sported a bra that shot bullets.

Adams himself admitted the series wasn't well considered. He asked the network to show the better, later episodes first and postpone broadcasting the undistinguished pilot until the show had built up an audience. Fox ignored the request and found itself fighting with the young lead, Andy Dick. Dick was committed to the new *GS* show when he got a chance to appear in another comedy series, *Talk Radio*. *GS* producers let him do *Talk Radio*, which was tantamount to admitting that the new *GS* series had little or no chance of being renewed. To ensure this, Dick made a point of bad-mouthing *Get Smart Again* whenever he was interviewed by the press.

Likely, this was the last incarnation of the war between Control and KAOS starring the original players. Plans for a *GS* film surface from time to time, as in 1999 when Warner Brothers bought a Nick Marine script called "Spyville," which the studio rewrote to be a *Get Smart* movie. Rights to the project have changed hands several times since. One play entitled *Get Smart* is in circulation (Dramatic Publishing), based on the "Mr. Big" pilot and another episode, "Diplomat's Daughter."

Get Smart remains part of twenty-first-century consciousness. In a syndicated June 9, 2002, Columbia News Service article, Baltimore video engineer Carl Birkmeyer, the creator of www.wouldyoubelieve.com, the most definitive website for *GS* fans, or "Smartians," was interviewed. According to Birkmeyer, about two thousand fans from sixty-three countries log on each month. Don Adams faithfully reads letters posted at the site, and Leonard Stern was moved to tears by some fan responses. TV Land reported that over 200,000 viewers catch the 8:00 A.M. airings of the show. In 2003, Sideshow Toys released new collectible figures of Smart and the Chief, and fans quickly supported the publication of Barbara Feldon's new autobiography, *Living Alone and Loving It*.

Attempts to create new television spy spoofs in the spirit of *GS* include *Adderly*, which appeared during the mid-1980s secret-agent revival as part of CBS's late night schedule. Winston Rekert played V. H. Adderly, a secret agent who injured his left hand. Demoted to routine assignments in the Department of Miscellaneous Affairs basement, he found danger and intrigue from the most banal of assignments. Based on creator Elliot Baker's 1971 novel, *Pocock and Pitt*, the show was produced in Canada, which provided local scenery that could look like Russian wilderness settings. *Adderly* didn't like to admit his name was Virgil Homer Adderly after his parent's love for Greek classics, was aided and comforted by department secretary Mona, and had an ongoing battle with his supervisor who didn't like minor assignments converted into major spy cases. *Adderly* was successful enough to run for forty-three episodes until 1988. According to some viewers, the series improved in its later episodes, moving away from predominant quirky humor into a more *U.N.C.L.E.* mix of such humor with a level of realism.

A later mid-season attempt to revitalize the spy comedy for network TV was 1997's *Spy Game* (ABC), in which the Cold War was over, and downsized ex-spies without pensions turned on each other. These resentful new terrorists and rogue spies inspired the U.S. president to create E.C.H.O. (Emergency Counter-Hostilities Organization). Attempting to emulate *The Avengers*, the agents Lorne Cash (Linden Ashby) and Max Landon (Allison Smith) were first seen in *Avengers*-like opening titles, and Patrick Macnee played a brief cameo in the first episode. Created by John McMamara, Sam Raimi, and Ivan Raimi, *Spy Game* also featured Bruce McCarty as Micah Simms, E.C.H.O.'s harried chief, who invested half his time in computer espionage and half worrying about ever-decreasing budgets. Ironically, during the Cold War, these combined areas of expertise were not valued in the intelligence community, and he was promoted when post–Cold War tactics changed.

Some plots were homages to *Mission: Impossible*, and reviewers noted the tongue-in-cheek approach was somewhat reminiscent of *U.N.C.L.E.* Even *Adderly* got a nod when Winston Rekert played a father figure in the show.

Other spies from television's past included Peter Lupus and Robert Culp. *People Magazine* liked the pilot so much that its reviewer gave the series a B-plus. Many critics noted this formula could have worked well had the execution and scripts been better. For some reviewers, *Spy Game* wasn't the comedy it claimed to be, and it died a quick death despite its intriguing premise, pilot, and potential.

To date, the most memorable post–*Get Smart* efforts are feature films and television sketches that don't require the talents needed for a weekly humorous outing. *Saturday Night Live* (*SNL*), in particular, has aired a number of sketch parodies, such as having comic Steve Martin play James Bond on a tightly limited expense account, forcing him to save bullets and curtail his expensive habits. In films, Leslie Nielsen, the star of *Police Squad* and a number of parodies of other film genres, took his turn as bumbling secret agent WD-40 in *Spy Hard*, an ineffectual *Mad Magazine*-inspired attempt to lampoon the already lampooned. TV spies were in *Spy Hard*'s sights, including the obligatory parody of the *Mission: Impossible* self-destruct messages. The film featured a walk-on by *I Spy*'s Robert Culp as an unnamed businessman. Much more successful were the Mike Myers's Austin Powers efforts, in which Myers brought new vitality to the form with an unexpected freshness.

In the first of these efforts, *Austin Powers, International Man of Mystery*, costarring Elizabeth Hurley, Myers wrote, directed, coproduced, and starred as various roles in a unique homage to spy films, TV shows, and the jet-set aspects of the 1960s in general. Among the many Bond parodies was the incomplete Dr. Evil lair, which came from a *Saturday Night Live* sketch based on a similar joke. In one of *SNL*'s many Bond parodies, the late actor Phil Hartman encountered the evil Zoran, who promised many dire threats while his headquarters was being built around them by bumbling construction workers. Myers incorporated this idea into the finale of *Austin Powers*. The "fembots," sexy robots firing bullets from their breasts, were inspired, said Myers, by the Matt Helm and Derek Flint movies. However, the device more resembled similar robots in episodes of *U.N.C.L.E.* and *The Bionic Woman*. While the DVD version of the first *Austin Powers* film contains a list of 1960s secret agent TV series, no commentary connected them to specific material in the film. Still, many viewers observed Hurley's leather suit echoed Emma Peel. One *U.N.C.L.E.* fan described the last fight scene, with the strains of "Secret Agent Man" in the background, as being very like the finale in *The Prisoner*'s "Fallout." *Austin Powers*, above and beyond its sight gags and bathroom humor, was a logical updating of *Get Smart*, giving a new generation the chance to see both the old and new views of spy parodies.

Spy humor continues in such films as *The Adventures of Rocky and Bullwinkle* (2000), in which the duo's perennial adversaries, Boris, Natasha, and Fearless Leader, plotted to take over the United States with RBTV (Really Bad Television), which broadcast twenty-four-hour spy adventures, turning viewers into zombies. To yet another revised version of the "Secret Agent Man" theme, RBTV programming included "Three Funny, Wacky Spies and Their Horse Who Will Also Be a Spy"! Spies and humor, it seems, should have a healthy life in the twenty-first century.

CHAPTER 11

Also-Rans and New Branches: Network Secret Agents from 1963 to 1980

BACK TO THE FIFTIES

Look, Al, I'm not asking you to spy. I'm just asking you to steal.
—Noah Bain in second season titles for *It Takes a Thief*, 1969

In the 1960s, imitation proved that nothing is as successful as someone else's success. Some TV series became classics, many others became also-rans. One group of shows now largely forgotten were essentially updates of 1950s styles and formulas, usually thirty-minute adventures set in World War II and filmed in Europe. Producers had good reason to think such outings would appeal to an audience watching both WWII dramas and comedies, from *Combat* and *Rat Patrol* to *Hogan's Heroes*. Series with a 1950s flavor, like the return of *Dragnet* and the continued presence of earlier series like *I Led Three Lives* in syndication, seemed to indicate a market still existed for spy series outside of the Fleming-inspired pop phenomenon. However, these shows tended to last only one season, much like many of the shows they copied.

One British-made series debuted in America and died before the *Man from U.N.C.L.E.* forever altered the TV spy genre. *Espionage*, produced by Herbert Hirschman and George Justin, was a 1963 to 1964 ITV throwback to the old rewritings of law enforcement files. This anthology series was more somber than its 1960s counterparts, even using newsreel footage mixed with location shootings in Europe (Vahimhei 1997). Using stories from WWII and the Cold War, twenty-four episodes were taped on 35-millimeter black-and-white film and aired on Saturday nights on ABC. Most actors were European and unknown on American television, but some members of underground resistance cells and government agents from times past were played by Dennis Hopper, Jim Backus, and Anthony Quayle. Bernard Lee, M from the Bond series, made one appearance. The final episode, "A Camel to Ride," aired on March 28, 1964, after being postponed from its original air date of November 23, 1963, the day after the assassination of President John F. Kennedy. (According to Tim Brooks and Earle Marsh's 1999 *The Complete Directory to Prime Network and Cable TV Shows*, Ian Fleming was an extra in one scene, but I was unable to confirm this. Reportedly, all episodes still exist.)

Blue Light, seen from January to August 1966 on ABC, featured David March (singer Robert Goulet) and Susan Duchard (Christine Carère) fighting Nazis behind German lines as members of the Code: Blue Light team. March, like many previous WWII spies, posed as a foreign correspondent who had supposedly renounced his American citizenship. His assignment was to infiltrate German High Command, keeping one step ahead of their counterintelligence organizations and Allied agents alike. His cover was so deep, even other agencies were unaware of his pose. This series, shot on location in Germany, was quickly canceled despite the star power of Goulet, then well known for his role as Lancelot in Broadway's first run of *Camelot*.

CBS's *Jericho* (1966–1967), coproduced by *U.N.C.L.E.*'s Norman Felton, was clearly influenced by the earlier British effort, *Four Just Men*, which featured agents of four countries battling evil after WWII. In this case, three undercover agents, working as Allied troubleshooters during World War II, represented three countries as a unit that was code-named "Jericho." Captain Franklin Sheppard (Don Francks) worked for American Army Intelligence, Jean-Gaston André (Marino Masé) was an officer in the Free French Air Force, and Nicholas Gage (John Leyton) was a lieutenant in the British Navy. Early in the war, these three had trained together in sabotage, ambush, rescue missions, and intelligence gathering.

According to Eric Barnouw, *Jericho* was an example of new network thinking regarding its World War II programs. In Barnouw's opinion, networks wanted their dramas to avoid overt references to Germany and Italy because these countries were now friends, NATO allies, and, more important, buyers of America's commercial products and television series. In addition, the networks suspected younger viewers didn't know who de Gaulle, Churchill, or even Hitler were. Thus WWII series like *Jericho* referred to nebulous enemies, which gave the stories something of a timeless, symbolic feel and made anti-Nazi adventures metaphors for the Cold War (Barnouw 1990, 375). Although *Jericho* didn't pass muster, Francks guest starred on *The Wild Wild West, Mission: Impossible,* and *U.N.C.L.E.* In the 1990s, he joined the ensemble cast of *La Femme Nikita*.

Shades of Biff Baker were evident in *The Baron* (ABC, 1966–1967). This series revolved around John Mannering (Steve Forrest), the title character who drew his name from his family's manor in Texas. Based on stories by John Creasey and filmed in England, the series cast Mannering as an owner of antique shops in London, Paris, and Washington, D.C. British intelligence called on Mannering whenever priceless art exhibits were involved in espionage, blackmail, or murder. John Alexander Templeton Green (Colin Gordon) was his contact, and beautiful agent Cordelia Winfield (Sue Lloyd) often assisted him. While the show's few fans remembered the stylish antique cars Mannering drove, writer Brian Clemens felt the series was an example of why *The Avengers* stood out. "The standards of scripts for *The Avengers* were very high whereas its contemporaries such as *Man in a Suitcase*, *The Baron*, and *The Champions* were all rather flat" (Sutcliffe 1984, 30). The series didn't lack for talent, with its creator being Monty Berman (*The Saint*) and scripts by Terry Nation (*The Avengers*). The series quickly disappeared, although it spun off one feature film in 1968, *Mystery Island*, using the original TV cast.

Another series with connections to the shows of the 1950s, *Man of the World*, was seen only in England from 1962 to 1963 and starred the former Peter Gunn, Craig Stevens. Produced by Harry Fine, these twenty hour-long episodes featured the music of Henry Mancini, composer of the *Pink Panther* and *Peter Gunn* themes. The adventures of Mike Strait (Stevens) were billed as "the assignments of a freelance photographer-cum-journalist Mike Strait, a man with the world in his lens and his finger on the trigger" (Vahimhei 1997). His svelte sidekick Maggie (Tracy Reed) usually assisted Strait in locations from Indochina to the Amazon. Several episodes were re-edited into made-for-TV movies. One early story, "The Sentimental Agent," was spun off into another British series of that name. Thirteen episodes, of the spin-off were aired in 1963 and starred Carlos Thompson as an import-export specialist finding dangers related to his cargo à la Biff Baker.[1] Three episodes of this popular show were edited into a feature film, *Our Man in the Caribbean* (1962), featuring future spy girls Shirley Eaton and Diana Rigg (Lisanti and Paul 2001, 118). "Carlos's Theme" from *The Sentimental Agent* is available on CD.

In the fall of 1965, *The Mask of Janus* featured Richard Cadell (Dinsdale Landen) and Anthony Kelly (Simon Oates) as British agents during the Cold War. Retitled *Spies* in 1966, the show was distinguished by a Max Harris title track still available on CD. Produced by Terence Dudley, only four of the original eleven episodes still exist and none was ever broadcast in America. Similarly, recalling the premises of *The Man from Interpol*, in 1968 ATV/ITC offered *Department S* for British viewers. For twenty-eight episodes, Peter Wyngarde, Joel Fabiani, and Rosemary Nicols starred as talented troubleshooters for the fictional "Department S," the alleged elite Paris-based wing of Interpol, working on cases the parent organization couldn't solve. The dandified, hedonistic Jason King (Wyngarde) was a thriller writer who occasionally applied the modus operandi of his literary creation, Mark

Caine, to his own investigative work. His sidekicks were Stuart Sullivan (Fabiani) and Annabelle Hurst (Nicols), the latter resembling *The Avengers'* Tara King in style. She was the scientific brain using logic and computer printouts, a precursor to agent Dana Scully in *The X-Files* (Lisanti and Paul 2001, 230). Like *The Avengers*, their cases tended to be those too baffling or surreal for the conventional police force. Three years after the series demise, Peter Wyngarde returned to fly solo for twenty-six episodes as Jason King in a series considered far more pedestrian and mundane than its imaginative forebear (Vahimhei 1997). All episodes of both series exist, and some are available on U.K. VHS and DVD. (The theme for *Department S*, composed by *Saint* and *Secret Agent's* Edwin Astley, is available on CD.)

The Man Who Never Was (1966–1967) starred Robert Lansing, who had come to television prominence as Brigadier General Frank Savage, a character who'd died bravely in the WWII series, *12 O'Clock High*. Lansing's second series was also based on the World War II, *The Man Who Never Was* being the title of Ewen Montagu's 1953 account of an actual British intelligence operation in which the body of a homeless man was given a false identity and false papers telling the Germans the Allies were planning to invade Greece instead of their true target, Sicily. Beyond the title, however, nothing of the clever ruse carried over into the television series.

In the first episode of the Cold War–era show, American agent Peter Murphy (Lansing) was fleeing from enemy agents hot on his trail in East Berlin when he hid in a handy bar. There, he came across his exact lookalike, millionaire playboy Mark Wainright. Wainright, mistaken for Murphy, was killed. Murphy quickly assumed Wainright's identity, taking on his wealthy lifestyle as a perfect cover for his undercover work. Wainright's wife, Eva (Dana Wynter), knew he was an imposter but assisted him in his role to keep the family fortune from going to Wainright's grasping, suspicious half-brother, Roger (Alex Davion). Eva ultimately fell in love with Murphy, but Roger remained wary. The only other person to know of the ruse was Murphy's boss, Colonel Jack Forbes (Murray Hamilton).

Like other such programs, the glamorous locations were filmed in London, Athens, and other European cities. The show didn't last long, but Lansing went on to work in such series as *The Equalizer* in the 1980s.

In the final analysis, the 1960s spy boom is defined by the series explored in-depth in this book, and few subsequent efforts would ever again attempt to regain the glories of the World War II and early Cold War eras. Most 1960s imitators looked to each other for concepts and characters, and the two most scrutinized successes were *The Man from U.N.C.L.E.* and *The Avengers*, and two related series point to the problems of such imitation.

The team behind ABC's successful *Burke's Law* (1963–1966) thought they had several marvelous ideas. First, Richard Levinson and William Link took their clever series starring Gene Barry as a witty, womanizing Los Angeles chief of homicide noted for traveling in his trademark Rolls Royce limousine, and made him *Amos Burke, Secret Agent* in 1965. Originally, actor Dick Powell had introduced the Burke character in one episode of his *Dick Powell Show* in a mystery titled "Who Killed Julie Grier?" When the idea became a series for Barry, all his episodes had the "Who Killed . . ." in the title. But the switch from policeman to spy didn't work for the popular Amos Burke. Instead of Barry making aphorisms with his trademark catch phrase, "That's Burke's law," Burke reported to "The Man" (Carl Benton Reid) and tried to be Napoleon Solo. Or perhaps Jim West—the show's most noted villain popped up in the seventh episode, the ruthlessly sadistic Mr. Sin, played by the former Miguelito Loveless himself, Michael Dunn.

Gene Barry had come to prominence starring in TV's stylish *Bat Masterson* (1958–1961), a Western gunslinger known for his bowler hat, walking cane, and quick pistol. Converting his twentieth-century California detective into a spy, however, did nothing for Barry's reputation. According to Eric Barnouw, the series was an example of network programmers attempting to appease government watchdogs during the escalation of the Vietnam conflict. In one *Amos Burke* episode, for example, enemy agents of Sekor, Burke's archenemy, planned to paralyze Washington, D.C., by placing chemicals into gasoline that would spread into the air. Thus the White House, the State Department, and worse—Burke's Washington, D.C., based agency—would be neutralized (Barnouw 1990, 70). The unwitting carriers of this gas would be antiwar demonstrators. But "who killed Amos Burke" was no mystery—it was *I Spy* that clobbered its distant cousin in the ratings.

At the same time, Levinson and Link took note of the pre-Rigg success of Cathy Gale from *The Avengers* and decided to make a series with Honor Blackman in mind. Blackman's Pussy Galore fame made her even more attractive, but the actress wasn't available or interested in the new project. Looking around for a Blackman lookalike, Levinson and Link found Ann Francis and tried her out as Honey West in an April 1965 episode of *Burke's Law*. Based on the Honey West novels by Gloria and Forrest Fickling, the TV version featured one of the first female leads in small-screen action adventure (Lisanti and Paul 2001, 129).

At the time, Francis was a well-liked up-and-coming actress who had captured male attention in the SF classic *Forbidden Planet* (1956). Her Honey West was the daughter of a police officer who opened her own private detective agency. Her partner, Sam Bolt (John Erickson); her Cobra sports car; and her pet ocelot, Bruce the Cat, made for interesting visuals. Francis was not only reminiscent of Cathy Gale; the producers made even stronger Bond connections by giving her numerous gadgets. West had tear-gas earrings, garter-belt gas masks, immense sunglasses with two-way radio frames, a walkie-talkie in her compact, and a radio-transmitting lipstick.

Fifty thousand dollars was budgeted for her wardrobe, including a tiger-skin bathing suit with matching cape and an all-black ensemble consisting of leotards, boots, turtleneck shirt, and gloves (Lisanti and Paul 2001, 129). She was very much a West Coast version of an *Avengers* girl, although she relied more on looks, charm, and guile than martial arts. Unlike her British inspiration, a man invariably bailed West out in the last act. The stories enjoyed the humorous touch of writer Ken Kolb, who also scripted some of the better *Wild Wild West* adventures.

In her brief run, West disguised herself as a Gypsy, battled robots, and encountered a would-be Robin Hood in the California woods. She didn't last past the season, although Francis was nominated for an Emmy. Ironically, according to Francis, her series was canceled because ABC found it cheaper to purchase *The Avengers* rather than produce a series of its own (Lisanti and Paul 2001, 129). After the success of her film *Legally Blonde*, in August 2001 Miramax Studios announced plans to make a Honey West film starring Reese Witherspoon.

In 1972, Gene Barry made another attempt to recapture the style of Amos Burke in the syndicated ITV program *The Adventurer*. Like its sister Gerry Anderson project, Robert Vaughn's *The Protectors*, Barry's series exploited the marquee draw of star names with production values from the syndicated bargain basement (McNeil 1996). Barry played Jim Bradley, a multimillionaire who pretended to be an international film star in order to work on secret missions near film locations or pleasure resorts. Ex-*Fugitive* detective, Barry Morse, played his contact, Mr. Parminter, passing himself off as Bradley's producer-manager. Filmed in the south of France and England, the show was something of a throwback to the 1950s *The Falcon* series, which puzzled viewers who wondered how a character could be billed as "the famous secret agent." In the opinion of some, the similar premise of *The Adventurer* damned the twenty-six short episodes. How does one pretend to be a film star, Barry's ostensible cover? More likely, however, the series perished as the 1960s spy boom was waning, and the show couldn't survive despite theme music by Bond composer John Barry and production input by *Saint* producer Monty Berman.

Not all the also-rans were efforts in bad form. *Man in a Suitcase* was a 1967 to 1968 series about a former U.S. intelligence officer turned freelance investigator. McGill (Richard Bradford), working for $500 a day plus expenses, carried a suitcase with no more than a change of clothes and a gun. He'd been falsely accused of treason, and his quest was to track down the man who had betrayed him. The series became something of a cult classic based on its truth-versus-illusion themes similar to its SF-oriented sister project, *The Prisoner*.

The thirty hour-long shows aired from September 1967 to April 1968 in the U.K., and it was syndicated in the United States throughout the following year. Produced by Lew Grade's ITV Studios, this series especially benefited from the end of *Danger Man*'s run, as half its crew moved on to *The Prisoner*, and half worked on *Suitcase*, including line producer Sidney Cole. Dennis Spooner, responsible for *The Champions*, also created *Suitcase*. Ron Grainer's jazzy piano-driven title track was released as a single and is one of the most treasured collector's items for spy buffs. In 1967, one two-part episode, "Variation on a Million Bucks," was re-edited as a ninety-seven-minute TV movie, *To Chase a Million*. Videos of this film are rare, and they command high prices on the eBay auction website.

Before the 1960s boom busted, Alexander Mundy (Robert Wagner) became one of the earliest secret agents recruited from a life of crime as a jewel crook because government intelligence supervisor Noah Bain felt "it takes a thief," the name of Wagner's sanitized series from 1968 to 1970. In the pilot, "The Magnificent Thief," four agents of the SIA (the acronym's meaning was never specified) were killed trying to steal a case with potentially sensitive information. Noah Bain (Malachi Throne) proposed to his boss that they use a thief to make the heist because his regular agents hadn't been successful. Bain suggested that Mundy, the best thief Bain had ever seen, be paroled from prison to pull off the caper. During these discussions, Mundy was in San Jobel Prison planning an escape attempt. Then, Mundy learned of his parole and asked Bain incredulously, "Let me get this straight. You want me to steal?" Like many spies to follow, the deal was simple—steal for the government or go back to prison.

Thief producers Gene Coon (*Star Trek*, *The Wild Wild West*) and Glen Larson (*Battlestar Galactica*, *Buck Rogers*) admitted they borrowed much from *The Man from U.N.C.L.E.* and *Mission: Impossible*. For one thing, *U.N.C.L.E.*'s Dean Hargrove was the primary script consultant for the series, and, ironically, *Thief* premiered on ABC just a week before *U.N.C.L.E.* was taken off by NBC. Influences from *Mission: Impossible* were evident in the show's format and use of plot contrivances. For example, Mundy's talents were most often needed in impossible circumstances. In the first part of each episode, viewers saw Mundy plan his escapade, but were shown only enough to pique their interest. Then the caper was unfolded in a manner similar to *MI*'s format. Occasionally, the first part of the show involved a failed attempt, with success occurring after a second try. Action sequences were rare as the show focused on the suspense of the situation. In fan Ed Johlman's opinion, some of the best scenes followed Mundy, in total silence and with no soundtrack, as he stealthily made his way through the caper.[2]

It Takes a Thief had strong first and second seasons, but most viewers and critics felt the show declined in its third year after Malachi Throne left the show. In the first two seasons, Mundy was essentially under house arrest, with most of the character conflicts between Mundy and Bain. But this device was relaxed as new plots became hard to come by. According to Ed

Johlman, "There are only so many foreign nations with things that needed to be stolen and only so many ways to steal them." In a special coup, the series tried for new life by bringing in song-and-dance star Fred Astaire to play Mundy's con-artist father, Alistair Mundy, the master thief who taught Alexander all he knew. However, the chemistry between Astaire and Wagner didn't rival the duels between Wagner and Throne, so the series faded. Still, the plot device of converting criminals into agents became a contrivance used in later shows, from *La Femme Nikita* to *The Invisible Man* (the SciFi Channel's 2000 version, that is).

SUPERSPIES IN THE SKY AND WONDER WOMEN IN THE 1970s

For the most part, television secret agent shows in the 1970s updated older formats and concepts, leaning on new technologies for their premises. But the same efforts didn't employ the important characteristics that made many 1960s series special. In particular, few characters were memorable. Most 1970s secret agents were handsome and capable but had little personality. In addition, the sophisticated style of the past now seemed dated, yet there was nothing to replace it.

Ironically, *U.N.C.L.E.* creator Sam Rolfe himself participated in this trend with his *Delphi Bureau* (1972–1973). This series featured unconventional and reluctant agent Glenn Garth Gregory (Broadway actor Laurence Luckinbill) as a researcher with one weapon, his photographic memory. According to Rolfe, who thought *U.N.C.L.E.* was more a police drama than spy adventure, Gregory wasn't so much a spy as "a funny government investigator" (Magee 1986a, 12). Ostensibly doing research for the president, Gregory found himself on secret missions with only one government contact, a Washington, D.C., socialite named Sybil Van Loween (Ann Jeffreys played the role in the series after Celeste Holm played the character in the pilot). She always claimed she had "this little thing" for Gregory to do, which always ended up complicated and important. The pilot featured lines from a poem seen just before each commercial break, with the complete poem shown at the end of the episode. Don Medford, who helped with the U.N.C.L.E. pilot, directed this episode.

The *Delphi Bureau* was a hastily produced series that alternated with two other rotating adventure shows collectively called "The Men," which included *Assignment: Vienna*. Originally intended to be set in Munich, according to some sources, the *Assignment: Vienna*'s location was changed after the September 5, 1972, "Black September" attack at the Munich Olympics, in which PLO terrorists kidnapped and then murdered eleven Israeli athletes (McNeil 1996, 65). However, series star Robert Conrad claimed these events had nothing to do with the setting change. He recalled attending the Olympics while filming the series, and that the switch to Vienna was due to the romance of the Austrian capital. In a 2002 interview with me, Conrad said, "Munich sounds a bit Aryan to me . . . as opposed to Viennese beautiful waltz music, it's closeness to Strasbourg, it's a great city."

The pilot film, "Assignment: Munich," had starred film actor Roy Scheider, later of *Jaws* fame. As Scheider didn't wish to work in television, Conrad got the last minute nod and accepted the project because of its Vienna setting. The concept showed promise, crafted by some of the best writers for *Mission: Impossible*, including Jerry Ludwig. *MI* connections also included casting Lesley Ann Warren.

In the quickly revamped *Assignment: Vienna*, special agent Jake Webster (Conrad) worked in Vienna for U.S. intelligence under the cover as owner of Jake's Bar and Grill. According to Conrad, Webster was a very different character from James West. "The guy ran a joint, a club, was an agent." He was in the typical trap of Alexander Mundy and many subsequent spies. If he didn't work for the government, he'd go to jail. Charles Cioffi played Major Bernard Caldwell, Webster's primary contact, and Anton Diffring played Inspector Hoffman of the Austrian police. But, like *The Delphi Bureau*, Jake Webster quickly disappeared after eight episodes, despite its relatively high ratings. *Assignment: Vienna*, on its own, couldn't carry "The Men."

Conrad tried for secret agent success one last time in the much awaited *A Man Called Sloane* for Quinn Martin Productions. From 1979 to 1980, the gimmick of a giant African American assistant named Torque (Ji-Tu Cumbuka) with a mechanical hand didn't help the disco-flavored clothing and lazy acting of most of the guest stars and the lead himself as the impulsive Thomas Remington Sloane III, agent of UNIT. The show was a pastiche of such gimmicks from all over the spy map, with many nods in particular to *The Man from U.N.C.L.E.*

For example, UNIT's headquarters was hidden behind a toy store in the manner of *U.N.C.L.E.*'s Del Floria's Tailor Shop. Sloane's partner, Torque, was simply the villainous bodyguard Tee Hee from the Bond film *Live and Let Die* converted into a good guy, also tall, African American, and endowed with a deadly mechanical hand. More interesting than Conrad or Torque were the split skirts, nightgowns, and bathing suits of female guest stars like Morgan Fairchild and Edie Adams. Like *U.N.C.L.E.*, sexy women worked for Unit, against Unit, and for anyone else involved with Sloane. As Unit was apparently based in California—a wise move as most masterminds seemed to operate out of Los Angeles or San Francisco and were likely to threaten Nevada more so than the East Coast—Sloane was most often found in beauty salons, health spas, and hot tubs. Most episodes ended with Sloane finally getting a romantic moment with one of these women just as the Director (Dan O'Herlihy) or Torque tracked him down with a new assignment. Even Unit's computer, Effie, had a sexy disembodied voice prone to flirt with her favorite agent, despite the fact she was a "Series 3000 multifunction computer occupying twenty-seven square feet and weighing six and one-half tons." (Effie's voice was provided by actress Michelle Carey.)

The few notable male guests included Roddy McDowell and Robert Culp. Whereas most villains were agents of the THRUSH-like organization, The Cartel, McDowell enjoyed the hammiest of the bad guy roles, playing Manfred Baronoff in "The Night of the Wizard." This overt nod to *The Wild Wild West* featured McDowell doing his best to play a petulant, childish Miguelito Loveless impersonation in a story about exploding pellets and robots very reminiscent of Conrad's first secret agent show. (Peter Allen Fields, a scripter for the first season of *U.N.C.L.E.*, wrote this episode.) Other SF elements included a blue crystal that could enslave millions and microbes from Venus too hot to handle, even by The Cartel.

In a 2002 interview with me, Conrad admitted that, twenty-three years after the show's demise, he couldn't talk about it with a straight face. "It was silly, trite television." According to Conrad, the show was originally created to star young actor Robert Logan, "a surfer, a real good-looking kid who made a lot of family-oriented movies." After Logan completed the pilot, "Fred Silverman didn't particularly care for him in that role and he said 'Go get Conrad.'" The actor was wooed with a paycheck that made Conrad dub himself "the King of Second Choices" (referring to both his *Sloane* and *Assignment: Vienna* roles). He directed one of the twelve episodes ("Shanghai Syndrome") and admitted there was nothing to the Sloane character. "I was walking around looking real cute, I was kind of a James Bond television character. It was just sort of silly, I thought."

On March 5, 1981, the Robert Logan pilot was aired as a TV movie, *Death Ray 2000*, the new title chosen to distance the film from the long-canceled, low-rated series. Since then, it has been aired sporadically, usually on the USA Network.

In 1973, NBC launched the short-lived *Search*, featuring rotating leads Hugh Lockwood (Hugh O'Brian), Nick Bianco (Tony Franciosa), and Christopher R. Grover (Doug McClure). All worked for a Washington, D.C.-based organization called Probe (later changed to the World Security Organization) headed by V. C. R. Cameron (Burgess Meredith). These agents carried transmitters in their ears, implanted monitors under their skin, and cameras in rings and tiepins to keep in contact with the red-lighted computerized headquarters. Dr. Barnett (Ford Rainey) was the Q-like research director, providing all the marvels that meant the agents never had to track down leads, with rooms full of computer technicians doing the legwork for them. O'Brian starred in half the episodes; the other two leads plied their wares from time to time in the other half. Typical of such efforts, the format was more interesting than the mundane plots and rather ordinary adversaries.

COMIC BOOK SPIES

> Craig Sterling, Sharon Macready, and Richard Barrett—*The Champions*.
> Endowed with the qualities and skills of superhumans. Qualities and
> skills, both physical and mental, to the peak of human performance.
> Gifts given to them by the unknown race from the lost city of Tibet.
> Gifts that are a secret to be closely guarded. A secret that enables them
> to use their powers to their best advantage as the Champions of law,
> order, and justice as operators of the international agency of Nemesis.
> —Opening narration, *The Champions*, 1968

Taking the notion of superspies blessed with helpful technology to its next
logical step, a series of shows appeared that either put the modern wizardry inside the agents themselves or simply endowed superspies with powers taken right out of comic books. One show more popular in England than
in the United States, partly because its first American appearance was as
a 1968 summer replacement series on NBC, was *The Champions*. It was a
series that should have had a good shot, created by Monty Berman (*The
Saint*) and Dennis Spooner, a former *Avengers* scriptwriter. *Danger Man* creator Ralph Smart and *Avengers* producer Brian Clemens both contributed
scripts. Other *Avengers* alumni included writer Donald James and stunt coordinator Ray Austin, who served as second unit director for *The Champions*. Broadcast in England between September 1968 and April 1969, The
thirty episodes of *The Champions* were also distinguished by a memorable
theme tune by Tony Hatch, released as a single in both England and the
United States. In addition, the show featured incidental music by Edwin
Astley, the composer for *Department S*, *The Saint*, and *Secret Agent*.

In the beginning, two concepts were sandwiched together to create the
show. Dennis Spooner wanted a realistic secret agent series, and Monty
Berman wanted to employ metaphysical elements. To appease Spooner, the
powers granted the Champions were underplayed, resulting in confusion as
to why these special abilities were needed. To appeal to an international
audience, ITV asked one lead be an American, so Stuart Damon, who'd
starred with Lesley Ann Warren in the 1966 *Cinderella*, was cast as Craig
Sterling. Shooting for the series mostly took place on soundstages, although
some footage was drawn from travel documentaries and unused film footage. As a result, the pilot earned critical praise for its feature film look. As
the series progressed, however, budgetary constraints resulted in problems.
For example, because of the cost in building a submarine for one story, the
set was used again repeatedly, forcing *The Champions* to go underwater more
than any other such show (Phillips and Garcia 1996, 154).

In the pilot, three agents of the international law enforcement organization Nemesis escape from China after stealing a lethal bacteria. Flying in a
plane then shot down by the Chinese, they crashed into the mountains of

Tibet and nearly died. But pilot Craig Stirling (Damon), cryptographer Richard Barrett (William Gaunt) and biologist Sharron McReady (Alexandra Bastedo) were rescued by the secret ancient people of the Himalayas. They gave the agents special powers of extrasensory perception, telekinesis, and superstrength to become "the Champions of law, justice, and order." In each subsequent episode, a voice-over narrator briefly retold this story, and after *The Avengers*-like title scenes, one of the agents demonstrated an ability in a low-key situation. After these introductions, the chief of Geneva-based Nemesis, Tremayne (Anthony Nicholls), unaware of his agents' special gifts, sent them off to bring in evildoers. Nemesis was a small but powerful agency supported by all countries of the world but answerable to none, dedicated to preserving the balance of power. Thus, all missions were of international consequence, from assassinations to political turmoil to evil scientists. The Champions worked from Austria to Australia to the Antarctic.

Despite all the creative powers in the production team, *The Champions* was one of the driest series created for the genre. Despite the physical attractions of all three stars, none of the agents showed any personality. No character development or relationships were ever explored. Their powers were not especially visual, most often no more than expressions of concentration as the agents sent messages to each other via ESP. Taking on bad guys without matching abilities, these agents seemed the heirs of radio's one-dimensional costumeless heroes designed for children. Notable guest stars included Bernard Lee, M of the Bond series, as a dying general. After the series demise, the pilot and one episode, "Interrogation," were spliced together to create a TV movie, *The Legend of the Champions*. In decades to come, more viewers saw the series in spotty syndication than those who'd viewed the original broadcasts, especially in England.

> Steve Austin, astronaut. A man barely alive. Gentlemen, we can rebuild him. We have the technology. We have the capability to make the world's first bionic man. Steve Austin will be that man. Better than he was before. Better, stronger, faster.
> —Oscar Goldman's narration in the title credits for
> *The Six Million Dollar Man*

The Champions did however turn out to be slightly ahead of its time. In the 1970s, a wildly popular fad began with Lee Majors starring as former astronaut Steve Austin in ABC's *The Six Million Dollar Man*. In a decade where literal comic books began to upgrade their scripts and artwork to appeal to college readers, Steve Austin clearly was oriented for a younger audience. According to scriptwriter Alan Caillou, the show's genesis showed how television's creative process had changed from his days on *The Man from U.N.C.L.E.* In the 1960s, he turned in scripts and later discovered they were in production before he had a chance to ask if rewrites were needed. In

1972, he wrote the pilot for *The Six Million Dollar Man*, at first titled "Cyborg," and submitted it. Twenty-seven writers later, he got the revised script back for his approval. Only one line of his dialogue remained. That's the sort of committee writing, he told *Starlog* magazine in 1998, that drains off the creativity television used to enjoy (Weaver 1988, 76–83).

According to Eric Barnouw, this shift in the creative process reflected sponsors' desires to shape TV programming to appeal to specific audience demographics. High ratings no longer mattered. The long-running *Red Skelton Show* and *Gunsmoke* were canceled despite consistent high ratings, as new advertising surveys showed such programs appealed to rural, older audiences, not the young consumers commercials were geared for. Therefore, series like *The Six Million Dollar Man*, *Happy Days*, *Laverne and Shirley*, and *Charlie's Angels* were designed to appeal to young women who were buying cosmetics, toiletries, processed foods, soft drinks, and drugstore candies (Barnouw 1990, 471). During the 1970s, no network was as successful in these goals as ABC, the network of *The Six Million Dollar Man*.

In the beginning, the concept was based on Martin Caidin's novel, *Cyborg*, which provided many of the character names and ideas for the show. Oscar Goldman was based on an unnamed real-life mentor, and Dr. Rudy Wells was based on a real-life bionics expert with that name, the real Wells reportedly flattered by his portrayal on television. The first producers, Kenneth Johnson and Leonard Siegal, wanted to cast actor Monty Markum as a Bondian character, but the nod went to the more athletic Lee Majors, an ex-football star who would look good in the physical, slow-motion scenes showcasing the bionic man's superpowers. Majors had a bit of a TV track record, having played major roles in the Western *The Big Valley* and the legal drama, *Owen Marshall*. (Markum later played the "seven million dollar man" in two episodes, Austin's psychologically troubled archnemesis.) No one thought much of Majors's acting, including Majors himself. When he negotiated his contracts, he joked if not for his TV roles, he'd be coaching high school football somewhere.

The concept was first tried out as two ninety-minute movies produced by Glen Larson, who made the films with a Bondian flair in mind, surrounding the suave, sophisticated Steve Austin with beautiful women. Michael Sloan, later the producer for *The Return of the Man from U.N.C.L.E.* and *The Equalizer*, was given credit for the two scripts, the first film starring Martin Landau, the second Robert Lansing. The movies didn't get much viewer response, so producer Harve Bennett was called in to see if he could resuscitate the project in the same way he had reenergized the *Star Trek* franchise with the second feature film, *The Wrath of Khan*. He noticed Majors walking in one scene with a match in his teeth, and decided to remold the character as a Gary Cooper Western hero. In this incarnation, Steve Austin was a man of few words—which suited Majors's desire for minimal dialogue—

a modest, patriotic man in the midst of high-tech gadgetry (Phillips and Garcia 1996, 344).

The early adventures explained how, after a testing accident, pilot Austin became an atomic-powered half-man, half-machine cyborg. In a secret government lab, he was rebuilt with bionic legs, a bionic arm, and a superpowered eye. He became an agent for the OSI (Office of Scientific Information) headed by Oscar Goldman (Richard Anderson). For all his improvements, however, *The Six Million Dollar Man* nearly died off a second time in his first year. ABC was so unhappy with its entire Friday-night lineup that it canceled all its shows airing that night, including Austin's adventures. But ABC was equally unhappy with the new pilots offered by other producers, so the network moved the show to Sunday nights, where it became an instant hit.

From 1974 to 1978, Austin fought terrorists, spies, fellow bionic men, and extraterrestrials. As *Get Smart* had tapped into the talents of comedians for its guest stars, *The Six Million Dollar Man* drew its guests from figures representing mainstream Americana. These included Cathy Rigby, football star Larry Csonka, announcer Frank Gifford, and personalities like Sonny Bono, Stephanie Powers, and Greg Morris. One popular character, "Bigfoot," was first played by wrestler André the Giant and later by Addams Family star Ted Cassidy. The series gained valuable publicity when frequent guest star Farrah Fawcett married Majors and became a celebrity in her own right on *Charlie's Angels*.

The show also benefited from being a Universal Studios production. As *U.N.C.L.E.* creators explored MGM's back lots for location sets, the creators of the bionic adventures looked over similar Universal stages and developed scripts based on existing sets. But as time progressed and ratings faltered, the show clearly needed changes. By the third year, ABC knew it had to attract adult viewers, so humor became an important ingredient. Austin was seen mowing his lawn bionically. He fell on his butt when pulling up tree stumps. More important, the producers decided to give him a love interest and created Jaime Sommers, a bionic woman (Phillips and Garcia 1996, 346).

At first, Kenneth Johnson and Harve Bennett intended Jaime Sommers to be a temporary character. Ex-tennis pro Sommers, played by TV newcomer Lindsay Wagner, was romantically involved with Austin, and the two were engaged to be married. After her own bionic upgradings, she suffered a skydiving accident that led to her death. After this episode, Universal was inundated with telegrams protesting the "tragedy." A noted psychologist told them children were shaken by such deaths, and it was cruel to introduce a perfect role model for women only to kill her off (Phillips and Garcia 1996, 64). Immediately, plans were made to bring her back, and the story line had her put in cryogenic suspended animation. When she recovered, she had amnesia and had forgotten her attraction for Austin. Thus, viewers could sympathize with Austin for his unrequited love, admire his stoic self-sacrifice as he held back his affections, and become engaged in the new soap opera as the two slowly started all over again.

After her return, Sommers was given her own series, *The Bionic Woman*, although Wagner had to be cajoled into taking the role. She was more interested in films than television. The producers considered various replacements, including Sally Fields and Stephanie Powers. But Bennett wanted Wagner, as she conveyed a sense of physical competitiveness unlike other actresses. To get her, Bennett had to offer a salary that made Wagner became the highest paid woman in a dramatic series. Despite the money, she was unhappy at having to play the role, and Majors worried that the spin-off would detract from his own series. To appease him, Majors was given a percentage of *Bionic Woman*. Other rivalries sprang up as the spin-off was allowed to film its episodes in seven days, the original limited to six. Despite such behind-the-scenes misgivings, the two series complemented each other, both enjoying the benefits of crossover stories. For a time, *The Six Million Dollar Man* was number one in the ratings and *The Bionic Woman* was number three.

In her show, Sommers too had two bionic legs and one bionic arm, but her hearing was atomic-powered, not her sight. For her cover, she was taken off the tennis court and made a schoolteacher on an air force base. This allowed for comic moments, as when Sommers overheard conversations in the back of the classroom. As her parents were long deceased, she lived in Ojai, California, with Austin's parents (Martha Scott and Ford Rainey). In addition, she had a bionic boy hanging around with Max, the bionic dog who was afraid of fire. He could outrun bicycles and chew up rifle barrels. Sommers worked undercover as a nun, a lady wrestler, a roller derby queen, and battled the "Fembots of Las Vegas," adversaries borrowed from *U.N.C.L.E.* According to Robert Fulton, one standout three-part adventure, "On The Run," was a "splendid spoof of *The Prisoner* . . . in which she resigned and was sent to a special camp for ex-agents" (Fulton). Looking after her physical, technological, psychological, and potential romantic needs was Rudy Wells (Martin E. Brooks). Taking another page from *U.N.C.L.E.*, in which two series starred the same chief, Richard Anderson played the role of Oscar Goldman on both *The Bionic Woman* and *The Six Million Dollar Man*.

Because the series leads had very different personalities, each show came to have distinct characteristics. Whereas Austin was quiet and reserved, Sommers was more emotional, and Wagner fought for better relationships and scripts. *Bionic Woman* tended to be more dramatic than action adventure, playing down her bionic abilities in favor of stories addressing more social issues, notably pacifism (Phillips and Garcia 1996, 45). In the opinion of some viewers, she was less kitschy than characters on *Wonder Woman* or *Charlie's Angels*, as she wore no superhero costume and was rarely seen in bikinis or short skirts (Douglas 1993, 212). A reward for such concerns was Wagner's winning an Emmy as best actress for the episode "Mirror Image."

This emphasis on realism included limits placed on Sommers's abilities. She could leap to a second floor, not the third, and could turn over a car, but not lift a truck. The show's most famous special effect was Sommers's bionic leaps, a stunt filmed by having a stuntwoman jump backward onto an airbag. But despite the fact that the show came in at number fourteen after its first season, to everyone's surprise, ABC inexplicably canceled the show.

NBC quickly picked up the program, but changes had to be made. Most obviously, crossovers were no longer possible, so the romantic subplot between Austin and Sommers was dropped. For another season, the dramatic adventures continued featuring guest stars like Andy Griffith, Stephanie Powers, and world-famous daredevil Evil Knievel, who played himself. Long-time Miss America announcer Bert Parks appeared in one beauty pageant episode. Recurring guest Melinda Fee earned screen credit before moving over to a sister show, *The Invisible Man*. Helen Hunt, later to become one of the most successful actresses in Hollywood, claimed she wished she could burn the tapes of her *Bionic Woman* appearance. For one year, Richard Anderson had the distinction of being the first actor to play the same character simultaneously on different networks.

But the second season didn't fare well, so Wagner asked for a final episode to be written with some commentary, ending with a mission Jaime Sommers refused to accept. Wagner, tired of her series, and Sommers, tired of being a reluctant secret agent, mirrored each other's concerns. In the grand finale, the government, angry at her refusal, tried to frame her for murder, tried to shoot hypodermics into her, tried to kidnap her, drugged her dog, and fired Oscar Goldman. Despite all this, the script added a coda having Sommers agree to do one more mission, leaving the door open for sequels.

Meanwhile, the last season of *The Six Million Dollar Man* almost didn't get off the ground. Majors, too, was tired of his role. The producers looked around for replacements and considered Gil Gerard and Bruce Jenner. Even Harrison Ford did a screen test before he was signed to *Star Wars*, but was deemed unsuitable for action adventure. Majors returned for one more season of SF adventures, including one in which he worked on the dark side of the moon. Although most of these episodes were broadcast in England, one story about an Irish terrorist group, "Outrage," was only seen in southern England before being banned (Fulton). In 1979, both bionic programs were unplugged.

The bionic couple returned in a series of TV movies beginning with NBC's *The Return of the Six Million Dollar Man and the Bionic Woman* (1987) and *Bionic*

Showdown: The Six Million Dollar Man and the Bionic Woman (1989). The series concluded with *Bionic Ever Afterward* (1994) on CBS, in which Sommers was infected with a computer virus. With the final film, the bionic couple had appeared on all three major networks. In 2001, the voice of Oscar Goldman returned with his opening narration to the original show backed with *The Six Million Dollar Man* theme now used to sell Chevy Trailblazer trucks built to be stronger and faster. We have the technology.

During its heyday, *The Six Million Dollar Man* was one of the most influential shows on television. In May 1975, NBC aired a ninety-minute movie starring David McCallum as *The Invisible Man,* a scientist named Daniel Westin working for a West Coast think tank called the Klae Corporation. Researching molecular reduction and transformation in laser experiments, Westin discovered the secret of invisibility. After using himself as a guinea pig, Westin learned the process had one major flaw: visibility could occur at any time without advance warning.

In the adult-oriented pilot, Westin was idealistic and naive, becoming horrified when his discovery was financed and controlled by the military. Destroying his lab, Westin went underground but ultimately agreed to work as a secret agent with his wife, Dr. Kate Westin (Melinda Fee) in exchange for the Klae Corporation's agreement to help him find a cure for his condition. In the pilot, Walter Carlson (Jackie Cooper), the head of the sinister Klae Corporation, provided Westin with gloves and a special mask of his old face so both viewers and cast members could see Westin when not on duty.

The film was a ratings success, so that fall twelve episodes followed. Despite a pilot written by Steven Bochco, a premise with promise was eroded by the network's desire to emulate Steve Austin. At first, according to McCallum, the idea of the character was total fantasy, a fusion of Superman, *Mission: Impossible*, and Claude Rains (the first movie Invisible Man). Later, he said he'd signed on to play the Fugitive and ended up playing Topper (Scott 1975). To make the series lighter than the film, Jackie Cooper was replaced by father-figure Craig Stevens, who gave the Klae Corporation a more benevolent flair than in Bochco's concept. According to Fee, "The pilot was geared more to the lurking Feds scrambling to steal the formula of invisibility. It had the proverbial car chase, ending in a huge crash-and-burn sequence. The series centered on the relationship of Daniel and Kate" (Phillips and Garcia 1996, 156).

There was no lack of talent in the creative team—the show even boasted a theme by legendary composer Henry Mancini. Craig Stevens was a popular actor, the former TV detective *Peter Gunn*. Newcomer Fee was excited by her role, later claiming Kate Westin came along about the same time as women's liberation. "She represented what women were striving for, separate professions, equality, recognition of intelligence and education" (Phillips and Garcia 1996, 156).

But most U.N.C.L.E. fans, seeing a new vehicle for McCallum at last, found the attempt a missed opportunity. From the beginning, producers Bochco, Harve Bennett, Leslie Stevens, and Robert O'Neill admitted they were imitating The Six Million Dollar Man. As a result, more effort went into the gimmicks than the characters or stories. Fee's most difficult job was playing to an invisible husband, which at that time wasn't as easy as it would become in subsequent decades thanks to improved special effects. Shooting a simple scene in which a hypodermic needle was passed from hand to hand could take half a day to film. It was difficult for an unseen agent to express emotion. And to let viewers know where he was, the invisible man bumped into pots and furniture so often, he seemed the clumsiest man on earth.

Ironically, like U.N.C.L.E. before it, the show quickly fell into comedy, only in a considerably shorter time. According to Robert O'Neill, "The Invisible Man was really a one-joke show. The minute you've taken the wrapping off his head, you've seen the joke" (Scott 1975). Creator Harve Bennett had a different take. "By today's standards it was very crude, but in 1975 it allowed us tremendous opportunities. It was a very noble experiment, and I'm very proud of the series" (Phillips and Garcia 1996, 156).

Some of the less satisfactory outings included McCallum going undercover for a cleaning woman, and one effort had him held in a small town by a corrupt sheriff for bogus traffic violations. The nadir of the series was one episode titled "Pin Money," which featured bank robbers with Frankenstein monster masks. The writer, James Parriott, admitted he was asked to write the script in the mold of the Six Million Dollar Man.

In this climate of overall silliness, commentators were reduced to speculating about the sexual possibilities for the couple. As the invisible man had to be naked to be unseen, he was often shivering and complained about freezing in public. Twenty-five years later, one fan recalled an episode in which Westin rode on a bicycle through a town, no doubt a most uncomfortable experience. One odd controversy arose when representatives from America's Bible Belt in the Midwest complained that the show was obscene because it featured a naked, if unseen, man on TV. Writers tried to build sympathy for the characters by having Fee forced to seduce enemies as her husband looked on.

For most observers, the format simply didn't jell, and some attempted to lay the blame on McCallum. Harve Bennett noted networks were still uneasy about British leads on American television, and some felt McCallum was better suited to a supporting "color" character like Illya Kuryakin rather than a straight lead. Most believed the Tuesday-night timeslot was McCallum's number one adversary, as MTM's double-shot of Rhoda and Phyllis were ratings champions. Whatever the case, the show enjoyed great popularity in Europe, especially England, where the ratings soared after the cancellation.

Although this incarnation of the premise quickly disappeared, NBC thought enough of the concept to try it again the following year in the *Gemini Man*. The same production team, headed by Harve Bennett and Leslie Stevens, created and cast the show, even using unused *Invisible Man* scripts. The network said it wanted more humor and physical action adventure than had been evident in the McCallum series, so actor Ben Murphy, star of the 1971 to 1973 Western hit, *Alias Smith and Jones*, was cast as Sam Casey.

In this attempt, Casey was an agent of the government think tank and operations center Intersect, a group specializing in secret missions. On a diving assignment, Casey was affected by the radiation in an underwater explosion. The resulting invisibility could only be controlled by the combined efforts of computer technician Abbey Lawrence (Katherine Crawford) and the no-nonsense boss of Intersect, Leonard Driscoll (William Sylvester). They gave Casey a watchlike device that kept him visible, which he could turn off for short periods of time. If he exceeded 15 minutes in any twenty-four-hour period, he would die. The series lasted slightly longer, one month.

By all accounts, Murphy wasn't the actor McCallum was, but perhaps more important, the scripts were rip-offs of the network's bionic series. A case in point was one script about the agent undergoing plastic surgery, an idea that had been revamped from a plot already used in *The Bionic Woman*. As it happened, *The Bionic Woman*'s plastic surgery episode was rerun the same week as *The Gemini Man*'s retelling of the plot, drawing angry fire from viewers who felt their intelligence had been insulted. Before the series vanished, it offered one interesting moment when the invisible Casey leaped into a railway sleeping car with actress Kim Basinger.

But before the supercharged spy fad fizzled completely, ABC tapped into DC Comics and revamped World War II heroine *Wonder Woman*. The first attempt occurred in a 1974 TV movie that badly miscast blond-haired Cathy Lee Crosby, who neither resembled the comic book Amazon from Paradise Island nor wore the world-famous outfit of red, white, and blue. In 1976, the same year *The Bionic Woman* and *Charlie's Angels* debuted, Warner Brothers producer Douglas Cramer gave the concept a second try, this time going for a campy approach similar to the 1960s *Batman* series, including a *Batman*-like bouncing theme song by Charles Fox. *The New, Original Adventures of Wonder Woman* sent poster queen Lynda Carter, a 1973 Miss USA beauty pageant winner, after Nazi agents and space aliens with her invisible plane, her rope that compelled those wrapped in it to tell the truth, and her bullet-bouncing bracelets.

In the pilot, Major Steve Trevor (Lyle Waggoner) was on a secret mission and crash-landed on Paradise Island, the hidden refuge of the ancient Amazons who mistrusted men and forbade them from their stronghold.

Learning of the Nazi threat worldwide, the Queen held a competition to see which Amazon would go into the world of men to help in the cause. Her daughter, Diana, was the clear champion. Taking on the secret identity of Diana Prince (like Clark Kent, her only disguise was her thick, horn-rimmed eyeglasses), Diana joined Major Trevor to help quash the Japanese and Germans in the 1940s. In following adventures, Prince would disappear into a private place, spin in circles, and a gold flash exploded around her. Suddenly, viewers saw Wonder Woman garbed in a gold-braided satin bustier, star-studded blue satin short-shorts, and her red knee-high satin high-heeled boots. As it happened, Steve Trevor was a character taken from the comics, but his TV personality, such as it was, was crafted especially for Lyle Waggoner, who asked the producers to develop the role for him after the cancellation of *The Carol Burnett Show*, on which he'd been a stock player.

One year later, *Wonder Woman* and her secret-identity alter ego moved to NBC and forward in time to the 1970s as an agent for I.A.D.C. (Inter-Agency Defense Command). The producers decided present-day settings would open up story possibilities that would appeal to a generation that didn't remember World War II. James Bond might seem ageless, but the Amazon from Paradise Island was centuries old, so there were no problems for her to survive WWII into the 1970s without a single crow's foot. However, her leading man, Steve Trevor, couldn't do likewise, so his son, Steve Trevor Jr. (also Lyle Waggoner) was Prince's supervisor in the second incarnation, after he too crash-landed on her home island. Like his father, he never suspected his Girl Friday was also his agency's best secret weapon.

By 1979, this trend ran its course and new directions replaced this light-hearted genre. One short-lived 1970s offering owed much more to the popularity of TV detectives than fictional espionage. In yet another spy series called *Hunter,* this one airing in 1977, the title character (James Franciscus) was a former bookstore owner who was now a government agent. His partner was Marty Shaw (Linda Evans), and they reported to a general named Baker (Ralph Bellamy). Airing Friday nights at 10:00 on CBS, the hour spy drama lasted about three months.

THE OTHER SIDE OF THE COIN

> Our battles are not fought at the ends of parachutes. Our battles are won in drab and dreary offices in Westminster.
> —Neil Bernside in *The Sandbaggers*

During the 1970s, *The New Avengers, The Return of The Saint, The Professionals,* and other British imports attempted to make names for themselves on traditional networks, and each were clearly products of their time. Others were harbingers of things to come in the 1980s. For example, from 1978 to 1979, Yorkshire Television produced *The Sandbaggers*, a commercial effort that would have been an appropriate addition to any PBS station's lineup. No other American network at that time would have touched a series that occasionally showed blood coming from murdered agents or blamed the FBI for the assassinations of John F. Kennedy and Martin Luther King Jr. Writer Ian Macintosh's seventeen scripts for producer Michael Ferguson emphasized the behind-the-scenes planning in offices more so than featuring action in the field. A measure of *The Sandbaggers*'s quality was that, in August 2001, it joined the American DVD market in a series of three boxed sets, despite the fact few Americans had either seen or heard of the show.

Beginning with the opening moments of its first episode, "First Principles," with London bureaucrats boarding buses for their morning commute, *The Sandbaggers* was clearly a series more about administrative and political intelligence decision making than personal, physical danger for secret agents. Former Sandbagger Neil Burnside (Roy Marsden) led this small (two to four agents) team of highly experienced S.I.S. (Secret Intelligence Service) operatives, while steering his way through intelligent, well-spoken, but often ambitious diplomats and politicians. Unlike le Carré's jaundiced portrayal of shadow governments, *The Sandbaggers* cast a measure of favorable light on those involved in espionage, although not without its own criticism of the secret world.

For example, Burnside represented those who felt intelligence operations should be run by those experienced in the field, not civil servants with personal agendas. His most dominant characteristic was his wariness and caution about putting his "Sandbaggers" in harm's way if he couldn't see a worthy reason for their sacrifice. The Sandbaggers were to be called upon only in special circumstances, notably those with political sensitivity. The qualities of such agents were so high level that it could take Burnside eight months to find suitable replacements. They spent most of their time, as Burnside put it, in "months of boredom, moments of panic." Burnside saw the intelligence business as "more cloak than dagger" and once noted eighteen months could go by without his agents needing to be armed in the field.

This is not to say the series lacked the drama or danger of international espionage. As the series progressed, most Sandbaggers died in the trenches, leaving Sandbagger One, Willie Caine (Ray Lonnen) the recurring voice of resentment and independence, while being known as the best field agent in the business. Like John Drake, Caine despised violence and avoided romantic entanglements. An ex-paratrooper trained in incursion and infiltration, Caine was Burnside's number two and often debated the morality and choices of his superiors. He was the agent most often dropped behind enemy lines, sent out to retrieve defectors, or kill enemy agents anywhere in the world.

The series thus had a noticeable dimension of believability, characterized by its frequent use of administrative abbreviations. (This usage was so prevalent the DVD versions include a glossary of terms to assist new viewers.) The low-key but fast-paced and earnest tone of the ongoing story lines had an almost documentary feel, as no incidental music punched up the action or added unnecessary poignancy to the rise and fall of relationships in the Secret Intelligence Service. On one hand, Burnside had to determine the validity of covert actions weighed against political consequences. In other cases, he advocated for special operations when he had little evidence to prompt such actions. In some instances, Burnside simply didn't have the staff to fulfill expectations and fortunately had a good relationship with the CIA who often worked well with his team.

Although Burnside fought for better pay for his team, he was never queasy about using dirty tricks to retain his agents, as in one episode in which he hounded the girlfriend of an agent who was hoping to quit the service. In another story, Burnside insisted his group would never fall into the world of assassination and violence seen in the American CIA. But by episode's end, temptation has taken hold, when he plotted the death of a potential prime minister known to be a KGB agent.

Like Len Deighton's later Bernard Sampson stories, Burnside was forced to work with family members deeply ensconced in the intelligence community, notably his sophisticated ex-father-in-law, Sir Geoffery Wellingham (Alan MacNaughtan), a friend of the prime minister. In one very Deighton-like adventure set in East Berlin, Burnside was forced to set up the murder of his own lover, Laura Dickens (Diane Keen), the only female Sandbagger, to preserve the "Special Relationship" between the S.I.S. and the CIA. Adding depth to this tragedy was the level of involvement Burnside had with Dickens during the four episodes before the climactic moment. The following episode, set exactly twelve months later, showed a Burnside so reluctant to send Sandbaggers out into the field that his most frequent phrase was "No more dead Sandbaggers."

According to Mike Vincitore, *The Sandbaggers* consisted of three series totaling twenty episodes, primarily by the show's creator and principal writer, Ian Mackintosh. Mackintosh, like Ian Fleming, had been a lieutenant commander in the British Royal Navy, with an intelligence background (Vincitore 1994). He'd written the first sixteen episodes and the twentieth, when, in July 1979, he and his girlfriend were lost in a light aircraft over the Gulf of Alaska after sending a distress signal. No traces were ever discovered. Other writers penned three additional episodes, but these scripts, although filmed, were not considered promising enough to persuade the producers to continue the series. It aired twice in the U.K. and appeared on some PBS stations up until 1992 (Vincitore 1994).

While Burnside's battles with budgets and bureaucracy were rarely transplanted to American television, such concerns had much to do with espionage in the 1980s. With the inauguration of President Ronald Reagan, high-flying exploits gave way to issues and story lines more domestic, grounded, and a far cry from the superspies of the 1970s. In the spy revivals of the 1980s, the contexts and tones of both American and British products had little to do with Steve Austin. Whereas new offerings would be fewer in number, the quality of TV espionage in the 1980s would be a step above the bionic, invisible, and supercharged agents that quickly disappeared from the small screen, even in syndication.

CHAPTER 12

Reagan, le Carré, Clancy, Cynicism, and Cable: Down to Earth in the 1980s and 1990s

MORALITY PLAYS

> I can't let you do it. It's a tough world out there, and there's all kinds of people who need help, all the time. And we've got our own world, our own little shadow world. You can't just walk away from it.
> —"Control" to Robert McCall in the pilot of *The Equalizer*, 1985

In 1971, Roger Moore began the decade as Lord Brett Sinclair in *The Persuaders*. He ended the 1970s with his fourth James Bond opus, *Moonraker* (1979). In 1978, the rebirth of old TV friends began on American television with the return of John Steed in *The New Avengers* and *The Return of The Saint* in the same year. In 1979, four years after a *Wild Wild West* imitator, William Shatner's *Barbary Coast*, sank without a trace, the first of two *WWW* reunions was aired as a TV movie. But the spy revival began in earnest in the 1980s with the return of Maxwell Smart and the men from U.N.C.L.E. in made-for-TV and feature films. *Mission: Impossible* and *The Saint* briefly returned as new television series. Accompanying these reunions was the burst of publications, comics, and videos in a new market for fictional espionage. Even Sean Connery returned as 007 in *Never Say Never Again* (1983).

Beyond the nostalgia for old spies, however, American network television showed little interest in creating new secret agents. One likely reason was that newscasts in both the 1970s and 1980s were filled with ongoing revelations of misdeeds in the actual intelligence community. New public awareness of such activities discouraged networks from seeking heroes in a realm that fostered more controversy than respect. In what some called a "stagnant fog of conflict" between the superpowers, the media dubbed 1985 "The Year of the Spy," when a series of news stories seemed to blend into one long espionage soap opera (Richelson 1995, 390).

More important, perhaps, according to Todd Gitlin, TV network executives looked to the 1980 election of Ronald Reagan as an indication that the country was moving to the right, and thus programming should reflect this trend (Gitlin 1983, 231). Feeling the United States would be more anti-foreign and more protectionist in the new era, in the spring of 1980 new CBS vice president Scott M. Zieglar commissioned a pilot script for a series to be called *The CIA* (Gitlin 1983, 221). Zieglar ordered a pilot by Sam Rolfe to be called "Quarrel" about an American spy tripped up by a Soviet mole. Neither project bore fruit, as other executives believed a return to basic values didn't include espionage duplicity. Simultaneously, just as political forces had pressured radio broadcasters to reflect isolationist ideology before World War II, similar political pressures were brought to bear on CBS in 1980, when Republicans feared *Hawaii Five-O* plots about nuclear bombs might fuel the "anti-nuke" movement of the era and adversely affect that year's presidential election. After the election, Reagan sought massive build-ups in military spending, most notably his Strategic Defense Initiative, dubbed "Star Wars." According to Susan Douglas, such thinking quickly permeated television advertising, notably for women's cosmetics. Suddenly, facial creams were now weapons described as protective barriers, shields, and delivery systems, employing anti-aging agents "presumably trained by the CIA to terminate wrinkles with extreme prejudice" (Douglas 1993, 260).

In this climate, network television moved from camp and spoof to more domestic, down-to-earth spy adventures. But, unlike decades before or since, the offerings were fewer, although some series, notably *Scarecrow and Mrs. King*, *The Equalizer*, and *MacGyver*, enjoyed longer stays on network television than many of their espionage-oriented cousins. Such shows featured characters who renounced or questioned the activities of covert operations. Most stayed close to home bases rather than doing much globe-trotting. Antiviolence groups had a noticeable impact on network programming, as seen in the new breed of Westerns in which heroes stayed out of saloons and instead lived in the Little House on the Prairie and were tended by Dr. Quinn, Medicine Woman. With the exception of *The A-Team*, which appealed to youngsters largely because of the colorful casting of Mr. T as a Mohawk-haired streetwise rebel, the TV spies of the 1980s didn't make much of an impression on popular culture. By and large, the 1980s were a time for reunions and revivals and not for kindling many new flames in the secret agent universe.

Ironically, the first TV offering was born in the ashes of one failed *Man from U.N.C.L.E.* movie. In 1980, writer-producer Danny Biederman and Oscar-winning special effects artist Robert Short had approached MGM with a proposal for a new *U.N.C.L.E.* feature film. Signed on to the project were series alumni Robert Vaughn, David McCallum, composer Gerald Fried, and cinematographer Fred Koenekamp. *U.N.C.L.E.* creator Sam Rolfe supported the project (Sabo 2000). In the treatment, Laura Antonelli was slated to play Serena, a character brought back from the original series. Bond veterans Jane Seymour and designer Ken Adams were scheduled to participate. However, MGM dropped the feature film idea saying that, despite the interest in the new *Star Trek: The Motion Picture*, the men from U.N.C.L.E. couldn't compete with James Bond. Biederman's script was then considered for a TV film, but Michael Sloan's team won the contract instead.

MGM producer Leonard Goldberg read the U.N.C.L.E. script and liked the idea. He hired Biederman and cowriter Robert Short to work on his new series, *Gavilan*. In this 1982 to 1983 NBC outing, Robert Gavilan (Robert Urich) played a semicynical ex-CIA operative who now worked as an inventor and consultant for the De Witt Oceanography Institute. Specializing in underwater rescue operations, Gavilan found himself working in the very covert world he had tried to escape. Marion "Jaws" Jaworski (Kate Reid), dean of the institute, liked her employee, but was bothered by his tendency to get involved with despots, international agents, and beautiful women. Adding to the star power of the series, former Avenger Patrick Macnee played the conniving travel agent and sometime actor Milo Bentley who shared Gavilan's Malibu beach house and his adventures.

According to Biederman, the show was based more on Urich's personality than any nods to past series. However, one episode he cowrote "had inside references to both *U.N.C.L.E.* and *The Avengers*. With Patrick Macnee in the series, it behooved me to make references to *The Avengers*. The title of the episode was 'The Proteus Affair,' and I'm sure you can see an *U.N.C.L.E.* connection right there. Macnee replaced the ailing Fernando Lamas as Gavilan's house guest."[1] But little viewer interest surfaced, so *Gavilan* was the first series canceled in March 1983.

HITS AND MISSES

> I feel like I was lying and sneaking.
> You are lying and sneaking. You're working for the government.
> —Amanda King and "Scarecrow"

In 1983, *Scarecrow and Mrs. King* took the concept, popularized by *The Man from U.N.C.L.E.*, of an innocent being dragged into the secret world to a new level. In the first episode of this popular series created by Eugenie Ross-Lemming and Brad Buckner, government agent Lee Stetson, codenamed "Scarecrow" (Bruce Boxleitner), was under pursuit by enemy agents. He handed a package to Amanda King (Kate Jackson, formerly of *Charlie's*

Angels), a recently divorced housewife. After they met and he recovered the package, Mrs. King decided she liked the thrill of playing a part-time unofficial agent.

The show's main strength in its early years was its balancing of the deadly world of Stetson and the domestic innocence of King, with both dramatic and humorous tones. But the series was far from a throwback to the 1960s. Although Scarecrow, like John Steed, was a professional with an amateurish partner, nothing beyond this superficial similarity connected the series to *The Avengers*. Stetson was the eight-year veteran professional; King was the raspy-voiced intuitive enthusiast who saw through deceptions because of her ability to judge character. Stetson was a world-class womanizer with four black books filled with names and addresses of his romantic contacts. King spent hours listening to agency tapes learning spycraft, while her mother and children bustled around her asking unanswerable questions about her studies. Unlike Emma Peel, King was the worst shot known on the firing range. Naturally, her inquisitive nature led her into situations forcing Scarecrow to bail her out of danger.

Unlike *U.N.C.L.E.*, *Scarecrow and Mrs. King*, filmed in Washington, D.C., kept close to home. Little of the international intrigue typically associated with the spy genre was ever evident. The emphasis was more on the innocent, day-to-day life of suburbia. The show only went on exotic locations for season finales or sweeps weeks outings (Brooks and Marsh 1999, 892). But, like *U.N.C.L.E.*, Scarecrow's mysterious organization was housed in a secret underground headquarters where secretaries placed special badges on guests and agents when they entered. Scarecrow's "Mr. Waverly" was an African American supervisor, William Melrose (Mel Stewart). On the other side of the street, Beverly Garland played Amanda's mother, a prize-winning cook. By the final season, King was no longer innocent and was a trainee for full-time work. Stetson and King married in February 1987, ending the series before it would presumably become "Mr. and Mrs. Scarecrow."

Similarly, from December 1983 to April 1984, ABC's *Masquerade* mixed *Mission: Impossible* with *U.N.C.L.E.* in a Glen Larson creation. This short-lived effort centered around NIA (National Intelligence Agency) agent Lavender (Rod Taylor). In the premiere episode, Lavender's archenemy at the KGB (Oliver Reed) identified all of NIA's agents and killed them off. In response, as in *Scarecrow and Mrs. King*, Lavender took *U.N.C.L.E.*'s notion of employing innocents a step further and specifically targeted American tourists, asking them to act as part-time agents. In a concept taken out of actual 1950s anti-Communist government schemes, Lavender's idea was that Americans abroad would be patriotic enough to serve their country and, as they were unknown to any enemy, would be excellent agents. They could perform specific tasks without costly training. To assist him, Lavender brought along two professional rookies, Danny (Greg Evigan) and Casey (Kirstie Alley). William Read Woodfield, one of the principal architects of

Mission: Impossible, was a script consultant for the show. Although the series concept certainly reflected the conservative values the networks thought Americans wanted, the only contribution *Masquerade* made to TV history was providing Kirstie Alley a screen credit to her resume before she joined the cast of *Cheers*.

MISFIT SPIES

> In 1972, a crack commando unit was sent to prison by a military court for a crime they didn't commit. These men promptly escaped from a maximum-security stockade to the Los Angeles underground. Today, still wanted by the government, they survive as soldiers of fortune. If you have a problem, if no one else can help, and if you can find them, maybe you can hire The A-Team.
> —Opening narration to *The A-Team*, 1983

In 1983, *The A-Team* was also introduced, a show turning the concepts of *Mission: Impossible* upside down. From 1983-1987, Jim Phelps was remolded into Col. John "Hannibal" Smith (George Peppard), and Templeton "Faceman" Peck (Dirk Benedict) was the inheritor of the acting wiles of Rollin Hand. Willy Armitage was updated into Sargent Bosco "B.A." Baracus (Mr. T). B.A. not only out-toughed anyone else on television, sporting his trademark Mohawk haircut and gold chains, he created the most memorable catch-phrase of the decade, "I pity the fool." He was also the team's Barney Collier, building machine guns out of washing machines, rocket launchers out of used water heaters, and an armored truck from a broken-down school bus. Other eccentric characters came and went, including Dwight Schultz as "Howling Mad" Murdock.

Unlike the cerebral *Mission: Impossible*, for 128 episodes, the A-Team were masters of weekly demolition derbies (Brooks and Marsh 1999, 5). At first they were soldiers of fortune for hire, but after plummeting ratings, the A-Team became secret agents after General Hunt Stockwell (Robert Vaughn) caught up with them and put them in the obligatory vise of many other media spies—work for me or go to jail. (See discussion of Vaughn in *The A-Team* in Chapter 2). Very popular in its early years, *The A-Team* was the only NBC series to crack Nielsen's top twenty in the 1982 to 1983 season.

In the spring of 1984, CBS offered *Airwolf*, a series partly created by *Invisible Man* veterans James Parriott and Alan J. Levi. *Airwolf* was a high-tech attack helicopter that outraced conventional jets at the speed of sound. It could travel halfway around the world carrying an array of fourteen weapons systems. In its two-hour opener, the machine's sadistic creator stole *Airwolf* and delivered it to Mu'ammar al-Gadhafi in Libya, one of the rogue nations then acceptable as a villainous enemy in network television. The scientist used *Airwolf* to fight the French in Chad and then sank a U.S. destroyer in a scene later echoed in an actual terrorist attack on the U.S.S. *Cole* in 2000.

The Firm, a nebulous secret agency, recruited reclusive pilot Stringfellow Hawke (Jan-Michael Vincent) to get *Airwolf* back. Hawke was a psychologically damaged warrior who had lost a childhood love in a boating accident and his brother in Vietnam. Hawke believed he was doomed to be able to return from missions unscathed while others paid the ultimate sacrifice with their lives. He refused a million dollar bounty to recover the copter, but instead insisted the government find his brother or his remains in Vietnam. After recovering *Airwolf*, Hawke refused to return it until the Firm provided him with hard evidence of his brother's condition. He struck a bargain, promising to do missions for the Firm while they continued to try to meet his demand. Each week, Hawke took *Airwolf* out of its southwestern desert hideaway to retrieve agents, defectors, stolen technology, or to rescue children held captive by the Russians.

Much of the show's success was due to its character-driven drama rather than high-tech special effects overkill. For example, Hawke enjoyed Impressionist art, played the cello, and loved animals. Women found this handsome, uncommunicative, and insolent loner fascinating. But he kept aloof, feeling relationships led only to pain and death. Hawke's contact at the Firm was the suave, mysterious Michael Archangel (Alex Cord), who wore a white suit, eye patch, and carried a cane. He sympathized with Hawke's feelings about his brother and worried the Firm was less likely to meet its promises than Hawke was his. The pilot's sensible, middle-aged war buddy, Dominic Santini (Ernest Borgnine), was Hawke's most reliable assistant. Dominic both helped fly *Airwolf* and played undercover roles he disliked, such as a janitor on a military base. Various Firm agents, notably beautiful women like Marella (Deborah Pratt), also assisted in undercover operations. (Pratt was married to series creator Donald Bellisario).

In 1987, CBS dropped the series, but it was quickly picked up by the USA Network in its bid to expand its action-adventure lineup. To meet the budgetary constraints of cable television, the show's production moved to Canada and *Airwolf*'s cast was completely changed. In the story line, Dominic was killed and Stringfellow badly injured when one of their regular helicopters, sabotaged by foreign agents, exploded. A talented but hard-to-control young agent, Major Mike Rivers (Geraint Wyn Davies), took *Airwolf* on a mission to rescue Stringfellow's brother, Saint John Hawke (Barry Van Dyke). After his rescue, Saint John took over for his injured brother as head of the *Airwolf* team. Other new team members included Dominic's niece, Jo Santini (Michele Scarabelli), and Jason Locke (Anthony Sherwood), the new government liaison. They still hid the *Airwolf* from the Firm (now called "the Company"), but were willing to use it on assignments of their choosing. Either because of or due to these changes, *Airwolf* was quickly grounded on USA, but the series retained a syndication afterlife into 2001 on TV Land's afternoon and weekend lineup.

In September 1984, Glen Larson's *Cover Up*, a clear update of *I Spy*, debuted on CBS. In the series, Dani (Jennifer O'Neill) was a fashion photographer who had been married to a government agent. Mac (John-Erik Hexum), her primary model, was a former Green Beret who'd served in Vietnam and was an expert in karate, chemical interrogation, and foreign languages. In their first team-up, they avenged the death of Dani's husband for the mysterious organization headed by Henry Towler (Richard Anderson), who loosely supervised the pair. In subsequent adventures, they traveled the world and helped out Americans who conveniently were having difficulties near sexy fashion shoots.

The series suffered a tragic turn when, on October 12, 1984, the twenty-six-year-old Hexum accidentally shot himself in the head on the set while playing around with a loaded prop gun. After his heart was used in a transplant, Anderson read a tribute to the actor on the air. In November, Australian Anthony Hamilton took on the male-model role as Jack Stryker. The CBS run ended in 1985, but *Cover Up* enjoyed a syndicated afternoon rebirth in the early 1990s on the Lifetime Network.

In January 1985, NBC trotted out *Code Name: Foxfire*, another derivative series about a trio of female agents taking orders from a male boss à la *Charlie's Angels*. Advertisements for the series were not subtle about the obvious connections: "These are the hottest team of hellcats since you-know-who." Connections to *Mission: Impossible* were also evident. Liz "Foxfire" Towne (Joanna Cassidy) was the female version of Jim Phelps, a former CIA agent who formed the team to take on special assignments for the United States. She'd served four years in prison for a crime she hadn't committed, and she was keenly interested in tracking down her former lover who had set up her imprisonment when he abandoned her in Bogota. Maggie "the Cat" Bryan (Sheryl Lee Ralph), a reformed thief from Detroit, was the combat expert and safe cracker. Danny "the Driver" O'Toole (Robin Johnson) was the team's version of Willy Armitage, the transportation expert and a resourceful, streetwise former New York hansom cab driver. Larry Hutchins (John McCook) was the president's brother who gave them their missions. He'd been the one who sprung Towne from jail to create a counterespionage team reporting directly to him.

In a *TV Guide* interview, Ralph tried to downplay the *Charlie's Angels* aspects, claiming *Foxfire* was more believable and down to earth. According to Ralph, this team could be elegant and sophisticated, but they could also be tough and hard-nosed, unlike the more glamour-oriented Angels (Brooks and Marsh 1999, 170). Others saw the series as using overt rip-offs of James Bond movie shenanigans. But most viewers didn't notice any aspects one way or the other. After the two-hour pilot, the show lasted six weeks.

An updated approach to the retired agent theme was *The Equalizer*, which ran on CBS for four seasons (1985–1989). For British viewers, the series was largely a reworking of the Thames Production *Callan* (1967–1973), an English series that had also starred Edward Woodward as a world-weary spy with a conscience. Described by Woodward as a "working class spy," David Callan had been an agent with a license to kill for a secret section of British intelligence specializing in bribery, blackmail, frame-ups, and assassinations. Killing was Callan's main calling card, and he suffered emotional and moral wounds for his work. He was brooding, solitary, and had few friends save for petty crook Lonely (Russell Hunter). His one hobby was collecting toy soldiers. He tended to rebel and argue with his bosses, but showed compassion and concern during his assignments. The series was popular in Britain, spinning off a theatrical film, *Callan* (1974), and a television special, *Web Job* (1981).

Produced by Michael Sloan (*The Return of the Man from U.N.C.L.E.*), *The Equalizer* seemingly dealt with a Callan-like character ten years later. *The Equalizer* was also clearly inspired by another British television hit, *Man in a Suitcase*. Like *Suitcase* and *Callan*, the very successful *Equalizer* featured a former cold-blooded assassin, Robert McCall (Woodward), who regretted his former career in the CIA. He felt espionage was "a dirty little game that no one ever won." Not surprisingly, reviewers easily equated McCall with John le Carré's George Smiley, who shared these views. (As it happened, le Carré was one of Woodward's favorite authors.)

After becoming the first agent to find a way to retire from the agency, McCall sought to atone for his past by becoming an "equalizer" who worked free of charge for the weak and innocent. As a result of this characterization, the series was also often compared with Sam Rolfe's Western outing, *Have Gun, Will Travel*, in which Paladin (Richard Boone) advertised his services with the show's title on calling cards. Similarly, McCall placed ads in New York newspapers alerting victims to his willingness to work for justice: "Got a problem? Odds against you? Call the Equalizer."

Typically, McCall took on situations conventional law enforcement wouldn't or couldn't address. In many episodes, McCall worked on two cases simultaneously. In one, he helped individuals with personal problems like stopping stalkers or assisting a young man fighting bullies. Simultaneously, he took on adversaries who posed more widespread threats to New York or the nation. In these story lines, he battled blackmailers with classified access to congresspeople and the Pentagon or helped the daughter of a former agent defect. He was often assisted by African American soul mates Steven Williams as Lieutenant Jefferson Burnett and Ron O'Neil as Lieutenant Isadore Smalls. The ex-Man That Never Was, Robert Lansing, played Control, McCall's former supervisor who attempted to pressure McCall into staying inside the agency. At first, Control labeled McCall a dangerous rogue elephant. But by the end of the first episode, Control grudgingly told his former colleague he'd been down-graded to Condition Yellow—dangerous but tolerable. McCall agreed to help the agency out from time to time, and Control agreed to provide backup for McCall when appropriate.

Looking for their Equalizer, producers of the show wanted an actor who could convey a sense of muted violence, a volcano waiting to be tapped.[2] Originally seeking a James Coburn-type (*Our Man Flint*), CBS executives wanted the Equalizer to have Coburn's laconic delivery, grace of movement, and catlike sensuality. In this light, actor Ben Gazzara was the front-runner for the role. But Sloan, a lover of *Callan* during his youth in England, wanted Woodward despite CBS's desire for an American rather than British personality. But Woodward, who looked like an unlikely physical enforcer, had starred in the successful film, *Breaker Morant*, and was given the nod after the insulting request from CBS that he read for a screen test. Woodward agreed, seeing an appalling anger in McCall, a man filled with bitterness about the life of a secret agent. Sounding very much like Neil Burnside in *The Sandbaggers*, Woodward thought such agents spent months sitting around a desk catching up on paperwork. Suddenly, they're in the middle of Nicaragua involved in mayhem and carnage, a situation unbalancing to the mind. In one interview, he claimed he based his role on one line from *Romeo and Juliet*: "A plague on both your houses."

The first episode aired September 18, 1985, but a full season hadn't yet been shot. For the first season, CBS seemed uncertain about the show's future, moving its time slot, preempting it for other programming, and ordering new episodes almost at the last minute. Precariously close to cancellation at the end of the season, *The Equalizer* picked up in summer reruns. To attract new viewers in the second year, the character was further developed. Often surrounded by friends and family, McCall demonstrated a change in television's perspective of the now more domesticated lone wolf, deemphasizing the independence of characters such as McGill and Simon Templar. Like other private detectives of the era, McCall was as much social worker as crime fighter, more personally involved with his cases and the conditions that seemingly entrap all innocents. Viewers saw McCall's interaction with his violin-playing teenaged son Scott (William Zabka) and saw McCall dating, although with a pronounced effort to give him love interests close to his own age (fifty-seven in the first year), and not the younger women prevalent in other series. (In one poll, Woodward was found "the sexiest man in television.") Employing Woodward's musical talents, McCall was often seen playing the piano to give his character a dimension of moodiness and introspection.

When Woodward suffered a heart attack in 1987, several new characters were brought in to fill the void, including Harley Gage (Richard Jordan) and Manhattan café owner Pete O'Phelan (Maureen Andermen), both former federal colleagues in the spy business. After winning one Golden Globe for *The Equalizer*, Woodward later rejoined the TV spy universe as "Flavius" Jones, the unscrupulous father of La Femme Nikita.

ABC's MacGyver (1985–1992) was another contribution to family-oriented television, with occasional nods to the spy genre. This creative effort, with a pilot written by *Mission: Impossible* and *Assignment: Vienna* veteran Jerry Ludwig, starred Richard Dean Anderson as agent Angus MacGyver, although his first name was kept secret. Anderson came to the role when casting directors noticed he was unafraid to use his glasses during his audition. His manner showed a lack of pretension that the creative team wanted in their lead. Anderson's MacGyver, allegedly born in Minnesota in January 1951, was claimed to be a former Special Forces member. As MacGyver had refused to carry a gun since the death of a childhood friend, this military service seemed doubtful. Still, he became an agent for DXS (Department of External Services), occasionally reporting to Peter Thornton (Dana Elcar), Director of Operations. More often, MacGyver worked for the Phoenix Foundation as a troubleshooter and as a freelance private investigator.

For 144 episodes, a distinctive motif of the show was the use of "MacGyverisms." In each adventure, MacGyver, an imaginative and innovative expert in chemistry and physics, created simple uses for ordinary items to create escape mechanisms and bombs. He used paper clips to disarm missiles and hotwire cars, plugged a sulfuric acid leak with milk chocolate, repaired a fuse with a gum wrapper, duct-taped a map to a hot air balloon to stop a leak, and placed magnets in his shoes to screw up a roulette table. A newspaper, cotton, engine fuel, and fertilizer made a useful bomb. A newspaper, magnifying glass, and watch crystal worked as a telescope. Whereas most secret agents relied on high-tech gadgetry, MacGyver only carried his Swiss Army knife and duct tape. Aware that children imitated MacGyver and tried to build his simple devices at home, the creative team made a point of leaving out crucial elements in their memorable gimmicks, working to establish a nonviolent mood for the series.

Writers like Rick Drew based such ideas on what items they found on location, along with concepts from scientific advisers John Koivula, Jim Green, and ex-FBI agent and Watergate-burglar-turned-actor G. Gordon Liddy. Another writer of note was Dave Ketchum, the former Agent 13 on *Get Smart*. This staff looked to real events for story inspirations, as in the episode in which riding crops contained ultrasonic devices used to confuse racehorses. Designed to appeal to younger audiences, story lines and character development employed a didactic, moralizing tone. One stereotypical episode had MacGyver aiding an aging Native American who was trying to preserve the values of the old ways as trophy hunters ransacked a sacred site. In another, two contemporary issues were fused in a plot involving a psychologically damaged Vietnam vet fighting mob-related toxic waste dumpers. This series enjoyed a long life on ABC, in reruns on the USA Network, and in many foreign countries. One fan website is based in the Netherlands. Anderson also starred in and coproduced two *MacGyver* television movies filmed in London. *MacGyver: Lost Treasure of Atlantis* and *MacGyver: Trail to Doomsday* both aired in 1994.

PBS/BBC SPIES

> So far as I can ever remember of my youth, I chose the secret road because it seemed to lead straightest and furthest towards my country's goal. The enemy in those days was someone we could point at and read about in the papers. Today, all I know is that I have learned to interpret the whole of life in terms of conspiracy. That is the sword I have lived by and as I look around me I see it as the sword I shall die by as well. These people terrify me but I am one of them.
>
> —(George Smiley in John le Carré's
> *The Honorable School Boy*, 1978, 233)

As with the classic series of the 1960s, many British TV spies of the 1980s were quite different from their Hollywood counterparts. In particular, it can be said that British novelist John le Carré's George Smiley, reserved, meticulous, dumpy, eyeglass-polishing, and nonviolent, is the BBC/PBS spy. Le Carré's world of shadow governments and suspicious double-dealings within intelligence organizations can also be seen as the precursor to many shows with similar themes such as *The Equalizer*, *The X-Files*, and *La Femme Nikita*.

In his seventeen novels from 1961 to the present, le Carré has been credited with rescuing espionage thrillers from the romance of Fleming. Unlike Fleming and the "Clubland" authors, le Carré's "circus" worldwide organization of spies didn't reflect high morals or singular purpose but was instead a perverted, corrupt family. Le Carré stated that his creative desire was to be credible, not authentic, using the "furniture of espionage" to deal with the literary themes of doubts, paranoia, morality, honor, and decency in murky circumstances (Hoffman 2001, 41–43). For him, the "metaphysical secret world" addresses the universals of real life, as in the conspiratorial relationships people have with spouses and employers.

Tinker, Tailor, Soldier, Spy (1974) was the first novel of the famous "Search for Karla" trilogy. In 1979, the September to October television adaptation made actor Sir Alec Guinness synonymous with George Smiley in the highly accredited BBC miniseries, broadcast on American Public Broadcasting in 1980. It was le Carré's choice to use television for this complex tale, feeling that a movie would be too restrictive. Seven fifty-minute episodes allowed the complex yarn to develop and retain the flavor of the numerous characters and episodes required to flesh out the plot. Reportedly, le Carré liked Arthur Hopcraft's restructuring of the story line to make the narrative clearer for TV viewers (Gianakos 1987).

Its sequel, the six-part *Smiley's People* (which was published in 1980) became in 1982 another critically acclaimed television success for Guinness. Le Carré was so happy with Guinness's acting in *Tinker* that he had the actor in mind when he wrote *Smiley's People*, bringing some of Guinness's insights regarding the role into the follow-up novel. In a 1996 profile of Guinness, le Carré warmly praised the actor and recalled watching him prepare for the role of Smiley:

> After lunch with Sir Maurice Oldfield, a retired head of the British Secret Service, who was not Smiley but resembled him, Alec hastened out into the street to watch him walk away. The clumsy cuff links and the poorly rolled-up umbrella were added to Smiley's properties chest from then on. Watching him putting on an identity is like watching a man set out on a mission into enemy territory. (Guinness 1996 i–ii)

A non-Smiley project, *The Perfect Spy* (1986), was televised in 1987 in the same BBC fashion, with another teleplay by Arthur Hopcraft. It starred Peter Egan as Magnus Pym, the sympathetic monster who betrays friends, family, and his country. Le Carré's second novel, *A Murder of Quality* (1962) was filmed for television in 1991. More an intellectual mystery than spy drama, this George Smiley (Denholm Elliott) uncovered clues at a boys' school where sexual misconduct and British snobbery lead to murder. In 1992, the film was nominated for an Edgar Allan Poe Award for best television feature or miniseries. In 2003, both Guinness series were finally released on video.

Le Carré wasn't the only British author to address such themes, and other English TV projects combined espionage with critiques of Great Britain's class system. One example was Dennis Potter's 1971 British TV play, *Traitor*. Later, Potter's *The Blade on the Feather* aired in England as part of a London Weekend Television trilogy in 1980, starring Tom Conti and Donald Pleasence. Like le Carré's BBC miniseries, *Feather* aired on American PBS stations, but on an ad hoc basis. In 1989, it was released in America on video, retitled *Deep Cover*.

The British class system and spies of England's past were also of recurring interest to playwright Alan Bennett, as in his *The Englishman Abroad*, which aired on PBS's *Great Performances* in April 1984. Bennett's TV movie cast Alan Bates as actual exiled British spy Guy Burgess, using comedy and memories of those who knew him to humanize a defector who saw himself as a Marxist simply wanting his home country to change. In this hour-long teleplay, the Englishness of Burgess led some reviewers to complain that being vulgar was apparently worse than being a traitor, and that charm seemed to be laudable even for pitiful characters. Still, the project earned thirteen international awards and a British best acting award for Bates. In June 1992, Bennett's study of fellow Cambridge alumnus Sir Anthony Blunt (Tony Alexander) was the subject of *A Question of Attribution*, which explored the traitor's relationship with the Queen (Mary Alexander). While video versions of Bennett's television dramas are rare, the two scripts were collected in one volume, *Single Spies*, which is now used in classrooms.

From January 19 to April 5, 1984, PBS's *Mystery* series aired the twelve-part "Reilly: Ace of Spies," based on facts and legends about Russian-born British secret agent Sidney Reilly. Drawing from the Book *Ace of Spies* by Robin Bruce Lockhart and produced by Chris Burt, the series starred Sam Neill, Jeananne Crowley, and *Prisoner* veteran Leo McKern. Dramatizing the career of the principal British intelligence agent in St. Petersburg during the first decades of the twentieth century, the series joined a host of books on the man and his myth, which purported he was the best spy that ever was. In this account, the agent attracted the notice of Soviet dictator Vladimir Lenin (Kenneth Cranham) and his successor, Josef Stalin (David Burke). According to Vincent Price's introduction to another *Mystery* outing, the "Adventures of Sherlock Holmes," the fictional detective's ingenuity and ability to completely size up situations influenced Reilly. Reilly was reported to have been an expert assassin with eleven passports and a wife to go with each, but the truth is both less certain and certainly less fanciful (Richelson 1995, 12). Still, the miniseries about him was well made and a worthy addition to the spy genre on its own merits.

In the 1960s, when Bond coproducer Harry Saltzman looked for a new project, he turned to the character of Harry Palmer in the Len Deighton novels and produced a successful trilogy starring Michael Caine. These included *The Ipcress File*, *Funeral in Berlin*, and *The Billion Dollar Brain*. Two decades later, Deighton's connections to television began with his Bernard Samson books, which featured a British spy involved in ongoing Cold War family dramas in trilogies beginning with *Berlin Game* (1984), *Mexico Set* (1984), and *London Match* (1985). For television, these books became the 1988 thirteen-part miniseries, *Game, Set, and Match*, directed by Patrick Lau. Ian Holm played Bernard Samson, and Mel Martin played Fiona, Sampson's wife, who spends years behind enemy lines as a high-level double agent. Amanda Donohoe was Gloria Kent, Bernard's love interest while his wife abandoned her family to tend to the cause of Queen and country.

The changing roles of secret agents and the growing importance of cable channels were also evident in two further Harry Palmer films, *Bullets to Beijing* (1995) and *Midnight in St. Petersburg* (1995), again starring Michael Caine. Although it is uncertain how much Deighton was involved in these projects, the films, ostensibly made-for-TV projects, were first seen in America in 1997 on the American Movie Channel and later on the Mystery Channel. However, they were in fact productions first aimed at theatrical release and were seen in Canadian and Russian cinemas in 1995. But Disney

Productions felt Harry Palmer couldn't compete against the new James Bond epic *Goldeneye*, the new *Mission: Impossible*, and the new *Saint* starring Val Kilmer. For one thing, the new Harry Palmer films were not high-tech, special-effects-driven stories. Instead, Michael Caine's laconic character was very unlike Bond and was showing signs of age. The action was slow paced, the characters gritty, and plot twists, not computer effects, drove the dramas.

In *Bullets to Beijing*, the once reluctant spy is forced into early retirement as part of post–Cold War downsizing. As in *The Equalizer* and *Man in a Suitcase* before him, Palmer became a freelance agent taking on projects for hire. In *Bullets*, Palmer is in Russia, but emulating the comic premise of TV's *Spy Game*, the enemies are the new Russian mafia, populated by ex-KGB agents battling ex-CIA operatives. Another character showing the contrasts between generations was the son of a female Russian agent and a British spy he had never met, possibly Palmer himself, played by Jason Connery, Sean's son.

Caine and Connery returned in *Midnight in St. Petersburg*, a televised sequel to *Bullets*, in which freelance Harry Palmer and Associates are open for business. As with other such efforts, the protagonists are old spies now without jobs or country, exploring what such agents can do with skills and techniques no longer valued in their nation's service. In this tastefully done drama, Palmer is now a permanent resident in the new Russia. He helped out a major Russian art museum and stopped a load of radioactive plutonium from leaving the country. No longer the irreverent, rebellious agent, Palmer has become the father figure for his younger associates, including his own Russian employees.

Another take on the independent agent in the post–Cold War era was the CBS drama *The Exile*, which had two runs, the first from 1991 to 1993. It reappeared from 1993 to 1995 as part of the network's late night adventure shows ("Crime Time after Prime Time"), competing against the talk shows on other channels. Jeffrey Meek played Jon Stone, a DCS U.S. intelligence officer thinking he's going home with the end of the Cold War. But an unknown fellow agent framed him for murder, so two ostensible friends, one in the American embassy and one with French security, fake his death and give him a new identity, John Phillips. Emulating the 1950s series, *Foreign Intrigue*, the Paris-based exile performed undercover work for his friends and sought out the traitor who had framed him. In the end, it was his American embassy buddy who did the dirty deed. In 1995, Stone finally went home as a hero.

But all the rules changed, in literature, the large screen, and television with the rise of novelist Tom Clancy. His arch-hero, Jack Ryan, may have been compared to James Bond both within and outside of the books themselves, but this character was fresh and new on a variety of levels. For one thing, Jack Ryan's values were never uncertain. He reflected Clancy's own deeply conservative perspectives, especially his fondness and support of military thinking and purpose. Not surprisingly, as John F. Kennedy had enjoyed Ian Fleming, President Ronald Reagan praised Clancy's first novel, *Hunt for Red October*, which became a successful 1990 film starring Alec Baldwin and Sean Connery. Ryan's concerns were both domestic and professional, seeking a balance between home life and the calls of the nation.

Partly due to creative differences Clancy had with film producers, the novelist turned to television, designing new projects with the small screen in mind. In 1995 with collaborator Steve Pieczenik, Clancy created a new four-hour miniseries for ABC, *Tom Clancy's Ops Center*, which yielded a highly successful stream of new novels based on the concept. Directed by Lewis Teague, the cast of the television version featured Harry Hamlin, Wilford Brimley, and Rod Steiger. *Ops Center* focused on international dilemmas mirroring domestic difficulties for highly specialized team of crisis management analysts and agents.

In 1998 Clancy and Pieczenik created another four-hour miniseries for ABC, *Net Force*, which was a specialized stand-alone FBI unit organized to combat online espionage and terrorism. Set in the year 2010, this project starred Scott Bakula as Alex Michaels, the new chief of the group. Costars included Joanna Going, Kris Kristofferson, Brian Dennehy, and Judge Reinhold. The SF flavor of the series, notably Kristofferson as a hologram downloaded from a sophisticated home page, brought together many elements more associated with romantic than realistic espionage. As of 2003, this miniseries was the last of small screen adaptations of Clancy's world, although, like *Ops Center*, *Net Force* became a new vehicle for a series of novels that featured spy adventure, romantic twists and turns, and the home lives of both agents and their teenage offspring. In the foreword to one sequel, *Hidden Agendas* (1999), the authors praised the producers of the original miniseries, along with "the brilliant screenwriter and director Rob Lieberman, and all the good people at ABC." Presumably, this note indicated good feelings from Clancy regarding his TV projects, and perhaps others may be produced in the future.

This ongoing interest of placing spies in home-based settings returned to network TV in *Under Cover* (1991), a series clearly aware of Clancy's influence in the modern realm of secret agents. In *Under Cover* (not to be confused with the 2001 series of the same name), a husband and wife team, Dylan and Kate Del'Amico (Anthony John Denison and Linda Purl), balanced professional obligations and globe-trotting for the NIA with domestic day-to-day circumstances, including children in their Washington, D.C., home. Very unlike the lighter and far more romantic settings in *Scarecrow and Mrs. King*, the NIA was clearly intended to be a fictional representation of the CIA, with the officers seen embroiled in office discussions and bureaucratic flare-ups as often as fieldwork. In a clear shift of sexual roles, Kate is reactivated after ten years in office work, and Dylan is seen deferring to her judgment when she is in charge of missions. The two spouses worry about each other in the field and are portrayed as nurturing parental figures for young agents on their first assignments. Viewers saw the Del'Amico's' relaxing after dinner with old friend and fellow agent Flynn (John Rhys-Davies). Rhys-Davies played the hard-edged field operative who paused between assignments to sing bass in spontaneous, poignant sing-alongs of old rock songs with his colleagues in their kitchen.

Choosing plot lines close to headlines, however, made ABC uneasy. In January 1991, one episode seemed too close for comfort. In that two-part adventure, Iraq planned to bomb Israel with a missile loaded with a virus. But the actual Iraq War broke out the same month, and the nonstop coverage on CNN showed a series of SCUD missiles being fired on Israel from Iraq, although without the deadly chemicals in the *Under Cover* story. A key moment in the final scenes was the sacrifice of one agent on his first mission who must keep a telemetry signal open to guide a U.S. missile to his location. A prolonged radio dialogue between this agent and his Washington contacts tragically dramatized the human cost in covert and overt war.

Because of the sensitive nature of this program in the midst of hostilities, the network held back broadcast of the episode until the war was over, and made the two-parter a TV movie retitled *Before the Storm*. Despite the above-average and cinematic quality of this effort, including feature-film-worthy music and camera work, the realism of this series was too much for ABC. The network quickly canceled the well done and thoughtful effort.

Since 1995, another series owing much to the popularity of Tom Clancy has been *JAG*, primarily a fusion of courtroom drama with military settings, characters, and story lines with a positive spin on military personnel and objectives. However, series lead Commander Harmon Rabb (David James Elliott), a lawyer with the Judge Advocate General Corps of the U.S. Navy, often butted heads with CIA deputy director of counter intelligence Clayton Webb (Steven Culp). In his many guest appearances since 1997, Webb was both adversary and aid to Rabb, a continual deceiver usually showing up when the CIA needed help. Still, when Rabb searched for his father in Russia, Webb was indispensable, as he was when Rabb needed assistance getting his half-brother, Sergei, out of prison. In one of their many debates, Webb was upset that Rabb had become involved in a CIA operation, but the lawyer responded Webb should have clued him in sooner instead of "playing the Man from U.N.C.L.E." Similarly, in a February 2002 espionage drama, Rabb uncovered a Webb operation in naval security but learned secrecy was vital in spite of Rabb's desire to clear a friend's name.

Not all of *JAG*'s espionage-oriented dramas involved Webb, as in one episode in which Rabb defended an admiral in charge of navy intelligence's "Psychic Spy" program. In one very Clancyesque drama, Rabb left the courtroom to help track down an overzealous security officer who had stolen a submarine and threatened to destroy the Statue of Liberty. In one adventure, Rabb helped U.S. citizens sneak out of Cuba, and in another, he helped prevent an assassination plot against Russia's Boris Yeltsin. In early episodes, the Chinese captured and tortured Rabb with mind-altering drugs, and Rabb helped track down a North Korean spy on a navy ship harboring dangerous new technology. *JAG* aired new episodes on CBS and in nightly reruns on USA into the spring of 2003 and seemed destined for continuation. Its May 2002 season finale made the show's connections to Tom Clancy overt. In the two-part episode about a rogue Russian submarine commander, one JAG colleague referred to himself as Jack Ryan in a nod to *Hunt for Red October*.

Most American-produced spy shows of the 1980s, and the above examples from the 1990s, demonstrated that a new era of conservatism had resulted in a new branch of TV spies. Many such series emphasized family relationships, questions about the aftermath of the Cold War, and a deep sense of cynicism regarding U.S. government intelligence activities. One subgenre of this trend was Tom Clancy's theme of patriotic values without the worries about undue government misdeeds. However, in the last decade of the century, the more fantasy- and escapist-oriented TV series tended to retain cynicism to the extreme in shows like *The X-Files*, *VR.5*, and *La Femme Nikita*, which brought science fiction back into the secret agent realm. More important, perhaps, this fresh hybrid came to prominence on new cable stations rather than the traditional networks. In the 1990s, fantasy returned in force to television's secret agent genre, but such shows were quite different from their forebears. The sophisticated fun of the 1960s and the seeming innocence of the 1970s could never be duplicated. Television's new agents, in a sense, merged the trends of the past forty years in a new mix of imagination and social commentary.

CHAPTER 13

The Return of Fantasy and the Dark Nights of Spies: *The X-Files, La Femme Nikita,* and the New Millennium

SOCIAL SCIENCE FICTION

> What about hunches, Scully? The element of surprise, random acts of unpredictability? If we fail to anticipate the unforeseen or expect the unexpected in the universe of infinite possibilities, we may find ourselves at the mercy of anyone or anything that can not be programmed, categorized, or easily referenced.
>
> —Fox Muldar in *The X-Files: Fight the Future*

In November 1997, the *Diagnosis: Murder* reunion of Patrick Macnee, Robert Culp, Barbara Bain, and Robert Vaughn tapped into nostalgia for spies now in their sixties and seventies. In 1994, *I Spy* returned with its original team, and Patrick Macnee gave new series, *Spy Game*, a send-off by appearing in its first episode. In the late 1990s, *Get Smart* returned both as a TV movie and a short-lived series, and *Secret Agent Man* made a brief rerun foray, although in name only. Mostly, the original Bond fraternity now lived in feature film remakes, with *The Saint*, *The Avengers*, and *Mission: Impossible* competing with Pierce Brosnan's 007 for box office draw at the end of the decade. The 1990s showed many changes in the spy genre as a whole, with most quality TV efforts moving from the traditional networks to cable channels and espionage fantasy becoming incorporated into a blossoming TV science-fiction trend. Again, networks looked to old ways for new programs, but any standout adventures on ABC, NBC, or CBS tended to be broadcast in the form of made-for-TV movies or miniseries.

In September 1992, the syndicated *James Bond, Jr.* joined the 007 universe. As if to draw the youngest generation into the Bond merchandising bonanza, the animated TV series found Bond's nephew cavorting with Q's grandson, I.Q., and American buddy Felix Leiter's son, Gordo, in the war against S.C.U.M. Although teenage offspring fighting evildoers in sneakers on skateboards hocking comic books, videos, and games wasn't designed to appeal to anyone over ten, the old mythology found new ways to reinvent itself. Television never ignores a solid product.

Due to lawsuits involving the television and video rights to Bond films, for the first half of the decade, the adult James Bond was more active in the John Gardner books than on screen. Instead, old Bond movies were aired during holiday marathons on cable station TBS ("15 Days of 007") and in two made-for-TV projects. Jason Connery, son of Sean, joined the world of Bond in *Spymaker: The Secret Life of Ian Fleming*, a fictional 1990 television movie for TNT. Made purely for fun and not historical accuracy, *Spymaker* featured a young Ian Fleming gathering around him a circle of supporting characters meant to be younger versions of Q and Miss Moneypenny. In the previous year, a low-key, slow-paced, and less fanciful version of Fleming's life, *Goldeneye: A Story of James Bond*, was a syndicated television movie starring Charles Dance. Filmed in London MGM lots and on location in Fleming's Jamaica retreat, which Fleming had named Goldeneye, this film emphasized James Bond's creator's days in World War II and his courtship with his wife, Annie. This low-budget project was unrelated to the later Pierce Brosnan film of the same name, which in 1995 reenergized the Bond franchise.

The Brosnan *Goldeneye* was set in the milieu of a changing Russia, a film reflecting the historical changes after the end of the Cold War. The actual KGB had been disbanded in 1991, and the fictional profiteers in Moscow now operated in a chaotic world without government control. The threats now came from and targeted computer technology and energy resources. The film's follow-up, *Tomorrow Never Dies*, reflected changes also seen in post–Cold War John le Carré novels in which the writer "replaced his cast of spies with corporate villains, supplanting those who had acted lawfully in the name of national security and ideology with those acting in the name of profit and position, the latter capable of much greater damage" (Hoffman 2001, 238). *The World Is Not Enough* (1999) showed the retreat of Soviet power into its former provinces, placing the distribution of oil in jeopardy when patriotic ethnic groups sought independence by gaining their power from natural resources, not fantastic technologies. Still, unlike Timothy Dalton, Brosnan brought back a Connery-inspired mix of humor, fantasy, and action, all elements reflected in new TV spies.

Airing on Fox in the fall of 1994, *Fortune Hunter*, starring Mark Frankel as Carlton Dial, was one 1990s attempt to merge 007 with *U.N.C.L.E.* Dial was a dashing former spy for British counterintelligence, now taking assignments from the Intercept Corporation, a San Francisco recovery firm headed by Mrs. Brady, who was played by the former Honey West, Anne Francis.

John Robert Hoffman played Harry Flack, the computer nerd who monitored Carlton's activities with high-tech telemetry equipment worn by the agent. This effort lasted one month. In 1996, *Mr. and Mrs. Smith* starred series regulars Scott Bakula and Maria Bello as two corporate spies specializing in protection for the secret "Factory." This show had its *Avengers*-like charms, including the costars' unusual relationship. Both worked for the same company but were not allowed to know about each other's backgrounds or their real names. In one episode never aired in the United States, "The Impossible Mission," David McCallum guest starred as bad guy Ian Felton (as in Ian Fleming and Norman Felton), who was planning to steal currency plates. Robert Vaughn was scheduled to star as Mr. Rolfe (as in Sam), but these plans fell through.

Another short-lived program came in 1998 on the WB Television Network entitled *Three*, starring Jonathan Vance as Edward Atterton, Amanda Webb as Julie Bowen, and Marcus Miller as Bumper Robinson. Using the old ploy of so many other shows, these three criminals were blackmailed into becoming secret agents by getting the choice of prison or performing covert work for a top-secret government organization. They were asked to assist both government and business interests, as their superiors saw little difference between the two worlds. One week they stopped nuclear attacks, the next, computer crime using *Mission: Impossible*–like teamwork and carefully planned sting operations. In *Three*, Atterton was the classic jewel thief à la *The Saint* and Alexander Mundy; Bowen was the angry, sexy con artist à la Cinnamon Carter; and Robinson was the computer hacker with a Robin Hood complex à la Barney Collier. Each had been a loner before being forced to join this team, but all three found comforts in a Manhattan brownstone where they lived together opulently.

In the early 1990s, the fledgling USA Network began building a reputation for creating its own dramatic series. One of its first offerings was the underappreciated *Counterstrike*, which starred Christopher Plummer as Canadian billionaire Alexander Addington. He updated *Mission: Impossible* by organizing his own strike force to assist justice when normal law enforcement couldn't or wouldn't deal out legal vengeance. From 1990 to 1993, Peter Sinclair (Simon MacCorkindale), who had quit Scotland Yard when politicians forbade him from bringing certain killers to justice, led Addington's team, comprising a series of beautiful women agents and American ex-military strongmen housed in a stylish and sophisticated jet plane. This plane, ready for service at a moment's notice, was equipped with a special video link to Addington's headquarters for orders and mission communications.

At first, the team looked for Addington's missing wife, but the missions quickly took on international criminals and espionage capers, often miffing law enforcement agencies who wanted secrets kept buried. Many stories had more depth than average TV fare, as in one episode where the team took on La Morte, an international assassination organization that brainwashed women and placed electrodes in their brains to monitor these involuntary agents. The team captured a seemingly savage killer before learning of her condition and helped to see that she was deprogrammed rather than killed. By episode's end, the brutal villain became the subject of sympathy and compassion in very realistic scenes of torment, a marked departure from most other such efforts.

This USA series ran for seventy-six episodes, one of the longer-running independent post-IMF shows. In the final episode, political forces unhappy with Addington's independence finally stopped his efforts when he was forced to break up the team to save the life of the imprisoned Peter Sinclair. In a thoughtful scene, the show's motto, "We must stop evil, no matter what the cost," was questioned when Addington met Sinclair in his cell, who was forced to serve five years as a punishment for the team's extralegal work. Addington was moved by the sacrifice, grieving over the cost of Sinclair's freedom. In the epilogue, we see Sinclair released from jail, with his former teammates waiting for him. Clearly, they plan to continue the fight without Addington's money, no matter what the cost.

Another *Mission: Impossible* update with a more military style was the syndicated *Soldier of Fortune, Inc.* (1997–1999). In this Canadian production filmed in Montreal, Major Matthew Shepherd (Brad Johnson), formerly of Special Forces, led a team of mercenaries made up of former military types on secret missions where the possibility of deniability was paramount. Xavier Trout (David Selby), an adviser to the NSA, gave them these missions at their refurbished warehouse in Venice Beach, California. The highly specialized team included Christopher C.J. Yates (Mark A. Sheppard), who was the pilot, formerly of the British Special Air Services. He was also the demolitions and electronics surveillance expert. Benny Ray Riddle (Tim Abell), a former marine staff sergeant, was the crack shot and weapons expert. He was the ladies' man, a former CIA case officer, covering cryptography and languages. Jason Chance Walker (Real Andrews) was another former pilot, an expert in close-quarters combat.

In their second season, the show was remade as *Special Ops Force* without Yates and Walker. Deacon "Deke" Reynolds was the new pilot and demo man played by professional basketball player and media bad boy, Dennis Rodman. Nick Delvecchio (David Eigenberg) was the new agent who enjoyed undercover work. The warehouse was now the "Silver Star Bar," a more colorful cover for their special operations. With a nod to the Iran hostage crisis, their first mission was to rescue four British soldiers whose helicopter had crashed in Iraq. Later, they captured war criminals in Bosnia, prevented Cuban leader Castro's assassination by an AWOL marine, rescued hostages in Chile, and freed a KGB officer in Moscow to protect American secret assets in Russia. In the series finale, Debbie (Julie Nathanson), a recurring character as a waitress in the bar, turned out to be an enemy agent keeping tabs on the crew.

> I was falsely accused of a hideous crime and sentenced to life in prison. One night, I was taken from my cell to a place called Section One, the most covert anti-terrorist group on the planet. Their ends are just, but their means are ruthless. If I don't play by their rules, I die.
> —Opening narration to *La Femme Nikita*

In 1996, *La Femme Nikita* debuted on USA, and the series quickly became basic cable's highest rated series, reaching approximately two million viewers in its first season (Edwards 1998, 3). In two films and in the USA Network series, a young girl, convicted of a murder she didn't commit, was given a life sentence, but released to a clandestine and ruthless agency promising her a new life if she becomes a secret agent and assassin for them. Her choices were limited—if she refused to kill terrorists, she would die.

La Femme Nikita was first filmed in 1991 as a highly regarded, R-rated French film directed by Luc Besson and starring Anne Parillaud. In this version, Nikita was a cold-blooded drug addict who was a woman drained of sentiment. For the director, Nikita represented anyone who does not like or cannot change the life they are given, but is given a second chance. A Warner Brothers Hollywood remake, *Point of No Return*, starring Bridget Fonda, was released in 1993, also R-rated. Critical reception to this incarnation wasn't kind, as Hollywood's version both toned down the grittiness of the original and essentially remade it shot-for-shot without subtitles. In 1996, Peta Wilson became the character for television under two titles. A coproduction of America's Warner Brothers and Canada's Fireworks Entertainment, Canadian stations dropped the "La Femme" from the title to avoid confusion with French-language Quebec programming. Airing Sunday and Monday nights, the show retained the tragic and realistic aspects of the original film, recasting some scenes from the French production in late evening episodes.

In the first season, the televised *Nikita* was considerably more innocent than her film inspiration, although the young girl was clearly a streetwise but unsophisticated survivor, unwanted and unloved by her mother and molested by her mother's boyfriends. She was depressed, awkward, and insecure. After she attempted to stop a murder, she was blamed for the crime when police found her with a bloody knife in her hands. After her sentence, the extremely ruthless Section One faked Nikita's suicide in jail and began remolding her into an agent. While the girl went through two years of training as a reluctant operative code-named "Josephine," Section One learned of her innocence but kept this information secret to retain their hold over her. One theme of the series was Nikita's desire to leave Section One, while it continually contrived to keep her under control. Along the way, she decided to make reforming Section One one of her personal quests as she tried to discover why she'd been recruited in the first place.

Nikita was the series' moral compass, and her relationship with fellow agent Michael Samuelle (Roy Dupuis) was the central character interaction. Born in 1970, Peta Wilson had been the third actress to read for the role, and was immediately the top contender for the part.

As Wilson had been raised partially in the bush of New Guinea and Australia, the producers saw a "wild child" in the actress. Wilson claimed that changing homes and environments during her childhood helped prepare her for the role. She equated Nikita's situation to being an animal in a zoo, once wild but beaten into submission. Her Nikita was the surprising killer, the beautiful woman no one expects to find in the situations ordered by Section One. Canadian actor Roy Dupuis played the unemotional manipulator Michael, Nikita's long-term love interest. To show that his character was a survivor who kept his feelings buried, the actor decided Michael would only convey his emotions through his eyes. This technique of using vision as a means to reveal character was also employed in Nikita's wearing sunglasses when she was on a job. When a mission was completed, she removed them to reveal the agent beneath the continual killings, or "cancellations," and manipulations.

From the beginning, Producer Joel Surnow planned to focus the series on Section One. Other characters in the ensemble cast established in the first year included Madeline (Alberta Watson), the master strategist who specialized in emotional and psychological aspects of missions, probing the psyches and motives of opponents. The rebellious computer hacker was Birkoff (Matthew Ferguson) who lived in Section One headquarters. After his first killing, he became afraid to go out into the world. Section One's technological wizard was Walter (Don Francks), who had a mysterious presection background with Operations (Eugene R. Glazer), and Operations respected Walter for whatever had happened between them. Walter was Section One's father figure, especially for Nikita and Birkoff. In turn, Operations began to obsess over Madeline, a subplot with interesting consequences in the final season.

Surnow and his team established one of the most uniquely stylized milieus in the spy genre, putting considerable effort into developing a rhythmic moodiness to each hour. To allow the actors to become familiar with each other and establish their interactions from the first episode on, the pilot was the third episode filmed. To have a visual style not quite realistic, actors didn't always wear clothing expected in normal situations. To establish the ruthless nature of these agents, all dialogues were romantic or dangerous conversations, avoiding snappy dialogue. All characters talked like Section members even if they were not part of the humorless organization. Although the names of actual groups such as the NSA or IRA were occasionally mentioned, the series avoided any direct connections to real-world dilemmas, attempting to establish a futuristic feel by being "five minutes ahead" of headlines. The settings were never mundane and the circumstances were always earth threatening. For example, the Glass Curtain, a highly specialized terrorist group seeking chaos and destruction, had a device capable of altering patterns on radar screens, causing planes to collide. Most locations were unspecified, subterranean, or in locales that neither looked nor felt familiar. Each episode ended ambiguously, each hour part of ongoing story arcs without final resolutions.

The producers worked within these story arcs to both establish continuity and have the characters transform after traumatic situations. Nikita, in particular, evolved from an uncertain trainee to a highly disciplined trainer within her first season. In her first assignment as a trainer, she mentored a new agent named Karen, who enjoyed killing to the point of murdering her own grandmother. Nikita decided Karen was unstable and therefore must be canceled. But Nikita was always kept off balance. In "Escape," Nikita found an opportunity to leave Section One, but was uncertain if she was facing a test, while Michael maneuvered her by promising a stronger romantic liaison. Nikita chose to stay, but found in the end Section One was very much aware of her opportunity and that Michael had manipulated her feelings to trap her in the organization. One venture into sci-fi, with a nod to *The Prisoner*, was "Brainwashed," in which Nikita explored a mind-altering helmet called a "phasing shell," which programmed her to be an assassin for the other side.

Throughout the series, Nikita and the other characters were constantly torn between their desires, especially to have a normal life in the midst of sanctioned murder. Like THRUSH, Section members were not permitted to have families and relationships, which led to problems for all members of the organization. In one episode, Nikita was attracted to Chandler (*Counterstrike*'s Simon MacCorkindale), who was suspected of money laundering on behalf of a children's charity. He turned out to be running a child slavery ring and tried to sell Nikita as well. Early in the series, Nikita was attracted to Michael, but was forced to assist his wife, Simone. Later, Adam, Michael's son, was born as a result of a deep cover mission to root out Simone's terrorist father. Nikita's feelings regarding her mother came out in an episode about an arms merchant named Helen Wick who'd never seen her daughter and had a trigger for a nuclear bomb. Nikita played the lost daughter, became attached to Wick, but had to ultimately "cancel" her.

At the end of the first season, Nikita became rebellious, and Section One sent her on a suicide mission to eliminate the risk. In a rare, unmanipulative move, Michael helped her create a new identity, and she went on the run for two episodes during the second season before returning to the fold. She then advanced in the organization. Alongside Michael and the rest, Nikita battled terrorist groups like the Glass Curtain and the Red Cell. The Red Cell in particular became so dangerous that Section One lured the group into its own headquarters to entrap the terrorists. In one two-parter, Nikita pretended to be recruited by Adrienne, the founder of Section One who had been forced out in a power play. More ruthless, seemingly, than Madeline, Adrienne wanted to destroy her creation because she feared its goal had become power for its own sake. In the end, Adrienne and Nikita both learn the scale and scope of Section's reach. It had, in one example, gone so far as to support Iraqi president Saddam Hussein because Operations believed the stability of the world depended on leaving him in place.

The series was scheduled to complete its four-year run in May 2000, but after a remarkable wave of interest from viewers, USA decided to order one more season. Fans from over forty countries, lead by an online group called "First Team," deluged the network with 25,000 e-mails and letters, 100 pairs of sunglasses, $3,000 in cash, and a flood of cookies with Michael's face. In the added season, new revelations revolved around Nikita being uncovered as a three-year agent for Center, the organization that controlled a number of Sections. Mr. Jones (*The Equalizer*'s Edward Woodward), code-named "Flavius," turned out to be the central member of the ruling committee who promised Nikita she could reform Section One and that he would reveal why she was recruited. In the wave of these changes, Madeline killed herself, leaving all to wonder why she took this action. A hologram of her was created to keep Operations under control and to help him cope with his obsession. Michael defected to a new terrorist organization, The Collective, after Nikita had faked his death in a suicide mission. Simultaneously, Nikita learned Jones was her father.

All these plots came to a head in the concluding two-parter in March 2001. By the grand finale, The Collective was on the verge of major victory, and Nikita had become second in command. Operations was killed while trying to save Michael's son, Adam. In the final ironic moments, Jones sacrificed his life to save Adam in return for Nikita's promise that she will become the new "Operations" and ultimately replace him as the head of Center. In the end, Nikita learned she'd been recruited to step into her father's shoes.

In March 2000, one off-beat updating of *I Led Three lives*, by way of *Scarecrow and Mrs. King*, was the USA Network's *Cover Me: Based on the True Life of an FBI Family*. The darkly humorous project was created, written, and produced by Shaun Cassidy, the former 1970s teen idol. Aired on Sundays at 8:00 P.M., the show told fictionalized yarns allegedly based on a real family that had come together to serve as undercover agents for the FBI. In the pilot, FBI agents Danny Arno (Peter Dobson) and his wife Barbara (Melora Hardin) learned of the murder of a fellow agent's family. They then decided they could better protect their three children by making them agents in the undercover world.

Cameron Richardson, a fashion model for numerous products and magazines, played Celeste Arno, the incurably romantic sixteen year old. Antoinette Picatto played bubbly, outspoken fifteen-year-old Ruby, and Michael Angarano played mischievous eleven-year-old Chance, who idolized his father. Each hour-length adventure was told from Chance's adult perspective, as he reminisced about his childhood.

As Chance recalled, instead of cheerleading practice and football games, the teenagers participated in mob infiltration and espionage, forced to find innovative ways to protect their cover. To explain why their home was filled with handcuffs, nunchuks, and night-vision glasses, they told classmates their parents worked for the IRS. They learned to live with various last names and know which of the ten phones in the house matched up with any given cover name. To root out dishonest council members, the girls babysat for their children. As Chance remembered with bemusement, the bedtime stories were case histories of his parents' successes.

Promoting the show, Cassidy claimed the family on which the series was based wished to maintain secrecy, although he admitted the father had been killed in mysterious circumstances. Still, Cassidy said he attempted to portray a healthy family undergoing bizarre situations. One side of the series was its 1960s-flavored humor signaled by the guitar-driven surf music theme, but the other was the often poignant human drama of the family. In one story, Danny tracked down the killer of his latest partner, only to discover that a young teenager going through a gang initiation had shot him. In another, the family was threatened by a former child pornographer, who blamed Barbara for his failures in life. Although she believed his imprisonment had been just, she felt guilt over the way she'd betrayed him and thought his punishments outside of jail far exceeded his crimes. Far less dark than *La Femme Nikita*, Cassidy was probably right when he said the role of the children would serve as wish fulfillment for youngsters everywhere who would prefer more interesting lives than most enjoy. While this wish fulfillment didn't take with any audience, Cassidy moved from the FBI to the CIA when he helped produce 2001's new spy series, *The Agency*.

"THE TRUTH IS OUT THERE"

But, by the close of the 1990s, the TV secret agent genre had largely been absorbed into sci-fi offerings, and times had changed for the breed. On one level, this was all to the advantage of the espionage realm. Unlike the often light-hearted "Spy-Fi" series of the 1960s, a modern distinction seen in series like *The X-Files* and *VR.5* was the loss of good guy versus bad guy plots. THRUSH, KAOS, and Miguelito Loveless were polar opposites of the agents that defeated them, but similar forces of virtue largely no longer succeeded U.N.C.L.E., CONTROL, and the U.S. Secret Service. By the 1990s, "Spy-Fi" shows were more clearly descendants of *The Prisoner* and John le

Carré. By the 1990s, fantasy no longer tended to descend into juvenile Steve Austins, as shown in the extremely popular *X-Files*, which premiered on September 10, 1993, on Fox. *The X-Files* established the trends for similar series in tone, attitude, and a clear desire to appeal to adult audiences.

The X-Files, produced in Vancouver during its first five years, revolved around cases assigned to FBI agents Fox Mulder (David Duchovny) and Dr. Dana Scully (Gillian Anderson, a fan of *The New Avengers*). Muldar, the true believer and dubbed "Spooky" by his colleagues, was known for his wry wit. Forensic pathologist Scully, originally the by-the-book skeptic, was assigned to keep an eye on her maverick partner. To qualify as an "X-File," a case had to deal with phenomena and situations defying conventional explanations, including UFOs, telepaths, genetically altered beings, mutants, and clones. Beyond such staples, *The X-Files* involved continuing plot lines about alien visitations and abductions connected to suspected government cover-ups, which spilled into the private lives of its lead characters. Various subplots and supporting characters in what the writers called the show's "mythology" created a realm of spies, counterspies, traitors, and double agents within various levels of the intelligence community.

The creator of *The X-Files* was writer-producer Chris Carter, who was interested in producing a frankly scary show combining elements from TV's past. He admitted being influenced by the Carl Kolchack character played by Darren MacGavin in the film *The Night Stalker* (1971) and the subsequent 1974 series of the same name (Edwards 1997, 5–7). Other inspirations came from a psychologist friend who told Carter about an alien abduction syndrome seen in three out of 100 people who believe they've been kidnapped by extraterrestrials. Carter thought this was a good starting point, and wrote the pilot introducing Mulder's belief that his sister had been so kidnapped.

Another acknowledged influence was *The Avengers*, which had much to do with the casting choices for Mulder and Scully. "I loved that show," Carter said. "I loved that relationship between Steed and Emma Peel, the intensity of the stories. It's sort of the way I instinctively write, so that has fed into my ultimate concept of the show" (Edwards 1997, 11). Under the surface, Carter added, a smart man and a smart woman in the same room create sexual tension, and he wanted this element in *The X-Files*. Duchovny, for example, had a background in English literature and was working on his Ph.D. when acting drew him away from academia. His most famous role before *The X-Files* was as a transvestite FBI agent in David Lynch's surreal series, *Twin Peaks*. Anderson, on the other hand, was a young and relatively inexperienced actress. She was a hard sell to the network, which would have preferred a more traditional blond bombshell. Carter put his show on the line to sign her, wanting someone who demonstrated vulnerability and intelligence against the usual type.

From the beginning, Carter established a creative atmosphere, resulting in a unique loyalty from his cast and crew. He recruited directors Howard

Gordon and Alex Ganza, who had worked on the fantasy series *Beauty and the Beast*. Rob Bowman, a director of *Star Trek: The Next Generation*, left that series feeling stifled, and came aboard Carter's more flexible project. Writing team Glen Morgan and James Wong, both *Night Stalker* fans, became long-term contributors. Carter had a three-year scheme in mind, feeling that unsuccessful shows weren't given sufficient planning. But he left his team enough creative leeway to add their own ideas and concepts for the series (Edwards 1997, 4–9). For example, in the second season he established the policy of allowing directors to be their own producers, feeling that directors had the best vision for their own episodes. As a result, director-producers like David Nutter became more committed to the show. To have a feature-film look in his project, Carter hired a second unit crew to film exterior shots that didn't need the principal actors. This decision allowed the crew to effectively expand the eight-day workweek into ten, providing the editors with more footage that would improve the show's look. Because composer Mark Snow stayed with the series for its entire run, he provided a continuity in tone and musical subtexts that gave the series a special moodiness, despite other changes over the years.

From the beginning, Carter wanted to make it clear the series wasn't only about aliens or the paranormal, and he worked to demonstrate that *The X-Files* would be difficult to categorize. For example, the Carter-written pilot episode, "Silence Coming," dealt with four teenagers abducted by a UFO. The next adventure, "Deep Throat," introduced the theme of government cover-ups. The third outing, "Squeeze," introduced the "Monster of the Week" premise with a liver-eating carnivore. Other episodes expanded the notion of what an X-File would be, as in "Ghosts in the Machine," which had nothing to do with the paranormal, but rather dealt with a house-sized computer gone amok. Carter and his scriptwriters looked to newspapers for such story ideas, as in the case of "Fresh Bones," based on accounts of several U.S. servicemen who inexplicably killed themselves in Haiti. Scriptwriters saw an opportunity to take this story, add a voodoo plot line, and create a typical *X-Files* episode. To ground the series, writers had to find ways to use both sci-fi and social science to give Scully rational explanations for the strange phenomena, keeping her skeptical and off-balance. *The X-Files* sought continual ambiguities, wanting to demonstrate the good guys don't always win. In "The List," a reincarnated killer comes back for revenge, but Scully and Mulder do not solve the case. In another story, Scully sees a demon, but it's not clear if it's a psychological terror or paranormal phenomenon.

As the seasons progressed, the "mythology" story arcs snowballed into prominence. These included stories interlinked to government conspiracies, the back stories of Scully's and Mulder's pasts, and the ongoing interest in aliens and their influence on the characters. Part of this direction came in the second season, when Anderson was pregnant and the show had to work

around her. This situation offered increased exposure for some of the supporting cast, which gave substance and depth to the show. Notable figures
included Mulder's boss, Assistant Director Walter Skinner (Mitch Pileggi) and
the "Lone Gunmen" (Bruce Harwood, Tom Braidwood, and Dean Haglund).
The latter became so popular that a spin-off centered on this computer-
hacker team was considered in 2000. Alex Krycek (Nicholas Lea) was an
evolving antagonist, a one-armed novice FBI agent who was part of the
cadre put together by the "cigarette smoking man" (William B. Davis).

Telling friend from foe was always a murky proposition. For example,
Skinner once told Mulder that he walked the professional and ethical line
Mulder often crossed, but it was rarely certain what motivated Skinner's
decisions. In some cases, he supported his agents, in others he created the
obstacles to their investigations.

By the third season, this mythology became the driving force of the show,
which was both advantage and problem for the creative team. Continuing
story arcs allowed for the now de rigueur season-ending cliffhangers, as in
the close of the first season when the informant "Deep Throat" was killed
and the X-Files were closed. Perhaps the most discussed cliffhanger ended
the second season, when Mulder found a boxcar of either alien corpses or
humans altered through genetics. But before he could uncover the truth, an
explosion destroyed the train and Mulder was either killed or abducted, a
source of much Internet debate that summer. But continuity often broke
down when stand-alone episodes seemed to break up the story arcs. Still,
the mythology made for a linking scaffold, giving the myth episodes a power
the stand-alone episodes didn't have. By the fourth season, some of these
subplots had become repetitious, as Scully had been abducted twice, beaten,
and given brain cancer in a season that rarely dealt with this issue. Still,
as the show leaped around from genre to genre, from horror, suspense,
comedy, espionage, and sci-fi, the mythology plots gave viewers something
consistent to hook onto. The stand-alone episodes, in turn, were successful in syndication and gave the ongoing series something of a double life.

Unlike major network programs, The X-Files was allowed to progress
because it was on Fox, a then new network wanting to do experimental
projects. Fox never expected the show to achieve the ratings it did, reaching both the top twenty and top ten in its second and third years. At its
height, The X-Files was as close to a national phenomenon in the 1990s as
U.N.C.L.E. and Star Trek had been in earlier decades. In 1995, Fox began
special promotions for the series at six hundred Musicland stores, selling
X-Files apparel and phone cards. The same year, they began syndicating
the series for late-night viewers on both the Fox and FX Networks.

Simultaneously, on-line discussions took a more serious tack, with en-
gineers and aerospace experts debating the plausibility and likelihood of the
alien technologies seen in the series (Genge 1995). Carter and others quickly
realized one reason for their show's success was that it debuted at the same

time the Internet began to take hold, and the show received over 10,000 fan postings a week in its first years. This possibility for immediate interaction established a trend followed by later series that capitalized on the Internet to spread the word about their series, gauge viewer response, and allow for dialogue between producers and fans.

Whereas other television movies made for theatrical release were produced after the original series had ended and used new casts and concepts, uniquely, *The X-Files* appeared as a major motion picture, *The X-Files: Fight the Future*, in 1998 while the series was still airing. Costarring Martin Landau, the film was deliberately both able to stand on its own and be tied into events in the ongoing adventures of Scully and Mulder. By the fifth season, some worried Carter was spreading himself too thin as he worked on *The X-Files* film, his new series, *Millennium*, and the scripts for the fifth season of the series, which all ostensibly led up to the events in the film. Because of this crossover, thirty-three different magazines ran cover stories on the movie.

Simultaneously, *Star Trek* convention dealers' rooms began offering *X-Files* collectibles from Mulder and Scully I.D. badges and masks, to the small Topps comic books stapled into issues of *TV Guide*. A logical extension of these sales were Creation Productions prepackaged *X-Files* conventions, featuring one room of props on display, one room of dealer merchandise, and an auditorium where video clips and performances by supporting actors were offered to fans. As the principal leads were rarely available for such weekends, minor characters and extras such as cigarette smoking man and the Lone Gunmen sat at autograph tables, while Creation hocked its new fan club, offering videos of repetitive interviews and glossy photos and newsletters. The conventions and fan club didn't last long, but the series didn't disappear.

Carter knew fans were watching both the unfolding dramas in the series and the behind-the-scenes goings-on with the principal leads. He used such situations to stir viewer interest and create speculation about the show's direction, when Duchovny expressed his wishes to distance himself from the show and appear in fewer episodes. Jeffrey Spender (Chris Owens) was cast as a new recurring character, a sort of anti-Mulder figure with nebulous ties to "cigarette smoking man." As fans wondered about Mulder's future in the series, Spender's presence helped fuel speculation about him replacing Mulder (Meisler 1999, 3). However, to appease Duchovny, who wanted to work closer to his home in Los Angeles, and because production costs were no longer a problem, Carter moved the series base to Los Angeles at the close of the fifth season. In addition, important changes were made to the lead characters. Mulder found everything he believed in and all his preconceptions were too suspect to be credible. He became the skeptic while Scully became more spiritual, now the believer Mulder had once been. Duchovny now participated in script writing, and Anderson's desire for more hopeful scripts about life after death and spiritual awakenings were incorporated into the series. She too wrote and directed, and asked composer Mark Snow to provide music with a more New Age, spiritual tone to add a new dimension to her episodes.

As *The X-Files* became an important flagship for the Fox Network, it enjoyed a special place at Universal Studios, where Stage 5 housed various permanent sets, and Stage 6 was used for new backgrounds. Production time allowed for eight days' prep time and eight for filming. The cast and crew totaled nearly four hundred members. However, in the 2000 to 2001 season, Duchovny began phasing out his Fox Mulder character, only appearing in eleven episodes during the eighth season. Camera crews were forced to schedule occasional scenes with Mulder in the few days the actor made himself available. To retain story connections to past mythology, flashbacks both kept the actor on screen and old story arcs alive.

His replacement was Robert Patrick as John Doggett. Designed to be a new foil for Scully, who was now in love with Mulder, the two began an emotional manhunt for Scully's former partner, apparently kidnapped by aliens in the seventh season. Executive producer Frank Spotnitz felt it was time to return gravity to the series after some forays into light comedy, and the Doggett character was an ex-cop whose common sense and streetsmarts made him a different kind of skeptic (Mason 2000, 13). At first, Scully was uneasy with her new partner, but she came to rely on Doggett and respect his character and work ethic. Simultaneously, Scully was not only pregnant, she became more impulsive, as she was now the reluctant senior agent in the X-Files department (Perenson 2001, 38–43). However, Spotnitz knew the series was taking on a major risk, as replacing Mulder was possibly the biggest gamble in television history.

By the end of the season, Mulder was back, literally resurrected from the grave. After some uncertainties about Doggett's loyalties, Mulder teamed with the new agent. In Duchovny's opinion, this pairing allowed for a new buddy relationship that was quite different from the male-female counterpoints between Scully and Mulder (Spelling 2001, 40). In the season finale, Scully gave birth, and Mulder seemingly had his final showdown with Krycek, the murderer of his father. In the final moments, we saw Doggett and a new female agent, Monica Reyes (Annabeth Gish) arguing with new department director Alvin Kersh (James Pickens Jr.) about the future of the X-Files. (Reyes had been earlier introduced as an old friend of Doggett's, an expert in ritualistic crime with clear psychic abilities.) Clearly, they are the new team. Meanwhile, Mulder and Scully met in her apartment admiring their new baby, who was to be named William after Mulder's father. The season ended with a family kiss, the least ambiguous moment of the show's first eight years.

Debuting November 11, 2001, the ninth and final season of *The X-Files* was considered by some reviewers largely a new series, but such conclusions only pointed to a change in the male lead, not all the other aspects that had made the series what it was for eight years. The first hour, set forty-eight hours after the episode ending the eighth season, had Doggett seemingly on his own in his investigation of Deputy Director Kersh. Mulder had mysteriously disappeared, and Scully was among those telling Doggett to back off from his investigation. Skinner and the Lone Gunmen made appearances, and Cary Elwes joined the cast as Assistant Director Brad Follmer, an old flame of Agent Reyes who advised her to avoid working with Doggett. Mulder might have vanished, but conspiracies within the FBI continued, Scully's personal life was jeopardized by her work, and a new mutant (Lucy Lawless) was on the prowl. Adding to these predicaments, *The X-Files* had a new competitor in the Sunday night time slot, the new ABC spy caper, *Alias*.

Although plans had been made for another season, by January 2002, *The X-Files* was clearly in its last phase. Interest in the show had waned, largely due to the increasing number of imitators, including shows like *Dark Skies*, *Nowhere Man*, *The Pretender*, and *Special Unit 2*, which all combined SF elements with government conspiracies. In the final five episodes of the show that started it all, Duchovny returned, first as a director, then as Agent Mulder in the May 19 two-hour finale. Important moments included the deaths of the Lone Gunmen, who sacrificed themselves to save Washington, D.C., from a plague. Just before Mulder's final return, Scully gave up William for adoption to protect him from the aliens. After putting Mulder on trial for a murder he didn't commit, the conspirators chased the four X-File agents into the desert where the last mystery was revealed—the aliens are coming in force in 2012. But few viewers learned this truth, as even the end of *The X-Files* couldn't compete with the last three-hour segment of the fourth *Survivor* series, the new ratings king on CBS.

VR FILES

One series often compared with *The X-Files*, *Le Femme Nikita*, and *The Prisoner* was the 1995 Fox SF spy drama, *VR.5*. *VR.5* was crafted for adult audiences merging *U.N.C.L.E.*'s device of drawing innocents into the covert world, *Nikita*'s premise of ruthless and factionalized secret organizations, and *The Prisoner*'s themes of brain games and deceptive realities. The central character was Sydney Bloom (Lori Singer), a telephone lines operator and computer hacker who was drawn into the convoluted and conflicting games of the secret "Committee" when she discovered how to enter and manipulate the subconscious dreamworld of virtual reality. Sydney could type out a desired destination on her screen, use her phone to call someone she wanted to take along on a journey to another dimension, and when the caller answered, she slammed the phone into the computer modem. A swoosh of special effects sent them into the fifth realm of virtual reality.

Produced by John Sacret and Thania St. John, the creative team was noted for its high quality special effects that didn't overpower the moody continuing plot line of Sydney Bloom seeking answers about her past and family connections to the Committee. In the early episodes, Bloom believed her father, Dr. Joseph Bloom (David McCallum), a pioneering neurobiologist, and her twin sister were killed in a car accident. But eventually she learned they were alive and under the power of one faction of the Committee that had placed false memories of the accident in her mind. In the dreamlike *VR.5* world, Bloom could alter physical reality and was therefore of considerable intrigue to various characters, including her love interest, Oliver Sampson (Anthony Stewart Head), with whom she had a relationship similar to that of Nikita and Michael.

Because of the show's focus on mind games, secret governmental duplicity, and alternate realities, the show gained a fan base generating detailed web pages on a par with *The Prisoner*. In fact, it can be said that *VR.5* was *The Prisoner* of the 1990s. The Committee is similar to the watchers of Number Six, omnipresent and frightening, using the alternating guises of toughness and tenderness. In one episode of *The Prisoner*, Number Six endured a personality transfer from one body to another, and in *VR.5*, Sydney's father had apparently done the same. Like the 1960s series, *VR.5* had a second life on the SciFi Channel in 1997, including first airings of three episodes not broadcast on the original Fox run. Nods to other earlier spy dramas were evident in details such as the names of Sydney's goldfish— Steed and Mrs. Peel.

Another example of such shows was Paramount's *7 Days*, starring Jonathan LaPaglia as Frank B. Parker. As previous secret agents had been veterans of Korea and Vietnam, Parker was a former CIA agent who had had a breakdown after being tortured in Somalia. After spending time at Hanson Island, a high-level mental institution, Operation Backstep recruited him, a top-secret project that had harvested an alien piece of technology from a crashed spacecraft at Roswell, New Mexico. Partly because of his individual ingenuity and photographic memory, but more so for his high tolerance for pain, which allowed him to suffer what had killed previous "chrononauts," Parker could be sent seven days back in time in a special sphere. Thus, Parker (code-named "Conundrum") could change events such as assassinations, technological and scientific disasters, and political turmoil. Partly because he might be needed at a moment's notice, partly because of his suspected psychological instability, and partly because of his tendency to enjoy life a little too much, Parker was largely confined to the Backstep base.

In the now de rigueur format of ensemble casts, *7 Days* found ways to use its various stars to be more than specialists in one arena. Showcasing different backgrounds and philosophies, most outings found the Backstep crew debating choices and alternatives about what they should or shouldn't do during their missions. For example, nods to the aftermath of the Cold War were seen in the character of Dr. Olga Vukavitch (Justina Vail), a former Russian Communist who had worked on a similar time travel experiment in her homeland. Beyond being the obvious TV descendant of Illya Kuryakin and the obligatory love interest for Parker, Olga's background led to conflicts with other zealous patriots in the team. In one May 2001 episode, her loyalties were tested when Russia suffered a major nerve gas attack that inspired her to share Backstep technology with her former Russian colleagues. However, these agents turned out to be the forces behind the disaster in a plan to pressure her to help Russia regain superpower status. Parker's Backstep allowed her to have a second chance, a recurring motif of the series.

Both Parker and Olga, along with most of the Backstep team, continually butted heads with Nathan Ramsey (Nick Searcy), an ex–CIA operative in charge of Backstep's security. Ramsey was the professional conservative who worried about nonmilitary behavior in others, especially the freewheeling Parker. Balancing his extremism was Captain Craig Donovan (Don Franklin), a straight-arrow ex–Navy Seal who remained a high-level intelligence officer serving as Parker's backup. Whereas he was as conservative as Ramsey, Donovan was more even-tempered and able to befriend Parker and support him. Little use was made of Issac Mentnor (Norman Lloyd), the senior scientist who solved technological dilemmas, but Bradley Talmadge (Alan Scarfe), the head of the Backstep team, had a higher profile role than most espionage supervisors. While ostensibly taking his orders from the NSA, Talmadge occasionally called for unauthorized backsteps when humanitarian needs outweighed national policy. He was continually forced to make decisions that were challenged by one or more of his team members, and he provided the needed balance in the team. This theme was demonstrated in one 2001 story when Ramsey took charge of the project, and the rest of the team mutinied to get Bradley back. At episode's end, Ramsey himself realized a cool, mature mind was needed to guide a program that had powerful implications.

This cast was more than a set of supporting characters providing background and character depth in the show. Some interaction was the usual bickering among various personality types; other debates pointed to alternative perspectives regarding issues of deeply felt points of view. *7 Days* showed teamwork in a realistic sense that grounded the fantastic adventures in more than two-dimensional human dramas. Unfortunately, behind-the-scenes relationships were reportedly less benign. According to some sources, conflict among the leads led to the show's cancellation in 2001.

From 1999 to 2000, UPN also offered an alleged update to *Secret Agent*, although the new *Secret Agent Man*—billed by the network as "ultra-cool"— had more to do with series like *U.N.C.L.E.* and *The Avengers* than the gritty adventures of John Drake. Filming the homage to the spies of old in

Vancouver, *Men in Black* and *Wild Wild West* producers Barry Sonnenfeld, Barry Josephson, and Michael Duggan tried to capitalize on their 1990s sense of tongue-in-cheek action adventure. But sadly, they created one of the shortest-running and lowest-rated spy series in the genre, despite considerable preplanning. Originally scheduled to debut in February 1999 with the agents working for P.O.I.S.E., the series didn't premiere until May 2000 after a string of casting and scripting changes.

When the show appeared, P.O.I.S.E. had been dropped in favor of "The Agency," and the new agents were far more amoral than their 1960s inspirations. Instead of John Drake, Costas Mandylor played Monk, a fashion-conscious smart-aleck Casanova. Holiday (Dina Meyer) was his sexy, reluctant partner who always knew where he could be found. Holiday invariably interrupted Monk's amours to let him know it was time to get back to work for their boss, Brubeck (Paul Guilfoyle). Davis (Dondre Whitfield) was the obligatory high-tech whiz. Monk's first and most frequent adversary was Prima (Musetta Vander), his ex-lover. Appearing in the opening scene of the pilot, she claimed she wanted to defect to Monk's unnamed agency from their adversary, Trinity, led by villain Vargas (Jsu Garcia). Evoking THRUSH's high-tech propensity, Vargas unveiled his electromagnetic gun to black out all of Manhattan. He had only one demand—he wanted Prima back for what would undoubtedly be a fatal reunion.

Throughout the series, these two sides dueled (Prima does not defect) with campy technology, thin character development, and a style meant to find the mix of adventure and humor of *U.N.C.L.E.* But Monk was the most forgettable figure in the cast, with no characteristics to distinguish him and nothing especially unique in the realm in which he and Holiday operated. Holiday herself seemed designed to be the 1990s version of Emma Peel: assertive, independent, and unimpressed by Monk's roving eye. But she seemed more a mirror image of Monk, a pastiche of former glories. *Secret Agent Man* must be relegated to the pile of shows like *A Man Called Sloane* and *Search*, which ended up being more premise than promise. The new *Secret Agent* could have been the revival show all spy buffs craved, but after two short seasons in two different time slots, *Secret Agent Man* disappeared.

In September 1999, Executive Producer Glenn Gordon Caron, creator of the wildly successful private eye series *Moonlighting*, attempted to repeat his formula of crime-fighting fantasy using secret agents in the short-lived *Now and Again*. Billed by CBS as "an action-comedy-drama-romance," the show was canceled after only one season of twenty-two episodes, despite considerable favor among TV critics.

In *Now and Again*, former *Roseanne* star John Goodman played Michael Wiseman in the pilot, a pudgy, middle-aged insurance executive killed by a subway train. Borrowing elements from *The Six Million Dollar Man*, Wiseman's brain was saved by a government agency who put it in the body of a handsome bioengineered twenty-six-year-old (Eric Close). After the operation, Dr. Theodore Morris (Dennis Haysbert, later to star in *24*) told Wiseman the government would keep his brain alive only if he agreed to take part in a secret government experiment, an attempt to manufacture supermen to perform hazardous tasks. Wiseman was forbidden to contact his wife, Lisa (Margaret Colin), his daughter, Heather (Heather Matarazzo), or his best friend, Roger Bender (Gerrit Graham). From the beginning, Wiseman's quest was to reunite with his family while battling the enemies of the United States. CBS didn't have much patience with the series, especially as it was expensive to produce in Caron's lavish hands. Wiseman and his family disappeared in May 2000 after defeating "Egghead" in an episode guest starring World Wrestling Federation superstar, Mankind.

Another such series found success on the SciFi Channel, yet one more incarnation of *The Invisible Man*. Created by producer Matt Greenberg, this version debuted on June 10, 2000, to that network's largest audience viewing an original program. In this incarnation, French-Canadian Darien Fawkes (Vincent Ventresca) was reminiscent of *Now and Again*'s Michael Wiseman in that he was a prisoner forced to be a guinea pig in a secret government experiment. Once again, *The Invisible Man* worked for an invisible agency without a name, which gave them unscrupulous power over his life and mind. A synthetic gland secreting light-bending "quicksilver" was inserted into his brain allowing him to become invisible, but it also began destroying his higher mental capabilities. A loose cannon by nature, the new chemical aggravated Fawkes's stability, driving him slowly insane and making him dependent on counter-drugs administered by Claire, "The Keeper" (Shannon Kenny). Fawkes's quest in the series was to find a means to have this gland safely removed.

Like *La Femme Nikita*, the personality of Fawkes's mysterious organization was seen through the various supporting characters, including his partner, Bobby Hobbs (Paul Ben-Victor), a bantering buddy who was streetwise but unsophisticated. Alex Monroe (Brandy Ledford) was the lead female agent. She'd transferred to the Agency after her newborn son was kidnapped, and her ongoing quest was to recover him. She had considerable difficulty working with others, so Monroe typically operated alone. Albert Eberts (Michael McCafferty) was the obligatory comic computer nerd wishing for opportunities to perform fieldwork. Administrating this small and underbudgeted group was "The Official" (Eddie Jones), who controlled all the secrets.

Rough-hewn and without the flair or urbanity of spies of old, Fawkes was clearly well-read, often inserting quotes from famous authors in off-camera asides or in final moments when he commented on the meaning of his latest adventure. For example, one 2001 quote was, "As Tennessee Williams once said, we have to distrust each other. It's our only defense against betrayal." (A list of Fawkes's quotes is available at the "Invisible Man" homepage at www.scifi.com.) This observation would apply to many episodes, as Fawkes, like Number Six, was on the receiving end of many biological and chemical weapons. For example, using modern themes, in one 2001 episode the enemy organization, Chrysalis, infected him with a nanobug allowing them to see and hear what he does. This was done by having the bug transported through sexual transmission.

Chrysalis was the twenty-first-century version of THRUSH. In one *U.N.C.L.E.* episode, we were told THRUSH raised many of its agents from childhood; in *The Invisible Man*, Fawkes infiltrated a school for such children, who were stolen from their mothers and who had been implanted with DNA from Chrysalis masters. Further, the interferon that ages humans was removed from the unwitting youngsters, who would grow up to become agents of destruction with bodies that never exceeded age thirty. While Fawkes and his fellows captured this school, it became clear there were more, an indication of the size and power of Chrysalis against an agency noticeably understaffed and underfinanced. In one outing, Alex Monroe learned her lost son was in fact the child of the alleged head of Chrysalis, Gerard Stark. In the series finale, viewers learned the superchildren were the primary aim of Chrysalis, a technological superpower able to patiently wait its turn to take over the world.

Like *The X-Files*, the Agency had adversaries within the U.S. government itself. In "Insensate," Fawkes met the leaders of the S.W.R.B. (Secret Weapons Research Branch), an agency so ruthless it intimidated and frightened The Official. In that episode, Fawkes learned his government was willing to conduct illegal chemical and biological experiments on innocent civilians, resulting in a secret building of humans robbed of their senses. ("Insensate" received special promotion from the SciFi channel, as it featured a rare guest appearance by Armin Shimerman, the former Ferengi bartender, Quark, on *Star Trek: Deep Space 9*.)

Geared for a broad audience, especially eighteen to forty-nine year olds, *The Invisible Man* was considerably lighter than *La Femme Nikita* or *The X-Files*, each hour characterized by departmental bickering. In one episode, the agency tracked down stolen sperm from a Nobel Prize winner's sperm bank, recapturing, as it were, the "crème de la crème." From the beginning, the producers avoided overworked sci-fi subjects like aliens or alternate universes, so the show kept close to its secret-agent foundations without veering off into matters becoming overly familiar on other programs. The last four SciFi Channel episodes were aired in January 2002, although, as of this writing, UPN has reportedly expressed interest in picking up the show. When word of the cancellation was released, the now obligatory online letter campaign began, including postcards and flyers ready-made for use by disappointed viewers. This response led to an unusual request from the network after the 2001 anthrax scare. The network posted a note to "Invisible Maniacs" asking that they not send "packages of Kool-Aid and glitter (or any other powdery substance). Due to the state of heightened security throughout the country and the U.S. Postal system, any and all questionable mail is being met with extreme scrutiny."

Several trends in spy dramas seemed apparent as the new century opened. *7 Days*, as *TV Guide* noted, was considered one of the last of a dying breed; that is, imaginative action adventure in general on network TV. Such claims, as it turned out, were premature. Instead, *7 Days* reflected a more general change in modern entertainment themes. The Backstep crew, despite personality conflicts, sexual tensions, and interdepartmental debates, was a group clearly meant to be "the good guys" without the bleakness or questionable ethics found in other shows in the last decade of the twentieth century. Outside of *7 Days* and *The Secret Adventures of Jules Verne*, however, virtually every other pre-2001 espionage-oriented series featured reluctant heroes forced under threat to engage in televised covert wars. Continuing the trends of the 1980s, more often than not modern spies were seen to oppose both evil and the murky conditions of corrupted secret services. Such themes reflected real-life concerns, as intelligence agencies battled to retain their influence and power after the end of the Cold War (Hoffman 2001, 6). Characters like "The Official" in *The Invisible Man* personified this perspective. Darien Fawkes was as much prisoner of his agency's need to exist as an agent of it.

In addition, 1990s heroes worked for such agencies while pursuing a deeper, personal quest that was a theme of their adventures. Fox Mulder sought the truth about his government, family, and apparent alien connections to both. *Now and Again* and *The Invisible Man* featured heroes in search for cures or a way out of their entrapment. Likewise, Nikita looked for a means of escape from her enforced servitude, and Sydney Bloom looked for the truth about her family background. Such quests would continue in the new series of 2001, when personal, family, and world-threatening situations would merge in ongoing story lines that lasted a season or better.

Much had changed since the 1950s when patriotism, professionalism, and clear distinctions set professional and amateur alike off to war against the opposition. One question remains to be answered: What will our heroes be like as the new century progresses?

CHAPTER 14

Active and Inactive Files: Alias, 24, The Agency, and Twenty-First-Century Spies

SPYING IN THE POSTMODERN WORLD

> The CIA must learn to kill silently when necessary to protect a vital mission . . . secret agents have molded our destiny.
> —*A Man Called X*, 1956

Fifteen years before the 2001 New Year's Eve millennium celebrations, media observers had dubbed 1985 "The Year of the Spy" due to the number and variety of news stories regarding the real-world intelligence community. Thirty-five years before the turn of the century, 1965 had also been a "Year of the Spy." In the wake of the success of The *Man from U.N.C.L.E.*, 1965's fall season had introduced *Amos Burke, Secret Agent, Get Smart, Honey West, I Spy, The Wild Wild West,* and the first American airings of *Secret Agent.* However, for a number of reasons, 2001 had an even more valid claim to the title "Year of the Spy" in both actual and fictional realms of espionage. Even before September 11, when four hijacked planes transformed America, 2001 marked an important shift in cultural views on the use of what some called "the world's second oldest profession."

For one thing, as the new century dawned, time hadn't forgotten the secret agents of the 1960s or their television descendants. New generations of TV watchers turned on cable networks from TV Land to the Mystery Channel to view *Get Smart, The A-Team, Airwolf,* and, of course, *The Avengers.* In larger markets with more local stations, viewers could catch reruns of *Scarecrow and Mrs. King, MacGyver,* and *The Equalizer.* By 2001, *The Avengers, The Prisoner, The Sandbaggers, Secret Agent, I Spy,* and *The X-Files,* among others, had all joined the American DVD market. Video releases of series such as *I Led Three Lives*, *The Six Million Dollar Man*, *Mission: Impossible*, and *The Wild Wild West* were available in both single cassettes and boxed set editions. Collectors found copies of their old favorites through both eBay auctions and trades with fellow fans on a growing number of Listservs and websites for aficionados. For younger viewers, everything old was, or would be, new again.

Without question, the history of these TV spies and the films that inspired them had already made an indelible impression on our collective consciousness, and the influence of spies of old continued to crop up in unexpected ways. For example, during the Gulf War, *New York Post* TV critic David Bianculli turned on an A&E broadcast of a black-and-white *Avengers* episode for a distraction. But one 1960s-style dialogue about the arms race was so prescient that he couldn't relax (Miller 1998, 25). In one August 2001 broadcast of ABC's *Politically Incorrect*, host Bill Maher lampooned a government antiporn campaign, saying "Operation: Avalanche" sounded more like a *Man from U.N.C.L.E.* episode than a legitimate attack on Internet sex. Earlier that year, in February, various CNN commentators on *Talk Back Live* noted fifteen-year double agent Robert Hanssen admitted being influenced as a child by Russian master spy Kim Philby. Hanssen's story seemed, to some, full of Cold War anachronisms. In one commentator's opinion, Hanssen had apparently watched too many *Get Smart*s, mixing together a psychology of fictional and actual worlds of espionage. It was a perfect tale for a TV movie. In December 2002, it was, *Masterspy: The Robert Hanssen Story*, starring William Hurt.

These blends of fact and fancy had much to do with the past fifty years of television's secret agents, and they dominated TV screens in 2001 on both news and entertainment channels. For example, various news magazines reported one interesting discussion after the September 11 attack on America. October articles suggested government intelligence officers and Hollywood scriptwriters should collaborate on actual antiterrorism plans because TV and movie creators had already thought through any number of possible scenarios. As fans of Napoleon Solo and Illya Kuryakin observed in online discussions, the new international collaboration, or coalition, against terrorism sounded very much like a new world order needing an U.N.C.L.E.-like organization. The shows of the past now seemed prophetic. Television fiction had gone where reality was forced to follow.

Then again, headlines now seemed to shape new plot lines. In April 2001, a Chinese jet hit a U.S. Navy spy plane, which was working for the NSA, over the China Sea, an incident reminiscent of the opening scenes in the Bond film *Tomorrow Never Dies*. In the Pierce Brosnan adventure, an evil media kingpin had wanted to start a war between China and the United States by staging just such a confrontation to boost the ratings of his new CNN-like network. In the real world, CNN indeed devoted considerable coverage to the unfolding drama. We watched as the Chinese scoured the wreck for insights into U.S. intelligence and listened to reactions while the Chinese held the twenty-four crew members as political hostages for eleven days. In November, these events would be fictionalized in a multipart story line in the CBS military law series, *JAG*. Similarly, on April 23, a Peruvian pilot working for the CIA shot down a suspected drug-smuggling plane, only to learn it carried American missionaries. This incident was later dramatized in the second episode of the new TV series, *The Agency*. After September 11, few dramatic series could avoid references to the new war on terrorism, and such connections between the real world and broadcast fiction would be most evident in new TV spies.

A NOD TO THE FIFTIES

> In the acting job that we do as part of our workaday world, it's very similar to the notion of role-playing and acting in Hollywood. The difference is that, here, when somebody says "cut," they're talking about stopping the action. For us, it could be your throat.
> —Chase Brandon, September 1, 2001, on *CNN Saturday Morning*

In the fall 2001 TV season, three new spy shows debuted and gained early critical and viewer interest. *The Agency* (CBS) in particular earned special consideration, as the CIA for the first time allowed scenes for the series to be partially filmed on its premises. At first, *The Agency* brought the genre of TV spies full circle, taking fictional espionage back to the days of adventure-as-propaganda.

In a televised report on *The Agency* by CNN's David Ensor, twenty-five-year CIA veteran Chase Brandon said, "They really have got all of the pieces of how we live and work and perform our duties here every day. They have all that down in their scripts."[1] Praising the filmmakers, Brandon admitted, "You don't get to come in here and film in our hallway and use our facilities if you're going to typecast us as ugly, nefarious people. If you want to capture that sense of bravery and service, we'll consider it on a case-by-case basis." According to Ensor, reasons for this new interplay between Hollywood and the CIA included the absence of a Cold War adversary forcing the agency to find new ways to drum up public support and create interest for new recruits. Ironically, Ensor's comments were made before the events in September, after which widespread interest in the intelligence community sprouted in all directions overnight. Tragically, *The Agency* seemed perfectly timed to participate in a climate geared to rehabilitate, upgrade, and expand the presence of the CIA in the new war against terrorism.

For some reviewers, this interplay was problematic, a throwback to the collusion of law enforcement and entertainment in the 1950s. For example, Lewis Lapam's review of *The Agency* in the July 2001 *Harper's Magazine*, "The

Boys Next Door," saw the series as an unwarranted propaganda piece for an intelligence community Lapam found reprehensible. Lapam said CBS had an ambitious project, attempting to legitimatize an agency well-known for corruption and stupidity (Lapam 2001, 10). He noted the filming in April at CIA headquarters was directed by CIA propaganda director (Lapam's term), Chase Brandon, whose feelings echoed the principal writer for the series, Michael Becker. In Becker's words, the show was "more about the families and lifestyles and personal day-to-day lives of the men and women of the CIA" (Lapam 2001, 11). In each episode, the covert action should be successfully completed before the last commercial and "everyone will come to know that America is defended, if not in fact at least in fiction, by an aging and increasingly dysfunctional family of patriots who remain capable despite the distractions of lost dogs and extra-marital love affairs" (Lapam 2001, 12).

Ironically, the September 10 *TV Guide* review of the series found this attention to the workaday world so undramatic as to be unentertaining. *Newsday* critic Diane Werts agreed, noting the fall 2001 spy shows didn't have the style of the past. "The genre's ubiquitous computers and electronic surveillance are hardly the pie-in-the-sky gadgetry of some 'U.N.C.L.E.' scheme. They're everyday elements of our own lives, right here, right now." The stakes, she felt, were similarly mundane, "closer to home and more realistically probable than those old souped-up supercapers" (Werts 2001).

The Agency was put together by some of the best talents in television, including producer Shaun Cassidy who had just attempted to give the FBI a family-oriented context in *Cover Me: Based on the True Life of an FBI Family*. *The Agency* was the first television series for feature film director Wolfgang Peterson (*The Perfect Storm, Das Boot*). He admitted the series was designed to compliment the CIA, and in interviews promoting the show he pointed to the attractive cast as evidence of the producers' intentions. Gil Bellows starred as Matt Callan, the occasionally action-oriented troubleshooter. In the first episodes, one subplot was Callan's search to find the truth about the death of his brother, Eric, who had disappeared during the war in Kosovo. In the first episodes, Director Alex Pierce (Ronny Cox) was a career agent worrying about the changing role of the CIA, complaining that former directors would be repulsed by what he was forced to do. This shift was evident in the first aired episode when the CIA not only had to save the life of its longtime target Fidel Castro, it had to stop assassins they had themselves contracted and trained in previous administrations for that very purpose.

The supporting cast included Pierce's deputy and hatchet man, Carl Reese (Rocky Carroll). Eight years previously, Reese had abandoned his wife and son in favor of his job. Jackson Haisley (Will Patton, a veteran of *VR.5*) was a father of two who wanted to get into fieldwork but found himself confined to desk duty. He was the lonely agent who fell in love with an Iranian al-Qaeda terrorist. New recruit Terri Lowell (Paige Turco) was the computer whiz, able to knock out counterfeit passports at a moment's notice. Like Rollin Hand before her, she crafted latex masks to help disguise informants. She even used these skills to counterfeit documents to pressure her ex-husband into a less bellicose divorce and learned how to manufacture Tibetan mildew to help fake a Chinese manuscript. Joshua Nankin (David Clennon) was Lowell's crafty boss, and Lisa Fabrizzi (Gloria Reuben) headed the counterterrorism team. She had moral qualms about her job and briefly saw a CIA therapist to work out her concerns. She quit the CIA after September 11, when she felt she had left the country down by not seeing the attacks coming.

CBS didn't plan on *The Agency* becoming a number-one show right out of the box, scheduling the series against long-running Thursday night hit, *E.R.* Citing the show's use of modern technology and gimmicks, network executives hoped *The Agency* would prove to be a worthy follow-up to lead-in series, *CSI*, which employed similar behind-the-scenes crime-fighting techniques. Further comparisons were obvious to ABC's 1990 to 1991 *Under Cover*, which had also merged field action with domestic duties blended into topical story lines. *Under Cover* had run into trouble with plots too close to current events, and *The Agency* was intended to premiere on September 20, but was held up one week in the wake of the September 11 tragedy.

Between September 11 and 20, CBS, along with the other networks offering new spy shows, chose to not promote these series, as they worried about national sensitivity regarding intelligence matters. CBS postponed the actual pilot because it contained frequent references to al-Qaeda terrorists. Although this episode established the characters and set up key plot lines, the "Viva Fidel!" hour was substituted for the premiere. Ironically, when the pilot was aired on November 1, the story line had already become too tame to prompt controversy. As early reviewers had noted, the hour's emphasis was on human drama and not much field action. Many viewers were puzzled because events in the lives of the characters hadn't been broadcast in order, so one character's divorce problems, resolved the week before, suddenly seemed to begin anew. More pointedly, the terrorist plot to blow up a London department store paled in comparison after September 11.

Despite such problems, CBS benefited from the new interest in intelligence agencies. After the series debut, promos for the show stated, "Now, more than ever, we need the CIA." However, news broadcasts continued to force *The Agency* to rethink and reschedule its offerings. Like the pilot, the show's third episode was pushed back to accommodate an hour-long presidential press conference dealing with terrorism and the war in Afghanistan. Ironically, CBS had worried about the subject of this episode, an anthrax attack in Belgium that moved across the ocean to Washington, D.C. As it happened, news reports were already covering concerns about an actual anthrax outbreak in south Florida. The following day, the first reports appeared about a New York NBC employee contracting the disease by way of infected powders in a mysterious envelope. While promos for the next episode of *The Agency* indicated the next broadcast would be the anthrax outing, by airing time, CBS had substituted another episode about power plays in Indonesia. By November, the network chose to air its belated stories after it seemed clear fact had far outpaced fiction, and no prepackaged drama could compete or compare with unfolding events. When the anthrax episode was finally broadcast, jokes on *Saturday Night Live* and by late night comedians had already taken the edge off the issue. *The Agency*'s use of the disease seemed only a MacGuffin in an otherwise well-trodden story line about revenge and *Mission: Impossible* sting operations.

By December, it seemed the series had abandoned all the domestic subplots in favor of in-house problems with more emphasis on spies than spouses. In the final episode of 2001, the plot harkened back to the Cold War, when the CIA found itself needing to bail out an old Russian mole now in need of new cover. Although the Russian repeatedly stated, "This is a war long gone," apparently an old story line was not. Still, *The Agency* gave the incident a modern spin, having one Russian bribed with a new source of seduction—basketball tickets. When Pierce tried to spin the incident for better news coverage, he lost his job, as the CIA didn't need good headlines—it desired none at all.

On January 17, 2002, multiple Emmy Award–winner Beau Bridges joined the cast as new the new director, former Senator Thomas Gage, after a short transitional period featuring Acting Director Robert Quinn (Daniel Benzali). In his first appearance, Quinn was shown to have been an aggressive, and disliked, director of the Agency before Pierce. Temporarily back in the saddle, Quinn quickly made himself disagreeable to his subordinates. In his second episode, Quinn ruthlessly fired a number of department heads without warning and forced out one counterterrorist agent when he learned she wouldn't lie for him under oath. As the inexperienced Senator Gage took over and began earning his spurs, the demoted Quinn, now the official liaison between the CIA and the Homeland Security Department, began making plans to return to the top. By May 2002, the battle between Gage and Quinn spilled over into the CBS law series *The District*, when Washington, D.C., detectives uncovered a potential CIA cover-up. At that time, *The Agency* had moved to Saturdays, airing after its new crossover partner. In the new year, clearly changes would be occurring in *The Agency*. In less than half a season, the series once both touted and criticized as propaganda, a voice against "ugly and nefarious types," had evolved into a very different show.

> It was during the fall of my freshman year. A man approached me. He told me that the U.S. government might be interested in talking with

me. When I asked, 'why me,' all he told me was that I fit a profile. I
didn't feel that I belonged anywhere, even in college. And I needed the
money anyway. . . . After my first month, I asked if I could try for agent
training. They said I was a natural, and maybe I was.
—Sydney Bristow in the pilot of *Alias*, 2001

On Sunday, September 30, three days after *The Agency* debut, ABC's *Alias*
premiered in a special sixty-six-minute episode without commercial breaks.
Alias centered on the life of after-school agent and graduate college student Sydney Bristow (Jennifer Garner). Energetic and athletic, the once shy
and lonely Bristow had been recruited in her freshman year by SD-6, allegedly a secret division of the CIA. At first, Bristow jumped at the chance
to do something beyond introductory freshman comp classes and hoped her
new life would fill the void left by the apparent death of her mother and
her increasing dislike for her remote father, Jack (Victor Garber). She soon
became an expert in "smash-mouth kick-boxing." However, seven years
later, her boyfriend, Danny, proposed to her, and Sydney violated the car-
dinal rule of SD-6 by telling him about her covert connections. While Sydney
was away on an assignment, SD-6 agents killed Danny to prevent potential leaks. In rage and pain, Sydney attempted to quit.

Like Nikita before her, Sydney went on the run, aided by her father.
Estranged for years, Sydney learned Jack too was an agent for SD-6, and
that this agency was in fact an enemy of the CIA. After three months of hiding, she returned to SD-6 before secretly meeting with the CIA to become
a double agent for the good guys. In the final moments of the opening episode, Sydney learned her father too was a highly placed double and discovered she would have to work with him while despising the man she felt
had betrayed her.

In subsequent episodes, subplots included friends attempting to find out
more about Danny's death while Sydney discouraged their help. During
continuing story lines about international life-and-death bouts, she coun-
seled a friend about her suspicions regarding her boyfriend while falling
behind in her schoolwork. She chose her own CIA contact, Agent Michael
Vaughn (Michael Vartan), over the objections of the section chief. This relationship became complicated when Sydney learned her mother, not her
father, had been a KGB agent. Sydney's own birth was part of her mother's
cover before Mrs. Bristow killed Vaughn's father two decades previously.
Now impulsive and rash, Sydney hoped to destroy SD-6 within two months
to get out of her secret life, but she discovered her quest was going to be a
long-term battle. Preferring to work alone and on her own terms, she discovered that her work had to be coordinated by those who knew more than
she and that her education in spycraft had only just begun.

By the fourth episode, Bristow had become so confused in the crossfire
between the CIA, SD-6, and the archenemy of both, the "K-Directorate," she

broke down in tears before Vaughn. What was true and what was illusion? Surrounding all this pathos, with the Cold War long gone, scriptwriters were forced to come up with new twists to old plots. In one story, Sydney helped a scientist, who had vaccines against bioterrorism, escape from Berlin. He wasn't a captive of any behind-the-Iron-Curtain government, but was rather hostage to a harsh corporation not wishing to lose its secrets. With a personal quest motif interwoven with such plots, Sydney couldn't simply track down an assassin. He would naturally be the killer of her fiancé, but he had been so ruthlessly programmed by SD-6 that Sydney felt sympathy for him and helped him escape.

Unlike *The Agency*, *Alias* had no pretensions of realism and thus had few problems launching after the September 11 tragedy. According to *The Agency* cast member Ronny Cox, *Alias* was addressed to a younger audience, was anti-CIA, and was therefore anti-*The Agency*. Preview materials had promised "no camp but real emotions," and *Entertainment Weekly* magazine dubbed the show the best new dramatic series of the fall season. Other critics weren't so certain, and early ratings didn't indicate a fast hit. Diane Werts felt the series reflected "TV's longtime trend toward delayed drama gratification. Trying to reflect reality and deepen character, plots can stretch for weeks." For Werts, *Alias* undercut its human narrative of father-daughter trust with so much "disjointed kiss-kiss-bang-bang that the show plays like a movie trailer" featuring "nerdy high-tech gadgetmakers designed less as persons than animate collections of quirk. The machinery they're there to explain is more real than they are" (Werts 2001).

Others saw a sense of style and fantasy in *Alias* that was missing from more realistic series like *The Agency*. Some pointed to parallels between Sydney and the equally active fighter Emma Peel. Most obviously, updating the "Emma Peelers," Garner wore latex skin-tight outfits, which forced her to put on a layer of baby powder to be able to get into and out of her costumes. Unlike Rigg, Garner worked on her martial arts skills for a month before her audition to be prepared for any physical action the casting directors might have liked to see.

Alias also relied on sound to give its stories another dimension in tone and pace. Creator and executive producer J. J. Abrams claimed he listened incessantly to the soundtrack of the cult German film *Run Lola Run* while he wrote the pilot for *Alias*. This influence was apparent in the modern rock soundtrack for *Alias*, which punched up the emotional level of the action sequences. Abrams also clearly had watched USA Network's *La Femme Nikita*, a series that established many of the premises reworked in *Alias*. Clearly attempting to appeal to eighteen to forty-nine year olds, the primary audience for cable network adventure shows, ABC promoted *Alias* with spots aired during *The Invisible Man* on the SciFi Channel.

Alias attracted a loyal audience in early 2002, along with special guest stars such as actor-director Quentin Tarantino (*Pulp Fiction*), who appeared in a two-part drama playing a former operative of SD-6 who was bent on revenge. In the same month, ABC proudly touted the fact that *Alias* had won the fall 2001 People's Choice Award for most favorite drama and that Jennifer Garner had won the Golden Globe for the year's best television actress. On March 1, *Alias* debuted a second time, beginning its cable rerun life on the Family Channel. Its March 9 episode gained special notice, as it featured Roger Moore as a guest villain. In the new season, *Alias* introduced a fresh twist to the spy drama. Sydney's mother wasn't dead. Instead, the Bristows found themselves a family spying on each other, spying together, and never sure when or whom to trust.

> I sure wish you hadn't called for backup. Cops have to play by the rules.
> I'm going to have to break a few to get this guy.
> —Jack Bauer to police officer in *24*, 2001

As noted in one David Ensor CNN report, the creators of Fox's *24* didn't ask for CIA help in its preproduction and wouldn't have gotten it if they had. Starring Keifer Sutherland as Jack Bauer, the head of an elite CIA Counterterrorist unit, *24* depicted the agency working inside the United States to protect the life of a presidential candidate—duties that are actually the responsibility of the Secret Service. This is not to say the highly praised show wasn't attempting a new style of realism. Debuting Tuesday, November 6, 2001, *24* had Sutherland working to stop an assassination in real time; that is, each episode dealt with activities in a real hour of time. One case was thus spread over twenty-four episodes, beginning on midnight of the California presidential primary.

Twenty-four was designed to be an experiment on several levels. To underline the fast pace and scope of each hour, countdown clock visuals appeared on the screen. Executive producers Ron Howard, Joel Surnow (*The Equalizer*), and Robert Cochran (with Surnow, a veteran of *La Femme Nikita*) wanted an edgy pressure cooker for their agent. As Bauer tried to divide his limited time between his duty and his wife and runaway teenager, the screen was split to show two activities happening at once. These visuals, coordinated by director Stephen Hopkins, were designed to be most effective on large-screen televisions.

In the pilot, Bauer was seen tracking down information about a hired European killer, while talking to his wife, Teri (Leslie Hope), about her search for their teenager and digging up dirt on one supervisor to blackmail him into giving up information, while worrying about a potential mole in the agency. Because of potential leaks, Bauer wasn't permitted to share his mission with his own team and had to establish interfaces with other law enforcement agencies to bypass the suspected traitor. At the same time, viewers saw Senator David Palmer (Dennis Haysbert, an alumnus of *Now and Again*) working on his campaign, while the CIA noted, if elected, he planned to gut the agency. Because Palmer is African American, Bauer is keenly aware that any failure to protect him could have major repercussions in the U.S. electorate. Simultaneously, the young Kim Bauer (Elisha Cuthbert) was seen with her friend, Janet York, slipping out to party with two young men they'd met on the Internet. At the same time, the assassin flew into the United States regaling a fellow passenger about his prowess as a photographer. In the final moments, a plane exploded over Los Angeles. All this in the first hour.

The concept and the star together inspired Fox to quickly snap up the project. Their belief in the series prompted the network to air the show on the most contested time slot of the season, Tuesdays at 9:00 P.M., and to repeat the premiere Friday, November 9, again on Fox, and then twice the following Sunday and Monday on FX. Later episodes were aired on both Tuesday and Friday nights, with Tuesday watchers being advised to spread the word and tell their friends about the encore broadcasts. Like *The Agency*, *24* found itself in need of retooling after the events of September 11. Originally, one subplot involved the hijacking of a jet airliner. Expecting strong viewer distaste for such a story line, the plot line was toned down and the premiere was backed up from its original broadcast date of October 30.

As producers of *24* wanted to establish suspense for the viewing audience, promoting the series led to unusual problems. Appearing on *The Tonight Show* with Jay Leno on November 12, Sutherland inadvertently slipped up by telling Leno about situations not yet aired. He admitted filming *24* was a unique challenge as the characters had to appear unchanged for the duration of the production. For example, he noted actress Elisha Cuthbert described the cast as being something like *The Simpsons* because they always wore the same clothes. In his second appearance on the Leno show in May 2002, Sutherland admitted he got into some trouble for his earlier slip-up, so the producers filmed three different endings to be certain the final hour would be a complete surprise for the audience. In January 2002, Sutherland won a Golden Globe for the best actor in a dramatic series. By the premiere of the new fall season, *24* was already offered as a DVD boxed set collection, including an unaired alternative ending to its first year.

A SEASON OF SPIES

> Spy scripters are stuck. They seem to want timely substance, but also timeless style. They want authentic texture, but also Hollywood polish. They want real people who resonate like superheroes. These diametrics are hard to reconcile.
> —Diane Werts, October 2001, www.newsday.com

In 2001, new TV spies were not limited to the three new network outings. On December 4, the American Movie Channel aired "Into the Shadows:

The CIA in Hollywood," a ninety-minute special that presented stories about how prop masters helped create disguises for intelligence operations. Then, the look into espionage and Hollywood examined the changes felt after September 11. The documentary noted that, like *The Agency* and *24*, other Hollywood projects already in production before September 2001 had to be rethought. More generally, the show reported, the industry felt pressure, both from the government and from networks and studios, to think about creating more positive, patriotic messages. For some, the age of irony and cynicism was over. Perhaps, some commentators speculated, action adventure would now have to show more brains and more of a conscience. After September 11, "Into the Shadows" observed, horrifying spectacles could no longer be used for mindless entertainment. Others saw these conclusions as premature. One May 2002 episode of the legal drama *First Monday* found the CIA attempting to manipulate the Supreme Court over the publication of a former agent's memoirs. In the final moments, one lawyer was apparently assassinated for her double-dealing actions. Perhaps the drive for more patriotic imagery couldn't withstand deeper roots of mistrust established over forty years.

As to the spies of the past and present, for television viewers, the fall 2001 season included three new series with secret agent characteristics and two returning series with new episodes (*The X-Files, Invisible Man*), not to mention reruns of shows from the ubiquitous *Avengers* and *Get Smart* to *La Femme Nikita*. Clearly, the spy genre showed a strong presence on the small screen in five hours a week of new programs, and ten to possibly thirty hours of reruns, depending on the market and local cable offerings. If New Year's Day 2002 was any indication, secret agents had another good year to look forward to. On January 1, 2002, two Encore channels ran *Avengers* marathons simultaneously, while one sister Western channel rebroadcast the first Jim West and Artemus Gordon reunion, *The Wild Wild West Revisited*. New documentaries for the year included the History Channel's "The Gadgets of James Bond," which aired January 29, 2002. This hour went behind the scenes, showing how the vehicles and weapons in the 007 films were created and how they were used in both fact and fancy . One gadget demonstrated was a pair of sunglasses equipped with a camera used in the original *Mission: Impossible*. Later, in May 2002, the Discovery Channel aired Danny Biederman's study of spy gadgets in fact and fiction. It featured interviews with Robert Vaughn and Robert Conrad one week after Vaughn's *Man from U.N.C.L.E.*, *Get Smart*, and *I Spy* were honored as part of NBC's 75th anniversary special.

From February to April 2002, the "James Bond ABC Picture Show" aired on Saturday nights, rerunning the first thirteen 007 flicks. As the network knew most viewers had seen these films either in countless airings on TBS or on video and DVD, ABC attempted to capture old and new viewers by adding trailers and comedy sketches hosted by the likes of Jim Belushi,

Brandy, Robert Wagner, and the cast of *The View*. Roger Moore himself hosted *Live and Let Die* on March 7. The cast of *Alias* hosted *From Russia with Love*, linking the original gentleman spy with his newest television imitator, allowing the former to promote the latter. Wedding the signature Bond theme with the ABC musical logo, clips and jokes were used to make the new broadcasts something more than simply offering what was already widely available. One addition to the broadcast was a new technology in censorship. To protect viewers from one second of nudity in *Diamonds Are Forever*, Lana Woods's Plenty O'Toole was given digitally enhanced clothes.

In March, Fox offered *American Embassy* on Mondays at 9:00 P.M. The central character was twenty-eight-year-old Emma Brody (Arija Bareikis) who yearned for adventure and meaning in her life. In the pilot, Brody became a vice counsel at the U.S. embassy in London. Before arriving at her new job site, Emma met and was captivated by a staple of any embassy— its CIA operative. In this case, handsome and charming Doug Roach (David Cubitt) turned out to be both mysterious and dedicated. Roach added a touch of *Scarecrow and Mrs. King* to a series largely about a career girl meeting an ensemble of eccentric English-speaking types while writing about them in letters home.

Two months later, British television viewers saw previews for another new show, *Spooks*, yet one more attempt to dramatize the work of MI-5. Debuting Mondays on BBC-1, *Spooks* was created by producer Stephen Garrett who was inspired by browsing through a section of John le Carré books in his local bookstore.[2] Gunning for grittiness, and occasional grim violence, the show benefited from MI-5 insiders like Nick Day, who emphasized that true spooks don't work on one case at a time, but rather have four or five files open at any given moment. Thus, the series was fast-paced and complex.

The spooks included intelligent and steel-nerved former army officer Harry Pearce (Peter Firth), the head of the department, the MI-5 father figure to his various counterintelligence teams. Dedicated professional Tom Quinn (Matthew MacFadyen) led the Section B group including Zoe Reynolds (Keeley Hawes), a fast-rising star, and Danny Hunter (David Oyelowo), a very young technical genius who is the group's loose cannon. Tessa Phillips (Jenny Agutter) was the cynical twenty-year veteran heading a counterterrorism section. Helen Flynn (Lisa Faulkner) was the clerk dreaming for her day in the field. In July 2003, *Spooks* came to the American A&E cable network, retitled *MI-5* in the spirit of other acronym titles like *CSI*, *JAG*, and the new *NCIS*. To promote the show, the A&E website featured information about the series and an online game asking visitors to see if they have what it takes to be a spy.

Also in 2002, in the same spirit as *Charlie's Angels* and *Code Name: Foxfire*, Executive Producer Vince Manze created *She Spies* for NBC, claiming he wanted to do *Lethal Weapon* or *Rush Hour* with leggy women (Sonseca 2002,

40). In his concept, a team of ex-cons included D. D. (Kristen Miller), the gorgeous computer hacker, and Shane (Natashia Williams), the no-nonsense agent. The series star was Cassie (Natasha Henstridge), the con artist who headed the team that was forced to work for a clandestine government agency infiltrating crime rings such as bogus charity organizations. Jack (Carlos Jacott) was the government contact who kept the girls in line, gave them their assignments, and reminded them of jail cells awaiting those who disobeyed orders. Targeted for young males, story lines weren't the point; the show was considered "campy distaff" entertainment. In promos for the show, Henstridge described the series as a mix of *Alias* and *Austin Powers*, a tongue-in-cheek "drama-ody" that broke the fourth wall as the characters spoke to the audience. *She Spies* debuted on NBC's 2002 summer schedule for four "sneak peek" episodes in a unique ploy to build up a national audience before the first twenty adventures were aired in syndication and then as late-night broadcasts after *Saturday Night Live*.

And TV spies were present outside of the small screen. From February 16 to July 14, Danny Biederman, in cooperation with the CIA, exhibited his Spies: Secrets from the CIA, KGB, and Hollywood collection at the Ronald Reagan Presidential Library in Simi Valley, California. This exhibit included part of Biederman's "Spy-Fi" archives, showcasing such items as the prop shoe phone from *Get Smart*, the pen radio from *The Man from U.N.C.L.E.*, secret documents from *Mission: Impossible*, James West's suit and sleeve-gun device from *The Wild Wild West*, a pair of leather trousers worn by Diana Rigg as Mrs. Peel, and the original storyboard concept art for the opening titles of *I Spy*. Biederman's "Spy-Fi" exhibit had earlier been staged from August 2000 through January 2001 at CIA headquarters in Langley, Virginia. Side by side, mementos of fact and fancy sat on display showing that espionage, in popular culture, was now one extended family of mutually attracted spheres of interest. On an even larger scale, as thousands of visitors found renewed interest in the new International Spy Museum in Washington, D.C., commentators wondered just why so many people are even more fascinated now by the realms of factual and fictional espionage than during the heyday of the 1960s. So, to complete this file, a few more questions are worthy of some thought. After the first half-century of TV spies, looking back should give us clues as to what to expect.

Conclusion: The Past, Present, and Future of TV Espionage: Why Spies?

THE MEANING OF TV SPIES

> Those vintage shows endure because they've got cool to burn. If it wasn't studly Napoleon Solo and Jim West packing lethal gizmos under tuxedos and skin-tight leather, it was "Avenger" Emma Peel's catsuit karate or John Steed's chipper quips. . . . These shows had a dashing-ness about them, a devil-may-care attitude, despite their threat of world annihilation.
>
> —Diane Werts, October 2001, www.newsday.com

In the twenty-first century, spies will clearly be seen in new ways, but equally as clearly, some aspects of our interest in broadcast espionage will be continued from the days of *U.N.C.L.E.*, *The Avengers*, and the rest. So why do we still find secret agents, in whatever guise, continually intriguing? Some simple answers seem obvious. There's certainly a level of nostalgia for the heroes of old. As Linda Thorson put it twenty-three years after the demise of *The Avengers*, the 1960s can be seen as a mythic time when fashion, music, color, and pleasure worked together to transcend the given stuff of life, and these still look good to despondent children in the 1990s. One reason for continued imitation, according to Thorson, is that those shows established the style of choreographed, ironized violence mixed with the trappings of popular culture (Miller 1998, 131). Another view is seen in John Javna's definition of cult TV, the title of his 1985 overview of many beloved television series. To move beyond popularity into cult status, Javna claimed, fans need to gravitate toward friendships between stars, whether buddy shows or ensemble casts. Special production values and usage of satire typify a cult classic. An unfortunate by-product of this status is, in Javna's opinion, fan reluctance to accept actors in new roles, and he cites Don Adams and Barbara Feldon as examples. By this definition, the spy shows of the 1960s easily fit this mold, and Javna indeed included *The Avengers, Get Smart, Mission: Impossible, The Man from U.N.C.L.E., The Prisoner,* and *The Wild Wild West* in his overview (Javna 1985, 13).

In February 2002, I asked Robert Vaughn why devoted fans still love his old series. He replied, "I think it relates definitely to the ongoing success of the James Bond pictures. Obviously, they're still making them and still making a lot of money. It is generally that genre that *U.N.C.L.E.* was supposed to emulate, which was an international roguish kind of spy who operates around the world with a lot of attractive women, and I guess that's why it's still going on. There were a lot of attractive women in the 1960s that are still on film. They may date but not the film." He added, "I don't know what it all meant, philosophically or intellectually. I know it was good fun for us to do and good fun for people to see."

In 1965, Vaughn's old partner, David McCallum, offered a formula accounting for the success of *U.N.C.L.E.* Some of his ideas seem pertinent to why his series worked so well in the 1960s; others suggest why such series still play a role in the twenty-first century. First, as many have noted, he proposed connections between the spy boom and the Beatles, a unique fusion of pop phenomena (Wolfe 1965). He thought Westerners were disturbed by great uncertainty due to many unknowns about what was happening behind the Iron Curtain. His Russian character came along looking like a nonthreatening customer at a go-go dance hall. Beyond this reassuring image, with the breakup of traditional families, young people were forced to become loners, and characters like Illya Kuryakin made loners look attractive and even well-paid for their aloofness. "With rumors of war all about, with the climate of brinkmanship in which we live, the division between newspaper reality and U.N.C.L.E. fiction tended to wobble," and viewers thought spy shows were glimpses into what was really going on (Wolfe 1965).

But the spy genre is more than the heroes of one decade. Before and after the 1960s, it has always been simple fun to see a hero sort out mysteries in less than an hour in an otherwise complicated world. Many have said it before—James Bond and his fraternity provide a wealth of wish fulfillment for both genders. Children (*Cover Me*), college students (*Alias*), housewives (*Scarecrow and Mrs. King*), and businessmen (*Biff Baker,* Barney Collier in *Mission: Impossible*) have all had turns at playing spies. And, as Simon Templar put it, we like to see others do the dirty work we ourselves would never consider. It takes a hero to put order into chaos. Heroes of all stripes conquering insurmountable odds remain entertaining and reassuring, taking headlines away from cold newsprint and transforming them, as McCallum suggested, into fantastic and therefore less frightening stories.

Other analysts find deeper meanings in the genre as a whole. Some see the detective story, of which secret agents are considered a part, as modern extensions of psychological dramas, notably the Oedipus story. After all, the Greek king had to solve a murder and uncover hidden truths found within himself. *The Avengers*, in particular, has been psychoanalyzed from every angle, and there is a fountainhead of academic articles on the sexual meanings in the characters and relationships. Series producer Brian Clemens was proud of this interest, as he claimed the Freudian symbolism was deliberately built into the scripts and designs of the Rigg seasons. On a sociological level, some see such tales as tribal rituals in which repetitive rites of good versus evil are fought and won again and again between commercials, cleansing us of guilt and restoring our sense of justice (Symons 1972, 8–9).

On a historical level, we can see spy dramas as mirrors of our national identities, time capsules of our past visions of political interactions. In the 1940s and 1950s, as explored in Chapter 2, secret agents were characters in propaganda wars, first against Nazis and then Communists. In the 1960s, secret agents were both dramatizations of what we perceived the Cold War to be and larger-than-life escapes from it. The 1970s saw spies as both comic-book heroes and players in the morality tales of le Carré and his fellow novelists. After one decade of secret agents reduced to demoralized and hard-hitting figures in the 1980s, ostensibly reflecting our interests in quasirealism, the last years of the twentieth century saw a return to a blending of fantasy and fact. These series often tended to emphasize our interest in new technology and what it means in our lives, while continuing to dramatize our interest in both the private and professional lives of the defenders of the West. After years of featuring reluctant agents drawn into espionage against their will, it is interesting to note that the three new series in 2001 centered on professional and semiprofessional spies more akin to their predecessors of the 1950s, as opposed to more recent agents in *The Invisible Man* and *La Femme Nikita*, whose main characters were both world weary and suspicious of their superiors and their opponents. Perhaps *The Agency*, *24*, and *Alias* signaled an important shift in our collective thoughts on the need for less tarnished heroes. Again, time will tell.

On the other hand, according to Cawilti and Rosenberg, our fascination for covert activities is now largely a hangover from Watergate and publicized CIA misbehavior. We now live, they believe, in a climate of "clandestinity," in which bureaucracy and corporate structures make outsiders of us all. In this view, we respond to modern spies because we work in seemingly disconnected, compartmentalized cubicles resulting in alienation, moral ambiguities, and uncertainties about organizations and culture. Like spies, we work under the eyes of security cameras, while supervisors claim the right to oversee what electronic correspondence comes and goes from our computers. In this view, we use fictional characters like secret agents to project our own frustrations with corporate superiors, bureaucratic regulations, or professional conventions (Cawilti and Rosenberg 1987, xi–xii, 43).

Actor David McCallum had a similar notion when he observed in 1965 that one reason for *U.N.C.L.E.*'s success was "maybe because we all live in an atmosphere of intrigue. These days there's as much scheming in the dry goods wholesalers or the college classroom as in the UN. To the degree that we're daily schemers, we strive to be invisible, since you can't pull any fast ones if you're very much in sight and can be seen through" (Wolfe 1965). In 1998, Ted Edwards described an example of just such thinking. In his overview of *La Femme Nikita*, he reported viewers sent the producers mail favorably responding to the cold-to-the-core attitude and atmosphere of the show. These viewers felt their own working situations in the corporate world reflected a similar hard edge (Edwards 1998, 4).

On a less haunted level, to make one last *Star Trek* connection, Captain Kirk himself, William Shatner, has repeatedly confessed his puzzlement over the phenomenon *Star Trek* became. Ultimately, in a number of interviews, he said he finally decided the series had become a new mythology, meeting the needs of modern generations who like recurring characters who are larger than life, able to beat insurmountable odds, and always show the best of the human spirit. Such must also be the case for the fictional world of secret agents. Myths of heroes of skill, durability, technology, ingenuity, and a taste for the best of life have resounded with readers, viewers, and people of every vocation and background for half a century. Although the faces on the chess pieces may change, the game goes on, and the new myths don't disappear. They adapt.

Secret agents, in the main, symbolize the immortal classic battles of the best versus the worst in us, the united forces of the Protectors versus those who choose to do us harm. The armed David must conquer the powerful Goliath, the dragon must meet Saint George, and Moriarity must lose to Sherlock Holmes. The arena of espionage is but another backdrop to ancient wars, and this coliseum is now entrenched in the imagination of modern humans. On one hand, we have the grays of morality and uncertainty in George Smiley, on the other we have Napoleon Solo and James West riding off to crush an unmistakable evil that wears its arrogance on its sleeve. As long as there are forces of oppression, militarism, and greed, there will always be a man, a woman, and organizations formed to leap into the fray. After the 1960s, all such heroes will owe something to Jim Phelps, Alexander Scott, Illya Kuryakin, Emma Peel, and Agent 99, even if they are unaware of their forebears. The best we can hope for is that their children will be as entertaining, engaging, and as memorable as those who went before.

Notes

CHAPTER 3

1. See Jon Heitland's 1988 *The Man From U.N.C.L.E.: The Behind the Scenes Story of a Television Classic*. As I rely on him frequently, I've omitted constant page references. I here thank Jon for reading this chapter and correcting my misinterpretations of some situations.

2. These references came from interviews with Vaughn for the 1989 New Year's Eve "All Night U.N.C.L.E. Affair" broadcast on TNT.

3. My interview with Robert Vaughn took place at the Montgomery Antique Fair in Gaithersburg, Maryland, on February 9, 2002.

CHAPTER 4

1. As many *Avengers* sources duplicate information presented here, I haven't cited details now accepted as credible. The best *Avengers* website, *The Avengers Forever*, is far more reliable than many of the print sources listed here. The site's address is http://theavengers.tv/forever/. Throughout this chapter, I have used many quotes from the twenty-five minute documentary, "Avenging the Avengers," originally produced in 1992 by England's Channel 4 for its program *Without Walls*.

CHAPTER 5

1. Although Sheldon Leonard claimed in his 1995 autobiography *And the Show Goes On: Broadway and Hollywood* that his remembrances were 90 percent accurate, some of his memories fall short of that percentage. For example, claiming *I Spy* would be unique by using location footage makes little sense considering the number of 1950s series filmed in Europe. If he meant non-European locations, as in the Far East, he would be closer to fact. In one passage of his memoir, Leonard

described a garden pub scene shot in England and how an unnamed actor got more and more drunk with each reshoot. There is no evidence any *I Spy* scene was ever shot in England. The few English actors who appeared on the show had no scenes similar to the one Leonard recalled. In one *TV Guide* interview, Leonard claimed Culp didn't write any scripts until the second season, which, as mentioned, is far from correct.

2. Thanks to Chantal Ni Laoghaire, I was able to ask Earle Hagen via e-mail a few questions about the *I Spy* theme and his thoughts on spy music in general. Regarding *I Spy*, he recalled, "The mood and the spirit of the theme for *I Spy* was dictated solely by the film. I worked to a 'story board' of the graphic art. If [the viewer] looks at it carefully, he will see that the theme doesn't start until you see the words *I Spy* on the screen. I use the film to dictate the style and the substance of whatever I write. Sheldon had no input at all. He never interfered with the music. . . . When you analyze the themes and scores to shows like *Mission: Impossible* and compare them to *Secret Agent* or *The Avengers* you have to come to the conclusion that the film dictates the style of the music."

CHAPTER 6

1. An extended interview with Bernie Williams is on the fourth DVD set of *The Prisoner* episodes. Set five contains *The Prisoner Video Companion* documentary cited throughout this chapter. In addition, the disc contains behind-the-scenes home movies, including shots of the original "Rover."

2. According to some sources, McGoohan had seven episodes in mind that he considered the core of the series: "Arrival," "Free for All," "Dance of the Dead," "Checkmate," "The Chimes of Big Ben," "Once Upon a Time," and "Fall Out" (Phillips and Garcia 1996, 222). According to *The Prisoner Video Companion*, Lew Grade wanted McGoohan to produce twenty-seven episodes to make syndication easier; they agreed on seventeen as a compromise.

3. "Living in Harmony" had the distinction of being the first Western adventure filmed for British television. Scriptwriter Ian Rakoff claimed he based the concept on his love of 1940s Western comic books. In the program's first American run, CBS would not air this episode because McGoohan's sheriff refused to carry a gun. The network worried the episode could be construed as an antiwar statement during the Vietnam conflict. To cover their intent, according to *The Prisoner Video Companion*, the network cited the presence of hallucinogenic drugs in the episode as their reason for banning the show. However, as other *Prisoner* episodes also used such drugs, the explanation seemed specious.

CHAPTER 8

1. To be fully accurate, in the first season, the tapes didn't self-destruct. Dan Briggs was usually instructed, "Please dispose of this recording in the usual manner." The recordings were then dropped into some sort of acid or liquid.

2. Patrick White's 1991 *The Complete Mission: Impossible Dossier* is widely felt to be one of the best books on television published to date. I agree. Of all the secret agent shows of the 1960s, *MI*'s history was certainly the most complex. White's

explanation of the process is exactly what any interested reader could ask for, and this chapter relies heavily on White's work.

3. In 1968, Lucille Ball's new series *Here's Lucy* featured her own spoof of *Mission*. In "Lucy's Impossible Mission," Lucy blundered into a phone booth and heard a taped message with the voice of Bob Johnson, which proceeded to self-destruct. She then met the tall, white-haired man the message was intended for, Captain Geller, who recruited Lucy and her family to help thwart an enemy agent.

CHAPTER 9

1. I hereby freely admit that 75 percent of the information I have regarding the production history of *WWW* came from Susan Kesler's 1988 *The Wild Wild West: The Series*. The heart of Kesler's overview is a detailed episode-by-episode chronological synopsis of the series, including critical responses to each episode, some flattering, some not.

2. From a telephone interview by this author with Robert Conrad, January 21, 2002. Other comments by Conrad dealt with his other spy series, *Assignment: Vienna* and *A Man Called Sloane*, and are included in discussions of those series in Chapter 11.

CHAPTER 10

1. From a transcript of "Caesar's Hour Revisited," a Writer's Guild of America West seminar broadcast on PBS, 1996. Reproduced in Gelbart 1998, 20. In the last sections of this book, Gelbart included scenes from his play "Mastergate," a hilarious parody of congressional inquires into covert actions.

CHAPTER 11

1. One 1963 British children's show, *Sierra 9*, deserves an "honorable mention" here. The thirteen thirty-minute color adventures were about three scientific troubleshooters described by Roger Fulton as a cross between *The Avengers* and *The Professionals*. Sierra 9 was a watchdog organization looking for any problems that might threaten the scientific equilibrium of the age, be it stolen missiles, secret formulas, or new weapons. Sir Willoughby Dodd (Max Kirby), an aging eccentric scientist, led Sierra 9. His creator, scriptwriter Peter Hayes, described Willoughby as "a nutcase at first sight." Peter Chance (David Sumner) and Anna Parsons (Deborah Stanford) were the two young assistants who worked from an exotic office off Trafalgar Square in London. For more details, see Fulton (1997).

Fulton's helpful overview also describes one Gerry Anderson project that also deserves an "honorable mention" here, even if it was only aired in parts of England and never seen in the United States. *Secret Service* was a children's show, a curious blend of live action and puppets. In the fall of 1969, Lew Grade financed thirteen episodes until he decided the high costs were too much, despite the clever blend of human stars with puppet doubles. Puppets were used for close-ups and studio work, while the actors stood in on long shots and locations allowing the characters to be seen walking and moving properly. The premise had a fifty-seven-year-old country vicar working for the bishop, who was a priest for the British Secret Service.

A special device hidden in a book allowed the clergyman to miniaturize his gardener, a highly trained agent. The bishop carried him around in a briefcase equipped with a chair, periscope, and miniature tool kit. Again, for more details, see Roger Fulton's *Encyclopedia of TV Science Fiction* (1997).

2. Much of this summary came from *It Takes a Thief* fan Ed Johlman, who sent me information in a private e-mail. For those interested in further details regarding *It Takes a Thief*, see http://www.epguides.com/ItTakesaThief/.

CHAPTER 12

1. Details about *Gavilan,* as well as the unsold *U.N.C.L.E.* movie, came from Danny Biederman himself in a series of e-mails with me.

2. I hereby thank Jim Benson, owner of Jim's TV Collectibles and coauthor of a book on *Night Gallery* for sending me rare interviews from and videos of *The Equalizer*.

CHAPTER 14

1. Broadcast September 1, 2001, on *CNN Saturday Morning*.

2. Details about *Spooks* can be found at http://www.bbc.co.uk/drama/spooks/.

References

BOOKS

Anderson, Robert. *The U.N.C.L.E. Tribute Book*. Las Vegas, NV: Pioneer, 1993.

Bamford, James. *Body of Secrets: Anatomy of the Ultra-Secret National Security Agency from the Cold War to the Dawn of a New Century*. New York: Doubleday, 2001.

Barer, Beryl. The Saint *in Print, Radio, Film, and Television, 1928–1992*. Jefferson, NC, and London: MacFarland and Co., 1993.

Barnouw, Eric. *Tube of Plenty: The Evolution of American Television*, 2nd rev. ed. New York: Oxford University Press, 1990.

Black, Jeremy. *The Politics of James Bond: From Fleming's Novels to the Big Screen*. Westport, CT: Praeger, 2001.

Bogle, Donald. *Prime Time Blues*. New York: Farrar, Straus, and Giroux, 2001.

Brooks, Tim and Earle Marsh. *The Complete Directory to Prime Network and Cable TV Shows: 1946–Present*, 7th ed. New York: Ballantine Books, 1999.

Buchan, John. *The Four Adventures of Richard Hannay: The 39 Steps, Green Mantle, Mr. Standfast, The Three Hostages*. Introduction by Robin W. Winks. Boston: D. R. Godine, 1988.

Buxton, David. *From* The Avengers *to Miami Vice: Form and Ideology in Television Series*. Manchester, England: Manchester University Press, 1990.

Cangey, R. M. *Inside* The Wild Wild West. Foreword by Robert Conrad. Cypress, CA: Cangey Press, 1996.

Carraze, Alain and Helene Oswald. The Prisoner: *A Televisionary Masterpiece*. New York: Barnes and Noble, by arrangement with Virgin, 1995.

Carraze, Alain and Jean-Luc Putheaud. The Avengers *Companion*. London: Titan Books, 1987.

Cawilti, John G. and Bruce A. Rosenberg. *The Spy Story*. Chicago: University of Chicago Press, 1987.

Charteris, Leslie. The Saint: *Five Complete Novels by Leslie Charteris*. New York: Avenel Books, 1983.

Cohen, Joel H. *Cool Cos: The Story of Bill Cosby*. New York: Scholastic Services, 1969.

Cornell, Paul, Martin Day, and Keith Topping. The Avengers *Dossier: The Definitive, Unauthorized Guide*. London: Virgin, 1998.

Donovan, Paul. *Roger Moore: A Biography*. London: W. H. Allen, 1983.

Douglas, Susan J. *Where the Girls Are: Growing Up Female with the Mass Media*. New York: Times Books, 1993.

Dunning, John. *On the Air: The Encyclopedia of Old Time Radio*. New York: Oxford University Press, 1998.

Edwards, Ted. *La Femme Nikita* X-Posed: The Unauthorized Biography of Peta Wilson and Her On-Screen Character. Rocklin, CA: Prima Books, 1998.

———. The X-Files *Confidential: The Unauthorized X-Philes Compendium*. Boston: Little, Brown and Co., 1997.

Fulton, Roger. *Encyclopedia of TV Science Fiction*. London: Macmillan, 1997.

Gelbart, Larry. *Laughing Matters: On Writing* M*A*S*H, Tootsie, Oh God!, *and a Few Other Funny Things*. New York: Random House, 1997.

Genge, N. E. *The Unofficial X-Files Companion*, part 2 (audio book). Minneapolis, MN: Audioscope, 1995.

Gerani, Gary with Paul Schulman. *Fantastic Television*. New York: Harmony Books, 1977.

Gianakos, Larry James. *TV Dramatic Series Programming: The Comprehensive Chronicle*, 5 vols. Lanham, MD: Scarecrow Press, 1980–1987.

Giblin, Gary. *James Bond's London: A Reference Guide to the Birthplace of 007 and His Creator*. Dunllen, NJ: Daleon Enterprises, 2001.

Gitlin, Todd. *Inside Prime Time*. New York: Pantheon Books, 1983.

Green, Joey. *The* Get Smart *Handbook*. Toronto: Collier Books of Canada, 1993.

Guinness, Sir Alec. *My Name Escapes Me: The Diary of a Retiring Actor*. Preface by John le Carré. New York: Penguin Books, 1996.

Heitland, Jon. The Man from U.N.C.L.E.: *The Behind the Scenes Story of a Television Classic*. London, England: Titan Books, 1988.

Hoffman, Todd. *John le Carré's Landscape*. Montreal: McGill-Queen's University Press, 2001.

Javna, John. *Cult TV*. New York: St. Martin's Press, 1985.

Kesler, Susan E. The Wild Wild West: *The Series*. Downey, CA: Arnett Press, 1988.

Kiel, Richard. *Making It Big in the Movies: The Autobiography of Richard "Jaws" Kiel*. Kew Gardens, England: Reynolds and Hearn, 2002.

Le Carre, John. *The Honorable School Boy*. New York: Bantam Books. 1978

Leonard, Sheldon. *And the Show Goes On: Broadway and Hollywood*. New York: Limelight Editions, 1995.

Lisanti, Tom and Louis Paul. *Film Fatales: Women in Espionage Films and Television, 1962–1973*. Jefferson, NC: McFarland and Co., 2001.

Lumley, Joanna. *Stare Back and Smile*. New York: Viking, 1989.

MacDonald, J. Fred. *Blacks and White TV: Afro-Americans in Television since 1948*. Chicago: Nelson-Hall, 1983.

———. *Don't Touch That Dial: Radio Programming in American Life (1920–1960)*. Chicago: Nelson-Hall, 1979.

———. *Television and the Red Menace: The Video Road to Vietnam*. New York: Praeger, 1985.

Macnee, Patrick and Dave Rogers. The Avengers *and Me*. New York: TB Books, 1997.

McCrohan, Donna. *The Life and Times of Maxwell Smart*. New York: St. Martin's Press, 1988.

McNeil, Alex. *Total Television: The Comprehensive Guide to Programming from 1948 to the Present*, 4th ed. New York: Penguin Books, 1996.

Meisler, Anthony. *Resist or Serve: The Official Guide to* The X-Files. New York: HarperCollins, 1999.

Meyers, Richard. *Murder on the Air*. New York: Mysterious Press, 1989.

Miller, Toby. *The Avengers*. British Film Institute, 1998.

Newcomb, Horace, ed. *Museum of Broadcasting Communications Encyclopedia of Television*, 3 vols. Chicago: Fitzroy, Dearborn, 1997. (Available online at http://www.museum.tv/archives/etv/S/htmlS/spyprograms/spyprograms.htm.)

Pearson, John. *The Life of Ian Fleming*. New York: McGraw-Hill, 1966.

Peel, John and Glenn A. Magee. *The U.N.C.L.E. Files Magazine: "The Second Year."* Canoga Park, CA: New Media Books, 1985.

Phillips, Mark and Frank Garcia. *Science Fiction Television Series: Episode Guide, Histories, and Cast and Credits for 62 Prime Time Shows from 1959 to 1989*. Jefferson, NC: McFarland and Co., 1996.

Polmar, Nolman and Thomas B. Allen. *Spy Book: The Encyclopedia of Espionage*. New York: Random House, 1997.

Rakoff, Ian. *Inside* The Prisoner: *Radical Television and Film in the 1960s*. London: Somerset, Butler and Tanner Ltd for B. T. Bates Ford Ltd, 1998.

Richelson, Jeffrey T. *A Century of Spies: Intelligence in the Twentieth Century*. New York: Oxford University Press, 1995.

Rogers, Dave. *The Complete* Avengers. New York: St. Martin's Press, 1989.

Shaw, Tony. *British Cinema and the Cold War: The State, Propaganda, and Consensus*. New York: St. Martin's Press, 2001.

Smith, Ronald L. *Cosby: The Life of a Comedy Legend*. New York: Prometheus Books, 1997.

Snelling, O. F. *007 James Bond: A Report*. New York: New American Library, 1964.

Solomon, Ed et al. *Men in Black: The Script and the Story Behind the Film*. New York: New Market Press, 1997.

Strada, Michael and Harold Troper. *Friend or Foe: Russians in American Film and Foreign Policy (1933–1991)*. Lanham, MD: Scarecrow Press, 1997.

Symons, Julian. *Mortal Consequences: A History from the Detective Story to the Crime Novel*. New York: Harper & Row, 1972.

Tiger, John. *Mission: Impossible*. New York: Popular Library, 1967.

Vahimhei, Tise, comp. *Your Guide to Over 1,100 Favourite Programmes: British Television, News and Drama, Documentaries and Comedies*. Oxford: Oxford University Press, 1997.

Weinstein, Allen and Alexander Vassiliev. *The Haunted Wood. Soviet Espionage in America: The Stalin Era*. New York: Random House, 1999.

White, Patrick J. *The Complete* Mission: Impossible *Dossier*. New York: Avon Books, 1991.

ARTICLES AND CHAPTERS

Alvarez, Maria. "Feminist Icon in a Catsuit." *New Statesman* 127, no. 43 (14 August 1998): 16–17.

Beatie, Bruce. "The Myth of the Hero: From *Mission: Impossible* to Magdalenian Caves." In *The Hero in Transition*, ed. Ray B. Browne, and Marshall W. Fishwick (pp. 46–49). Bowling Green, Kentucky: Bowling Green University Popular Press, 1983.

Caruba, David. "An Interview with Sydney Newman." *Daredevils* no. 14 (1985): 18–21.

Crighton, Kathleen. "The Real Man from U.N.C.L.E." *Epi-log Journal*, no. 13 (February 1993) (2 August 2002).

Ephron, Nora. "How Stephanie Powers Came to U.N.C.L.E." The Girl from U.N.C.L.E. *Digest* 1, no. 3 (April 1967): 102–9.

Eramo, Steven. "Honor Roles." *Starlog* 254, (September 1998): 24–28.

Freeman, Michael. "The Digital Frontier." *Mediaweek* 9, no. 23 (7 June 1999): 40–46.

Johnson, Ted. "Wry Spies." *TV Guide* (8–14 November 1997): 23–27.

Koenig, William. "The Other Spies" (1997) http://www.hmss.com (2 June 2003).

Lane, J.G. "Diana Rigg (1997) http://www.mindspring.com/ ~ jglane/riggbio.htm (23 February 2002).

Lapam, Louis. "The Boys Next Door." *Harper's Magazine* (July 2001): 10–13.

Lipton, Michael A. and Jeff Schnaufer. "The Impossible Years." *People Magazine* (20 May 1995): 46–53.

Magee, Glenn. "Sam Rolfe Interview: The Creator of *U.N.C.L.E.* Opens Channel D." *Top Secret* 1, no. 3 (April 1986a): 12–13.

———. "Sam Rolfe interview." *Top Secret* 1, no. 4 (July 1986b): 22–26.

Mason, M.S. "X-tra cool 'X-Files' premiere." *Christian Science Monitor*. (1 November, 2000): 13.

Olexa, Keith. "Avenging women." *Starlog* 254 (September 1998): 28–29.

———. "Master of the World, Revisited." *Starlog* no. 283 (February 2001a): 76–79.

———. "Victorian Secrets." *Starlog* no. 284 (March, 2001b): 56–59.

Perenson, Melissa. "*X-Files*' Brave New World." *Sci-Fi: The Official Magazine of the SciFi Channel* (June 2001): 38–43, 73.

Pringle, Kenneth. "J. Edgar Hoover No Fan of *U.N.C.L.E.*: FBI File Shows' Director Irked by TV Show" (24 August 2000) http://www.apbnews.com/media/gfiles/uncle/uncle0824_01.html (17 June 2003).

Sabo, Kristin. "*The Wild Wild West*: The Wildest Page: Danny Biederman Interview" (2000). Wild Wild West.org/default.asp (3 August 2003).

Said, Fouad, as told to Stanley Zipperman. "Interview." *American Cinematogropher* (March 1966): 180–183, 202–3.

Scott, Vernon. "'The Invisible Man' Really a Family Man" (1975) http://www.davidmccallumfansonline.com (2 July 2002).

"Six into One: The Prisoner File Story." *Prime Time: The Television Magazine* 1, no. 8 (Spring 1984): 26–28.

Smith, Ben. "Robert Conrad Interview," *Martial Arts Magazine* http://www.martial-arts-network.com/qa_robert_conrad.html (3 August 2003).

Sonseca, Nicholas. "She Spies." *Entertainment Weekly* (14 June 2002): 40.

Spelling, Ian. "Evolutionary Man." *Starlog* no. 289 (August 2001): 40–41.

Sutcliffe, McKennan. "Making a Killing: Interview with Brian Clemens." *Prime Time: The Television Magazine* 1, no. 8 (Spring 1984): 29–31.

Vincitore, Mike. "*The Sandbaggers* at HMSS" (1994) http://www.hmss.com (3 June
    2002).
Walker, Cynthia. "The Gun as Star and the *U.N.C.L.E.* Special." In *Bang Bang, Shoot
    Shoot: Essays on Guns in Popular Culture*, ed. Murray Pomerance and John
    Sakeris (pp. 187–97). Needham Heights, MA: Simon and Schuster, 1999.
Walters, David. "An Interview with Albert Elms" (Excerpted from *Once Upon a Time*,
    no, 32 (29 September 2002). http://www.the-prisoner-6.freeserve.co.uk/
    index_music_archive.htm (29 March 2001).
Weaver, Tom. "*Secret Agent* scribe." Interview with Alan Caillou. *Starlog*. no. 248
    (March 1988): 76–83.
Werts, Diane. "Time to Say 'U.N.C.L.E'" http://newsday.com/ (22 October 2001).
Williams, Grahamn. "Majestic Beauty: The Ultra-Modern, Glamorous, Tara King
    Explodes on *The Avengers* Scene." *Top Secret* 1, no. 4 (July 1986): 29–32.
Wolfe, Bernard. "The Man Called I-L-L-Y-A." *New York Times Magazine* (October
    24, 1965) http://www.davidmccallumfansonline.com/Man%20Called%20IL
    LYA.htm (2 December 2001).
Worland, Rick. "The Cold War Mannerists: *The Man from U.N.C.L.E* and TV Es-
    pionage in the 1960's." *Journal of Popular Film and Television* (Winter 1994):
    23–25.

Index